David Mo

WORLD'S AIRLINER REGISTRATIONS

LONDON

IAN ALLAN LTD

Fourth edition 1974
ISBN 07110 0548 6

Published by Ian Allan Ltd, Shepperton, Surrey
and printed in the United Kingdom by
Biddles Ltd, Guildford, Surrey

Contents

Introduction	4
Aérospatiale (Nord) 262	5
Aérospatiale (Sud) Caravelle	8
BAC One-Eleven	16
BAC/Vickers VC10	23
Beech 99	25
Boeing 707	30
Boeing 720	47
Boeing 727	52
Boeing 737	71
Boeing 747	79
Bristol Britannia	84
Canadair CL-44	89
Convair 540/Canadair 540	91
Convair 580	92
Convair 600	97
Convair 640	98
Douglas DC-8	99
Douglas DC-9	113
Douglas DC-10	128
Fairchild F-27	131
Fairchild FH-227	136
Fokker F-27	138
Fokker F-28	151
General Dynamics (Convair) 880	154
General Dynamics (Convair) 990	156
Handley Page Herald	158
Hawker Siddeley AW650 Argosy	160
Hawker Siddeley/DH Comet	161
Hawker Siddeley HS748	167
Hawker Siddeley HS748 (India)	173
Hawker Siddeley Trident	174
Lockheed Electra	176
Lockheed Hercules	183
Lockheed L-1011 TriStar	185
NAMC YS-11	187
Short Skyvan	190
Vickers Vanguard	193
Vickers Viscount	195
Soviet Airliners	213

Introduction

This fourth edition of World's Airliner Registrations has again increased in size, by comparison with the previous edition which appeared in 1971, and gives the full picture of the wide-body jets by including the Lockheed L-1011 TriStar and McDonnell Douglas DC-10 for the first time. The scope of the book, as before, embraces all types of turbine-engined airliners (turboprop, turbojet or turbofan) operated by regular airlines. The lists include therefore not only those types at present in production, but some which are now out of production but still in airline service.

The information is presented in the same manner as in the earlier editions of this title. For the benefit of new users, it may be explained that the first column lists the manufacturer's construction number, in numerical sequence (except in the case of the Convair 340/440s, converted from piston to turboprop power). This construction number (c/n) remains unchanged throughout the life of an aircraft and permits its identity to be traced regardless of the external identifying marks, ie its civil registration or military serial number. These external marks, shown in the second column of data, are given for the current (or latest known) owner, whose name appears in the third column. The next two columns provide information on the variant or series number and the date of initial delivery. The final remarks column traces, so far as possible, the history of the aircraft, with information on previous external identities and owners, individual aircraft names (shown in italics), and dates of write-offs or scrapping. Capital letter abbreviations used in the remarks column comprise D : delivered; FF : first flown; L : leased; WFS : withdrawn from service; and WO : written off.

This being the first occasion on which I have undertaken the compilation of World's Airliner Registrations, I have had some difficulty in creating effective lines of communication for the all-essential accurate information. My grateful thanks must go to the public relations department of the manufacturers whose products are included in this volume, and in particular to Jim Oughton and Alan Piper of BAC, Gordon Williams of Boeing, Mr H. Schwing of the Netherlands for details of the Fokker F-27 and F-28, Philip Birtles and Harry Holmes of Hawker Siddeley Aviation, Richard Martin and R. F. Turner of Lockheed-California, Jim White of Shorts and, last but far from least, my friend and colleague John W. R. Taylor.

Regretfully, it has proved impossible to make contact with Nihon of Japan who produce the NAMC YS-11, and this entry has therefore received very minimal updating, as has the brief and difficult to confirm information of Soviet airliners.

The contents of the book have been updated, so far as possible, to the end of 1973. It is appreciated that, however desirable, 100 per cent accuracy is very difficult to obtain. In consequence, the compiler will be most grateful for accurate news of errors or omissions. **David Mondey/ January 1974**

Aérospatiale (Nord) 262

C/n	Current Marks	Current Owner/operator	Model Series	Initial Delivery	Remarks
01	F–WKVR	Nord	262		Prototype, FF DEC–24–62
1	F–WLKE	Nord	262		Trials acft, FF MAY–7–63 reg. F–BLKA
2	F–BNGB	Rousseau Avn	262	9/10/65	Trials acft, FF as F–BLHQ. L to JDA 1965. L to Air Madagascar 1966 as 5R–MCC. To SFA as F–BNGB 1969. To Rousseau Avn, FEB–27–70 WO DEC–31–70
3	F–WZHR	CEV	262		Trials acft. L by Air Inter 1970 under reg F–BLHR. S to CEV APR–4–73.
4	F–BLHS	Air Inter	262B	21/7/64	D to Air Inter
5	F–BLHT	Air Inter	262B	18/8/64	D to Air Inter
6	F–BLHU	Air Inter	262B	18/9/64	D to Air Inter
7	F–BLHY	Air Inter	262B	21/1/65	D to Air Inter
8	PI–C-967	Filipinas Orient	262A	9/11/65	FF as F–BNDE. D to JDA as JA8646. S 1968
9	N26201	Ransome AL	262A	15/8/65	D to Lake Central/Allegheny as N26201. To BCA MAR–29–70 reg CF–BCU L to Ransome Airlines FEB–1972
10	7T–VSR	STA Algeria	262A	16/8/65	D to Lake Central/Allegheny as N26202. S to STA OCT–14–70
11	N26203	Allegheny AL	262A	15/9/65	D to Lake Central/Allegheny
12	7T–VSS	STA Algeria	262A	14/10/65	D to Lake Central/Allegheny as N26204. S to STA OCT–14–70
13	N26205	Allegheny AL	262A	20/11/65	D to Lake Central/Allegheny
14	7T–VSQ	STA Algeria	262A	17/12/65	D to Lake Central/Allegheny as N26206. S to STA MAR–23–71
15	PI–C–968	Filipinas Orient	262A	27/1/66	D to JDA as JA8652. S 1968
16	N26210	Ransome AL	262A	15/1/66	D to Lake Central/Allegheny as N26210. To BCA APR–15–69 reg CF–BCR. L to Ransome Airlines FEB–1972
17	N26211	Allegheny AL	262A	31/1/66	D to Lake Central/Allegheny
18	7T–VST	STA Algeria	262A	13/3/66	D to Lake Central/Allegheny as N26212. S to STA OCT–14–70
19	7T–VSU	STA Algeria	262A	1/4/66	D to Lake Central/Allegheny as N26213. S to STA OCT–14–70
20	F–BLHX	SFA	262A	6/4/67	L to Alisarda 1967–68
21	OY–BDD	Cimber Air	262A	26/11/69	FF as F–BNLI D to Europe Air Services F–BOFQ. S to Cimber Air SEP–16–71
22	PI–C–966	Filipinas Orient	262A	8/7/66	D to JDA as JA8663, S 1968
23	N26215	Ransome AL	262A	13/7/66	D to Lake Central/Allegheny as N26215. To BCA MAR–17–69 reg CF–BCS. L to Ransome AL FEB–1972

Aérospatiale (Nord) 262

C/n	Current Marks	Current Owner/operator	Model Series	Initial Delivery	Remarks
24	N26217	Ransome AL	262A	13/7/66	D to Lake Central/Allegheny as N26217. To BCA APR–22–69 reg CF–BCT. L to Ransome AL FEB–1972
25	OY–BDL	Cimber Air	262A	4/7/66	D to Alisarda as I–SARL *Costa Smeralda.* S 1970
26	F–BNTT	Rousseau Avn	262A	27/1/67	
27	F–BNMO	Rousseau Avn	262A	31/3/67	WO DEC–5–1970
28	F–YCKY	Aeronavale	262A	8/7/67	FF as F–WNMP
29	F–BTDQ	Rousseau Avn	262A	3/7/67	FF as F–BNKX. D to Air Ceylon as 4R–ACL. S to Dan-Air JUL–1970. reg G–AYFR. S to Rousseau Avn MAR–1972. L to Cimber Air.
30	F–BPNS	SFA	262A	16/3/67	FF as F–WNDA
31	SE–CCR	Linjeflyg	262A	8/5/67	
32	SE–CCS	Linjeflyg	262A	19/5/67	
33	OY–BCO	Cimber Air	262A	8/7/67	
34	OY–BDM	Cimber Air	262A	21/4/67	D to Alisarda as I–SARP *Gallura.* S 1970
35	F–BPNT	SFA	262A	27/7/67	FF as F–WNDB
36	F–WPXA	Nord	262C		Trials acft. Bastan VIIA
37	D–CADY	Interregionalflug	262A	11/8/67	FF as F–WNDC. D to LTU *Saarbrucken*. L to Cimber Air
38	F–BPNU	SFA	262A	28/7/67	FF as F–WOFA
39	F–BPNV	SFA	262A	1/3/68	FF as F–WNDC
40	F–BPNX	SFA	262A	28/2/68	FF as F–WNDD
41	5R–MCU	Air Madagascar	262A	2/9/68	
42	F–BPNY	Rousseau Avn	262A	22/3/68	FF as F–WOFD D to Air Camores. S to Rousseau Air AUG–17–71
43	F–YCKB	Aeronavale	262A	23/12/68	FF as F–WOFE
44	F–RBOA	Armee de l'Air	262A	8/1/69	WO JAN–21–71
45	F–RBOB	Aeronavale	262A	24/3/69	D to Armee de l' Air. Trans to Aeronavale MAR–21–69
46	F–RBOC	Aeronavale	262A	28/11/68	D to Armee de l'Air. Trans to Aeronavale SEPT–2–72
47	OY–BKR	Cimber Air	262A	15/11/68	
48	F–BSTN	Rousseau Avn	262A	7/11/69	D to Air Comores as F–OCOG S to Rousseau Avn AUG–17–71
49	F–BOHH	SFA	262A	6/1/69	
50	TS–LIP	Tunis-Air	262A	17/4/69	FF as F–OCNQ
51	F–RBOD	Aeronavale	262A	20/2/69	D to Armee de l'Air. Trans to Aeronavale OCT–7–71
52	F–RBOE	Aeronavale	262A	3/4/69	D to Armee de l'Air. Trans to Aeronavale SEP–28–71
53	F–RBOF	Aeronavale	262A	11/6/69	D to Armee de l'Air. Trans to Aeronavale OCT–4–71
54	D–CIFG	Interregionalflug	262A	29/3/69	L to Cimber Air
55	F–ZVMH	ENSA	262A	8/12/69	
56	SE–CCT	Linjaflyg	262A	30/10/69	
57	OY–IVA	CAA Danois	262A	30/9/70	
58		CEV	262A	24/3/71	
59	F–YCCM	Aeronavale	262A	16/12/69	
60	F–YCKC	Aeronavale	262A	16/2/70	
61		Aeronavale	262A	2/4/70	
62		Aeronavale	262A	6/4/70	
63		Aeronavale	262A	5/5/70	
64	F–ZJYV	Armee de l'Air	262D	22/7/70	
65		Aeronavale	262A	4/6/70	
66	F–RBAB	Armee de l'Air	262D		

C/n	Current Marks	Current Owner/operator	Model Series	Initial Delivery	Remarks
67	F–ZVMI	CEV	262A	3/6/70	
68	F–RBAC	Armee de l'Air	262D	16/6/71	
69	SE–CCU	Lynjeflyg	262A	21/9/70	
70		Aeronavale	262A	15/10/70	
71		Aeronavale	262A	24/10/70	
72		Aeronavale	262A	22/12/70	
73		Aeronavale	262A	25/2/71	
74	F–BSUF	SFA	262C	28/7/71	
75		Aeronavale	262A	22/3/71	
76	F–RBAD	Armee de l'Air	262D	9/7/71	
77	F–RBAE	Armee de l'Air	262D	19/7/71	
78	F–RBAF	Armee de l'Air	262D	16/7/71	
79		Aeronavale	262A	2/2/72	
80	F–RBAG	Armee de l'Air	262D	19/8/71	
81	F–RBAH	Armee de l'Air	262D	24/8/71	
82	TR–KJA	Gabonese Government	262C	30/7/71	
83	F–RBAI	Armee de l'Air	262D	30/9/71	
84	OY–BDR	Cimber Air	262A	4/4/71	
85		Aeronavale	262A	10/10/71	
86	F–RBAJ	Armee de l'Air	262D	21/10/71	
87	F–RBAK	Armee de l'Air	262D	30/9/71	
88	F–RBAL	Armee de l'Air	262D	30/1/72	
89	F–RBAM	Armee de l'Air	262D	27/1/72	
90	TR–KJB	Gabonese Government	262C	11/11/71	
91	F–RBAJ	Armee de l'Air	262D	10/2/72	
92	F–RBAO	Armee de l'Air	262D	15/3/72	
93	F–RBAP	Armee de l'Air	262D	10/4/72	
94	F–RBAQ	Armee de l'Air	262D	19/6/72	
95	F–RBAR	Armee de l'Air	262D	26/7/72	
96	SY–DCA	East African Community	262C	13/6/72	
97	TR–KJC	Gabonese Government	262C	12/1/73	

Aérospatiale (Sud) Caravelle

C/n	Current Marks	Current Owner/operator	Model Series	Initial Delivery	Remarks
01	F–BHHH	Sud-Aviation			Prototype FF MAY–27–65
02	F–BHHI	Sud-Aviation			2nd Prototype FF MAY–6–56
1	F–BHRA	Air France	III	2/4/59	*Alsace* Cvtd from Srs 1
2	F–BHRB	Air France	III	19/3/59	*Lorraine* Cvtd from Srs 1
3	LN–KLH	SAS	III	10/4/59	*Finn* Cvtd from Srs 1
4	SE–DAA	SAS	III	25/4/59	*Eskil* Cvtd from Srs 1
5	6–VFBC	Republic of Senegal	III	15/5/59	Cvtd from Srs 1. D to Air France as F–BHRC *Anjou* Cvtd from Srs 1. L Rep. of Senegal DEC–28–71
6	OY–KRA	SAS	III	5/5/59	*Vagn* Cvtd from Srs 1
7	LN–KLI	SAS	III	17/6/59	*Einar* Cvtd from Srs 1
8	F–BHRD	Air France	III	30/6/59	*Guyenne* Cvtd from Srs 1
9	F–BHRE	Air France	III	31/7/59	*Artois* Cvtd from Srs 1
10	TL–AAI	R.C. Africaine	III	16/9/59	D to Varig as PP–VJC. S to Air Vietnam as XV–NJA AUG–17–64. To Air France as F–BNGE JAN–1969. L to MEA to MAR–31–69. L to R. Air Maroc. S DEC–28–70
11	SE–DAB	SAS	III	18/10/59	*Ingemar* Cvtd from Srs 1
12	F–BHRF	Air France	III	17/10/59	*Auvergne* Cvtd from Srs 1
13	F–BHRG	Air France	III	6/11/59	*Berry* Cvtd from Srs 1
14	OY–KRB	SAS	III	18/11/59	*Orm* Cvtd from Srs 1 WO Ankara JAN–19–60
15	PP–VJD	Varig	III	7/12/59	Cvtd from Srs I. WO Brasillia SEP–27–61
16	F–BHRH	Air France	III	11/12/59	*Bourgogne* Cvtd from Srs 1
17	F–BHRI	Air France	III	22/12/59	*Bretagne* Cvtd from Srs 1
18	7T–VAG	Air Algerie	III	26/12/59	D as F–OBNG Cvtd from Srs 1
19	T–91	F.A. Argentines	VI–N	15/1/62	Prototype Srs III F–WJAQ cvtd to VI–N SEP–60. D as LV–PRR *Aldebaran* to Aerolineas, reg LV–HGX. S JUL–73
20	YV–C–AVI	Avensa	III	1/1/60	D to Air Algerie as Srs I F–OBNH. S to Varig as PP–VJI DEC–15–61. S Avensa AUG–13–64. Crashed and under investigation for possible repair AUG–21–73
21	F–BSRR	Aérospatiale	III	18/2/60	D to Finnair as OH–LEA Srs 1A *Sinilintu*. S to LTU FEB–18–65 as D–ABAF *Nordrhein-Westfalen*. to Aérospatiale AUG–68 S to Transavia as PH–TRM FEB–11–69. S to Air Inter as F–BSRR MAR–19–71 S DEC–1972
22	F–BJTR	Air France	III	30/3/60	D to Finnair as OH–LEB Srs 1A *Sinisiipi*. S to Air France AUG–31–64 *Vercors*
23	OD–AEM	MEA	III	2/9/60	D to Air France as Srs 1 F–BHRJ *Champagne*. L to MEA 1964 and WO APR–17–64
24	LN–KLP	SAS	III	8/3/60	*Trond* Cvtd from Srs 1A

C/n	Current Marks	Current Owner/operator	Model Series	Initial Delivery	Remarks
25	HS–TGI	THAI	III	11/3/60	D to SAC as Srs 1A. SE–DAC *Arne.* L to THAI 1967. WO Hong Kong JUN–30–67
26	F–BHRK	Air France	III	18/3/60	*Corse* Cvtd from Srs 1A
27	F–BJTS	Air France	III	5/5/60	D to Finnair as OH–LEC Srs 1A *Sininuoli* S to Air France OCT–1–64 *Principaute de Monaco.*
28	7T–VAI	Air Algerie	III	19/3/60	D to Air Algerie as F–OBNI, Srs 1A
29	OY–KRC	SAS	III	2/4/60	*Faste Viking* Srs 1A. L to THAI OCT–65 to 1970 as HS–TGH
30	LN–KLR	SAS	III	15/4/60	D to SAS as LN–KLR. *Hall.* Cvtd from Srs 1A. L to THAI AUG–67 as HS–TGJ. Rvtd to LN–KLR. L to THAI as HS–TGL 1969–MAY–70
31	F–BHRL	Air France	III	26/4/60	*Dauphine* Cvtd from Srs 1A
32	CN–CCV	R. Air Maroc	III	11/5/60	FF as F–WJAL. Srs 1A cvtd. WO APR–1–70. Casablanca
33	PH–TRO	Transavia	III	30/4/60	FF as F–WJAM. Srs 1A cvtd. D to Swissair as HB–ICW *Solothurn.* S OCT–15–69
34	HS–TGK	THAI	III	28/5/60	D to SAS as Srs 1A SE–DAD *Torolf.* L to THAI in 1964 and from DEC–67. WO JUL–9–69
35	I–DAXA	Alitalia	VI–N	28/5/60	*Altair* Cvtd from first Srs III
36	PH–TVW	Transavia	VI–N	19/5/60	*Aldebaran* Cvtd from Srs III to Alitalia as I–DAXE. L APR–73
37	F–BHRM	Air France	III	3/5/60	*Quercy*
38	B–1854	China	III	24/6/60	FF as F–WJAM. *Chur* D to Swissair on L from SAS as HB–ICX. S to Catair MAR–23–1971 S MAR–1973
39	F–BHRN	Air France	III	18/6/60	*Gascogne*
40	I–DAXI	Alitalia	VI–N	10/6/60	*Antares* Cvtd from Srs III
41	F–BHRO	Air France	III	29/6/60	*Ile de France*
42	F–BLKF	Air France	III	18/7/60	FF as F–BJOA; D to General Electric and cvtd to proto Srs VII N420GE *Santa Maria;* cvtd to Srs 10A demonstrator 1962. S Air France JUL–30–63; cvtd to Srs III *Angoumois*
43	PH–TRP	Transavia	III	0/7/00	D to Swissair as HB–ICY *Lousanne.* S NOV–11–69
44	PH–TVV	Transavia	VI–N	18/7/60	D to Alitalia as I–DAXO *Weneb.* L MAY–1973
45	F–BHRP	Air France	III	12/8/60	*Lanquedoc*
46	F–BHRQ	Air Inter	III	28/8/60	D to Air France. *Limousin.* L to Air Inter MAR–31–73. S APR–1–73
47	OY–KRD	SAS	III	30/7/60	*Ulf*
48	PH–TRR	Transavia	III	12/8/60	D to Swissair as HB–ICZ *Bellinzona.* L to Air Algeria 1969. S MAR–70
49	OY–KRE	SAS	III	21/9/60	D to SAS as OY–KRE *Knud Viking* L to THAI from MAR–26–64 to SEP–1970 as HS–TGG

Aérospatiale (Sud) Caravelle

C/n	Current Marks	Current Owner/operator	Model Series	Initial Delivery	Remarks
50	F–BHRR	Air Inter	III	23/9/60	D to Air France. *Lyonnais*. S MAR–1973
51	7T–VAE	Air Algerie	III	12/9/60	D as F–OBNJ. later F–BLCZ. L by Air Liban as OD–ADZ 1963
52	F–BHRZ	Air Inter	III	16/3/61	D to Air France *Flandre*. L to Air Inter APR–1–71. S JUL–1–72
53	XU–JTB	Air Cambodge	III	7/4/61	D to Air France as F–BJTA *Conte de Nice*, later *Antilles* S APR–10–73
54	F–BHRS	Air France	III	26/10/60	*Normandia*
55	F–BHRT	Air France	III	14/10/60	*Picardie*
56	SE–DAE	SAS	III	28/10/60	D to SAS as SE–DAE *Alric*. L to THAI from DEC–26–63 to JUN–1970 as HS–TGF *Suranaree*
57	CN–CCX	R. Air Maroc	III	25/2/61	
58	F–BHRU	Air France	III	10/10/60	*Poitou*
59	F–BHRV	Air France	III	22/10/60	*Provence*
60	F–BHRX	Air France	III	29/11/60	*Savoie*
61	F–BHRY	Air France	III	15/12/60	*Touraine*
62	PP–CJC	Cruzeiro do Sol	VI–R	6/8/63	Prototype, FF FEB–6–61 as F–WJAP; temporarily N2001U before D
63	F–WJAO	Sud-Aviation	10A		Prototype. FF AUG–31–62. Scrapped
64	OO–SRA	Sabena	VI–N	20/1/60	
65	OO–SRB	Sabelair	VI–N	1/2/61	
66	OO–SRC	Sabelair	VI–N	17/2/61	
67	OO–SRE	Sabena	VI–N	24/3/61	
68	F–BJTB	Air France	III	30/5/61	*Bearn* WO Rabat SEP–12–61
69	OO–SRD	Sabelair	VI–N	1/3/61	
70	VT–ECG	Air India	VI–N	12/7/61	D to Sabena as OO–SRG. S NOV–1973
71	I–DABA	Alitalia	VI–N	21/3/61	*Regolo*
72	I–DABE	Alitalia	VI–N	30/3/61	*Rigel*
73	7T–VAK	Air Algerie	VI–N	2/5/61	D as F–OBNK. WO JUL–26–69 Biskra
74	I–DABI	Alitalia	VI–N	22/4/61	*Sirio*
75	7T–VAL	Air Algerie	VI–N	20/6/61	D as F–OBNL
76	OO–SRF	Sabena	VI–N	28/4/61	
77	I–DABU	Alitalia	VI–N	17/5/61	*Vega*
78		Air India	VI–N	11/8/61	D to Sabena as OO–SRH. S NOV–1973
79	I–DAXU	Alitalia	VI–N	9/6/61	*Canope*
80	I–DAXI	Alitalia	VI–N	17/10/61	D to Alitalia *Pelluce*.
81	I–DABR	Alitalia	VI–N	19/1/62	*Bellatrix*
82	I–DABZ	SAM	VI–N	9/2/62	*Spica*. L to SAM
83	F–BKGZ	Air France	III	10/7/61	D as F–BJTC. L to Air Liban as OD–ADY. *Comte de Foix*
84	TS–IKM	Tunis Air	III	31/8/61	D as F–BJTD to Air France
85	I–DABT	SAM	VI–N	2/4/62	D to Alitalia *Denebola* JUL–1–68. L to SAM
86	N1001U	Litton Industries	VI–R	10/6/61	D to UAL. Toulouse S FEB–1971
87	PH–TRY	Transavia	VI–R	20/6/61	D to UAL as N1002U *Cahors* S MAY–1–70
88	OY–SAH	Sterling	VI–R	2/7/61	D to UAL as N1003U *Marseille* S NOV–11–71 *City of Copenhagen*
89	OY–SAL	Sterling	VI–R	6/7/61	D to UAL as N1004U *Paris*. S DEC–17–71 *City of Stockholm*

C/n	Current Marks	Current Owner/operator	Model Series	Initial Delivery	Remarks
90	–	Filipinas Orient	VI–R	31/7/61	D to UAL as N1005U *Grenoble.* S to Sterling JUN–1–72. S OCT–72.
91	OY–SBV	Sterling	VI–R	11/8/61	D to UAL as N1006U. *Saintes* S 1972 L to Transavia to OCT–1972
92	PH–TRX	Transavia	VI–R	30/8/61	D to United AL as N1007U *Coutances.* S JUN–70
93	PH–TVT	Transavia	VI–R	20/9/61	D to UAL as N1008U *Rochefort.* S to Sterling MAY–1972 S JUN–1973
94	OY–SBY	Sterling	VI–R	7/10/61	D to UAL as N1009U *Rouen.* S 1972 *City of Rome*
95	OY–SAM	Sterling	VI–R	20/10/61	D to UAL as N1010U *Strasbourg.* S JAN–10–72. *City of Athens*
96	PH–TRH	Transavia	VI–R	26/10/61	D to UAL as N1011U *Dijon.* S OCT–1971
97	–	Air Fret	VI–R	11/11/61	D to UAL as N1012 *Lille.* S JUL–1972
98	OY–SAN	Sterling	VI–R	23/11/61	D to UAL as N1013U *Arles* S JAN–1–72
99	OY–SAK	Sterling	VI–R	30/11/61	D to UAL as N1014U. *Nice* S DEC–10–72 *City of Brussels*
100	PH–TRS	Transavia	VI–R	8/12/61	D to UAL as N1015U *St. Nazaire.* S DEC–1970
101	F–BUFF	Catair	VI–R	29/12/61	D to UAL as N1016U *Nantes* S to Sterling JAN–31–72 S DEC–1972
102	PH–TRU	Transavia	VI–R	14/12/61	D to UAL as N1017U *Cannes* S FEB–1970
103	–	Filipinas Orient	VI–R	4/1/62	D to UAL as N1018U *Bordeaux.* S OCT–1972
104	OY–SAJ	Sterling	VI–R	6/1/62	D to UAL as N1019U *Lyon* S 1972 *City of Oslo*
105	F–BJTI	Air France	III	23/5/62	*Navarre.* L to KLA OCT–7–67 to NOV–11–67
106	I–DABS	Alitalia	VI–N	6/4/62	*Dubhe*
107	EC–ARI	Aviaco	VI–R	5/2/62	D to Iberia *Albeniz* S OCT–1973
108	B–2501	F.A.T.	VI–R	28/2/62	D to Iberia *Chapi* EC–ARJ. S 1973
109	EC–ARK	Aviaco	VI–R	30/3/62	D to Iberia *Granados* S 1973
110	B–2503	F.A.T.	VI–R	18/4/62	D to Iberia as EC–ARL *Manuel de Falla.* S 1973
111	F–BJTE	Air France	III	12/1/62	*Grenoble.*
112	SE–DAF	SAS	III	17/2/62	*Sven*
113	F–BJTF	Air France	III	7/3/62	*Orleanais*
114	OY–SBZ	Sterling	VI–R	24/2/62	D to UAL as N1020U *Calais* S 1972 *City of Reykjavik*
115	F–BJTG	Air France	III	4/5/62	*Rousillon* L by Air Charter International
116	F–ZACE	CEV Bretigny	III	23/2/62	D as OH–LED to Finnair *Sinipiika.* To French Air Forces DEC–1–64
117	CS–TCA	TAP	VI–R	16/7/62	*Goa*
118	PP–PDU	Panair do Brazil	VI–R	19/7/62	FF as F–WJAL *Antao Leme da Silva.* WO SEP–6–63
119	F–BJTJ	Air France	III	18/6/62	*Bourdonnais.* L by Swissair as HB–ICR 1963–1966 L by Air Charter International

Aérospatiale (Sud) Caravelle

C/n	Current Marks	Current Owner/operator	Model Series	Initial Delivery	Remarks
120	PP–PDV	Cruzeiro do Sul	VI–R	19/7/62	FF as F–WJAK. D to Panair do Brasil *Domingo Rodriguez de Carvalho.* Trsfd to Cruzeiro FEB–17–66
121	B–1850	China	III	17/3/62	D to Swissair as HB–ICS *Uri,* on L from SAS. S APR–8–71
122	B–1852	China	III	29/3/62	D to Swissair as HB–ICT *Schwyz,* on L from SAS. S JAN–8–71. WO NOV–20–71
123	OO–SBQ	Sobelair	III	14/4/62	D to Swissair as HB–ICU *Aargan,* on L from SAS S to Huygen OCT–20–70 L 1971
124	F–BJTH	Air France	III	10/5/62	*Franche-Comte* L by Air Charter International
125	CS–TCB	TAP	VI–R	24/7/62	*Damao*
126	PP–PDX	Cruzeiro do Sul	VI–R	16/8/62	FF as F–WJAN. D to Panair do Brasil. *Fernando de Camargo.* Trsfd to Cruzeiro FEB–17–66 WO at Sao-Luiz JUN–1–73
127	LV–HGY	Aerolineas	VI–N	7/6/62	*Sirius* WO JUL–3–63, Cordoba
128	VT–DPO	IAC	VI–N	21/12/63	FF as F–WLKJ *Pavandoot*
129	PP–CJA	Cruzeiro do Sul	VI–R	10/12/64	
130	VT–DPP	IAC	VI–N	17/1/64	*Akashdoot* WO New Delhi; FEB–15–66
131	PP–PDZ	Cruzeiro do Sul	VI–R	16/9/62	D to Panair do Brasil *Francisco* Diaz *de Avila.* Trsfd to Cruzeiro FEB–17–66
132	I–DABL	SAM	VI–N	28/11/64	D to Alitalia *Fomalhaut* L to SAM
133	PP–CJB	Cruzeiro do Sul	VI–R	13/12/62	
134	VT–DSB	IAC	VI–N	28/11/64	*Vayudoot* WO Bombay SEP–4–66
135	YU–AHB	JAT	VI–N	27/2/63	*Bled* WO near Titograd SEP–11–73
136	F–BTDL	Euralair	VI–R	13/5/66	Prototype, Sud-Lear Autoland as F–BLKI JAN–64 *Steiermark* S NOV 1971 to AUA, reg OE–LCU. S 1973
137	CS–TCC	TAP	VI–R	27/11/62	*Diu*
138	EC–AXU	Aviaco	VI–R		D to Garrett JUL–31–63 as N210G. S JAN–11–65 *Alfonso X el Sabia* S JUN–1973
139	YU–AHA	JAT	VI–N	11/1/63	*Dubrovnic*
140	CC–CCO	LAN–Chile	VI–N	6/3/64	
141	F–RAFG	G.T.L.A.	III	13/9/63	D as F–BJTK to Air France *Principaute de Monaco*
142	F–BJTL	Air France	III	15/3/63	*Aunis et Saintonge*
143	I–DABM	Alitalia	VI–N	27/5/64	Was F–WJSO, prototype Smiths Autoland DEC–62. D to Alitalia *Procione*
144	F–BJTM	Air France	III	9/4/63	*Maine*
145	XU–JTA	Royal Air Cambodge	III	18/4/63	D to Air France as F–BJTN *Comminges.* S JAN–19–69
146	I–DABY	SAM	VI–N	14/3/63	D to Alitalia *Acruz.* L JAN–1–69
147	HB–ICV	Swissair	III	19/10/62	*Schaffhausen.* L from SAS WO at Duerranaesch SEP–4–63

C/n	Current Marks	Current Owner/operator	Model Series	Initial Delivery	Remarks
148	F–BJTO	Air France	III	30/5/63	*Nivernais* L to Air Charter International
149	T–92	F.A. Argentines	VI–N	31/10/62	D as LV–PVU to Swissair *Rigel.* S to Aerolineas, re-reg LV–HGZ S JUL–1973
150	I–DABW	SAM	VI–N	1/4/63	D to Alitalia *Betelgeuse* L to SAM
151	YU–AHD	JAT	VI–N	31/5/63	*Opatija* WO Moganik SEP–11–73
152	F–BJTP	Air France	III	16/4/63	*Comat Venaissin*
153	OD–AEE	MEA	VI–N	26/4/64	WO Beirut DEC–28–68
154	CN–CCY	R Air Maroc	III	1/6/63	L by MEA JAN–23–69 to JUN–69
155	VT–DPN	IAC	VI–N	22/11/63	*Gagandoot*
156	LX–LGG	Luxair	VI–R	1/6/63	D to AUA as OE–LCE *Tyrol.* S MAY–1972
157	OD–AEF	MEA	VI–N	6/5/63	WO Beirut DEC–28–68
158	5A–DAA	Libyan Arab AL	VI–R	24/7/65	FF as F–BLHY. L by GLAM as F–RAFA before D to KLA
159	EC–AVZ	Iberia	VI–R	7/2/64	*Sarasate* WO OCT–24–73
160	CC–CCQ	LAN–Chile	VI–R	2/7/64	
161	F–BUFC	Catair	VI–R	18/2/63	D to AUA as OE–LCA *Wien.* S JAN–1973
162	5A–DAB	Libyan Arab AL	VI–R	28/7/65	FF as F–BJTD. L Finnair as OH–LER 1964 before D to KLA
163	EC–ATV	Iberia	VI–R	9/7/63	*Tomas L de Victoria* WO Ibiza JAN–7–72
164	CC–CCP	LAN–Chile	VI–R	4/5/64	
165	EC–ATX	Aviaco	VI–R	25/4/63	D to Iberia as *Turina.* S OCT–1973
166	LX–LGF	Luxair	VI–R	28/3/64	D to AUA as OE–LCI *Salzburg* S MAR–23–72
167	F–BSEL	Euralair	VI–R	22/4/65	D to AUA as OE–LCO *Karnten* S NOV–1971
168	PP–CJD	Cruzeiro do Sul	VI–R	8/7/63	
169	OH–LSG	Finnair	Super	6/6/66	Prototype, FF as F–WLKJ on MAR–3–64 *Jyvaskyla*
170	OY–KRF	SAS	III	3/3/64	*Torkild.* L to THAI 1968
171	EC–BBR	Iberia	VI–R	6/11/65	FF as F–WLKR *Padilla*
172	–	K.F.F.	III	17/12/64	D to SAS as SE–DAG *Dag.* S JAN–1971
173	EC–AVY	Iberia	VI–R	24/1/64	*Amadeo Vives* WO OCT–24–73
174	OD–AEO	MEA	VI–N	10/11/64	
175	OO–SRI	Sabena	VI–N	29/12/64	
176	FC–CAE	Aviaco	10R	1/4/66	Prototype, FF as F–BLKS on JAN–10–65. L to Iberia *Hilarion Eslava* as EC–BDC. S APR–1–72
177	F–BJTO	Air France	III	3/4/64	*Champagne II*
178	TS–TAR	Tunis Air	III	18/3/64	
179	I–DABF	Alitalia	VI–N	19/2/65	*Mizar.* WO AUG–2–69 Marseilles
180	T–93	FA–Argentines	VI–N	18/9/64	D as LV–PBJ *Antares.* S to Aerolineas, reg LV–III S JUL–1973
181	OH–LSA	Finnair	Super	22/7/64	*Helsinki,* L to Kar Air 1970
182	OH–LSB	Finnair	Super	4/8/64	*Tampere*
183	YR–ATC	Syrian Air	Super	20/3/65	D to Sterling as OY–STA. S JUN–6–71.
184	YK–AFA	Syrian Arab AL	Super	20/10/65	D to Sterling as OY–STA. S JUN–6–71
185	OH–LSC	Finnair	Super	27/8/64	*Turku*
186	YK–AFD	Syrian Arab AL	Super	4/4/66	D to Sterling as OY–STB. S NOV–26–71

Aérospatiale (Sud) Caravelle

C/n	Current Marks	Current Owner/operator	Model Series	Initial Delivery	Remarks
187	OH–LSD	Finnair	Super	10/9/64	*Oulu*
188	OH–LSF	Finnair	Super	12/3/66	*Pori*
189	OH–LSE	Finnair	Super	23/9/64	*Lahti*
190	YK–AFB	Syrian Arab AL	Super	30/6/66	*April 17*
191	YU–AJG	JAT	III	16/2/65	D to SAS as OY–KRG *Alf.* S JUN–69 to Transavia as PH–TRN. S 1972
192	I–DABP	SAM	VI–N	13/4/65	D to Alitalia *Castore* L to SAM
193	F–BRIM	Transunion	III	12/4/65	D to SAS as SE–DAH *Torgny* S to Sud. L to Transunion APR–30–69
194	YU–AHE	JAT	VI–N	10/7/65	*Budva*
195	CN–CCZ	R Air Maroc	III	25/6/65	
196	OO–SRK	Sabena	VI–N	29/4/65	
197	EC–AYD	Aviaco	VI–R	26/2/65	D to Iberia as *Juan Crisostomo Arriaga.* S to Aviaco
198	EC–AYE	Iberia	VI–R	2/4/65	*Jose Maria Usandizaga*
199	JY–ACS	Alia	10R	28/7/65	*Amman*
200	HB–ICK	SATA	10R	25/2/66	FF as F–BNFE *Jerusalem* D to Alia as JY–ACT. S MAR–21–73
201	F–BNRA	UTA	10R	28/2/66	
202	EC–BDD	Iberia	10R	29/4/66	*Jesus Gurudi.* WO NOV–4–67 Fernhurst
203	VT–DUH	IAC	VI–N	28/12/65	*Rashiradoot*
204	VT–DUI	IAC	VI–N	26/2/66	*Bharatdoot*
205	I–DABG	SAM	VI–N	28/5/66	D to Alitalia as *Arturo.* L to SAM
206	F–BNKA	Air Inter	III	28/6/66	S by Air France before D
207	TS–MAC	Tunis Air	III	18/3/66	
208	F–BNKB	Air Inter	III	13/4/66	S by Air France before D
209	F–BUFM	Tunis Air	III	17/12/65	D to SAS as LN–KLN *Trygve* S to Sud. L to Transunion MAR–15–70.
210	–	K.F.F.	III	10/2/66	D to SAS as SE–DAI *Alrik* S JAN–1971
211	OH–LSH	Finnair	Super	20/1/67	*Kuopio*
212	OY–STC	Sterling	Super	3/3/67	Was F–BOEE for UTA
213	VT–DVI	JAT	VI–N	28/10/66	*Meghdoot*
214	F–BNKI	Air Inter	III	6/12/66	D to LTU as D-ABAM. S JUN–5–68 WO JAN–4–71
215	TU–TCO	Air Afrique	11R	18/9/67	*Quagadougou*
216	VT–DVJ	IAC	VI–N	26/12/66	*Hansadoot*
217	F–BNKC	Air Inter	III	15/3/67	
218	YU–AHF	JAT	VI–N	29/3/67	*Split*
219	TU–TCY	Air Afrique	11R	18/9/67	FF as F–BJAK *Yaounde*
220	F–BNKD	Air Inter	III	25/2/67	
221	5A–DAE	Libyan Arab AL	VI–R	29/4/67	D to KLA
222	HB–ICQ	SATA	10R	7/3/67	D to UTA as F–BNRB. S JAN–15–73
223	EC–BIB	Aviaco	10R	7/6/67	F–WJAQ (re-used) before delivery *Teobaldo Power.* S to Aviaco
224	F–BNKE	Air Inter	III	31/3/67	
225	EC–BIC	Aviaco	10R	27/6/67	D to Iberia as *Emilio Arrieta.* S MAY–17–72. WO AUG–13–73 at la Corogne
226	EC–BIA	Iberia	VI–R	28/7/67	*Jeronimo Jimenez*
227	F–BNKF	Air Inter	III	25/11/67	
228	EC–BID	Air Inter	10R	7/7/67	D to Iberia as *Thomas Breton.* S MAY–17–72 WO Madere MAR–5–73

C/n	Current Marks	Current Owner/operator	Model Series	Initial Delivery	Remarks
229	F–BNKG	Air Inter	III	2/1/68	
230	EC–BIE	Aviaco	10R	21/7/67	D to Iberia as *Padre Antonio Soler* S MAY–17–72
231	VT–DWN	IAC	VI–N	3/11/67	*Shantidoot*
232	EC–BIF	Aviaco	10R	20/10/67	D to Iberia as *Francisco Tarrega* S MAY–17–72
233	YU–AHG	JAT	VI–N	10/1/68	*Ohrid*
234	HB–ICP	SATA	VI–R	3/3/70	D to Luxair as *Princess Maria Atrid,* LX–LGE. S MAR–23–72
235	D–ABAP	LTU	10–R	18/12/67	
236	JY–ADG	Alia	10–R	21/6/68	*Bethlehem*
237	YU–AHK	JAT	VI–N	7/6/69	L from Aérospatiale
238	OY–STD	Sterling	Super	23/2/68	
239	D–ABAW	LTU	10–R	18/7/68	
240	9Q–CLC	Air Congo	11–R	27/10/67	*Impala* later *Lumumbashi*
241	7–601	Jugoslav AF	VI–N	8/2/69	
242	F–BOHA	Air France	III	21/3/68	*Comte de Nice*
243	D–ABAV	LTU	10–R	28/2/68	
244	F–BOHB	Air France	III	19/4/68	WO SEP–11–68, off Cap d'Antibes
245	F–BOHC	Air France	III	17/5/68	*Aquitaine* later *Guyane*
246	TS–ITU	Tunis Air	III	16/2/68	
247	D–ANYL	LTU	10–R	31/12/69	
248	F–BNKH	Air Inter	III	15/3/68	L from Aérospatiale
249	OY–STE	Sterling	Super	9/4/68	
250	EC–BRJ	Transeuropa	10–R	3/3/70	
251	9Q–CLD	Air Zaire	11–R	18/10/68	*Bukavu*
252	F–BNKJ	Air Inter	III	11/10/68	L from Aérospatiale
253	HB–ICN	SATA	10–R	7/3/70	
254	CN–CCT	Royal Air Maroc	III	9/8/68	
255	HB–ICO	SATA	10–R	12/12/69	D to Sterling as OY–SAY. S FEB–12–71
256	F–BNKK	Air Inter	III	4/12/69	L from Aérospatiale
257	OY–STF	Sterling	10B3	12/2/69	D to Sterling as OY–STF. L to Aviaction
258	F–BSRY	Air Inter	III	8/6/70	FF as F–OCPJ. L to Tunis Air S DEC–1970
259	OY–STG	Sterling	10B3	14/3/69	
260	F–BNKL	Air Inter	III	24/1/70	L from Aérospatiale
261	EG–BRX	Transeuropa	11R	29/7/69	L from Aérospatiale
262	OY–STH	Sterling	10B3	4/4/69	
263	D–ABAF	LTU	10R	16/1/70	D to Sterling as OY–SAZ. S JAN–14–72
264	EC–BRY	Transeuropa	11R	20/9/69	L from Aérospatiale
265	OY–STI	Sterling	10B3	14/5/69	
266	OY–STK	Sterling	10B3	6/5/70	
267	OY–STL	Sterling	10B3	10/5/70	WO Dubai MAR–14–73
268	OY–STM	Sterling	10B3	16/6/70	
269	OY–SAC	Sterling	12	18/5/71	
270	OY–SAA	Sterling	12	12/3/71	
271	OY–SAB	Sterling	12	26/3/71	
272	OY–SAD	Sterling	12	7/6/71	
273	OY–SAE	Fly Kammanditselskabet	12	28/2/72	D to Sterling S MAY–22–73
274	F–BTOA	Air Inter	12	20/10/72	
275	OY–SAF	Sterling	12	19/5/72	
276	OY–SAG	Sterling	12	19/6/72	
277	F–BTOB	Air Inter	12	20/12/72	
278	F–BTOC	Air Inter	12	17/4/73	
279	F–BTOD	Air Inter	12	20/2/73	
280	F–BTOE	Air Inter	12	16/3/73	

BAC One-Eleven

C/n	Current Marks	Current Owner/operator	Model Series	Initial Delivery	Remarks
4	G–ASHG	BAC	200		FF AUG–20–63. WO Chicklade OCT–22–63
5	N734EB	Barwick Industries	201	11/10/65	D to BUA as G–ASJA. S Barwick Industries
6	G–ASJB		201		WO Wisley MAR–18–64
7	G–ASJC	British Caledonian	201	6/11/65	
8	XX105	RAE Bedford	201	5/8/65	D to BUA as G–ASJD. S to RAE Bedford for development flying
9	G–ASJE	British Caledonian	201	23/7/65	
10	G–ASJF	British Caledonian	201	22/5/65	
11	G–ASJG	British Caledonian	201	6/7/65	
12	G–ASJH	British Caledonian	201	17/4/65	
13	G–ASJI		201	15/4/65	
14	G–ASJJ		201	6/4/65	
15	N5LC	Stewart Lumber Co	203	10/8/65	G–ASUF before delivery to Braniff as N1541 Subsequent registrations N111QA and N541BN. S to Stewart Lumber Co.
16	N1542	Allegheny Airlines	203	20/4/65	D to Braniff S to Allegheny AL
17	N1543	Allegheny Airlines	203	11/3/65	D to Braniff S to Allegheny AL
18	N1544	Allegheny Airlines	203	6/4/65	D to Braniff S to Alleghney AL
19	N1545	Allegheny Airlines	203	12/5/65	D to Braniff S to Allegheny AL
20	N1546	Allegheny Airlines	203	2/6/65	D to Braniff S to Allegheny AL
29	N2111J	Allegheny Airlines	204	15/5/65	D to Mohawk which merged with Allegheny AL
30	N1112J	Allegheny Airlines	204	25/6/65	D to Mohawk which merged with Allegheny AL
31	N1113J	Allegheny Airlines	204	10/8/65	D to Mohawk which merged with Allegheny AL
32	N1114J	Allegheny Airlines	204	29/9/65	D to Mohawk which merged with Allegheny AL
33	G–ATPJ	Dan-Air	301	28/4/67	Built as 9K–ACI Kuwait AW D to British Eagle *Stalwart* S Dan-Air
34	G–ATPK	Laker Airways	301	24/6/66	Built as 9K–ACJ Kuwait AW D to British Eagle *Spur*. S Bahamas Air and registered VP–BCP. S Laker Airways.
35	G–ATPL	Dan-Air	301	22/7/66	Built as 9K–ACK Kuwait AW D to British Eagle *Superb*. S Dan-Air
39	9J–RCH	Zambia Airways	207	22/4/66	Built as VP–YXA. L to British Eagle as G–ATTP *Swift* Returned to Zambia AW
40	9J–RCI	Zambia Airways	207	27/4/66	Built as VP–YXB. L to British Eagle as G–ATVH *Serene* Later registered 7Q–YKE. Returned to Zambia Air
41	N1547	Allegheny Airlines	203	20/7/65	D to Braniff S to Allegheny AL
42	N1548	Allegheny Airlines	203	10/8/65	D to Braniff S to Allegheny AL
43	N1549	Allegheny Airlines	203	24/9/65	D to Braniff S to Allegheny AL

C/n	Current Marks	Current Owner/operator	Model Series	Initial Delivery	Remarks
44	N1550	Allegheny Airlines	203	5/10/65	D to Braniff S to Allegheny AL
45	N1134J	Allegheny Airlines	203	8/11/65	D to Braniff as N1551. S to Mohawk, since merged with Allegheny AL
46	N1135J	Allegheny Airlines	203	24/11/65	D to Braniff as N1552. S to Mohawk, since merged with Allegheny AL
49	EI–ANE	Aer Lingus-Irish	208AL	16/5/65	*St. Mel*
50	EI–ANF	Aer Lingus-Irish	208AL	12/6/65	*St. Malachy.* L to Lancia as AN–BBS. Returned to Aer Lingus
51	EI–ANG	Aer Lingus-Irish	208AL	31/7/65	*St. Declan*
52	EI–ANH	Aer Lingus-Irish	208AL	9/9/65	*St. Ronan*
53	G–ASYD	BAC	400		Development aft. FF JUL–13–65. Cvtd to Srs 500 proto FF JUN–30–67. Cvtd to Srs 475 proto FF AUG–27–70
54	N77CS	Chesapeake and Ohio Railway	410	8/9/66	Second Srs 400 development aft. FF SEP–16–65 as G–ASYE. S Victor Comptometer, reg N3939V. Later reg N4111X. S Chesapeake and Ohio.
55	N5015	National Aircraft Leasing	401	23/12/65	D American Airlines S National Aircraft Leasing
56	N5016	National Aircraft Leasing	401	22/1/66	D American Airlines S National Aircraft Leasing
57	N5017	Jet Travel	401	29/1/66	D American Airlines S Jet Travel
58	N5018	National Aircraft Leasing	401	15/2/66	D American Airlines. S National Aircraft Leasing
59	N5019	American Airlines	401	24/2/66	
60	N5021	National Aircraft Leasing	401	4/3/66	D American Airlines S National Aircraft Leasing
61	N5020	American Airlines	401	13/3/66	
62	N5022	American Airlines	401	17/3/66	
63	N5023	American Airlines	401	21/3/66	
64	N5025	American Airlines	401	7/4/66	
65	N5024	American Airlines	401	15/4/66	
66	G–A2MI	Orientair	401	23/4/66	D American Airlines as N5026 S Orientair
67	N5027	American Airlines	401	29/4/66	
68	N5028	American Airlines	401	10/5/66	
69	N5029	American Airlines	401	21/5/66	
70	N1553	Braniff	203	8/12/65	WO Falls City AUG–6–66
71	N1136J	Allegheny Airlines	203	22/12/65	D to Braniff as N1554. S to Mohawk since merged with Allegheny AL
72	N5030	National Aircraft Leasing	401	27/5/66	D American Airlines S National Aircraft Leasing
73	N111FL	Farmland Co	401	9/6/66	D American Airlines as N5031 S to Farmland Co.
74	VP–BDI	Bahamasair	401	21/6/66	Temporarily G–ATVU before delivery to American Airlines as N5032. Later registered AN–BHM. S Bahamasair
75	N5033	American Airlines	401	27/6/66	
76	N5034	American Airlines	401	9/6/66	
77	YR–BCG	TAROM–Romania	401	22/7/66	D American Airlines as N5035 S. TAROM
78	N5036	American Airlines	401	4/8/66	
79	N5037	National Aircraft Leasing	401	19/8/66	D American Airlines S National Aircraft Leasing

BAC One-Eleven

C/n	Current Marks	Current Owner/operator	Model Series	Initial Delivery	Remarks
80	N10HM	Jet Travel	401	8/9/66	D American Airlines as N5038 S to Jet Travel
81	N5039	American Airlines	401	13/10/66	
82	N1115J	Allegheny Airlines	204	21/11/65	D Mohawk, since merged with Allegheny AL
83	N502T	Tenneco	212	4/4/66	
84	D–ABHH	H. Horten GmbH	211	29/1/66	
85	G–ASTJ	British Caledonian	201	9/11/65	
86	N5040	American Airlines	401	28/10/66	
87	G–AXCP	Dan-Air	401	10/11/66	D American Airlines as N5041 S Dan-Air
88	N5042	American Airlines	401	19/11/66	
89	N5043	American Airlines	401	10/12/66	
90	G–AXCK	Dan-Air	401	16/12/66	D American Airlines as N5044 S Dan-Air
91	XX–919	RAE Farnborough	402	19/4/66	D Philippine AL as PI–C1121 S RAE Farnborough as development craft.
92	PI–C1131	Philippine Airlines	402	24/9/66	WO Manila SEP–12–69
93	YS–17C	TACA–El Salvador	407	14/12/66	
94	CF–QBR	Quebecair	402	16/1/67	FF as G–16–1 on JAN–3–67 L to Bavaria Fluggesellschaft as G–AYEJ. D to Philippine AL as PI–C1141. S to Quebecair
95	G–ASVT	BAC	201		Rebuild of c/n 6 G–ASJB, not completed.
96	N1130J	Allegheny Airlines	215	15/4/66	D to Aloha Airlines as N11181 *Queen Kapiolani* S to Mohawk, since merged with Allegheny AL
97	N1131J	Allegheny Airlines	215	7/6/66	D to Aloah Airlines as N11182 S to Mohawk, since merged with Allegheny AL
98	N1116J	Mohawk	204	5/8/66	*Discover America.* WO Blossburg JUN–23–67
99	N1117J	Allegheny Airlines	204	30/8/66	D to Mohawk, since merged with Allegheny AL
100	N1118J	Allegheny Airlines	204	26/9/66	D to Mohawk, since merged Allegheny AL
101	N1119J	Allegheny Airlines	204	15/10/66	D to Mohawk, since merged Allegheny AL
102	N1120J	Allegheny Airlines	204	24/1/67	D to Mohawk, since merged Allegheny AL
103	N1122J	Allegheny Airlines	204	17/8/67	D to Mohawk, since merged Allegheny AL
104	N1123J	Allegheny Airlines	204	30/12/67	D to Mohawk, since merged Allegheny AL
105	N1132J	Allegheny Airlines	215	31/5/67	D to Aloha Airlines as N11183 *Queen Kaahumanu* S to Mohawk, since merged Allegheny AL
106	YS–18C	TACA–El Salvador	407	21/2/67	
107	G–AVBW	Laker Airways	320L	25/2/67	
108	YS–01C	TACA–El Salvador	409	14/4/67	D to LACSA as T1-1056C. *El Tico.* S to TACA.
109	G–AVBX	Laker Airways	320L	8/4/67	
110	CF–QBN	Quebecair	304	18/4/67	D to British Eagle as G–ATPH S to Quebecair
111	AN–BBI	ICN Corporation	412	20/4/67	D to LANICA. S to ICN Corp.
112	CF–QBO	Quebecair	304	25/5/67	D to British Eagle as G–ATPI. S to Quebecair

C/n	Current Marks	Current Owner/operator	Model Series	Initial Delivery	Remarks
113	G–AVBY	Laker Airways	320L	9/5/67	
114	G–AVGP	Cambrian Airways	408	14/6/67	Built for Channel Airways. L before D to Cambrian
115	G–AWEJ	Channel Airways	408	10/5/68	
116	D–ALLI	Bavaria Fluggesellschaft	414EG	25/6/68	FF as G–AWGG and L to Bavaria Flug. before S. *Moritz von Schwind*
117	LV–JGX	Austral	420	25/9/68	D as LV–PKB
118	VC92–2111	Brazilian Air Force	423	10/10/68	FF as G–16–2 on OCT–12–67
119	PP–SRT	VASP	422	19/12/67	
120	N44R	Rockwell International	419	21/9/67	D Englehard Industries as N270E S Rockwell
121	G–AXOX	Gulf Aviation	432	11/11/68	FF as G–16–5 on AUG–28–68. D to Bahamas AW as VP–BCY. S to Gulf Aviation
122	LV–IZR	Austral	420	12/10/67	Temporarily G–AVTF before D as LV–PID
123	LV–IZS	Austral	420	8/11/67	D as LV–PIF
124	A12–124	RAAF	217	12/1/68	
125	A12–125	RAAF	217	8/2/68	
126	PP–SRU	VASP	422	19/12/67	
127	G–AZED	Dan-Air	414	29/12/67	D to Bavaria Fluggesellschaft as D–ANDY. S to Dan-Air
128	G–AWKJ	Hanson Trust	408	31/3/69	D to Channel AW. L to BUA S to Hanson Trust
129	G–AVOE	Cambrian Airways	416	19/3/68	D to Autair *Halcyon Days.* S to Cambrian
130	YR–BCA	TAROM–Romania	424	14/6/68	FF as G–16–4 on JAN–23–68. WO DEC–17–70
131	G–AVOF	Cambrian Airways	416	8/2/68	D to Autair *Halcyon Breeze.* S to Cambrian
132	G–AWBL	Cambrian Airways	416	1/5/68	D to Autair *Halcyon Dawn.* S to Cambrian
133	G–AVYZ	Laker Airways	320L	11/4/68	
134	N1124J	Allegheny Airlines	204	25/3/68	Temporarily G–AWDF before D to Mohawk, since merged Allegheny AL
135	N1125J	Allegheny Airlines	204	17/6/68	D to Mohawk, since merged Allegheny AL
136	G–AVMH	British Airways	510	12/6/69	D to BEA
137	G–AVMI	British Airways	510	2/4/69	D to BEA
138	G–AVMJ	British Airways	510	29/8/68	D to BEA
139	G–AVMK	British Airways	510	16/9/68	D to BEA
140	G–AVML	British Airways	510	4/10/68	D to BEA
141	G–AVMM	British Airways	510	25/10/68	D to BEA
142	G–AVMN	British Airways	510	25/11/68	D to BEA
143	G–AVMO	British Airways	510	27/11/68	D to BEA
144	G–AVMP	British Airways	510	11/12/68	D to BEA
145	G–AVMR	British Airways	510	5/5/70	D to BEA
146	G–AVMS	British Airways	510	13/1/69	D to BEA
147	G–AVMT	British Airways	510	28/3/69	D to BEA
148	G–AVMU	British Airways	510	19/3/69	D to BEA
149	G–AVMV	British Airways	510	21/4/69	D to BEA
150	G–AVMW	British Airways	510	2/5/69	D to BEA
151	G–AVMX	British Airways	510	20/6/69	D to BEA
152	G–AVMY	British Airways	510	21/7/69	D to BEA
153	G–AVMZ	British Airways	510	15/8/69	D to BEA
154	VC92–2110	Brazilian Air Force	423	13/5/69	
155	LV–JGY	Austral	420	17/12/68	D as LV–PKA
156	YR–BCB	TAROM–Romania	424	17/12/68	

BAC One-Eleven

C/n	Current Marks	Current Owner/operator	Model Series	Initial Delivery	Remarks
157	G–AXMU	Gulf Aviation	432	4/12/68	FF as G–16–14 on NOV–27–68. D to Bahamas AW as VP–BCZ. S to Philippine AL, registered PI–C1151. S to Gulf Aviation, registered G–AXMU.
158	D–AISY	Bavaria Fluggesellschaft	414EG	22/4/70	*Franz von Lembach*
159	YR–BCD	TAROM–Romania	424	30/7/69	
160	D–ANNO	Bavaria Fluggesellschaft	414EG	22/12/70	*Carl Spitzweg*
161	YR–BCH	TAROM–Romania	402	1/3/69	Intended as PI–C1151 for Philippine AL. L by BAC under registration G–AYHM. Later registered EC–BQF. S to TAROM
162	TI–1055C	LACSA–Costa Rica	409	13/11/69	FF as G–16–6 on FEB–14–69. L to Quebecair as G–AXBB. L to TAROM as YR–BCP. L to Germanair as G–AXBB. S to LACSA
163	D–AILY	Bavaria Fluggesellschaft	414EG	26/2/70	*Dominikus Zimmermann*
164					
165	YR–BCE	TAROM–Romania	424	23/11/69	
166	PK–PJC	Pelita	416	20/3/69	L to Autair as G–AWXJ *Halcyon Sun.* S to Aero-leasing, registered HB–ITK and L to Autair. Later registration 9V–BEF. S to Pelita
167	YR–BCC	TAROM–Romania	424	3/7/69	
168	YR–BCF	TAROM–Romania	424	13/12/69	
169					
170					
171					
172					
173					
174	G–AWYR	British Caledonian	501	11/4/69	
175	G–AWYS	British Caledonian	501	24/4/69	
176	G–AWYT	British Caledonian	501	13/5/69	
177	G–AWYU	British Caledonian	501	17/6/69	
178	G–AWYV	British Caledonian	501	26/6/69	
179	N1126J	Allegheny Airlines	204	2/8/68	D to Mohawk, since merged with Allegheny AL
180	N1127J	Allegheny Airlines	204	31/12/68	D to Mohawk, since merged with Allegheny AL
181	N1128J	Allegheny Airlines	204	21/1/69	D to Mohawk, since merged with Allegheny AL
182	N1129J	Allegheny Airlines	204	17/5/69	D to Mohawk, since merged with Allegheny AL
183	N503T	Tenneco	212	8/7/69	
184	G–AWWX	British Caledonian	509	29/3/69	*Isle of Skye*
185	G–AWWY	British Caledonian	509	31/3/69	*Iona*
186	G–AWWZ	British Caledonian	509	28/4/69	*Eriskay*
187	D–AMAS	Germanair	515FB	13/6/69	D Paninternational as D–ALAT. Later registered G–AZPY. S to Germanair
188	VP–LAP	LIAT	517	23/7/69	D Bahamas Airways as VP–BCN later registered G–AZEB. S to LIAT
189	G–AZEC	Court Line	517	29/7/69	D Bahamas Airways as VP–BCO. S to Court Line.
190	D–AMIE	Germanair	524FF	17/10/69	
191	G–AXJK	British Caledonian	501	5/3/70	

C/n	Current Marks	Current Owner/operator	Model Series	Initial Delivery	Remarks
192	LV–JNR	Austral	521	21/11/69	FF as G–16–7 on Oct–15–69. D to Austral. S to Sadia, registered PP–SDP later registered G–AYXB. S to Austral
193	PP–SDT	Trans Brasil	523	17/2/70	FF as G–16–8 on SEP–25–69. D British Midland as G–AXLL. S to Trans Brasil
194	LV–JNS	Austral	521	18/11/69	FF as G–16–19 on OCT–8–69 Temporarily G–AXPH before D.
195	D–AMUR	Germanair	524FF	16/12/69	Temporarily G–AXSY before D.
196	LV–JNT	Austral	521	25/11/69	FF as G–16–10 on NOV–6–69
197	D–AMOR	Germanair	524FF	20/3/70	FF as G–16–11. Temporarily G–AXVO before D.
198	VP–LAN	LIAT	517	20/6/72	FF as G–16–12 on JAN–12–70. Intended for Bahamas AW as VP–BCQ
199	G–AXLM	British Midland	523	5/3/70	
200	G–AXME	Court Line	518	5/12/69	*Halcyon Breeze*
201	G–AXMG	Court Line	518	18/12/69	*Halcyon Sky*
202	G–AXMH	Court Line	518	11/2/70	*Halcyon Sun*
203	G–AXMI	Court Line	518	24/3/70	*Halcyon Days*
204	G–AXMJ	Court Line	518	12/3/70	*Halcyon Night*
205	G–AXMK	Court Line	518	17/4/70	*Halcyon Star.* Has been L and registered as TG–ARA and VP–LAK
206	G–AXML	Court Line	518	30/4/70	*Halcyon Cloud* Has been L and registered as AN–BHJ
207	D–ALAR	Paninternational	515	13/5/70	WO SEP–6–71
208	G–AZPE	British Caledonian	515	20/3/70	D to Paninternational as D–ALAS
209	G–AXJL	British Caledonian	501	3/3/70	
210	G–AXYD	British Caledonian	509	18/3/70	*Isle of Arran*
211	G–AXLN	Court Line	523	12/3/70	D to British Midland. L to Court Line
212	HB–ITL	Phoenix	529	1/4/71	FF as G–16–3
213	PI–C1161	Philippine Airlines	527	26/10/71	Temporarily G–AYOS before D
214	G–AXJM	British Caledonian	501	25/3/70	
215	PI–C1171	Philippine Airlines	527	29/10/71	Temporarily G–AYKN before D
216					
217					
218					
219					
220					
221					
222					
223					
224					
225					
226	PI–C1181	Philippine Airlines	527	5/11/71	
227	D–AMUC	Bavaria Fluggeselleschaft	528	3/12/70	*Ludwig Thoma*
228	PP–SDQ	Trans Brasil	520	15/10/70	
229	D–AMAM	Germanair	515FB	12/3/71	D Paninternational as D–ALAQ Later registered G–AZPZ S to German air
230	PP–SDR	Trans Brasil	520	31/12/70	
231	TG–AZA	Aviateca-Guatemala	516	25/3/71	Intended for Philippine AL as PI–C1191 D to Aviateca

BAC One-Eleven

C/n	Current Marks	Current Owner/operator	Model Series	Initial Delivery	Remarks
232	G–AYOR	Court Line	518	18/3/71	
233	G–AYOP	British Caledonian	518	31/3/71	D to Court Line. S British Caledonian
234	D–ALFA	Bavaria Fluggesselschaft	528	26/2/71	*Jakob Fugger*
235	D–AMAT	Germanair	524FF	8/5/71	Temporarily G–AYSC before D.
236	PP–SDS	Trans Brasil	520	23/9/72	FF as G–16–15 on APR–30–71 before D
237	TI–1084C	LACSA–Costa Rica	531	26/5/71	Temporarily G–AYWB before D
238	D–ANUE	Bavaria Fluggesellschaft	528	15/3/72	*Albrecht Dürer*
239	OB–R–953	Faucett	476	23/7/71	FF as G–16–17 on APR–5–71 Temporarily G–AYUW before D
240	G–AZMF	British Caledonian	530	14/3/72	
241	G–AZUK	Faucett	476		FF as G–16–16 on JUL–5–71
242	TI–1095C	LACSA–Costa Rica	531	6/11/72	*Poas*
243	7Q–YKF	Air Malawi	481	23/2/72	
244	TI–1096C	LACSA–Costa Rica	531	15/5/73	
245	DQ–FBQ	Air Pacific	479	4/3/72	
246					
247					
248					
249					
250	DQ–FBV	Air Pacific	479	4/8/73	
251					
252					
253					
254					
255					

BAC/Vickers VC10

C/n	Current Marks	Current Owner/operator	Model Series	Initial Delivery	Remarks
803	G–ARTA	British Caledonian	1109	1/2/68	Prototype Srs 1100. FF JUN–29–62 as G–ARTA. Cvtd to production standard Srs 1109 and S Laker AW. L to MEA under registration OD–AFA. S BAC Re-registered G–ARTA. S BUA *Loch Ness.*
804	5N–ABD	Nigeria Airways	1101	8/12/64	D to BOAC as G–ARVA. S Nigeria AW WO Lagos NOV–20–69
805	G–ARVB	British Airways	1101	6/2/65	Formerly BOAC
806	G–ARVC	British Airways	1101	1/12/64	Formerly BOAC
807	G–ARVE	British Airways	1101	1/10/64	Formerly BOAC
808	G–ARVF	British Airways	1101	4/9/64	Formerly BOAC
809	G–ARVG	British Airways	1101	12/6/64	Formerly BOAC
810	G–ARVH	British Airways	1101	2/7/64	Formerly BOAC
811	G–ARVI	British Airways	1101	22/4/64	Formerly BOAC
812	G–ARVJ	British Airways	1101	23/4/64	Formerly BOAC
813	G–ARVK	British Airways	1101	2/5/64	Formerly BOAC
814	G–ARVL	British Airways	1101	16/6/64	Formerly BOAC
815	G–ARVM	British Airways	1101	22/7/64	Formerly BOAC
819	G–ASIW	British Caledonian	1103	30/9/64	D to BUA. Freight door
820	G–ASIX	British Caledonian	1103	31/10/64	D to BUA. Freight door
823	9G–ABO	Ghana Airways	1102	27/1/65	
824	9G–ABP	Middle East Airlines	1102	18/6/65	D to Ghana AW. Freight door. L to MEA. WO Beirut DEC–28–68
825	G–ATDJ	British Caledonian	1103	1/7/65	Freight door. Built as 9G–ABQ for Ghana AW. S to BUA
826	XR806	RAF Strike Command	1106	19/4/67	No.10 Sqdn. *George Thompson VC*
827	XR807	RAF Strike Command	1106	17/11/66	No.10 Sqdn. *Donald Garland VC; Thomas Gray VC*
828	XR808	RAF Strike Command	1106	7/7/66	No.10 Sqdn. *Kenneth Campbell VC*
829	G–AXLR	Rolls-Royce (1971) Ltd	1106	31/8/66	D to RAF Air Support Command as XR–809 No. 10 Sqdn. *Hugh Malcolm VC.* Cvtd to RB.211 test bed which FF MAR–6–70
830	XR810	RAF Strike Command	1106	21/12/66	No.10 Sqdn. *David Lord VC*
831	XV101	RAF Strike Command	1106	31/1/67	No.10 Sqdn. *Lanoe Hawker VC*
832	XV102	RAF Strike Command	1106	23/5/67	No.10 Sqdn. *Guy Gibson VC*
833	XV103	RAF Strike Command	1106	5/7/67	No. 10 Sqdn. *Edward Mannock VC*
834	XV104	RAF Strike Command	1106	3/8/67	No.10 Sqdn. *James McCudden VC*
835	XV105	RAF Strike Command	1106	20/10/67	No.10 Sqdn. *Albert Ball VC*
836	XV106	RAF Strike Command	1106	1/12/67	No.10 Sqdn. *Thomas Mottershead VC*
837	XV107	RAF Strike Command	1106	17/4/68	No.10 Sqdn. *James Nicolson VC*
838	XV108	RAF Strike Command	1106	18/6/68	No.10 Sqdn. *William Rhodes-Moorhouse VC*
839	XV109	RAF Strike Command	1106	1/8/68	No.10 Sqdn. *Arthur Scarf VC*

BAC/Vickers VC10

C/n	Current Marks	Current Owner/operator	Model Series	Initial Delivery	Remarks
851	G–ASGA	British Airways	1151	31/12/65	Formerly BOAC
852	G–ASGB	British Airways	1151	30/4/65	Formerly BOAC
853	G–ASGC	British Airways	1151	1/2/65	Formerly BOAC
854	G–ASGD	British Airways	1151	3/3/65	Formerly BOAC
855	G–ASGE	British Airways	1151	27/3/65	Formerly BOAC
856	G–ASGF	British Airways	1151	2/4/65	Formerly BOAC
857	G–ASGG	British Airways	1151	21/6/65	Formerly BOAC Autoland development until June 1967
858	G–ASGH	British Airways	1151	4/11/65	Formerly BOAC
859	G–ASGI	British Airways	1151	2/2/66	Formerly BOAC
860	G–ASGJ	British Airways	1151	3/3/67	Formerly BOAC
861	G–ASGK	British Airways	1151	27/10/67	Formerly BOAC
862	G–ASGL	British Airways	1151	25/1/68	Formerly BOAC
863	G–ASGM	British Airways	1151	9/4/68	Formerly BOAC
864	G–ASGN	B.O.A.C.	1151	7/5/68	WO Dawson Field, Jordan SEP–12–70
865	G–ASGO	British Airways	1151	27/9/68	Formerly BOAC
866	G–ASGP	British Airways	1151	6/12/68	Formerly BOAC
867	G–ASGR	British Airways	1151	29/5/69	Formerly BOAC
881	5X–UVA	East African Airways	1154	12/10/66	WO Addis Ababa APR–18–72
882	5H–MMT	East African Airways	1154	3/12/66	
883	5Y–ADA	East African Airways	1154	1/4/67	
884	5X–UVJ	East African Airways	1154	30/4/69	
885	5H–MOG	East African Airways	1154	28/2/70	

Beech 99

C/n	Current Marks	Current Owner/operator	Model Series	Initial Delivery	Remarks
LR–1	N599AT	Beech Aircraft	99		Prototype/demonstrator. FF July 1966
U–1	N7099N	Monmouth Airlines	99	29/6/70	Engineering prototype before D
U–2	N7199N	Bar Harbor Airways	99	20/9/69	Demonstrator before D to FAA S Bar Harbor Airways
U–3	N1032C	Pro Airlines	99	3/5/68	D to Commuter AL. S Pro Airlines
U–4	N8399N	Continental Oil Company	99	1/11/69	L to Varig as PP–VDY before delivery D to Keystone Commuter. S to Continental Oil Company
U–5	N1036C	Bar Harbor Airways	99	3/5/68	D to Commuter AL S to Bar Harbor Airways
U–6	N1038C	Air South	99	23/5/68	D to Commuter AL. S to Air South
U–7	N1048C	Pro Airlines	99	23/5/68	D to Commuter AL. S to Pro Airlines
U–8	N245V	Air Wisconsin	99	21/5/68	
U–9	N1049C	Altair Airlines	99	29/5/68	D to Commuter AL. S to Altair Airlines
U–10	N246V	Air Wisconsin	99	27/5/68	
U–11	F–BRUN	Air Alpes	99	9/2/70	Demonstrator N8499N before D
U–12	N3757Q	Brunei Shell Petroleum Co	99	24/7/68	
U–13	N8899M	MidState Air Commuter	99	13/6/68	
U–14	N651EX	Great Western Aircraft	99	2/7/68	Originally N614RV. D to Executive AL. S to Great Western Aircraft
U–15	N196HA	Henson Aviation	99	19/6/68	Was L formerly to Allegheny Commuter
U–16					
U–17	N845NS	Air South	99	28/6/68	
U–18		Touraine Air Transport	99	2/7/68	D to Coastal Aviation S to Reading Air Service. S to Touraine Air Transport.
U–19	F–BSRZ	Avia Taxi France	99	28/6/68	D to Executive AL as N650EX S to Avia Taxi France
U–20	N850SA	Shawnee Airlines	99	3/7/68	
U–21		Air Alpes	99	18/7/68	D Commuter AL as N1058C S Air Alpes
U–22	N985MA	Monmouth Airlines	99	18/7/68	
U–23	N740A	Altair Airlines	99	18/7/68	
U–24	N315VA	Vercoa Air Service	99	3/8/68	Was leased formerley to Allegheny Commuter
U–25	N851SA	Houston Metro Airlines	99	24/7/68	D Shawnee Airlines S Houston Metro Airlines
U–26	N746A	Altair Airlines	99	31/7/68	D to Ohio Aviation. S Altair Airlines
U–27	N7507N	Command Airways	99	1/8/68	
U–28	N699JM	Mackey International Air Taxi	99	6/8/68	
U–29	N7486N	Pennsylvania Commuter	99	13/8/68	Originally N488MD
U–30	N652EX	MidState Air Commuter	99	14/8/68	D Executive AL. S MidState Air Commuter

Beech 99

C/n	Current Marks	Current Owner/operator	Model Series	Initial Delivery	Remarks
U–31	N316BA	Vercoa Air Service	99	21/8/68	D Commuter AL. S Vercoa Air Services
U–32	N444T	Fairways Corporation	99	18/9/68	
U–33	N1128H	Hub Airlines	99	28/8/68	
U–34	N852SA	Shawnee Airlines	99	6/9/68	
U–35	N336PL	Pocono Airlines	99	5/9/68	Was leased formerly to Allegheny Commuter
U–36	N949K	Tulakes Aviation	99A	30/9/71	Originally Beech demonstrator before D
U–37	N7530N	Midwest Commuter	99	11/10/68	D Gopher Airlines. S Time Airlines. S Midwest Commuter
U–38	N1075C	Upper Valley Aviation	99	25/9/68	D Commuter AL. S Upper Valley Aviation
U–39	N7647	Skyway Aviation	99	25/9/68	
U–40	N910JM	Mackey International Air Taxi	99	27/9/68	
U–41	N853SA	Houston Metro Airlines	99	3/10/68	D Shawnee AL. S Houston Metro Airlines
U–42	N7799R	Air East	99	27/11/68	D Allegheny AL. S Air East
U–43	N899JM	Mackey International Air Taxi	99	10/10/68	
U–44					
U–45	N854SA	Rio Airways	99	3/10/68	D Shawnee AL. S Rio Airways
U–46	N855SA	Shawnee Airlines	99	16/10/68	
U–47	N7485N	Hub Airlines	99	23/10/68	
U–48	N7699N	S.M.B. Stage Line	99	25/10/68	Was L formerly to Air Pacific
U–49	N846NS	Air South	99	7/11/68	
U–50	N7940	Air New England	99	31/10/68	D Monmouth AL. S Air New England
U–51	N1031S	United Beechcraft	99	7/11/68	D Cal State AL. S United Beechcraft
U–52	N847NS	Air South	99	13/11/68	
U–53	N1032S	Altair Airlines	99	9/11/68	D Cal State AL. S Altair Airlines
U–54	N1129H	Hub Airlines	99	15/11/68	
U–55	N24KS	Kelly-Springfield Tire Co	99	26/2/69	D Coastal Aviation as N3116C S Kelly-Springfield Tire Co.
U–56	N7901R	Rio Airways	99	21/11/68	D Hood Airlines. S Rio Airways
U–57	F–BSUZ	Air-Rouergue	99	16/12/68	D Commuter AL as N1173C S Air-Rouergue
U–58	N7801R	Great Lakes Commuter	99	27/12/68	D Air Indies. S Great Lakes Commuter
U–59		Touraine Air Transport	99	19/12/68	D Tradewinds AL as N7834R. S Touraine Air Transport
U–60	N7888R	MidState Air Commuter	99	24/4/69	
U–61		Touraine Air Transport	99	9/7/70	D Arawak AL as N8110R. S Touraine Air Transport
U–62		Air Alpes	99	20/12/68	D Commuter AL as N1178C. S Air Alpes
U–63	N995E	Professional Air Transport	99	20/12/68	D Air Indies. S Professional Air Transport
U–64	N1033S	Altair Airlines	99	14/12/68	D Cal State AL. S Altair Airlines
U–65	PP–FSC	Ministerio do Interior, Brazil	99	26/12/68	
U–66	N451C	Altair Airlines	99	23/4/69	
U–67	N954SM	Golden West Airlines	99	31/12/68	D to Air Pacific. S Golden West Airlines

C/n	Current Marks	Current Owner/operator	Model Series	Initial Delivery	Remarks
U–68	N8068R	Skyway Aviation	99	26/3/69	Originally N1185C
U–69	N8012R	Great Lakes Commuter	99	11/6/69	D Trans Michigan AL. S Great Lakes Commuter
U–70	N8013R	Great Lakes Commuter	99	11/6/69	Originally N1191C. D Trans Michigan AL S Great Lakes Commuter
U–71	N1034S	Air New England	99	14/1/69	D Cal State AL. S Air New England
U–72	N317VA	Vercoa Air Service	99	23/1/69	D Shawnee AL as N8565A. S Vercoa Air Service
U–73	N796A	Altair Airlines	99	22/1/69	
U–74	N7655N	Crown Airways	99	30/1/69	
U–75	F–BIEM	Air Paris	99	29/1/69	D Shawnee AL as N857SA. S Air Paris
U–76	N983MA	Monmouth Airlines	99	3/2/69	
U–77	N848NS	Air South	99	6/3/69	
U–78	N7809R	Vercoa Air Service	99	7/4/70	Was leased formerly to Allegheny Commuter
U–79		Touraine Air Transport	99	13/2/69	D as N551 to Golden Pacific AL. Later registered N100GP. S to Touraine Air Transport
U–80	N653EX	Altair Airlines	99A	16/2/69	D Executive AL S to Altair Airlines
U–81	NK	John Roberts Ltd	99A	21/2/69	D Executive AL as N654EX.
U–82		Air Gaspe	99A	16/2/69	D Executive AL as N655EX. S to Air Gaspe
U–83	N656EX	Pennsylvania Commuter	99A	21/2/69	D Executive AL S to Pennsylvania Commuter
U–84	NK	John Roberts Ltd	99A	25/2/69	D Executive AL as N657EX.
U–85	N7862R	Aero Mech	99A	1/5/69	D Air Michigan S to Aero Mech
U–86		Touraine Air Transport	99	7/3/69	D as N671GP to Golden Pacific AL. Later registered N101GP. S to Touraine Air Transport
U–87		Touraine Air Transport	99	3/3/69	D Tradewinds AL as N7902R S to Touraine Air Transport
U–88	N7899R	Henson Aviation	99	27/5/69	Leased formerly to Allegheny Commuter
U–89	N658EX	Altair Airlines	99A	15/3/69	D Executive AL. S to Altair Airlines
U–90		Touraine Air Transport	99	21/3/69	D Golden Pacific AL as N921GP. S to Touraine Air Transport
U–91	N19991	Command Airways	99	3/4/69	D Golden West AL. L Golden Pacific AL. S Command Airways
U–92		Uni-Air	99	29/3/69	D Golden Pacific AL as N931GP. S Uni-Air
U–93	ZS–CHH	Air Cape	99A	11/4/69	
U–94	N981GP	Seagreen Air Transport	99	16/4/69	D Golden Pacific AL. S Seagreen Air Transport
U–95	N9995	Air New England	99	11/4/69	L from Golden West AL
U–96	N1920T	United Air Services Ltd	99A	24/2/70	D Texas International as N2858B. Re-registered N1920T. S United Air Services
U–97	N3990A	Air Midwest	99A	2/6/69	
U–98	NK	C Frank and Associates	99	1/5/69	D Golden Pacific AL as N991GP
U–99	N8099R	Keystone Commuter	99	11/6/69	

Beech 99

C/n	Current Marks	Current Owner/operator	Model Series	Initial Delivery	Remarks
U–100	N99100	Air New England	99	30/4/69	D Air Pacific S Golden West AL. S Air New England
U–101	N7961R	Rio Airways	99A	26/5/69	D Hood AL. S Rio Airways
U–102	N247V	Air Wisconsin	99	30/4/69	
U–103	N7994R	S.M.B. Stage Line	99	6/5/69	
U–104	N1922T	Marco Island Airways	99A	30/6/70	D Texas International as N4155A Re-registered N1922T L Marco Island Airways
U–105	N4099A	Air Midwest	99A	2/10/70	Beech Aircraft demonstrator before D
U–106					
U–107		Touraine Air Transport	99	16/5/69	D Tradewinds AL as N7986R S Touraine Air Transport
U–108	N8084R	Vercoa Air Service	99	1/7/69	D Travel Air. S Vercoa Air Service
U–109	N2880A	Cascade Airways	99	28/5/69	
U–110	N4212A	Henson Aviation	99A	4/6/69	D Air Michigan S Henson Aviation
U–111	N20FW	Cascade Airways	99A	17/6/69	D Flying W. S Wright Airlines. L to Cascade Airways.
U–112	N195R	Royale Airlines	99A	8/4/70	
U–113	N295R	Royale Airlines	99A	1/7/70	
U–114	N2860A	Cascade Airways	99	8/7/69	
U–115	N1924T	Rio Airways	99A	2/7/69	D Air Texas as N24AT. S Texas International AL. Re-registered N1924T. L Rio Airways
U–116	N860SA	Apollo Aviation	99A	3/7/69	D Shawnes AL. S Allegheny AL. L to Apollo Avaition
U–117	N21FW	Cascade Airways	99A	10/7/69	D Flying W. S Wright Airlines L Cascade Airways
U–118	N296HA	Henson Aviation	99A	1/7/69	Leased formerly to Allegheny Commuter
U–119	N7997R	Command Airways	99	25/11/69	
U–120	N9018Q	C. Itoh and Co	99	26/5/70	
U–121					
U–122	F–BRUX	Air Alpes	99	11/5/70	
U–123	NIOHA	Rio Airways	99A	11/12/69	D Hood Airlines S Rio Airways
U–124	N788C	Altair Airlines	99	15/7/69	
U–125	N3925A	Air East	99A	26/7/69	
U–126	N21AT	Rio Airways	99A	2/8/69	D Air Texas S to Rio Airways
U–127	N22AT	Colgan Airways	99A	2/8/69	D Air Texas S to Colgan Airways
U–128	N1921T	Marco Island Airways	99A	13/2/70	D Texas International S to Marco Island Airways
U–129	LN–LML	Air Alpes	99A	17/4/70	
U–130	LN–LMT	Air Alpes	99A	29/4/70	
U–131					
U–132	N1923T	Marco Island Airways	A99A	20/11/69	D Air Texas as N23AT. S Texas International Airlines re-registered N1923T. L Marco Island Airways
U–133	N2421A	Air East	99A	1/11/69	D Hub Airlines S Air East
U–134	N180Z	US Dept of Agriculture. Forest Service	99A	22/10/70	
U–135	N10RA	Rio Airways	99A	23/12/69	
U–136	PT–CIK	Central Eletrica De Furnas	99	19/12/69	
U–137	300	Ministerio de Defensa Nacional-Chile	99A	17/8/70	

C/n	Current Marks	Current Owner/operator	Model Series	Initial Delivery	Remarks
U–138	301	Ministerio de Defensa Nacional-Chile	99A	1/7/70	
U–139	302	Ministerio de Defensa Nacional-Chile	99A	2/7/70	
U–140	303	Ministerio de Defensa Nacional-Chile	99A	2/7/70	
U–141	304	Ministerio de Defensa Nacional-Chile	99A	17/8/70	
U–142	305	Ministerio de Defensa Nacional-Chile	99A	17/8/70	
U–143	306	Ministerio de Defensa Nacional-Chile	99A		
U–144	307	Ministerio de Defensa Nacional-Chile	99A		
U–145	308	Ministerio de Defensa Nacional-Chile	99A		
U–146	N4299A	Pacific Southwest Airlines	B99	3/4/72	
U–147	N147AE	Air East	99A	8/9/71	
U–148	N9399Q	Aero Mech	B99	24/11/71	
U–149	N3149W	United Air Services	B99	3/5/73	
U–150	N5SS	Scheduled Skyways	B99	15/11/72	
U–151	N338PL	Pocono Airlines	B99	23/2/73	
U–152					
U–153					
U–154					
U–155					
U–156					
U–157					
U–158					
U–159					
U–160					

Boeing 707

C/n	Current Marks	Current Owner/operator	Model Series	Initial Delivery	Remarks
17586	N708PA	PAA	121	1/12/58	*Constitution.* WO Montserrat SEP–17–65
17587	N707PA	PAA	121B	19/12/58	*Maria* Srs 121 cvtd. WFS
17588	N709PA	PAA	121	15/8/58	*Tradewind* WO Elkton DEC–8–63
17589	N710PA	PAA	121B	29/9/58	*America* Srs 121 cvtd. WFS
17590	N711PA	PAA	121B	16/10/58	*America*, later *Mayflower.* Srs 121 cvtd. WFS
17591	N712PA	PAA	121B	31/10/58	*Washington.* Srs 121 cvtd. WFS
17592	N714PA	PAA	321	28/8/59	*Golden Eagle*
17593	N715PA	Greyfin Leasing	321	19/7/59	D to PAA. *Liberty Bell.* S MAR–27–72
17594	N716PA	Pan Ayer	321	22/8/59	D to PAA. *Flying Eagle.* S SEP 1973
17595	N717PA	PAA	321	1/9/59	*Fleetwing*
17596	N718PA	PAA	321	22/9/59	*Invincible*
17597	G–AYBJ	British Midland	321	3/10/59	D to PAA as N719PA *Windward.* S APR–15–70
17598	G–AYVG	Donaldson International	321	6/10/59	D to PAA as N720PA *Fairwind.* S MAR–1–71
17599	G–AYSL	Dan-Air	321	19/10/59	D to PAA as N721PA *Splendid.* S MAR–1–71
17600	G–AZTG	Dan-Air	321	28/10/59	D to PAA as N722PA *Lark.* S MAY–16–72
17601	–	GATX/Boothe	321	27/10/59	D to PAA as N723PA *Viking.* S MAY–24–70
17602	G–BAEL	Donaldson International	321	8/12/59	D to PAA as N724PA *Mercury.* S NOV 1972
17603	N725PA	Greyfin Leasing	321	12/12/59	D to PAA as N725PA. *Aurora* S MAR–27–72
17604	N726PA	Leas Air Corporation	321	13/1/60	D to PAA as N726PA. *Westward Ho.* S AUG–15–72
17605	G–AZWA	Donaldson International	321	27/1/60	D to PAA as N727PA *Mohawk.* S JUN–22–72
17606	N11RV	International Controls Corp	321	6/3/60	D to PAA as N728PA *Peerless* S JUN–14–71
17607	N729PA	Greyfin Leasing	321	27/4/60	D to PAA as N729PA *Isabella.* S MAR–27–72
17608	G–AYXR	Donaldson International	321	28/4/60	D to PAA as N730PA. *Bald Eagle.* S MAY–14–71
17609	N70773	Continental AL	124	19/4/59	WO Kansas City JUL–1–65
17610	–	Israel Aircraft Industries	124	27/5/59	D to Continental AL as N70774. S to TWA DEC–22–67. S NOV–12–71
17611	N70775	Continental AL	124	17/7/59	WO MAY–23–62
17612	–	Israel Aircraft Industries	124	10/10/59	D to Continental AL as N70785. S to TWA DEC–31–67. S NOV–16–71
17613	F–BHSA	Air France	328	22/10/59	*Versailles.* WO Hamburg JUN–16–61
17614	F–BHSB	Air France	328	10/12/59	*Chambard*
17615	F–BHSC	Air France	328	23/12/59	Was N74615 before D *Fontaine Bleau*
17616	F–BHSD	Air France	328	29/1/60	*Chenonceaux*
17617	F–BHSE	Air France	328	20/3/60	*Rambouillet*
17618	F–BHSF	Air France	328	24/3/60	*Blois*
17619	F–BHSG	Air France	328	12/5/60	Was N5093K before D *Pau*
17620	F–BHSH	Air France	328	23/6/60	*Amboise*
17621	F–BHSI	Air France	328	11/7/60	*Josselin*
17622	F–BHSJ	Air France	328	29/7/60	*Chaumont*
17623	OO–SJA	Sabena	329	4/12/59	
17624	OO–SJB	Sabena	329	13/1/60	WO Brussels FEB–15–61

C/n	Current Marks	Current Owner/operator	Model Series	Initial Delivery	Remarks
17625	OO–SJC	Sabena	329	13/2/60	
17626	OO–SJD	Sabena	329	10/4/60	
17627	OO–SJE	Sabena	329	8/6/60	
17628	N7501A	American Airlines	123B	23/10/58	Was *Michigan* Srs 123 cvtd
17629	N7502A	American Airlines	123	4/5/59	*Oklahoma* WO Long Island JAN–28–61
17630	N7503A	American Airlines	123B	31/12/58	Was *California* Srs 123 cvtd
17631	N7504A	American Airlines	123B	23/1/59	Was *New York* Srs 123 cvtd
17632	N7505A	American Airlines	123B	31/1/59	Was *Illinois* Srs 123 cvtd
17633	N7506A	American Airlines	123B	12/2/59	Was *District of Columbia.* Srs 123 cvtd. WO New York MAR–1–62
17634	N7507A	American Airlines	123B	27/2/59	Was *Maryland* Srs 123 cvtd
17635	N7508A	American Airlines	123B	27/3/59	Was *Virginia* Srs 123 cvtd
17636	N7509A	American Airlines	123B	9/4/59	Was *Texas* Srs 123 cvtd
17637	N7510A	American Airlines	123B	23/4/59	Was *Massachusetts.* Srs 123 cvtd
17638	N7511A	American Airlines	123B	12/5/59	Was *New Jersey.* Srs 123 cvtd
17639	N7512A	American Airlines	123B	21/5/59	Was *Pennsylvania.* Srs 123 cvtd
17640	N7513A	American Airlines	123B	28/5/59	Was *Delaware* Srs 123 cvtd
17641	N7514A	American Airlines	123	5/6/59	*California.* WO Calverton AUG–15–59
17642	N7515A	American Airlines	123B	24/6/59	Was *Arizona* Srs 123 cvtd
17643	N7516A	American Airlines	123B	29/6/59	Was *Ohio* Srs 123 cvtd
17644	N7517A	American Airlines	123B	27/7/59	Was *Missouri* Srs 123 cvtd
17645	N7518A	American Airlines	123B	31/7/59	Was *Tennessee* Srs 123 cvtd
17646	PH–TVA	Transavia	123B	23/8/59	D to American Airlines as N7519A *Kentucky.* Srs 123 cvtd. S to Transavia MAR–21–72
17647	N7520A	American Airlines	123B	12/8/59	Was *Arkansas* Srs 123 cvtd
17648	N7521A	American Airlines	123B	14/9/59	Was *West Virginia* Srs 123 cvtd
17649	N7522A	American Airlines	123B	5/10/59	Was *Indiana* Srs 123 cvtd
17650	N7523A	American Airlines	123B	14/10/59	Was *Rhode Island* Srs 123 cvtd
17651	N7524A	American Airlines	123B	28/10/59	Was *Canada.* Srs 123 cvtd
17652	N7525A	American Airlines	123B	20/11/59	Was *Mexico.* Srs 123 cvtd
17658	–	Israel Aircraft Industries	131	29/1/59	D to TWA as N731TW. S Israel AI. DEC–20–71
17659	OO–TEC	Trans European	131	17/3/59	D to TWA as N732TW. S Israel AI. S to Trans European MAY–21–73
17660	–	Israel Aircraft Industries	131	30/3/59	D to TWA as N733TW. S Israel AI NOV–2–71
17661	N734TW	TWA	131	3/4/59	
17662	N735T	AirClub International	131	18/4/59	D to TWA as N735TW. S AirClub Int. MAR–8–71
17663	–	Israel Aircraft Industries	131	29/4/59	D to TWA as N736TW. S Israel AI DEC–6–71
17664	–	Israel Aircraft Industries	131	10/5/59	D to TWA as N737TW. S Israel AI DEC–13–71
17665	–	Israel Aircraft Industries	131	13/5/59	D to TWA as N738TW. S Israel AI DEC–15–71
17666	HS–VGA	Air Siam	131	28/5/59	D to TWA as N739TW. S Israel AI. S to Air Siam DEC–27–72
17667	–	Israel Aircraft Industries	131	24/5/59	D to TWA as N740TW. S Israel AI DEC–9–71
17668	N741TW	TWA	131	13/6/59	
17669	N742TW	TWA	131	1/7/59	WO Cincinatti NOV–6–67
17670	N743TW	TWA	131	10/7/59	
17671	HB–IEG	Phoenix Airways	131	14/7/59	D to TWA as N744TW. S Israel AI. S to Phoenix AW NOV–15–72

Boeing 707

C/n	Current Marks	Current Owner/operator	Model Series	Initial Delivery	Remarks
17672	OO–TED	Trans European	131	1/8/59	D to TWA as N745TW. S Israel Al NOV–26–71. S OCT–26–73
17673	N761TW	TWA	331	5/11/59	
17674	N701PA	PAA	331	4/11/59	*Donald McKay*
17675	N762TW	TWA	331	4/11/59	
17676	N763TW	TWA	331	25/11/59	
17677	N702PA	PAA	331	15/12/59	*Hotspur*
17678	N764TW	TWA	331	23/12/59	
17679	N765TW	TWA	331	18/1/60	
17680	—	Astroair Services	331	30/12/59	D to PAA as N703PA *Dash-away*. S to Astroair Services OCT 1973
17681	N766TW	TWA	331	29/2/60	
17682	N767TW	TWA	331	7/3/60	
17683	N704PA	PAA	331	23/3/60	*Defiance*
17684	N768TW	TWA	331	12/4/60	
17685	N769TW	TWA	331	9/5/60	WO Rome NOV–23–64
17686	N705PA	Air Holiday	331	8/4/60	D to PAA as N705PA *Wings of the Morning*. S to Air Florida. S to Air Holiday MAY–23–73
17687	N770TW	TWA	331	20/5/60	
17688	N771TW	TWA	331	22/6/60	
17689	N706PA	PAA	331	8/6/60	*Courier*
17690	N772TW	TWA	331	23/6/60	
17691	N7071	Braniff	227		WO Before delivery OCT–19–59
17692	9Y–TDO	British West Indian	227	3/12/59	D to Braniff as N7072. S FEB–9–71
17693	9Y–TDR	British West Indian	227	15/1/60	D to Braniff as N7073. S MAY–11–71
17694	9Y–TDP	British West Indian	227	21/1/60	D to Braniff as N7074. S MAR–27–71
17695	9Y–TDQ	British West Indian	227	10/2/60	D to Braniff as N7075. S APR–10–71
17696	CF–PWV	Pacific Western	138B	16/7/59	Was N31239 before D to Quantas as VH–EBA *Melbourne*. Srs 138 cvtd. S NOV–1967
17697	N790SA	Standard AW	138B	26/6/59	D Quantas as VH–EBB *Sydney*. Srs 138 cvtd. S MAY–6–67. L by El Al
17698	N791SA	Standard AW	138B	7/7/59	D to Qantas as VH–EBC *Canberra*. Srs 138 cvtd. S APR–1–67. L to Sudflug 1967. L to CPAL *Empress of Sydney* from 1967 until WO Vancouver FEB–7–68
17699	G–AVZZ	Laker Airways	138B	1/8/59	D to Qantas as VH–EBD *Brisbane*. Srs 138 cvtd. S JAN 1969
17700	N7935A	National Aircraft Leasing	138B	23/8/59	D to Qantas as VH–EBE *Perth*. Srs 138 cvtd. S to Pacific Western, reg CF–PWW. S SEP–15–71
17701	N792SA	Standard AW	138B	4/9/59	D to Qantas as VH–EBF *Adelaide*. Srs 138 cvtd. S 1968
17702	G–AWDG	Laker Airways	138B	18/9/59	D to Qantas as VH–EBG *Hobart* Srs 138 cvtd. S JAN 1969
17703	G–APFB	British Airways	436	8/4/60	Was N13241 before D to BOAC, now British Airways

C/n	Current Marks	Current Owner/operator	Model Series	Initial Delivery	Remarks
17704	G–APFC	British Airways	436	16/5/60	Was N5088K before D to BOAC, now British Airways
17705	G–APFD	British Airways Airtours	436	12/4/60	Was N5091K before D to BOAC, S British Airways Airtours.
17706	G–APFE	British Airways	436	19/4/60	Was N5092K before D. WO Mount Fuji MAR–5–66
17707	G–APFF	British Airways	436	14/5/60	D to BOAC, now British Airways
17708	G–APFG	British Airways Airtours	436	21/6/60	Was N5094K before D to BOAC. S to BEA Airtours, MAR–30–73. now British Airways Airtours.
17709	G–APFH	British Airways Airtours	436	14/7/60	D to BOAC. S to BEA Airtours JAN–15–72, now British Airways Airtours
17710	G–APFI	British Airways	436	23/7/60	D to BOAC, now British Airways
17711	G–APFJ	British Airways	436	21/9/60	D to BOAC, now British Airways
17712	G–APFK	British Airways Airtours	436	26/9/60	D to BOAC, S to BEA Airtours DEC–30–71, now British Airways Airtours
17713	G–APFL	British Airways Airtours	436	22/10/60	D to BOAC. S to BEA Airtours DEC–1–72, now British Airways Airtours
17714	G–APFM	British Airways	436	5/11/60	D to BOAC, now British Airways
17715	G–APFN	British Airways	436	16/11/60	D to BOAC, now British Airways
17716	G–APFO	British Airways Airtours	436	6/12/60	D to BOAC, S to BEA Airtours NOV–15–72. now British Airways Airtours
17717	G–APFP	British Airways	436	22/12/60	D to BOAC, now British Airways
17718	D–ABOB	Lufthansa	430	3/2/60	Was N31240 before D *Hamburg*
17719	D–ABOC	Lufthansa	430	9/3/60	*Berlin.* L to Condor
17720	D–ABOD	Lufthansa	430	24/4/60	*Frankfurt*
17721	D–ABOF	Lufthansa	430	30/9/60	*Munchen*
17722	VT–DJI	Air India	437	18/2/60	*Nanda Devi* WO
17723	VT–DJJ	Air India	437	17/2/60	*Annapurna,* later *Gauri Shankar*
17724	VT–DJK	Air India	437	8/3/60	*Bombay,* later *Everest*
17903	N76413	Air Vietnam	139B	13/5/60	D to PAA as N778PA. Srs 139 cvtd
17904	N779PA	PAA	139B	4/5/60	D as N74614 Srs 139 cvtd. WO New York APR–7–64
17905	PP–VJA	Varig	441	27/4/60	Was N5090K before D
17906	PP–VJB	Varig	441	15/6/60	WO Lima Nov–27–62
17918	F–BHSK	Air France	328	18/8/60	Was N5095K before D *Vizille*
17919	F–BHSL	Air France	328	19/8/60	*Maintenon*
17920	F–BHSM	Air France	328	21/9/60	*Sully.* WO Orly JUN–3–62
17921	F–BHSN	Air France	328	16/9/60	*Valencay*
17922	F–BHSO	Air France	328	16/9/60	*Anet*
17923	F–BHSP	Air France	328	7/11/60	*Villandry*
17924	F–BHSQ	Air France	328	22/10/60	*Compiegne*
17925	58–6970	USAF	153B	3/5/59	VC–137B cvtd from VC–137A
17926	58–6971	USAF	153B	30/5/59	VC–137B cvtd from VC–137A

Boeing 707

C/n	Current Marks	Current Owner/operator	Model Series	Initial Delivery	Remarks
17927	58–6972	USAF	153B	30/6/59	VC–137B cvtd from VC–137A
17928	ZS–SAA	SAA	344	13/6/60	D as ZS–CKC *Johannesburg*
17929	ZS–SAB	SAA	344	22/8/60	D as ZS–CKD *Capetown*
17930	ZS–SAC	SAA	344	22/8/60	D as ZS–CKE *Durban*
18012	–	Israel Aircraft Industries	124	17/3/60	D to Continental AL as N74612. S to TWA. S to Israel AI NOV–10–71
18054	N7526A	American Airlines	123B	25/5/60	
18055	VT–DMN	Air India	437	17/4/61	*Kanchenjunga* WO Alps JAN–24–66
18056	D–ABOG	Lufthansa	430	17/3/61	*Bonn*
18067	9Y–TDC	BWIA	138B	28/7/61	N93134 before D to Qantas as VH–EBH *Darwin.* S SEP–28–69
18068	N105BN	Regency Income Corp	138B	31/8/61	D to Qantas as VH–EBI *Winton.* S JUNE–28–69 to Braniff. S to Regency 1973
18069	N106BN	Regency Income Corp	138B	25/8/61	D to Qantas as VH–EBJ *Longreach.* S to Regency 1973
18070	4X–ATA	El Al	458	22/4/61	*Shehecheyanu*
18071	4X–ATB	El Al	458	7/6/61	
18083	G–AYVE	British Midland	321	16/5/61	D to PAA as N757PA *Pathfinder.* S JAN–1971
18084	VP–BDG	Bahama World Airlines	321	23/6/61	D to PAA as N758PA *Resolute* S to Lloyd International, reg G–AYRZ. S to Bahama World AL DEC–1972
18085	VP–BDF	Bahama World Airlines	321	11/7/61	D to PAA as N759PA *Freedom.* S to Lloyd International, reg G–AYAG. S to Bahama World AL DEC–1972
18245	F–BHSR	Air France	328	1/2/62	Was N93138 before D *Cheverny*
18246	F–BHSS	Air France	328	16/2/62	*Uzes*
18247	F–BHST	Air France	328	9/3/62	*Chantilly* WO Guadeloupe JUN–22–62
18334	9Y–TDB	BWIA	138B	2/2/62	D to Qantas as VH–EBK *Newcastle* S SEP–1969
18335	N760PA	PAA	321B	15/6/62	*Evening Star*
18336	N761PA	PAA	321B	13/6/62	*Friendship*
18337	N762PA	PAA	321B	12/4/62	*Endeavour*
18338	N763PA	PAA	321B	1/6/62	*Yankee*
18339	N764PA	PAA	321B	1/6/62	*Nautilus*
18357	4X–ATC	El Al	458	13/2/62	
18372	G–ARWD	British Airways	465	27/2/62	D to BOAC. Now British Airways
18373	G–ARWE	BOAC	465	6/7/62	WO Heathrow APR–8–68
18374	OO–SJF	Sabena	329	16/4/62	
18375	F–BHSU	Air France	328	11/5/62	*Versailles*
18385	N746TW	TWA	131B	29/3/62	
18386	N747TW	TWA	131B	10/4/62	
18387	N748TW	TWA	131B	30/4/62	
18388	N749TW	TWA	131B	18/5/62	
18389	N750TW	TWA	131B	23/5/62	
18390	N751TW	TWA	131B	31/5/62	
18391	N752TW	TWA	131B	16/6/62	
18392	N754TW	TWA	131B	28/6/62	
18393	N755TW	TWA	131B	23/7/62	
18394	N756TW	TWA	131B	2/8/62	
18395	N757TW	TWA	131B	1/8/62	

C/n	Current Marks	Current Owner/operator	Model Series	Initial Delivery	Remarks
18396	N758TW	TWA	131B	21/8/62	
18397	N759TW	TWA	131B	29/8/62	
18400	N781TW	TWA	131B	31/8/62	
18401	N782TW	TWA	131B	21/9/62	
18402	N783TW	TWA	131B	26/9/62	
18403	N784TW	TWA	131B	28/9/62	
18404	N785TW	TWA	131B	12/10/62	
18405	N773TW	TWA	331B	11/3/62	
18406	N774TW	TWA	331B	1/11/62	
18407	N775TW	TWA	331B	3/12/62	
18408	N776TW	TWA	331B	23/1/63	
18409	N778TW	TWA	331B	21/2/63	
18411	G–ARRA	British Airways	436	16/2/62	D to BOAC, now British Airways
18412	G–ARRB	British Airways	436	12/2/63	D to BOAC, now British Airways
18413	G–ARRC	British Airways	436	15/3/63	D to BOAC, now British Airways
18414	VT–DNY	Air India	437	6/3/62	*Dhaulagiri*
18415	VT–DNZ	Air India	437	12/4/62	*Nangaparbat*
18456	F–BHSV	Air France	328B	15/12/62	*Vincennes*
18457	F–BHSX	Air France	328B	11/1/63	*Grignon*
18458	F–BHSY	Air France	328B	17/2/63	*Luneville*
18459	F–BHSZ	Air France	328B	30/3/63	*Kerjean.* WO Caracas DEC–4–69
18460	OO–SJG	Sabena	329	19/1/63	
18461	62–6000	USAF	353B	9/10/62	VC–137C
18462	D–ABOV	Lufthansa	330B	28/2/63	*Berlin.* Was D–ABOS *Duisburg*
18463	D–ABOT	Lufthansa	330B	5/3/64	*Düsseldorf*
18579	N765PA	PAA	321C	8/6/63	*Gladiator*
18580	N766PA	PAA	321C	2/5/63	*Jupiter*
18582	HZ–ACE	Saudi Arabian AL	373C	16/7/63	D to World AW as N373WA S to Saudi Arabian AUG–15–73
18583	HZ–ACF	Saudi Arabian AL	373C	20/8/63	D to World AW as N374WA S to Saudi Arabian AUG–20–73
18584	VR–HGH	Cathay Pacific	351B	5/6/63	D to Northwest as N351US. S to Cathay Pacific JUN–30–71
18585	VR–HGI	Cathay Pacific	351B	19/6/63	D to Northwest as N352US. S to Cathay Pacific DEC–24–71
18586	VR–HGO	Cathay Pacific	351B	30/7/63	D to Northwest as N353US. S to Cathay Pacific AUG–27–72
18591	N767PA	PAA	321C	7/6/63	*Challenger*
18685	F–BLCA	Air France	328B	31/1/64	*Sully*
18686	F–BLCB	Air France	328B	13/1/64	*Chantilly*
18689	N7555A	American Airlines	323C	19/11/63	
18690	N7556A	American Airlines	323C	13/12/63	
18691	N7557A	American Airlines	323C	20/12/63	
18692	N7558A	American Airlines	323C	31/12/63	
18693	VR–HGN	Cathay Pacific	351B	9/9/63	D to Northwest as N354US. S to Cathay Pacific APR–29–72
18694	PP–VJJ	Varig	441	12/11/63	
18707	G–AYSI	Britannia Airways	373C	23/9/63	D to World Airways as N375 WA. S to Britannia AW FEB–28–71
18708	VT–DPM	Air India	337B	28/5/64	*Makalu*
18709	N789TW	TWA	373C	18/11/63	
18710	B–1828	China Airlines	351B	13/10/63	D to Northwest as N355US. S to China AL MAR–4–71

Boeing 707

C/n	Current Marks	Current Owner/operator	Model Series	Initial Delivery	Remarks
18711	N786TW	TWA	331C	24/4/64	
18712	N787TW	TWA	331C	19/5/64	WO Altantic City JUL–26–69
18713	N788TW	TWA	331C	11/6/64	
18714	N790PA	PAA	321C	26/2/64	*Courser*
18715	N791PA	PAA	321C	18/3/64	*Fidelity*
18716	N792PA	PAA	321C	27/3/64	*Good Hope*
18717	N793PA	PAA	321C	3/3/64	*Messenger*
18718	N794PA	PAA	321C	30/3/64	*Undaunted,* temporarily was *African Queen*
18737	LX–LGV	Luxair	348C	10/6/64	D to Aer Lingus as EI–AMW ***Lorcan O' Tuathail.*** S to Luxair JUN–23–72
18738	N790TW	TWA	373C	23/12/63	WO
18739	N107BN	Regency Income Corp	138B	6/8/64	D to Qantas as VH–EBL *Geelong* S to Braniff JUN–19–69. S to Regency 1973
18740	N108BN	Regency Income Corp	138B	1/9/64	D to Qantas as VH–EBM *Launceston.* S to Braniff JUN–24–69. S to Regency 1973
18746	CF–PWJ	Pacific Western	351C	9/4/64	D to Northwest as N356US. S to Pacific Western MAR–2–73
18747	VR–HHB	Cathay Pacific	351C	17/3/64	D to Northwest as N357US S to Cathay Pacific for D in 1974
18748	VR–HHD	Cathay Pacific	351C	12/6/64	D to Northwest as N358US S to Cathay Pacific for D in 1974
18756	N791TW	TWA	331C	22/7/64	
18757	N792TW	TWA	331C	24/8/64	
18758	N795TW	TWA	131B	9/10/64	
18759	N796TW	TWA	131B	26/10/64	
18760	N797TW	TWA	131B	10/11/64	
18761	N798TW	TWA	131B	3/12/64	
18762	N799TW	TWA	131B	8/12/64	
18764	N779TW	TWA	331B	14/1/65	
18765	N795PA	PAA	321C	29/4/64	*Jupiter Rex*
18766	N796PA	PAA	321C	8/5/64	*Mermaid*
18767	N797PA	PAA	321C	26/5/64	*Northwind*
18790	N798PA	PAA	321C	23/11/64	*Caribbean* WO Calcutta JUN–13–68
18808	VH–EBN	Qantas	338C	9/2/65	*Parramatta*
18809	9V–BFN	Singapore Airlines	338C	5/3/65	D to Qantas as VH–EBO *Townsville.* S to Singapore AL NOV–20–72
18810	VH–EBP	Qantas	338C	11/8/65	*Alice Springs*
18819	D–ABOX	Lufthansa	330B	8/1/65	*Köln*
18824	N799PA	PAA	321C	31/12/64	*Racer* WO Elmendorf DEC–26–68
18825	B–1832	China Airlines	321C	14/8/64	D to Continental Airlines as N17321. S to China AL AUG–10–73
18826	CF–PWZ	Pacific Western	321C	10/9/64	D to Continental AL as N17322. S to Pacific Western. WO
18832	N401PA	PAA	321B	3/2/65	*Dauntless*
18833	N402PA	PAA	321B	17/2/65	*Black Hawk*
18834	N403PA	PAA	321B	23/2/65	*Goodwill*
18835	N404PA	PAA	321B	4/3/65	*Seven Seas*
18836	N405PA	PAA	321B	10/3/65	*Stargazer*
18837	N406PA	PAA	321B	17/3/65	*Kingfisher*
18838	N407PA	PAA	321B	26/3/65	*Celestial* WO Rome DEC–17–73

C/n	Current Marks	Current Owner/operator	Model Series	Initial Delivery	Remarks
18839	N408PA	PAA	321B	15/4/65	*Morning Star*
18840	N409PA	PAA	321B	21/4/65	*Eclipse*
18841	N410PA	PAA	321B	27/4/65	*Argonaut*
18842	N412PA	PAA	321B	21/5/65	*Empress of the Skies*, was also *La Palma*
18873	VT–DSI	Air India	337B	12/3/65	Was N68655 before D *Lhotse*
18880	EI–ANO	Aer Lingus	348C	5/4/65	*St. Brigid*
18881	F–BLCC	Air France	328C	5/8/65	
18882	N7550A	American Airlines	123B	27/5/65	
18883	N7551A	American Airlines	123B	26/5/65	
18884	N7552A	American Airlines	123B	15/6/65	
18885	N7553A	American Airlines	123B	23/7/65	
18886	G–AZJM	British Caledonian	324C	17/6/65	D to Continental AL as N17323. S to Lloyd International. S to British Caledonian. MAR–7–73
18887	N17324	Continental Airlines	324C	21/6/65	
18888	VR–HHE	Cathay Pacific	351C	22/5/65	D to Northwest AL as N359US. S to Cathay Pacific for D in 1974
18889	VR–HHJ	Cathay Pacific	351C	12/6/65	D to Northwest AL as N360US. S to Cathay Pacific for D in 1974
18890	OO–SJH	Sabena	329C	18/4/65	
18891	ZS–SAD	SAA	344B	5/9/65	D as ZS–DYL *Bloemfontein*
18913	N760TW	TWA	331B	29/1/65	
18914	N780TW	TWA	331B	9/4/65	
18915	N793TW	TWA	331B	25/5/65	
18916	N8705T	TWA	331B	9/12/65	
18917	N8715T	TWA	331B	21/12/65	WO
18918	N8725T	TWA	331B	12/1/66	
18921	VR–HGR	Cathay Pacific	351C	14/8/65	D to Northwest AL as N361US. S to Cathay Pacific AUG–15–73
18922	VR–HGP	Cathay Pacific	351C	15/9/65	D to Northwest AL as N362US. S to Cathay Pacific NOV–18–72
18923	D–ABUB	Lufthansa	330B	4/8/65	*Stuttgart*
18924	G–ASZF	British Airways	336C	22/12/65	Was N2978G before D to BOAC, now British Airways
18925	G–ASZG	British Airways	336C	23/12/65	
18926	CC–CEA	LAN–Chile	330B	5/10/65	D to Lufthansa as D–ABUC *Bremen*. S to LAN–Chile APR–5–67
18927	D–ABUD	Lufthansa	330B	24/11/65	*Nürnberg*
18928	D–ABUF	Lufthansa	330B	1/1/66	*Hannover*
18929	D–ABUG	Lufthansa	330B	7/1/66	*Essen*
18930	D–ABUH	Lufthansa	330B	19/1/66	*Dortmund*
18931	D–ABUK	Lufthansa	330B	27/3/66	*Bochum*
18932	D–ABUE	Lufthansa	330C	11/3/66	*America*
18937	D–ABUA	Lufthansa	330C	10/11/65	*Europa*
18938	N7559A	American Airlines	323C	30/7/65	
18939	OD–AGD	Trans Mediterranean	323C	30/8/65	D to American AL as N7560A S to Trans Mediterranean AUG–27–73
18940	PP–VLP	Varig	323C	27/8/65	D to American AL as N7561A. S to Varig APR–20–73
18941	F–BLCD	Air France	328B	10/2/66	*Dampierre*
18948	SX–DBA	Olympic Airways	384C	11/5/66	*Athens*
18949	SX–DBB	Olympic Airways	384C	21/5/66	*Corinth*
18950	SX–DBC	Olympic Airways	384C	18/6/66	*Knossos*
18953	VH–EBQ	Qantas	338C	13/9/65	*Ballarat*
18954	VH–EBR	Qantas	338C	28/12/65	*Wollongong*
18955	VH–EBS	Qantas	338C	28/1/66	*Kalgoorlie*

Boeing 707

C/n	Current Marks	Current Owner/operator	Model Series	Initial Delivery	Remarks
18956	N414PA	PAA	321B	28/1/66	*Ann McKim*
18957	N415PA	PAA	321B	15/2/66	*Monsoon*
18958	N416PA	PAA	321B	25/2/66	*Paul Jones*
18959	N417PA	PAA	321B	20/5/66	*Winged Racer* WO Papeete JUL–23–73
18960	N418PA	PAA	321B	7/4/66	*Yankee Ranger*
18961	CS–TBA	TAP	382B	16/12/66	*Santa Cruz*
18962	CS–TBB	TAP	382B	8/6/66	*Santa Maria*
18964	VR–HGQ	Cathay Pacific	351C	15/11/65	D to Northwest AL as N363US. S to Cathay Pacific MAY–26–73
18975	G–AWTK	British Caledonian	349C	27/9/65	D to Flying Tiger Line as N322F. S to British Caledonian. MAR–31–69. *County of Angus*
18976	EI–ASN	Aer Lingus-Irish	349C	13/10/65	D to Flying Tiger Line as N323F. S to Aer Lingus MAY 1970 *St Evnan*
18978	N18701	TWA	331B	25/1/66	
18979	N18702	TWA	331B	3/2/66	
18980	N18703	TWA	331B	5/2/66	
18981	N18704	TWA	331B	5/3/66	
18982	N18706	TWA	331B	4/4/66	
18983	N18707	TWA	331B	15/4/66	
18984	N18708	TWA	331B	20/4/66	
18985	N18709	TWA	331B	23/5/66	
18986	N6720	TWA	131B	25/3/66	
18987	N6721	TWA	131B	17/4/66	
18988	N6722	TWA	131B	28/4/66	
18989	N6723	TWA	131B	6/5/66	
18991	N376WA	World Airways	373C	22/10/65	
19000	CC–CEB	LAN–Chile	385C	20/12/69	Originally Boeing-owned N68657
19001	EI–ANV	Aer Lingus-Irish	348C	21/4/66	*St Enda*
19004	4X–ATR	El Al	358B	7/1/66	
19034	VR–HGU	Cathay Pacific	351C	8/1/66	D to Northwest AL as N364US. S to Cathay Pacific NOV–14–73
19104	N7095	Trans Mediterranean	327C	26/5/66	D to Braniff as N7095. S to Trans Mediterranean
19105	N7096	Trans Mediterranean	327C	28/5/66	D to Braniff as N7096. S to Trans Mediterranean
19106	PP–VLJ	Varig	327C	19/6/66	D to Braniff as N7097. S to Varig NOV–25–71. WO.
19107	OD–AFX	Trans Mediterranean	327C	29/6/66	D to Braniff as N7098. S to Trans Mediterranean JUN–30–72
19108	OD–AFY	Trans Mediterranean	327C	26/7/66	D to Braniff as N7099. S to Trans Mediterranean OCT 1972
19133	ZS–SAE	SAA	344B	9/1/67	D as ZS–EKV *Windhoek*
19162	OO–SJJ	Sabena	329C	24/3/66	
19163	SX–DBP	Olympic Airways	351C	17/5/66	D to Northwest AL as N365US. S to Olympic AW MAY 1973 *City of Thebes*
19164	SX–DBC	Olympic Airways	351C	24/6/66	D to Northwest AL as N366US. S to Olympic AW MAR–26–73 *City of Lindos*
19168	–	Bangladesh Biman	351C	11/7/66	D to Northwest AL as N367US. S to Templewood Aviation. S to Bangledesh Biman for D DEC 1973

C/n	Current Marks	Current Owner/operator	Model Series	Initial Delivery	Remarks
19177	PP–VLN	Varig	324C	29/7/66	D to Continental AL as N17325. S to Varig APR–7–73
19178	B–1380	China Airlines	324C	22/8/66	D to Continental AL as N17326. S to China AL MAY–9–72
19179	N372WA	World Airways	373C	29/5/66	
19185	N7554A	American Airlines	123B	30/4/66	
19186	N7570A	American Airlines	123B	12/5/66	
19187	N7571A	American Airlines	123B	30/6/66	
19188	N7572A	American Airlines	123B	1/7/66	
19209	N368US	Northwest	351C	19/7/66	
19210	N369US	Northwest	351C	12/8/66	
19211	OO–SJK	Sabena	329C	30/8/67	WO Lagos JUL–13–68
19212	N5771T	TWA	331C	19/6/67	
19213	N5772T	TWA	331C	29/8/67	
19214	N5773T	TWA	331C	30/9/67	
19215	N6724	TWA	131B	23/11/66	
19216	N6726	TWA	131B	9/3/67	
19217	N6727	TWA	131B	2/4/67	
19218	N6728	TWA	131B	30/3/67	
19219	N6729	TWA	131B	15/4/67	
19220	N6763T	TWA	131B	23/5/67	
19221	N6764T	TWA	131B	13/5/67	
19222	N6771T	TWA	131B	28/5/67	
19223	N6789T	TWA	131B	13/7/67	
19224	N18710	TWA	331B	15/3/67	
19225	N18711	TWA	331B	5/4/67	
19226	N18712	TWA	331B	1/6/67	
19227	N18713	TWA	331B	5/8/67	
19235	N7562A	American AL	323C	31/8/66	
19236	N7563A	American AL	323C	28/9/66	
19237	N7564A	American AL	323C	30/9/66	
19238	LV–ISA	Aerolineas	387B	4/11/66	*Antártida Argentina*
19239	LV–ISB	Aerolineas	387B	16/12/66	*Almilán*
19240	LV–ISC	Aerolineas	387B	16/12/66	*Betelgeuse*
19241	LV–ISD	Aerolineas	387B	24/2/67	*Procion*
19247	VT–DVA	Air India	337B	12/10/66	*Annapoorna*
19248	VT–DVB	Air India	337C	12/2/67	*Kamet*
19263	N370US	Northwest	351C	19/8/66	
19264	N419PA	PAA	321B	6/11/66	*Gem of the Skies*
19265	N420PA	PAA	321B	8/11/66	*Monarch of the Skies*
19266	N421PA	PAA	321B	30/11/66	*Charmer*
19267	N445PA	PAA	321C	14/12/66	*Archer*
19268	N446PA	PAA	321C	20/12/66	*Climax*
19269	N447PA	PAA	321C	1/5/67	*Onward*
19270	N448PA	PAA	321C	8/5/67	*Pacific Raider*
19271	N449PA	PAA	321C	16/5/67	*Red Rover*
19272	N450PA	PAA	321C	24/5/67	*Borinquen*
19273	N451PA	PAA	321C	31/5/67	*Union*
19274	N452PA	PAA	321C	22/6/67	*Golden Fleece*
19275	N422PA	PAA	321B	28/6/67	*Mount Vernon*
19276	N423PA	PAA	321B	1/7/67	*Glory of the Skies*
19277	N424PA	PAA	321B	27/7/67	*Golden West*
19278	N425PA	PAA	321B	29/7/67	*Virginia*
19284	AP–AUN	PIA	340C	23/7/66	L to JAT
19285	AP–AUO	PIA	340C	20/10/66	L to MEA DEC–69. L to JAT
19286	AP–AUP	PIA	340C	21/9/67	
19291	F–BLCE	Air France	328B	7/3/67	*Chateau d'Usse.* L by Air Afrique as TU–TXL, FEB–68 and as TU–TXN MAR–68
19292	F–BLCF	Air France	328C	15/3/67	*Le Pelican 2* later *Chateau de Grusbois*
19293	VH–EBT	Qantas	338C	28/1/67	*Bendigo*

Boeing 707

C/n	Current Marks	Current Owner/operator	Model Series	Initial Delivery	Remarks
19294	VH–EBU	Qantas	338C	30/3/67	*Broken Hill*
19295	VH–EBV	Qantas	338C	7/9/67	*Tamworth*
19296	VH–EBW	Qantas	338C	11/10/67	*Armidale*
19297	VH–EBX	Qantas	338C	24/10/67	*Port Moresby*
19315	D–ABUL	Lufthansa	330B	31/12/66	*Duisburg*
19316	D–ABUM	Lufthansa	330B	30/1/67	*Bremen*
19317	D–ABUI	Lufthansa	330C	3/3/67	*Asia*
19320	PP–VJR	Varig	341C	29/12/66	WO Rio de Janeiro 1968
19321	PP–VJS	Varig	341C	29/12/66	
19322	PP–VJT	Varig	341C	22/3/67	
19323	N7573A	American AL	123B	11/11/66	
10324	N7574A	American AL	123B	16/12/66	
19325	N7575A	American AL	123B	5/1/67	
19326	N7576A	American AL	123B	24/1/67	
19237	N7577A	American AL	123B	4/4/67	
19328	N7578A	American AL	123B	23/3/67	
19329	N7579A	American AL	123B	14/4/67	
19330	N7580A	American AL	123B	28/4/67	
19331	N7581A	American AL	123B	8/5/67	
19332	N7582A	American AL	123B	26/5/67	
19333	N7583A	American AL	123B	5/6/67	
19334	N7584A	American AL	123B	16/6/67	
19335	N7585A	American AL	123B	20/6/67	
19336	N7586A	American AL	123B	27/6/67	
19337	N7587A	American AL	123B	7/7/67	
19338	N7588A	American AL	123B	14/7/67	
19339	N7589A	American AL	123B	20/7/67	
19340	N7590A	American AL	123B	15/9/67	
19341	N7591A	American AL	123B	2/3/68	
19342	N7592A	American AL	123B	12/3/69	
19343	N7593A	American AL	123B	28/3/69	
19344	N7594A	American AL	123B	22/4/69	
19350	PP–VLO	Varig	324C	2/12/66	D to Continental AL as N17327. S to Varig JUL–20–73
19351	9V–BEW	Singapore Airlines	324C	1/2/67	D to Continental AL as N17328. S to Singapore AL JUN–29–72
19352	9V–BEX	Singapore Airlines	324C	21/4/67	D to Continental AL as N17329. S to Singapore AL AUG–4–72
19353	9V–BEY	Singapore Airlines	324C	27/5/67	D to Continental AL as N17330. S to Singapore AL OCT–7–72
19354	VH–EBZ	Qantas	349C	21/6/66	D to FTL as N324F. S to Aer Lingus as EI–ASO. APR–2–69 *St Canice.* L to Quantas 1970–71
19355	G–AWWD	Caledonian AW	349C	8/2/67	D to FTL as N325F. L to El Al 1968. S DEC–68. *County of Argyll*
19361	N426PA	PAA	321B	21/9/67	*National Eagle*
19362	N427PA	PAA	321B	22/9/67	*Crystal Palace*
19363	N428PA	PAA	321B	22/9/67	*Star of Hope*
19364	N433PA	PAA	321B	29/9/67	*Glad Tidings*
19365	N434PA	PAA	321B	12/10/67	*Queen of the Sky*
19366	N435PA	PAA	321B	14/10/67	*Celestial Empire*
19367	N457PA	PAA	321B	28/10/67	*Phoenix*
19368	N458PA	PAA	321B	7/11/67	*Titian* WO Boston NOV–3–73
19369	N459PA	PAA	321B	28/11/67	*Western Continent*
19370	N460PA	PAA	321B	30/11/67	*Sovereign of the Seas*
19371	N461PA	PAA	321B	30/11/67	*Rising Sun* WO
19372	N462PA	PAA	321B	12/12/67	*Eagle*
19373	N463PA	PAA	321B	11/12/67	*Queen of the East*

C/n	Current Marks	Current Owner/operator	Model Series	Initial Delivery	Remarks
19374	N453PA	PAA	321B	19/12/67	*Universe*. L to Air Vietnam 1970
19375	N473PA	PAA	321B	1/1/68	*Pride of America*
19376	N454PA	PAA	321B	20/12/67	*Radiant*
19377	N474PA	PAA	321B	17/1/68	*Morning Glory*
19378	N455PA	PAA	321B	6/2/68	*Waverly*
19379	N475PA	PAA	321B	21/2/68	*Sea Serpent*
19380	N7565A	American AL	323C	12/10/66	No windows
19381	N7566A	American AL	323C	10/8/67	No windows
19382	N7567A	American AL	323C	2/10/67	No windows
19383	N7568A	American AL	323C	6/11/67	No windows
19384	N7569A	American AL	323C	21/11/67	No windows
19410	EI–APG	Aer Lingus	348C	1/7/67	L to Trans-Caribbean SEP–30–67 to 1968 as N8789R *St. Senan*
19411	N371US	Northwest	351C	6/12/66	
19412	N372US	Northwest	351C	18/3/67	
19415	CS–TBH	TAP–Portugal	399C	13/7/67	Formerly British Caledonian G–AVKA. S to TAP MAY 1973. *Pedro Nunes*
19416	G–ATZC	Caledonian AW	365C	14/4/67	Built for British Eagle as G–ATZC. L to Airlift as N737AL APR–67 to APR–70. L to Transavia as PH–TRW APR–JUN–70. *County of Stirling*
19417	G–AYEX	Caledonian AW	355C	19/5/67	D to Executive Jet as N625EJ. L to Airlift 1967; L to Air Bahama JUL–20–68. S JUL–70. *County of Perth.*
19433	PP–VLI	Varig	385C	6/12/66	Built for American Flyers. S before D to American AL as N8400. S to Varig SEP–3–71
19434	N373US	Northwest	351C	21/3/67	
19435	N5774T	TWA	331C	13/10/67	
19436	N6790T	TWA	131B	1/8/67	
19440	N7100	Trans Mediterranean	327C	16/2/67	D to Braniff. S to Trans Mediterranean
19441	N371WA	World AW	373C	22/12/66	
19442	N370WA	World AW	373C	3/8/67	
19443	N374US	Northwest	351C	12/8/67	
19498	G–ATWV	British Airways	336C	2/12/67	D to BOAC, now British Airways
19502	4X–ATS	El Al	358B	2/2/67	
19515	N7595A	American AL	323C	15/8/67	
19516	N7596A	American AL	323C	23/8/67	
19517	N7597A	American AL	323C	28/8/67	
19518	N7598A	American AL	323C	31/8/67	
19519	N7599A	American AL	323C	11/9/67	
19521	F–BLCG	Air France	328C	16/6/67	*Chateau de Lude*
19522	F–BLCH	Air France	328C	29/6/67	*Chateau de Hautefor*
19529	9M AQB	Malayan AL System	327C	9/10/67	D to Braniff as N7102. S to Singapore AL MAR–2–71. L Malayan AL
19530	9V BDC	Singapore Airlines	327C	18/10/67	D to Braniff as N7103. S to Singapore AL APR–23–71
19531	N7104	Trans Mediterranean	327C	20/11/67	D to Braniff S to Trans Mediterranean
19566	N15710	TWA	331C	26/6/68	
19567	N15711	TWA	331C	27/6/68	
19568	N16738	TWA	131B	11/3/68	
19569	N16739	TWA	331B	8/3/68	

Boeing 707

C/n	Current Marks	Current Owner/operator	Model Series	Initial Delivery	Remarks
19570	N28724	TWA	331B	16/2/68	
19571	N28726	TWA	331B	27/3/68	
19572	N28727	TWA	331B	22/3/68	
19573	N28728	TWA	331B	7/5/68	
19574	N8411	American AL	323C	21/5/68	
19575	N8412	American AL	323C	4/6/68	
19576	N8413	American AL	323C	17/6/68	
19577	N8414	American AL	323C	26/6/68	
19578	N8424	American AL	323C		Not built
19579	N8425	American AL	323C		Not built
19580	N8426	American AL	323C		Not built
19581	N8401	American AL	323C	31/10/67	
19582	N8402	American AL	323C	27/10/67	
19583	N8403	American AL	323C	29/11/67	
19584	N8404	American AL	323C	11/1/68	
19585	N8405	American AL	323C	26/1/68	
19586	N8406	American AL	323C	5/2/68	
19587	N8408	American AL	323C	15/3/68	
19588	N8409	American AL	323C	4/4/68	
19589	N8410	American AL	323C	26/4/68	
19590	G–ATZD	British Airways	365C	22/12/67	FF as G–ATZD. D to British Eagle as VR–BCP *Enterprise* and L to MEA. S to BOAC 1969, now British Airways
19621	VH–EAA	Qantas	338C	8/12/67	*Toowoomba*
19622	VH–EAB	Qantas	338C	10/1/68	*Winton*
19623	VH–EAC	Qantas	338C	5/2/68	*Longreach*
19624	VH–EAD	Qantas	338C	27/3/68	*City of Newcastle*
19625	VH–EAE	Qantas	338C	4/4/68	*City of Swan Hill*
19626	VH–EAF	Qantas	338C	4/5/68	*City of Townsville*
19627	VH–EAG	Qantas	338C	16/5/68	*City of Hobart*
19628	VH–EAH	Qantas	338C	12/6/68	*City of Launceston*
19629	VH–EAI	Qantas	338C	22/8/68	*City of Darwin*
19630	VH–EAJ	Qantas	338C	25/9/68	*City of Geelong*
19631	N375US	Northwest	351C	14/10/67	
19632	N376US	Northwest	351C	21/11/67	
19633	N377US	Northwest	351B	26/3/68	
19634	N378US	Northwest	351B	29/3/68	
19635	N379US	Northwest	351B		
19636	N380US	Northwest	351B	24/7/68	
19664	G–AXRS	Caledonian AW	355C	9/11/67	D to Executive Jet as N526EJ. L by Transavia as PH–TRF. *Prins Bernhard* from JUN–20–68. S to Caledonian NOV–69 *Caithness*
19693	N491PA	PAA	321B	8/2/65	***Chariot of Fame***
19694	N492PA	PAA	321B	22/2/68	***Eagle Wing***
19695	N493PA	PAA	321B	14/3/68	***Priscilla Alden***
19696	N494PA	PAA	321B	28/3/68	*Malay* WO Maiquetia DEC–12–68
19697	N495PA	PAA	321B	9/4/68	*Nor'wester*
19688	N496PA	PAA	321B	17/4/68	*Northern Eagle*
19699	N497PA	PAA	321B	24/4/68	*Victory*
19705	ZS–EUW	SAA	344C	22/2/68	*Pretoria*. WO Windhoek APR–20–68
19706	ZS–SAF	SAA	344C	2/4/68	D as ZS–EUX. *Port Elizabeth*
19715	N369WA	World AW	373C	7/11/67	
19716	N368WA	World AW	373C	13/11/67	
19723	F–BLCI	Air France	328C	17/1/68	*Chateau de Verteuil*
19724	F–BLCJ	Air France	328C	24/1/68	*Chateau de Voute-Polignac*, WO Guadeloupe MAR–5–68
19736	ET–ACD	Ethiopian AL	360C	8/4/68	L to Nigeria AW 1970
19737	9V–BBA	Malaysian AL	312B	28/5/68	

C/n	Current Marks	Current Owner/operator	Model Series	Initial Delivery	Remarks
19738	9V–BFB	Malaysian AL	312B	3/7/68	
19739	9V–BBB	Malaysian AL	312B	9/12/68	
19740	CS–TBC	TAP–Portugal	382B	19/2/68	*Cidade de Luanda*
19741	HK–1402	Avianca	359B	7/3/68	*Sucre*
19760	SX–DBD	Olympic AW	384C	5/6/68	*Sparta*
19767	CS–TBI	TAP–Portugal	399C	30/12/67	D to British Caledonian as G–AVTW *Ayr.* S to TAP APR–1973. D *Joao de Castro*
19773	N382US	Northwest	351C	3/5/68	
19774	N383US	Northwest	351C	11/5/68	
19775	N384US	Northwest	351C	18/7/68	
19776	N385US	Northwest	351C	24/7/68	
19777	N386US	Northwest	351C	28/8/68	
19789	CF–FAN	Wardair	311C	27/4/68	*C. H. Punch Dickens*
19809	HZ–ACC	Saudi Arabian AL	368C	8/1/68	
19810	HZ–ACD	Saudi Arabian AL	368C	19/1/68	
19820	ET–ACQ	Ethiopian AL	379C	20/5/68	Built for Saturn as N761U. L to Nigeria AW JUN to DEC–70
19821	G–AWHU	British Airways	379C	1/7/68	Built for Saturn as N762U
19822	PP–VJK	Varig	379C		Built for Saturn as N763U
19840	PP–VJY	Varig	345C	26/2/68	D to Seaboard as N7321S on L until FEB–28–69
19841	PP–VJZ	Varig	345C	3/3/68	D to Seaboard as N7322S on L until MAR–31–69 WO
19842	PP–VJX	Varig	345C	6/8/68	Built for Seaboard as N7323S
19843	G–AVBP	British Airways	336C	13/8/68	D to BOAC, now British Airways
19844	SU–AOU	United Arab AL	366C	21/10/68	
19845	SU–AOW	United Arab AL	366C	26/5/69	WO
19866	AP–AVL	PIA	340C	26/8/68	
19869	PP–VLM	Varig	324C	18/4/68	D to Continental AL as N N47331. S to Varig OCT–15–72
19870	PP–VLK	Varig	324C	21/4/68	D to Continental AL as N47332. S to Varig MAR–31–72
19871	PP–VLL	Varig	324C	16/5/68	D to Continental AL as N67333. S to Varig APR–15–72
19872	N381US	Northwest	351B	30/8/68	
19916	F–BLCK	Air France	328C	4/12/68	*Chateau de Laugeais*
19917	F–BLCL	Air France	328C	10/12/68	*Chateau de la Roche Courbon*
19961	LV–JGR	Aerolineas	387C	4/11/68	*Canopus*
19962	LV–JGP	Aerolineas	387C	4/11/68	*Achernar*
19963	N1501W	Western AL	347C		
19964	N1502W	Western AL	347C	25/7/68	
19965	N1503W	Western AL	347C	30/7/68	
19966	N1504W	Western AL	347C	10/9/68	
19967	N1505W	Western AL	347C	19/9/68	
19969	CS–TBD	TAP	382B	14/10/68	*Cidade de Lourenco Marques*
19986	F–BJCM	Air France	335C	12/12/68	D to Executive Jet as N527EJ. L to Air France 1970 *Chateau de Grosbois*
19988	VT–DXT	Air India	337C	21/8/68	*Trishul*
19996	OO–SJL	Sabena	329C	30/9/68	
19997	10–01	Luftwaffe	307C	30/9/68	
19998	10–02	Luftwaffe	307C	15/10/68	
19999	10–03	Luftwaffe	307C	21/10/68	
20000	10–04	Luftwaffe	307C	18/11/68	
20008	PP–VJH	Varig	320C	15/8/68	Originally Boeing demonstrator N707N
20016	N870PA	PAA	321C	12/12/68	*Dreadnought*
20017	N871PA	PAA	321C	25/10/68	*Sirius*
20018	N872PA	PAA	321C	22/11/68	*Swordfish*

Boeing 707

C/n	Current Marks	Current Owner/operator	Model Series	Initial Delivery	Remarks
20019	N880PA	PAA	321B	10/12/68	*Emerald Isle*
20020	N881PA	PAA	321B	13/12/68	*Reindeer*
20021	N882PA	PAA	321B	17/12/68	*Queen of the Pacific*
20022	N883PA	PAA	321B	18/12/68	*Cathay*
20023	N884PA	PAA	321B	8/1/69	*Nightingale*
20024	N885PA	PAA	321B	10/1/69	*Northern Light*
20025	N886PA	PAA	321B	24/1/69	*Sea Lark*
20026	N887PA	PAA	321B	31/1/69	*Flora Temple*
20027	N890PA	PAA	321B	6/2/69	*Gauntlet*
20028	N891PA	PAA	321B	6/2/69	*Gem of the Ocean*
20029	N892PA	PAA	321B	4/3/69	*Star King*
20030	N893PA	PAA	321B	11/3/69	*Whirlwind*
20031	N894PA	PAA	321B	14/3/69	*Polynesian*
20032	N895PA	PAA	321B	14/3/69	*Herald of the Morning*
20033	N896PA	PAA	321B	26/3/69	*Norseman*
20034	N897PA	PAA	321B	31/3/69	*Ocean Express*
20035	SX–DBE	Olympic AW	384B	19/12/68	*Pella*
20036	SX–DBF	Olympic AW	384B	23/1/69	*Mycenae*
20043	CF–ZYP	Wardair	396C	14/3/69	Originally ordered by Quebecair. *WR Wop May*
20056	N86740	TWA	131B	8/1/69	
20057	N86741	TWA	131B	23/1/69	
20058	N8729	TWA	331B	12/12/69	
20059	N8730	TWA	331B	15/1/69	
20060	N8731	TWA	331B	3/3/69	
20061	N8732	TWA	331B	7/3/69	
20062	N8733	TWA	331B	2/4/69	
20063	N8734	TWA	331B	7/4/69	
20064	N8735	TWA	331B	1/5/61	
20065	N8736	TWA	331B	7/5/69	
20066	N8737	TWA	331B	12/6/69	
20067	N8738	TWA	331B	17/6/69	
20068	N15712	TWA	331C	2/7/69	WO
20069	N15713	TWA	331C	16/7/69	
20076	N738AL	Airlift Int	372C	14/6/68	
20077	N739AL	Airlift Int	372C	11/7/68	L by Caledonian AW 1970
20084	9K–ACJ	Kuwait AW	369C	4/11/68	
20085	9K–ACK	Kuwait AW	369C	14/11/68	
20086	9K–ACL	Kuwait AW	369C	25/11/68	
20087	N8415	American AL	323C	5/7/68	
20088	N8416	American AL	323C	17/7/68	
20089	N8417	American AL	323C	30/8/68	
20097	4X–ATT	El AL	358B	22/1/69	
20110	ZS–SAG	SAA	344C	23/4/69	Initially allocated ZS–FKT *Durban*
20122	4X–ATX	El AL	358C	15/5/69	
20123	D–ABUJ	Lufthansa	330C	27/2/69	*Afrika*
20124	D–ABUO	Lufthansa	330C	8/5/69	*Australia*
20136	CS–TBE	TAP	382B	28/4/69	*Pedro Alvares Cabral*
20170	N8431	American AL	323B	9/4/69	
20171	N8432	American AL	323B	16/4/69	
20172	N8433	American AL	323B	30/4/69	
20173	N8434	American AL	323B	9/5/69	
20174	N8435	American AL	323B	23/5/69	
20175	N8436	American AL	323B	13/6/69	
20176	N8437	American AL	323B	31/7/69	
20177	N8438	American AL	323B	10/8/69	
20178	N8439	American AL	323B	9/9/69	
20179	N8440	American AL	323B	17/9/69	
20198	OO–SJM	Sabena	329C	17/6/69	
20199	OO–SJN	Sabena	329C	22/7/69	
20200	OO–SJO	Sabena	329C	3/12/69	
20224	OD–AFB	MEA	3B4C	18/11/68	
20225	OD–AFC	MEA	3B4C	18/11/68	WO Beirut DEC–28–68
20230	ZS–SAH	SAA	344C	1/9/69	Initially allocated as ZS–FKG *Pretoria*

C/n	Current Marks	Current Owner/operator	Model Series	Initial Delivery	Remarks
20259	OD–AFD	MEA	3B4C	1/10/69	
20260	OD–AFE	MEA	3B4C	29/10/69	
20261	B–1824	China AL	309C	7/11/69	
20262	B–1826	China AL	309C	26/11/69	
20275	AP–AWB	PIA	340C	10/8/70	
20283	ZS–SAI	SAA	344C	22/12/69	*East London*
20287	EP–IRL	Iranair	386C	1/70	
20288	EP–IRM	Iranair	386C	27/3/70	
20297	CS–TBF	TAP	382B	13/2/70	*Vasco da Gama*
20298	CS–TBG	TAP	382B	25/3/70	*Farnao de Magalhaes*
20301	4X–ATY	El Al	358C	26/1/70	
20315	13701	CAF	347C	28/2/70	Laid down as N1506W for Western AL
20316	13702	CAF	347C	18/2/70	Laid down as N1507W for Western AL. FF as N1785B
20317	13703	CAF	347C	4/3/70	Laid down as N1508W for Western AL
20318	13704	CAF	347C	10/3/70	Laid down as N1509W for Western AL
20319	13705	CAF	347C	11/5/71	
20340	HK–1410	Avianca	359B	24/4/70	*Bolivar*
20341	SU–APD	Egyptair	366C		
20342	SU–APE	Egyptair	366C	24/3/70	FF as N4094
20374	G–AXGW	British Airways	336C	8/3/70	D to BOAC, now British Airways
20375	G–AXGX	British Airways	336C	26/3/70	D to BOAC, now British Airways
20395	D–ABUY	Lufthansa	330C	15/11/70	*Essen*
20428	N1793T	TWA	331C	23/7/70	
20429	N794TW	TWA	331C	24/8/70	
20456	G–AXXY	British Airways	336B	18/2/71	D to BOAC, now British Airways
20457	G–AXXZ	British Airways	336B	17/4/71	D to BOAC, now British Airways
20487	AP–AVZ	PIA	340C	15/10/70	WO
20488	AP–AWA	PIA	340C		
20494	JY–ADO	Alia	3D3C	26/1/71	WO
20495	JY–ADP	Alia	3D3C		
20514	8801	Portuguese Government	3F5C	24/9/71	
20515	8802	Portuguese Government	3F5C	13/12/71	
20517	G–AYLT	British Airways	336C	28/5/71	D to BOAC, now British Airways
20518	71–1407	USAF	EC–137	9/2/72	AWACS prototype
20519	71–1408	USAF	EC–137	23/2/72	AWACS prototype
20522	HL–7406	Korean Air Lines	3B5C	6/8/71	
20546	9K–ACM	Kuwait Airways	369C	24/1/72	
20547	9K–ACN	Kuwait Airways	369C	26/2/72	
20629	TJ–CAA	Cameroon AL	3H7C	20/11/72	
20630	72–7000	USAF	353B	9/8/72	
20669	5N–ABK	Nigeria Airways	3F9C	18/1/73	
20714	2402	CAAC	3J6B	23/8/73	
20715	2404	CAAC	3J6B	17/9/73	
20716	2406	CAAC	3J6B		
20717	2408	CAAC	3J6B		
20718	2410	CAAC	3J6C	31/10/73	
20719	2412	CAAC	3J6C	14/11/73	
20720	2414	CAAC	3J6C		
20721	2416	CAAC	3J6C		
20722	2418	CAAC	3J6C		
20723	2420	CAAC	3J6C		
20741	EP–IRN	Iran Air	386C	27/3/73	
20760	SU–AVX	Egyptair	366C	30/3/73	*Tutankhamun*
20761	SU–AVY	Egyptair	366C	25/4/73	*Akhenaton*

Boeing 707

C/n	Current Marks	Current Owner/operator	Model Series	Initial Delivery	Remarks
20762	SU–AVZ	Egyptair	366C	29/6/73	*Mena*
20763	SU–AXA	Egyptair	366C	20/9/73	*Ramases II*
20803	YR–ABA	Tarom	3K1C		
20804	YR–ABB	Tarom	3K1C		
20805	YR–ABC	Tarom	3K1C		
20830	5–981	Imperial Iranian AF	3J9C		
20831	5–982	Imperial Iranian AF	3J9C		
20832	5–983	Imperial Iranian AF	3J9C		
20833	5–984	Imperial Iranian AF	3J9C		
20834	5–985	Imperial Iranian AF	3J9C		
20835	5–986	Imperial Iranian AF	3J9C		

Boeing 720

C/n	Current Marks	Current Owner/operator	Model Series	Initial Delivery	Remarks
17907	N7201U	Contemporary Entertainment	022	1/10/60	D to United AL as *Walter T. Varney*. S JAN–1973
17908	N7202U	United AL	022	29/7/60	
17909	N7203U	United AL	022	30/4/60	
17910	N7204U	United AL	022	21/5/60	*Phillip G Johnson*
17911	N7205U	United AL	022	25/5/60	
17912	N7206U	United AL	022	9/6/60	*T. Claude Ryan*
17913	N7207U	United AL	022	29/6/60	
17914	N7208U	United AL	022	25/6/60	
17915	N720CC	Cavanagh Communities Corp	022	27/7/60	D to United AL as N7209U. S to Cavanagh Communities MAY–18–73
17916	N7210U	United AL	022	5/8/60	
17917	N7211U	United AL	022	13/8/60	
18013	N7527A	American Airlines	023B	30/7/60	Was *Mississippi*. Cvtd from 023
18014	N7528A	American Airlines	023B	24/7/60	Was *Connecticut*. Cvtd from 023
18015	N7529A	American Airlines	023B	13/8/60	Was *Wisconsin*. Cvtd from 023
18016	N7530A	American Airlines	023B	22/9/60	Was *Alabama*. Cvtd from 023
18017	OD–AFP	MEA	023B	1/9/60	D to American AL as N7531A *North Dakota* Cvtd from 023. S to MEA MAY–4–71
18018	OD–AFR	MEA	023B	8/9/60	D to American AL as N7532A *South Carolina* Cvtd from 023. S to MEA OCT–27–71
18019	OD–AFS	MEA	023B	19/9/60	D to American AL as N7533A *South Dakota*. Cvtd from 023. S to MEA JAN–29–72
18020	OD–AFT	MEA	023B	10/10/60	D to American AL as N7534A *Colorado* Cvtd from 023. S to MEA MAR–3–72
18021	OD–AGB	MEA	023B	23/11/60	D to American AL as N7535A *Florida*. Cvtd from 023. S to MEA MAY–3–73
18022	N1R	Los Angeles Dodgers	023B	3/12/60	D to American Airlines as N7536A. S to L.A. Dodgers FEB–2–71
18023	HK–1973	Aerocondor	023B	27/4/61	D to American AL as N7537A S to Aerocondor DEC–20–72
18024	OD–AFQ	MEA	023B	3/2/61	D to American AL as N7538A S to MEA SEP–29–71
18025	OD–AFZ	MEA	023B	17/3/61	D to American AL as N7539A S to MEA OCT–17–72
18026	OD–AFW	MEA	023B	17/2/61D to	D to American AL as N7540A S to MEA MAR–31–72
18027	OD–AFN	MEA	023B	27/2/61	D to American AL as N7451A S to MEA OCT–10–70
18028	N7542A	American Airlines	023B	29/3/61	Was *Maine*
18029	OD–AFU	MEA	023B	28/3/61	D to American AL as N7543A *Minnesota*. S to MEA DEC–17–71
18030	OD–AFM	MEA	023B	10/4/61	D to American AL as N7544A S to MEA DEC–31–70
18031	N7545A	American Airlines	023B	17/4/61	
18032	N7546A	American Airlines	023B	20/4/61	
18033	N7547A	American Airlines	023B	23/5/61	

Boeing 720

C/n	Current Marks	Current Owner/operator	Model Series	Initial Delivery	Remarks
18034	OD–AFL	MEA	023B	22/6/61	D to American AL as N7548A S to MEA OCT–9–70
18035	OD–AFO	MEA	023B	9/6/61	D to American AL as N7549A S to MEA FEB–5–71
18036	N7550A	American Airlines	023B	2/7/61	
18037	N7551A	American Airlines	023B	20/7/61	
18041	N1776Q	American International Inc	048	24/10/60	D to Aer Lingus as EI–ALA *St Patrick* S to Air Club International, reg N734T S to American Int. MAY–1–73.
18042	N7081	Alaska Airlines	048	24/1/61	D to Aer Lingus as EI–ALB *St Briget* S to Western AL reg N7081. S to Alaska MAY 1973
18043	OO–TEB	Trans European	048	6/4/61	D to Aer Lingus as EI–ALC *St Brendan* S to Trans European AUG–10–72
18044	N7212U	Aero Specialities	022	22/12/60	D to United AL. S to Aero Specialities. SEP–10–73
18045	N7213U	United Air Lines	022	19/12/60	
18046	N7214U	United Air Lines	022	14/1/61	
18047	N7215U	United Air Lines	022	27/1/61	
18048	N7216U	Aero Specialities	022	2/2/61	D to United AL as *George R. Hamm.* S to Aero Specialties AUG–29–73
18049	N7217U	United Air Lines	022	13/2/61	
18050	N7218U	United Air Lines	022	5/3/61	
18057	–	Avianca	030B	8/3/61	D to Lufthansa as D–ABOH *Köln* S to PAA reg N783PA. *Bonita.* S Avianca JUL–28–73
18058	D–ABOK	Lufthansa	030B	28/4/61	*Dusseldorf.* WO Ebersheim DEC–4–61
18059	–	Avianca	030B	3/5/61	D to Lufthansa as D–ABOL *Stuttgart* S to PAA, reg N784PA, *Panama.* S Avianca APR–13–73
18060	YA–HBA	Ariana	030B	2/6/61	D to Lufthansa as D–ABOM *Nurnberg* S to PAA, reg N785PA, *Balboa.* S Ariana JUN–21–73
18061	HK–723	Avianca	047B	7/4/61	D to Western AL as N93141 S to Avianca OCT–23–69
18062	N93142	Western AL	047B	9/5/61	
18063	N93143	Western AL	047B	7/6/61	
18064	N736T	AirClub International	027	11/2/61	D to Braniff as N7076. S to AirClub Int. SEP–14–73
18065	N7077	AirClub International	027	22/3/61	D to Braniff as N7077. S to AirClub Int. SEP–19–73
18066	N113	FAA	061	12/5/61	Built as 720-027
18072	N7219	T. L. Corporation	022	1/12/61	D to United AL as N7219U S to T.L. Corp. Jul–5–73
18073	N7220U	United Air Lines	022	13/12/61	
18074	N7221U	United Air Lines	022	21/12/61	
18075	N7222U	United Air Lines	022	10/1/62	
18076	N7223U	United Air Lines	022	17/1/62	
18077	N7224U	United Air Lines	022	10/4/62	*William R Gruen*
18078	N7225U	Jet Set Travel Club	022	24/4/62	D to United AL L to Jet Set Travel OCT–19–73
18079	N7226U	United Air Lines	022	8/5/62	*Jack Vilas*
18080	N7227U	Aero Specialities	022	15/5/62	D to United AL as N7227U S to Aero Specialities. AUG–27–73

C/n	Current Marks	Current Owner/operator	Model Series	Initial Delivery	Remarks
18081	N7228U	Atlanta Skylarks	022	1/6/62	D to United AL. S to Atlanta Skylarks JUL–2–73
18082	N7229U	United Air Lines	022	12/6/62	
18086	HK–724	Avianca	059B	8/11/61	*Bolivar*
18087	HK–725	Avianca	059B	15/11/61	*Santander*
18154	N730T	AirClub International	027	9/8/61	D to Braniff as N7078. S to AirClub Int. OCT–16–73
18155	OO–TEA	Trans European	025	15/8/61	D to Eastern AL as N8701E. Returned to Boeing Co. SEP–1969. S to Trans European MAY–1–71
18156	N10VG	Voyager 1000	025	25/8/61	D to Eastern AL as N8702E. Returned to Boeing Co. S to Voyager MAY–19–70
18157	OY–DSK	Conair of Scandinavia	025	2/2/62	D to Eastern AL as N8703E. Returned to Boeing Co. S to Conair APR–30–71
18158	N3183B	Boeing Co	025	19/9/61	D to Eastern AL as N8704E. S to Trans-Polar, reg LN–TUW. *Richard Byrd.* Returned to Boeing
18159	OY–DSL	Conair of Scandinavia	025	27/9/61	D to Eastern AL as N8705E Returned to Boeing Co. S to Conair JUN–2–71
18160	HL–7402	Korean Air Lines	025	6/10/61	D to Eastern AL as N8706E. Returned to Boeing Co. S to Korean AL AUG–21–69
18161	OY–DSM	Conair of Scandinavia	025	17/10/61	D to Eastern AL as N8707E Returned to Boeing Co. S to Conair
18162	VP–YNN	Air Rhodesia	025	8/11/61	D to Eastern AL as N8708E. Returned to Boeing. S to Calair, reg D–ACIP. S to Jet Aviation. S to Rhodesia
18163	N15VG	Voyager 1000	025	23/10/61	D to Eastern AL as N8709E. Returned to Boeing. S to Voyager JAN–1973
18164	HL–7403	Korean Air Lines	025	23/10/61	D to Eastern AL as N8710E. Returned to Boeing. S to Korean AL FEB–19–69
18165	HZ–ACA	Saudi Arabian AL	068B	20/12/61	N93136 before D
18166	HZ–ACB	Saudi Arabian AL	068B	20/12/61	
18167	N93144	Western AL	047B	11/7/61	
18240	N8711E	Aero American Leasing	025	8/1/62	D to Eastern AL. S to Club American S to Aero American Leasing APR–1973
18241	OY–DSP	Conair of Scandinavia	025	13/11/61	D to Eastern AL as N8712E. Returned to Boeing. S to Conair JUL–14–71
18242	VP–YNL	Air Rhodesia	025	22/11/61	D to Eastern AL as N8713E. Returned to Boeing. S to Calair, reg D–ACIS. S to Jet Aviation. S to Rhodesia
18243	OY–DSR	Conair of Scandinavia	025	8/12/61	D to Eastern as N8714E. Returned to Boeing S to Conair AUG–14–71
18244	VP–YNM	Air Rhodesia	025	16/12/61	D to Eastern AL as N8715E. Returned to Boeing. S to Calair, reg D–ACIT. S to Jet Aviation. S to Rhodesia

Boeing 720

C/n	Current Marks	Current Owner/operator	Model Series	Initial Delivery	Remarks
18248	HK–749	Avianca	030B	5/1/62	D to Lufthansa as D–ABON *Hannover.* S to PAA, reg N786PA *Winged Arrow.* S to Avianca NOV–30–72
18249	D–ABOP	Lufthansa	030B	12/1/62	*Bremen* WO Nuremburg JUL –15–64
18250	JY–ADS	Royal Jordanian	030B	23/3/62	N93137 before D to Lufthansa as D–ABOQ *Essen* S to PAA, reg N787PA, *Guiding Star.* S NOV–15–72
18251	JY–ADT	Royal Jordanian	030B	27/2/62	D to Lufthansa as D–ABOR. *Dortmund.* S to PAA, reg N788PA, *Nonpareil.* S NOV–17–72
18351	–	Chinese Air Force	051B	26/5/61	D to Northwest as N721US. S to Templewood Aviation S to Chinese AF NOV–1971
18352	SX–DBG	Olympic Airways	051B	22/6/61	D to Northwest as N722US. S to Olympic MAR–5–72 *Axios River*
18353	SX–DBH	Olympic Airways	051B	12/7/61	D to Northwest as N723US. S to Olympic MAR–30–72 *Acheloos River*
18354	N724US	Northwest	051B	26/7/61	WO Florida FEB–12–63
18355	SX–DBI	Olympic Airways	051B	1/9/61	D to Northwest as N725US. S to Olympic APR–19–72 *Pinios River*
18356	SX–DBK	Olympic Airways	051B	5/10/61	D to Northwest as N726US S to Olympic MAR–15–72 *Strimon River*
18376	N720V	Alaska Airlines	062	23/3/62	D to Pacific Northern. Later Western AL. S to Alaska AL MAY–1973
18377	N720W	Alaska Airlines	062	18/4/62	D to Pacific Northern. Later Western AL. S to Alaska AL
18378	AP–AMG	PIA	040B	26/12/61	
18379	AP–AMH	PIA	040B	6/11/62	WO Cairo MAY–20–65
18380	AP–AMJ	PIA	040B	29/11/62	
18381	G–AZFB	Monarch Airlines	051B	23/7/61	D to Northwest as N730US. S to Monarch NOV–28–71
18382	G–AZKM	Monarch Airlines	051B	2/8/61	D to Northwest as N731US S to Monarch FEB–15–72
18383	G–AZNX	Monarch Airlines	051B	27/8/61	D to Northwest as N732US S to Monarch APR–12–72
18384	OY–APP	Maersk Air	051B	30/9/61	D to Northwest as N733US S to Maersk JAN–9–73
18416	N57201	Continental	024B	30/4/62	
18417	N57202	Continental	024B	27/5/62	
18418	ET–AFA	Ethiopian AL	024B	20/6/62	D to Continental as N57203. S to Ethiopian AL OCT–1–73
18419	–	Ethiopian AL	024B	7/7/62	D to Continental as N57204 S to Ethiopian AL for D in 1974.
18420	SX–DBL	Olympic Airways	051B	25/10/61	D to Northwest as N727US. S to Olympic FEB–6–72 *Evros River*
18421	OY–APN	Maersk Air	051B	15/11/61	D to Northwest as N728US. S to Maersk SEP–1972

C/n	Current Marks	Current Owner/operator	Model Series	Initial Delivery	Remarks
18422	OY–APO	Maersk Air	051B	13/12/61	D to Northwest as N729US. S to Maersk MAR–16–73
18423	N7079	AirClub International	027	10/5/62	D to Braniff. S to AirClub Int. SEP–28–73
18424	4X–ABA	El Al	058B	26/3/62	
18425	4X–ABB	El Al	058B	26/4/62	
18451	N93145	Western AL	047B	27/7/62	
18452	N93146	Western AL	047B	8/8/62	
18453	N93147	Western AL	047B	28/8/62	
18454	ET–AAG	Ethiopian AL	060B	2/11/62	*Blue Nile.* WO Beirut JAN–9–68
18455	ET–AAH	Ethiopian AL	060B	27/11/62	*White Nile*
18581	N733T	AirClub International	027	22/8/63	D to Braniff as N7080. S to AirClub Int. OCT–9–73
18587	N57205	Continental AL	024B	11/5/63	
18588	N93148	Western AL	047B	3/4/63	
18589	N93149	Western AL	047B	24/4/63	
18590	N93150	Western AL	047B	3/5/63	
18687	SX–DBM	Olympic Airways	051B	22/10/63	D to Northwest AL as N734US. S to Olympic JUL–1–72 *Aliakmon River*
18688	SX–DBN	Olympic Airways	051B	23/1/64	D to Northwest as N735US S to Olympic JAN–18–73. *Nestos River*
18745	AP–ATQ	PIA	040B	23/4/65	N68646 before D.
18749	N93151	Western AL	047B	21/5/64	
18763	N57206	Continental AL	024B	23/7/64	
18792	–	Maersk Air	051B	26/6/64	D to Northwest as N736US. S to Maersk AUG–1973
18793	N737US	Northwest	051B	24/7/64	
18818	N93152	Western AL	047B	25/9/64	
18820	N93153	Western AL	047B	21/1/65	
18827	N3154	Western AL	047B	10/3/65	
18828	N3155	Western AL	047B	19/5/65	
18829	N3156	Western AL	047B	2/6/65	
18830	N3157	Western AL	047B	17/6/65	
18831	HK–726	Avianca	059B	8/4/65	*Narino*
18963	N3158	Western AL	047B	21/7/65	
18977	ET–ABP	Ethiopian AL	060B	20/9/65	
19002	ET–AFA	Ethiopian AL	024B	16/2/66	D to Continental AL as N17207. S OCT–3–73
19003	N17208	Continental AL	024B	19/2/66	
19160	N3159	Western AL	047B	26/1/66	
19161	N3160	Western AL	047B	12/3/66	
19207	N3161	Western AL	047B	30/7/66	
19208	N3162	Western AL	047B	30/7/66	
19413	N3163	Western AL	047B	15/5/67	
19414	N3164	Western AL	047B	28/6/67	
19438	N3165	Western AL	047B	18/8/68	
19439	N3166	Western AL	047B	7/9/67	WO
19523	N3167	Western AL	047B	20/9/67	

Boeing 727

C/n	Current Marks	Current Owner/operator	Model Series	Initial Delivery	Remarks
18252	N8101N	Eastern AL	25	28/2/64	
18253	N8102N	Eastern AL	25	15/11/63	
18254	N8103N	Eastern AL	25	13/12/63	
18255	N8104N	Eastern AL	25	28/2/64	
18256	N8105N	Eastern AL	25	13/3/64	
18257	N8106N	Eastern AL	25	30/1/64	
18258	N8107N	Eastern AL	25	20/1/64	
18259	N8108N	Eastern AL	25	11/3/64	
18260	N8109N	Eastern AL	25	27/3/64	
18261	N8110N	Eastern AL	25	26/3/64	
18262	N8111N	Eastern AL	25	30/4/64	
18263	N8112N	Eastern AL	25	28/5/64	
18264	N8113N	Eastern AL	25	24/6/64	
18265	N8114N	Eastern AL	25	26/6/64	
18266	N8115N	Eastern AL	25	28/7/64	
18267	N8116N	Eastern AL	25	7/8/64	
18268	N8117N	Eastern AL	25	1/9/64	
18269	N8118N	Eastern AL	25	14/9/64	
18270	N8119N	Eastern AL	25	7/10/64	
18271	N8120N	Eastern AL	25	19/10/64	
18272	N8121N	Eastern AL	25	12/11/64	
18273	N8122N	Eastern AL	25	13/11/64	
18274	N8123N	Eastern AL	25	4/12/64	
18275	N8124N	Eastern AL	25	18/12/64	
18276	N8125N	Eastern AL	25	6/1/65	
18277	N8126N	Eastern AL	25	22/1/65	
18278	N8127N	Eastern AL	25	13/2/65	
18279	N8128N	Eastern AL	25	9/3/65	
18280	N8129N	Eastern AL	25	6/4/65	
18281	N8130N	Eastern AL	25	25/5/65	
18282	N8131N	Eastern AL	25	9/6/65	
18283	N8132N	Eastern AL	25	15/7/65	
18284	N8133N	Eastern AL	25	28/7/65	
18285	N8134N	Eastern AL	25	25/8/65	
18286	N8135N	Eastern AL	25	24/9/65	
18287	N8136N	Eastern AL	25	11/10/65	
18288	N8137N	Eastern AL	25	26/10/65	
18289	N8138N	Eastern AL	25	9/11/65	
18290	N8139N	Eastern AL	25	30/11/65	
18291	N8140N	Eastern AL	25	9/12/65	
18293	N7001U	United AL	22	6/10/64	
18294	N7002U	United AL	22	24/6/65	
18295	N68650	Piedmont	22		First flown as N7003U. L from Boeing by All Nippon AW. L by Iranair **1965–67**. L by Piedmont MAR–15–67 *Manhattan*. WO 19–7–67 Hendersonville
18296	N7004U	United AL	22	29/10/63	
18297	N7005U	United AL	22	27/11/63	Was N68644 before delivery
18298	N7006U	United AL	22	23/11/63	
18299	N7007U	United AL	22	18/12/63	
18300	N7008U	United AL	22	22/1/64	
18301	N7009U	United AL	22	11/3/64	
18302	N7010U	United AL	22	20/1/64	
18303	N7011U	United AL	22	7/2/64	
18304	N7012U	United AL	22	14/2/64	
18305	N7013U	United AL	22	20/3/64	
18306	N7014U	United AL	22	6/4/64	
18307	N7015U	United AL	22	16/4/64	
18308	N7016U	United AL	22	1/5/64	
18309	N7017U	United AL	22	27/5/64	

C/n	Current Marks	Current Owner/operator	Model Series	Initial Delivery	Remarks
18310	N7018U	United AL	22	9/6/64	
18311	N7019U	United AL	22	30/6/64	
18312	N7020U	United AL	22	16/7/64	
18313	N7021U	United AL	22	7/8/64	
18314	N7022U	United AL	22	15/9/64	
18315	N7023U	United AL	22	25/9/64	
18316	N7024U	United AL	22	8/10/64	
18317	N7025U	United AL	22	3/11/64	
18318	N7026U	United AL	22	3/12/64	
18319	N7027U	United AL	22	27/1/65	
18320	N7028U	United AL	22	5/5/65	
18321	N7029U	United AL	22	25/3/65	
18322	N7030U	United AL	22	7/4/65	WO NOV–11–65 Salt Lake City
18323	N7031U	United AL	22	23/4/65	
18324	N7032U	United AL	22	28/4/65	
18325	N7033U	United AL	22	12/5/65	
18326	N7034U	United AL	22	21/5/65	
18327	N7035U	United AL	22	21/5/65	
18328	N7036U	United AL	22	3/6/65	WO Lake Michigan AUG–16–65
18329	N7037U	United AL	22	25/6/65	
18330	N7038U	United AL	22	2/7/65	
18331	N7039U	United AL	22	14/7/65	
18332	N7040U	United AL	22	4/8/65	
18360	D–ABIB	Lufthansa	30	22/2/64	Was N68649 before D *Augsburg*
18361	D–ABIC	Lufthansa	30	19/3/64	*Saarbrucken*
18362	D–ABID	Lufthansa	30	2/4/64	*Braunschweig*
18363	D–ABIF	Lufthansa	30	7/4/64	*Mannheim*
18364	D–ABIG	Lufthansa	30	10/4/64	*Kiel*
18365	D–ABIH	Lufthansa	30	19/6/64	*Wiesbaden*
18366	D–ABIK	Condor	30	28/12/64	*Heidelberg* L from Lufthansa
18367	D–ABIL	Condor	30	3/2/65	*Lubeck*. L from Lufthansa
18368	D–ABIM	Condor	30	26/2/65	*Kassel*. L from Lufthansa
18369	D–ABIN	Lufthansa	30	19/3/65	*Munster*. L to Condor 1970
18370	D–ABIP	Condor	30	16/4/65	*Mainz*. L from Lufthansa
18371	D–ABIQ	Condor	30	26/5/65	*Karlsruhe*. L from Lufthansa
18426	N1970	American AL	23	26/2/64	
18427	N1971	American AL	23	17/2/64	
18428	N1972	American AL	23	20/2/64	
18429	N1973	American AL	23	27/3/64	
18430	N1974	American AL	23	14/4/64	
18431	N1975	American AL	23	31/5/64	
18432	N1976	American AL	23	13/5/64	
18433	N1977	American AL	23	25/5/64	
18434	N1978	American AL	23	16/6/64	
18435	N1979	American AL	23	30/6/64	
18436	N1980	American AL	23	16/7/64	
18437	N1981	American AL	23	24/7/64	
18438	N1982	American AL	23	21/8/64	
18439	N1983	American AL	23	20/8/64	
18440	N1984	American AL	23	28/8/64	
18441	N1985	American AL	23	18/12/64	
18442	N1986	American AL	23	22/1/65	
18443	N1987	American AL	23	10/2/65	
18444	N1988	American AL	23	23/2/65	
18445	N1989	American AL	23	23/2/65	
18446	N1990	American AL	23	18/3/65	
18447	N1991	American AL	23	3/4/65	
18448	N1992	American AL	23	9/4/65	
18449	N1993	American AL	23	27/4/65	
18450	N1994	American AL	23	14/5/65	
18464	N72700	Boeing Co	22		Prototype, FF FEB–9–63
18569	N850TW	TWA	31	29/4/64	

Boeing 727

C/n	Current Marks	Current Owner/operator	Model Series	Initial Delivery	Remarks
18570	N851TW	TWA	31	25/4/64	
18571	N852TW	TWA	31	2/5/64	
18572	N853TW	TWA	31	21/5/64	
18573	N854TW	TWA	31	6/6/64	
18574	N855TW	TWA	31	10/7/64	
18575	N856TW	TWA	31	14/7/64	
18576	N857TW	TWA	31	11/8/64	
18577	N858TW	TWA	31	31/7/64	
18578	N859TW	TWA	31	17/8/64	
18741	VH–TJA	TAA	76	28/9/64	*James Cook*
18742	VH–TJB	TAA	76	27/10/64	*John Forrest*
18743	VH–RME	Ansett–ANA	77	29/9/64	
18744	VH–RMF	Ansett–ANA	77	1/11/64	
18750	N849TW	TWA	31	3/9/64	
18751	N848TW	TWA	31	18/9/64	
18752	N847TW	TWA	31	21/9/64	
18753	N846TW	TWA	31	27/10/64	
18754	N845TW	TWA	31	30/10/64	
18755	N844TW	TWA	31	7/11/64	
18791	N7003U	United AL	22	3/8/65	
18794	N305BN	Braniff	78	22/12/64	D to BWIA as 9Y–TCO. S to Braniff AUG–1971
18795	N306BN	Braniff	78	13/1/65	D to BWIA as 9Y–TCP. S to Braniff APR–10–71
18796	N307BN	Braniff	78	28/1/65	D to BWIA as 9Y–TCQ. S to Braniff MAR–20–71
18797	N461US	Northwest	51	12/11/64	
18798	N462US	Northwest	51	24/11/64	
18799	N463US	Northwest	51	23/12/64	
18800	N464US	Northwest	51	11/2/65	
18801	N465US	Northwest	51	1/3/65	
18802	N466US	Northwest	51	31/3/65	
18803	N467US	Northwest	51	22/4/65	
18804	N468US	Northwest	51	23/7/65	
18805	N469US	Northwest	51	10/9/65	
18806	N470US	Northwest	51	7/10/65	
18807	N471US	Northwest	51	22/10/65	
18811	N4610	National AL	35	23/10/64	
18812	N4611	National AL	35	19/11/64	
18813	N4612	National AL	35	3/12/64	
18814	N4613	National AL	35	16/12/64	
18815	N4614	National AL	35	19/1/65	
18816	N4615	National AL	35	10/2/65	
18817	N4616	National AL	35	26/2/65	
18821	N124	Pacific Southwest	81	18/3/65	D to All-Nippon as JA8301. S to Pacific MAY–29–72
18822	JA8302	All-Nippon AW	81	27/3/65	WO Tokyo Bay FEB–4–66
18823	D–AHL	Hapag Lloyd	100	19/4/65	D to All Nippon AW as JA8303. S to Hapag Lloyd FEB–12–73
18843	VH–TJC	TAA	76	19/8/65	*Arthur Philip*
18844	VH–RMD	Ansett–ANA	77	19/8/65	
18845	N4617	National	35	2/9/65	
18846	N4618	National	35	24/9/65	
18847	N4619	National	35	11/11/65	
18848	N7041U	United AL	22	14/9/65	
18849	N7042U	United AL	22	15/9/65	
18850	N1631	Northeast AL	22	7/10/65	Initially to be N7043U for United AL
18851	N7044U	United AL	22	22/9/65	
18852	N7045U	United AL	22	5/10/65	
18853	N7046U	United AL	22	14/10/65	
18854	N7047U	United AL	22	27/10/65	
18855	N7048U	United AL	22	3/11/65	
18856	N7049U	United AL	22	21/12/65	
18857	N7050U	United AL	22	18/11/65	

C/n	Current Marks	Current Owner/operator	Model Series	Initial Delivery	Remarks
18858	N1632	Northern AL	22	17/12/65	Initially to be N7051U for United AL
18859	N7052U	United AL	22	14/12/65	
18860	N7053U	United AL	22	16/12/65	
18861	N7054U	United AL	22	28/12/65	
18862	N7055U	United AL	22	12/1/66	
18863	N7056U	United AL	22	3/2/66	
18864	N7057U	United AL	22	22/2/66	
18865	N7058U	United AL	22	18/2/66	
18866	N7059U	United AL	22	13/3/66	
18867	N7060U	United AL	22	30/3/66	
18868	N7061U	United AL	22	1/4/66	
18869	N7062U	United AL	22	15/4/66	L to Richard Nixon OCT–68 as *Tricia*
18870	N7063U	United AL	22	27/4/66	
18871	N7064U	United AL	22	28/4/66	
18872	N7065U	United AL	22	30/4/66	
18874	HL–7307	Korean Air Lines	46	15/6/65	D to JAL as JA8307 *Tome*. S to Korean AL JUL–13–72
18875	HL–7308	Korean Air Lines	46	19/11/65	D to JAL as JA8308 *Kono*. S to Korean AL AUG–1–72
18876	JA8309	JAL	46	7/1/66	*Chikugo*
18877	G–BAFZ	Dan-Air	46	31/1/66	D to JAL as JA8310 *Ishikari*. S to Dan-Air NOV–1–72
18878	G–BAJW	Dan-Air	46	2/3/66	D to JAL as JA8311 *Kiso*. S to Dan-Air OCT–31–72
18879	G–BAEF	Dan-Air	46	16/4/66	D to JAL as JA8312 *Tokachi* S to Dan-Air SEP–29–72
18892	ZS–SBA	SAA	44	3/6/65	D as ZS–DYM. *Tugela*
18893	ZS–SBB	SAA	44	8/7/65	D as ZS–DYN. *Limpopo*
18894	ZS–SBC	SAA	44	10/8/65	D as ZS–DYO. *Vaal*
18895	ZS–SBD	SAA	44	23/8/65	D as ZS–DYP. *Orange*
18896	ZS–SBE	SAA	44	10/10/65	D as ZS–DYR. *Letaba*
18897	N303BN	Braniff	51C		Proto cargo-convertible model, initially N2977G. L from Boeing APR–6–67 to SEP–24–68 by Piedmont as N7270C *Empire State*. L to Braniff 1969
18898	N490US	Northwest	51C	11/4/66	
18899	N491US	Northwest	51C	9/5/66	
18900	N1995	American	23	23/6/65	
18901	N1996	American	23	29/6/65	WO Cincinnati NOV–8–65
18902	N831TW	TWA	31	18/5/65	
18903	N833TW	TWA	31	16/6/65	
18904	N839TW	TWA	31	24/6/65	
18905	N840TW	TWA	31	12/7/65	
18906	N841TW	TWA	31	9/9/65	
18907	N842TW	TWA	31	29/1/66	
18908	XA–SER	Mexicana	14	3/4/65	D to PSA as N970PS. S to Mexicana SEP–27–69
18909	XA–SEU	Mexicana	14	22/5/65	D to PSA as N971PS. S to Mexicana JUN–17–69
18910	N972PS	Alaska AL	14	27/6/65	L from PSA
18911	XA–SEA	Mexicana	14	1/8/65	D to PSA as N973PS. S to Mexicana AUG–15–69
18912	XA–SEP	Mexicana	14	10/8/65	D to PSA as N974PS. L to All-Nippon, FEB–69 to JAN–70. L to Mexicana from MAR–70
18919	D–AHLM	Hapag Lloyd	100	26/7/65	D to All-Nippon AW as JA8305. S to Hapag Lloyd NOV–12–72
18920	HP–619	Air Panama	46	23/8/65	D to All Nippon AW as JA8306. S to Air Panama NOV–3–72

Boeing 727

C/n	Current Marks	Current Owner/operator	Model Series	Initial Delivery	Remarks
18933	D–ABIR	Condor	30	29/9/65	*Aachen.* L from Lufthansa
18934	D–ABIS	Lufthansa	30	21/1/66	*Freiburg*
18935	D–ABIT	Lufthansa	30	24/2/66	*Heidelburg*
18936	D–ABIV	Lufthansa	30	7/4/66	*Kassel*
18942	N472US	Northwest	51	9/11/65	
18943	N473US	Northwest	51	2/12/65	
18944	N474US	Northwest	51	17/12/65	
18945	N492US	Northwest	51C	12/5/66	
18946	N493US	Northwest	51C	27/5/66	
18947	N494US	Northwest	51C	13/8/66	
18951	HP–620	Air Panama	46	4/3/66	D to All-Nippon AW as JA8316. S to Air Panama MAR–26–73.
18952	D–AHLN	Hapag Lloyd	100	30/8/66	D to All-Nippon AW as JA8317. S to Hapag Lloyd DEC–12–72.
18965	N8141N	Eastern AL	25	15/12/65	
18966	N8142N	Eastern AL	25	21/12/65	
18967	N8143N	Eastern AL	25	15/1/66	
18968	N8144N	Eastern AL	25	25/1/66	
18969	N8145N	Eastern AL	25	29/1/66	
18970	N8146N	Eastern AL	25	10/2/66	
18971	N8147N	Eastern AL	25	15/2/66	
18972	N8148N	Eastern AL	25	18/3/66	
18973	N8149N	Eastern AL	25	15/4/66	
18974	N8150N	Eastern AL	25	15/4/66	
18990	–	Hapag Lloyd	14	7/3/66	D to Pacific Southwest as N975PS. S to Lockheed. S to Hapag Lloyd SEP–1973
18992	N314PA	PAA	21	18/12/65	*Sam Houston*
18993	N315PA	PAA	21	14/1/66	*White Falcon*
18994	N316PA	PAA	21	15/1/66	*Buena Vista*
18995	N317PA	PAA	21	20/1/66	*De Soto* WO Berlin NOV–15–66
18996	N318PA	PAA	21	19/2/66	*Inca*
18997	N319PA	PAA	21	28/2/66	*Ponce de Leon*
18998	N320PA	PAA	21	12/3/66	*Berlin*
18999	N321PA	PAA	21	16/3/66	*Koln-Bonn*
19005	N323PA	PAA	21	28/4/66	*Frankfurt*
19006	N324PA	PAA	21	4/5/66	*Munchen*
19007	N325PA	PAA	21	19/5/66	*Dusseldorf*
19008	D–ABIW	Lufthansa	30C	22/2/67	*Bielefeld*
19009	D–ABIX	Lufthansa	30C	6/3/67	*Wurzburg*
19010	D–ABIZ	Lufthansa	30C	17/3/67	*Gelsenkirchen*
19011	D–ABIA	Lufthansa	30C	31/3/67	*Pforzheim*
19012	D–ABIE	Lufthansa	30C	10/4/67	*Oberhausen*
19035	N326PA	PAA	21	27/5/66	*Nuremburg*
19036	N327PA	PAA	21	25/6/66	*Hannover*
19037	N328PA	PAA	21	22/6/66	*Hamburg*
19038	N329PA	PAA	21	29/6/66	*Lightfoot*
19079	N7066U	United AL	22	16/5/66	
19080	N7067U	United AL	22	19/5/66	
19081	N7068U	United AL	22	6/6/66	
19082	N7069U	United AL	22	9/6/66	
19083	N7070U	United AL	22	21/6/66	
19084	N7071U	United AL	22	19/12/66	
19085	N7072U	United AL	22	22/12/66	
19086	N7073U	United AL	22	23/1/67	
19087	N7074U	United AL	22	27/1/67	
19088	N7075U	United AL	22	9/2/67	
19089	N7401U	United AL	22QC	15/5/66	
19090	N7402U	United AL	22QC	29/6/66	
19091	N7403U	United AL	22QC	7/7/66	
19092	N7404U	United AL	22QC	16/8/66	
19093	N7405U	United AL	22QC	19/8/66	
19094	N7406U	United AL	22QC	22/9/66	

C/n	Current Marks	Current Owner/operator	Model Series	Initial Delivery	Remarks
19095	N7407U	United AL	22QC	9/9/66	
19096	N7408U	United AL	22QC	14/9/66	
19097	N7409U	United AL	22QC	20/9/66	
19098	N7410U	United AL	22QC	10/10/66	
19099	N7411U	United AL	22QC	26/10/66	
19100	N7412U	United AL	22QC	31/10/66	
19101	N7413U	United AL	22QC	21/11/66	
19102	N7414U	United AL	22QC	7/12/66	
19103	N7415U	United AL	22QC	17/12/66	
19109	N7270	Braniff	27C	27/5/66	L by American Flyers, DEC–67
19110	N7271	Braniff	27C	24/6/66	
19111	N7272	Braniff	27C	14/8/66	
19112	N7273	Braniff	27C	26/8/66	
19113	N7274	Braniff	27C	14/9/66	
19114	N7275	Braniff	27C	21/9/66	
19115	N7276	Braniff	27C	29/10/66	
19116	N7277	Braniff	27C	4/11/66	
19117	N7278	Braniff	27C	1/3/67	
19118	N7279	Braniff	27C	7/3/67	
19119	N7280	Braniff	27C	4/4/67	
19120	N7281	Braniff	27C	18/4/67	
19121	N475US	Northwest	51	5/5/66	
19122	N476US	Northwest	51	28/9/66	
19123	N477US	Northwest	51	12/11/66	
19124	N478US	Northwest	51	16/12/66	
19125	N479US	Northwest	51	25/1/67	
19126	N480US	Northwest	51	1/1/67	
19127	HK727	Avianca	59	14/3/66	*Córdoba*
19128	N1997	American AL	23	24/11/65	
19129	N1998	American AL	23	19/11/65	
19130	N1901	American AL	23	21/12/65	
19131	N1902	American AL	23	18/1/66	
19132	N1903	American AL	23	16/2/66	
19134	N339PA	PAA	21QC	21/7/66	*Stuttgart*
19135	N340PA	PAA	21QC	1/9/66	*Talisman*
19136	N341PA	PAA	21QC	27/9/66	*Plymouth Rock*
19137	N342PA	PAA	21QC	7/10/66	*Golden Age*
19138	JA8314	JAL	89	29/3/66	D to JDA *Tenryu*
19139	JA8315	JAL	89	19/4/66	D to JDA *Yodo*
19140	N7076U	United AL	22	14/2/67	
19141	N7077U	United AL	22	20/2/67	
19142	N7078U	United AL	22	30/7/67	
19143	N7079U	United AL	22	17/8/67	
19144	N7080U	United AL	22	30/8/67	
19145	N7081U	United AL	22	31/8/67	
19146	N7082U	United AL	22	5/9/67	L to Richard Nixon OCT–68 as *Julie*
19147	N7083U	United AL	22	12/10/67	
19148	N7084U	United AL	22	16/10/67	
19149	N7085U	United AL	22	31/10/67	
19150	N7086U	United AL	22	8/12/67	
19151	N7087U	United AL	22	20/12/67	
19152	N7088U	United AL	22	20/12/67	
19153	N7089U	United AL	22	20/12/67	
19154	N7090U	United AL	22	29/12/67	
19165	N4620	National	35	23/7/66	
19166	N4621	National	35	30/8/66	
19167	N4622	National	35	17/10/66	
19169	N797AS	Alaska AL	90C	21/10/66	
19170	N798AS	Alaska AL	90C	18/11/66	
19171	EP–IRA	Iranair	86	7/6/66	
19172	EP–IRB	Iranair	86	13/10/66	
19173	N18476	Continental	92C	3/10/66	D to Air Asia as N5055. S to Continental OCT–3–72

Boeing 727

C/n	Current Marks	Current Owner/operator	Model Series	Initial Delivery	Remarks
19174	CF–PXB	Pacific Western	92C	6/11/66	D to Air Asia as N5092. S to Pacific Western OCT–26–72
19175	B–1018	CAT	92C	10/12/66	D to Air Asia as N5093. WO Linklow FEB–16–68
19176	N127	FAA	61		
19180	N1905	American AL	23	15/4/66	
19181	N1906	American AL	23	25/5/66	
19182	N1907	American AL	23	12/5/66	
19183	N1908	American AL	23	19/5/66	
19184	N1909	American AL	23	24/6/66	
19191	N7416U	United AL	22C	31/3/67	
19192	N7417U	United AL	22C	10/4/67	
19193	N7418U	United AL	22C	17/4/67	
19194	N7419U	United AL	22C	25/4/67	
19195	N7420U	United AL	22C	11/5/67	
19196	N7421U	United AL	22C	16/5/67	
19197	N7422U	United AL	22C	23/5/67	
19198	N7423U	United AL	22C	5/6/67	
19199	N7424U	United AL	22C	12/6/67	
19200	N7425U	United AL	22C	19/6/67	WO
19201	N7426U	United AL	22C	27/6/67	
19202	N7427U	United AL	22C	30/6/67	
19203	N7428U	United AL	22C	30/7/67	
19204	N7429U	United AL	22C	25/7/67	
19205	N7430U	United AL	22C	3/8/67	
19206	N495US	Northwest	51C	24/8/66	
19228	N889TW	TWA	31	29/12/66	
19229	N890TW	TWA	31C	16/4/67	
19230	N891TW	TWA	31C	3/5/67	
19231	N892TW	TWA	31C	9/5/67	
19232	N893TW	TWA	31C	30/6/67	
19233	N894TW	TWA	31C	17/9/67	
19234	N895TW	TWA	31C	29/9/67	
19242	PP–CJI	Cruzeiro	11	25/4/66	D to Wardair as CF–FUN *Cy Becker*. S to Cruzeiro MAY–24–73
19243	N7282	Braniff	162	20/5/66	Built as N7271P for PNA
19244	N7284	Braniff	62C	24/11/66	Built as N2727 for PNA
19245	N7286	Braniff	62C	12/12/66	Built as N3727 for PNA
19246	N7287	Braniff	27C	10/6/67	Built as N4727P for PNA
19249	N1633	Northeast AL	95	25/8/66	
19250	N1634	Northeast AL	95	16/9/66	
19251	N1635	Northeast AL	95	29/9/66	
19252	N1636	Northeast AL	95	22/10/66	
19253	VH–RMR	Ansett–ANA	77	10/8/66	
19254	VH–TJD	TAA	76	10/8/66	*Gregory Blaxland*
19255	XA–SEJ	Mexicana	64	8/11/66	WO AUG–21–69 Mexico City
19256	XA–SEL	Mexicana	64	17/1/67	WO JUN–4–69 near Monterrey
19257	N355PA	PAA	21	17/3/67	*Andrew Jackson* later *Nurnberg*
19258	N356PA	PAA	21	13/4/67	*Belle of the Sky*
19259	N357PA	PAA	21	10/5/67	*Bessy Ross*
19260	N358PA	PAA	21	20/5/67	*David Crockett*
19261	N359PA	PAA	21	17/6/67	*Unity*
19262	N360PA	PAA	21	28/6/67	*Golden Rule*
19279	JA8318	JAL	46	1/67	*Tama*
19280	JA8319	JAL	46	17/2/67	*Kitayami*
19281	JA8320	JAL	46	25/2/67	*Sagami*
19282	JA8325	JAL	46	5/12/67	*Shinano*
19283	JA8326	JAL	46	11/12/67	*Kumano*
19287	N496US	Northwest	51C	12/3/67	
19288	N497US	Northwest	51C	28/3/67	
19289	N498US	Northwest	51C	22/4/67	

C/n	Current Marks	Current Owner/operator	Model Series	Initial Delivery	Remarks
19290	N499US	Northwest	51C	27/5/67	
19298	N8151G	Eastern AL	25C	17/12/66	
19299	N8152G	Eastern AL	25C	18/12/66	
19300	N8153G	Eastern AL	25C	21/12/66	
19301	N8154G	Eastern AL	25C	27/1/67	
19302	N8155G	Eastern AL	25C	2/2/67	
19303	HK1337	Avianca	59	16/1/67	*Camilo Torres*
19304	N2969G	Braniff	192	1/7/66	D to Pacific AL, later Air West. L to BWIA NOV–67 to NOV–68. L to Braniff MAR–69 to FEB–70 WO
19305	PP–CJH	Cruzeiro	193	4/8/66	D to Pacific AL, later Air West, reg N2979G. S to Cruzeiro NOV–1972
19310	D–ABII	Lufthansa	30C	18/4/67	*Wuppertal*
19311	D–ABIO	Lufthansa	30C	18/5/67	*Hagen*
19312	D–ABIU	Lufthansa	30C	18/5/67	*Ulm*
19313	D–ABIY	Lufthansa	30C	25/5/67	*Aachen*
19314	D–ABIJ	Lufthansa	30C	28/7/67	*Krefeld*
19318	ZS–SBF	SAA	44	9/1/67	D as ZS–EKW *Komati*
19319	ZS–SBG	SAA	44C	25/8/67	D as ZS–EKX *Swakop*
19356	N8156G	Eastern AL	25C	10/2/67	
19357	N8157G	Eastern AL	25C	7/2/67	
19358	N8158G	Eastern AL	25C	18/3/67	
19359	N8159G	Eastern AL	25C	24/2/67	
19360	N8160G	Eastern AL	25C	9/3/67	
19385	N1910	American AL	23	9/9/66	
19386	N1928	American AL	23	7/10/66	
19387	N1929	American AL	23	27/10/66	
19388	N1930	American AL	23	2/12/66	
19389	N1931	American AL	23	13/12/66	
19390	N1932	American AL	23	1/1/67	
19391	N297BN	Braniff	191	8/9/66	D to Frontier as N7270F. S to Braniff DEC–16–69
19392	N2988N	Braniff	191	4/10/66	D to Frontier as N7271F. S to Braniff DEC–3–69
19393	N299BN	Braniff	191	19/4/67	D to Frontier as N7272F. S to Braniff APR–16–69
19394	N300BN	Braniff	191	2/6/67	D to Frontier as N7273F. S to Braniff NOV–5–69
19395	N301BN	Braniff	191	5/7/67	D to Frontier as N7274F. S to Braniff NOV–16–69
19398	XA–SEN	Mexicana	14	16/12/66	D to PSA as N976PS. S to Mexicana JUN–10–69
19399	B–1818	China Air	109	3/3/67	
19400	OO–STA	Sabena	29	28/4/67	
19401	–	Hapag Lloyd	29	10/6/67	D to Sabena as 00–STC. S to Hapag Lloyd NOV–1973.
19402	OO–STB	Sabena	29C	6/6/67	
19403	OO–STD	Sabena	29C	27/7/67	
19404	CS–TBK	TAP	82	12/3/67	*Acores*
19405	CS–TBL	TAP	82	24/4/67	*Madeira*
19406	CS–TBM	TAP	82	11/7/67	*Algarve*
19427	XA–SEM	Mexicana	64	14/3/67	
19428	N1933	American AL	23	20/1/67	
19429	N1934	American AL	23	31/1/67	
19430	N1935	American AL	23	7/2/67	
19431	N1955	American AL	23	16/2/67	
19432	N1956	American AL	23	10/3/67	
19444	N1639	Northeast AL	295	29/1/67	L to TWA 1967
19445	N1640	Northeast AL	295	18/12/67	
19446	N1641	Northeast AL	295	11/12/67	
19447	N1642	Northeast AL	295	15/12/67	
19448	N1643	Northeast AL	295	8/1/68	
19449	N1644	Northeast AL	295	10/1/68	

Boeing 727

C/n	Current Marks	Current Owner/operator	Model Series	Initial Delivery	Remarks
19450	N4730	National AL	235	13/12/67	L to TWA
19451	N4731	National AL	235	19/12/67	
19452	N4732	National AL	235	27/12/67	L to TWA
19453	N4733	National AL	235	19/1/68	L to TWA
19454	N4734	National AL	235	23/1/68	
19455	N4735	National AL	235	25/1/68	
19456	N4736	National AL	235	30/1/68	
19457	N4737	National AL	235	31/1/68	
19458	N4738	National AL	235	16/2/68	
19459	N4739	National AL	235	23/2/68	
19460	N4740	National AL	235	27/2/68	
19461	N4741	National AL	235	6/3/68	
19462	N4742	National AL	235	12/3/68	
19463	N4743	National AL	235	29/3/68	
19464	N4744	National AL	235	27/3/68	
19465	N4745	National AL	235	3/4/68	
19466	N4746	National AL	235	18/4/68	L to TWA
19467	N4747	National AL	235	26/4/68	
19468	N4748	National AL	235	30/4/68	
19469	N4749	National AL	235	29/4/68	
19470	N4750	National AL	235	3/5/68	
19471	N4751	National AL	235	18/6/68	
19472	N4752	National AL	235	20/6/68	
19473	N4753	National AL	235	23/7/68	
19474	N4754	National AL	235	25/7/68	
19475	N6800	American AL	223	1/2/68	
19476	N6801	American AL	223	19/2/68	
19477	N6802	American AL	223	29/2/68	
19478	N6803	American AL	223	5/3/68	
19479	N6804	American AL	223	18/3/68	
19480	N6805	American AL	223	25/3/68	
19481	N6806	American AL	223	2/4/68	
19482	N6807	American AL	223	17/4/68	
19483	N6808	American AL	223	11/4/68	
19484	N6809	American AL	223	23/4/68	
19485	N6810	American AL	223	10/5/68	
19486	N6811	American AL	223	27/5/68	
19487	N6812	American AL	223	29/5/68	
19488	N6813	American AL	223	12/6/68	
19489	N6814	American AL	223	28/6/68	
19490	N6815	American AL	223	15/7/68	
19491	N6816	American AL	223	31/7/68	
19492	N6817	American AL	223	1/11/68	
19493	N6818	American AL	223	19/11/68	
19494	N6819	American AL	223	22/11/68	
19495	N6820	American AL	223	3/12/68	
19496	N6821	American AL	223	17/12/68	
19497	N7288	Braniff	27C	1/7/67	
19499	N7289	Braniff	27	10/8/67	
19500	N7290	Braniff	27	14/8/67	
19501	N7292	Braniff	27	29/8/67	
19503	TF–FIE	Icelandair	108C	22/6/67	*Enterprise* later *Gullfaxi*
19504	N690WA	World AW	173C	12/7/67	L to Ariana 1969. L to JAL 1970
19505	N691WA	World AW	173C	15/7/57	L to JAL 1969-70
19506	N692WA	World AW	173C	20/8/67	L to JAL 1970
19507	N693WA	World AW	173C	6/9/67	L by United AL OCT–8–67 to JUN–25–68. L to JAL 1970
19508	N694WA	World AW	173C	22/9/67	L by United AL OCT–8–67 to JUN–27–68. L to JAL 1970
19509	N695WA	World AW	173C	14/9/67	L by United AL OCT–8–67 to JUN–30–68. L by Ariana Afghan 1969

C/n	Current Marks	Current Owner/operator	Model Series	Initial Delivery	Remarks
19510	N88701	Continental AL	224		
19511	N88702	Continental AL	224	28/5/68	
19512	N88703	Continental AL	224	29/5/68	
19513	N88704	Continental AL	224	26/6/68	*Sheldon G Cooper*
19514	N88705	Continental AL	224	1/7/68	
19520	B–1820	China Air	109	27/9/67	
19524	HK–1271	Avianca	24C	1/7/67	L by Boeing as N5475. S to Avianca DEC–1971
19525	HK–1272	Avianca	24C	27/7/67	L by Boeing as N5472. S to Avianca NOV–1971
19526	HK–1273	Avianca	24C	3/8/67	L by Boeing as N2473. S to Avianca NOV–1971
19527	N5474	–	24C	16/9/67	L from Boeing by Continental as N2474 until AUG–20–68
19528	N2475	Air Micronesia	24C	24/9/67	L from Boeing by Continental to Air Micronesia 1968
19532	N7295	Braniff	27C	5/10/67	
19533	N7296	Braniff	27C	20/10/67	
19534	N7293	Braniff	27	6/9/67	
19535	N7294	Braniff	27	31/8/67	
19536	SX–CBF	Olympic Airways	200	–	Prototype Srs 200 long-fuselage, reg originally before D as N7270L
19537	N7620U	United AL	222		
19538	N7621U	United AL	222	31/5/68	
19539	N7622U	United AL	222	9/6/68	
19540	N7623U	United AL	222	12/6/68	
19541	N7624U	United AL	222	15/6/68	
19542	N7625U	United AL	222	18/6/68	
19543	F–BOJA	Air France	228	24/3/68	
19544	F–BOJB	Air France	228	23/4/68	
19545	F–BOJC	Air France	228	2/5/68	
19546	F–BOJD	Air France	228	21/5/68	
19557	N329K	Ford Motor Co	81	1/5/67	
19558	N12301	TWA	231		
19559	N12302	TWA	231		
19560	N12303	TWA	231		
19561	N12304	TWA	231		
19562	N12305	TWA	231	25/5/68	
19563	N12306	TWA	231	17/6/68	
19564	N12307	TWA	231	19/7/68	
19565	N12308	TWA	231	22/7/68	
19595	PP–VLQ	Varig	95	27/9/67	D to Northeast as N1637. Later Delta, later Charlotte Aircraft Corp. S to Varig MAY–11–73
19596	PP–VLR	Varig	95	23/10/67	D to Northeast as N1638. Later Delta, later Charlotte Aircraft Corp. S to Varig MAY–23–73
19597	CS–TBN	TAP	82	6/2/68	*Cicade de Porto*
19618	N530EJ	National Aircraft Leasing	155C	13/10/67	D to Executive Jet, later C.I.T. Corp. S to NAL APR–7–72.
19619	YA–FAW	Ariana	155C	27/10/67	D to Executive Jet as N531EJ S to Ariana JUN–24–71
19620	XY–ADR	Union of Burma AW	193	10/3/68	D to Pacific AL, later Air West as N878PC. L to Braniff FEB–69 to MAR–70. S to Union of Burma AW JUL–16–70
19662	HK–1400	Avianca	59	3/11/67	
19663	HK–1401	Avianca	59	15/11/67	

Boeing 727

C/n	Current Marks	Current Owner/operator	Model Series	Initial Delivery	Remarks
19665	CS–TBQ	TAP–Portugal	172C	24/10/67	D to Airlift Int. as N725AL. S to TAP MAR–10–73 *Bissau*
19666	PP–VLE	Varig	172C	31/10/67	D to Airlift Int. as N726AL. S to Varig APR–2–73
19683	F–BPJU	Air France	214	19/12/67	D to PSA as N528PS. S to Air France MAY–26–72
19684	F–BPJV	Air France	214	12/1/68	D to PSA as N529PS. S to Air France NOV–22–72
19685	N530PS	PSA	214	2/4/68	
19686	N531PS	PSA	214	3/5/68	
19687	N532PS	PSA	214	10/5/68	
19688	N533PS	PSA	214	11/6/68	
19689	N534PS	PSA	214	20/7/68	
19690	YA–FAR	Ariana Afghan AL	113C	25/3/68	WO Gatwick JAN–5–69
19691	SE–DDA	Scanair	134	18/11/67	D to Transair. To Scanair OCT–1–69 *Midnight Sun*
19692	SE–DDB	Scanair	134	30/11/67	D to Transair. To Scanair OCT–1–69 *Northern Light*
19700	N6822	American AL	223	2/1/69	
19701	N6823	American AL	223	14/1/69	
19702	N6824	American AL	223	17/1/69	
19703	N6825	American AL	223	30/1/69	
19704	N6826	American AL	223	13/2/69	
19717	N8161G	Eastern AL	25C	30/9/67	
19718	N8162G	Eastern AL	25C	17/10/67	
19719	N8163G	Eastern AL	25C	28/10/67	
19720	N8164G	Eastern AL	25C	10/11/67	
19721	N8165G	Eastern AL	25C	15/11/67	
19722	N8166G	Eastern AL	25C	20/11/67	
19728	N766AS	Alaska AL	90C	7/3/68	
19793	D–ABBI	Lufthansa	30C	20/1/68	*Mainz*
19797	N88706	Continental AL	224	3/7/68	
19798	N88777	Continental AL	224	25/7/68	Initially registered N88707
19799	N88708	Continental AL	224	23/7/68	
19800	N88709	Continental AL	224	2/8/68	
19801	N88710	Continental AL	224	7/8/68	
19802	N88711	Continental AL	224	14/8/68	*Capt O. R. Ted Hunter*
19803	N88712	Continental AL	224	20/8/68	
19804	N88713	Continental AL	224	28/8/68	
19805	N7431U	United AL	22C	14/3/68	
19806	N7432U	United AL	22C	25/3/68	
19807	N727AL	Airlift	172C	31/5/68	
19808	N732AL	Bank of America	172C		
19811	CC–CAG	LAN–Chile	116	2/2/68	
19812	CC–CAQ	LAN–Chile	116	7/2/68	WO
19813	CC–CFD	LAN–Chile	116C	11/6/68	
19814	CC–CFE	LAN–Chile	116C	11/6/68	
19815	XA–TUY	Mexicana	114	2/12/68	D to PSA as N977PS. S to Mexicana NOV–12–69
19816	EP–IRC	Iranair	86	19/12/67	
19817	EP–IRD	Iranair	86	16/2/68	
19818	XV–NJB	Air Viet Nam	121C	29/9/67	D to PAA as N388PA *Ganges* To Air Viet Nam JAN–4–68
19819	XV–NJC	Air Viet Nam	121C	16/1/68	D to PAA as N389PA *Golden Light.* To Air Viet Nam on JAN–23–69
19826	TF–FIA	Icelandair	185C	1/4/68	D to American Flyers as N12826. S to Icelandair MAY–18–71
19827	N308BN	Braniff	100C	20/2/68	D to American Flyers as N12827. S to Braniff DEC–2–71

C/n	Current Marks	Current Owner/operator	Model Series	Initial Delivery	Remarks
19828	N52309	TWA	231	29/7/68	
19829	N52310	TWA	231	17/9/68	
19830	N52311	TWA	231	20/9/68	
19831	N52312	TWA	231	27/9/68	
19832	N52313	TWA	231	11/10/68	
19833	N1957	American AL	35	7/11/67	
19834	N1958	American AL	35	14/11/67	
19835	N1959	American AL	35	28/12/67	
19836	N1962	American AL	95	5/12/67	
19837	N1963	American AL	95	19/12/67	
19838	N1964	American AL	123	29/3/68	
19839	N1965	American AL	123	8/3/68	
19846	OB–R–902	Faucett	63	9/4/68	
19850	N8167G	Eastern AL	25C	2/12/67	
19851	N8168G	Eastern AL	25C	9/1/68	
19852	N8169G	Eastern AL	25C	23/1/68	
19853	N8170G	Eastern AL	25C	1/2/68	
19854	N8171G	Eastern AL	25C	10/9/68	
19855	N8172G	Eastern AL	25C	20/9/68	
19856	N8173G	Eastern AL	25C	3/10/68	
19857	N8174G	Eastern AL	25C	15/10/68	
19858	N8175G	Eastern AL	25C	18/10/68	
19859	N1727T	Trans-International	171C	16/4/68	
19860	N1728T	Trans-International	171C	5/7/68	
19861	F–BOJE	Air France	228	28/1/69	
19862	F–BOJF	Air France	228	6/2/69	
19863	F–BPJG	Air France	228	19/2/69	
19864	F–BPJH	Air France	228	3/3/69	
19865	F–BPJI	Air France	228		
19867	N488US	Northwest	151C	9/1/68	
19868	N489US	Northwest	151C	7/2/68	L to UBA 1969
19873	N9516T	TWA	180C	23/6/68	
19874	N9515T	TWA	180C	19/2/68	
19890	N7433U	United AL	22C	19/9/68	
19891	N7434U	United AL	22C	20/9/68	WO Los Angeles JAN–18–69
19892	N7435U	United AL	22C	14/10/68	
19893	N7436U	United AL	22C	15/10/68	
19894	N7437U	United AL	22C	25/10/68	
19895	N7438U	United AL	22C	19/11/68	
19899	N7626U	United AL	222	16/8/68	
19900	N7627U	United AL	222	23/8/68	
19901	N7628U	United AL	222	6/9/68	
19902	N7629U	United AL	222	2/10/68	
19903	N7630U	United AL	222	4/10/68	
19904	N7631U	United AL	222	4/11/68	
19905	N7632U	United AL	222	8/11/68	
19906	N7633U	United AL	222	15/11/68	
19907	N7634U	United AL	222	21/11/68	
19908	N7635U	United AL	222	5/12/68	
19909	N7636U	United AL	222	12/12/65	
19910	N7637U	United AL	222	27/12/68	
19911	N7638U	United AL	222	27/12/68	
19912	N7639U	United AL	222	6/1/68	
19913	N7640U	United AL	222	6/1/68	
19914	N7641U	United AL	222	15/1/68	
19915	N7642U	United AL	222	3/3/69	
19968	CS–TBO	TAP	82C	23/11/68	*Costa Do Sol*
19970	N251US	Northwest	251	19/10/68	
19971	N252US	Northwest	251	2/11/68	
19972	N253US	Northwest	251	21/11/68	
19973	N254US	Northwest	251	27/11/68	
19974	N255US	Northwest	251	7/12/68	
19975	N256US	Northwest	251	4/1/69	
19976	N257US	Northwest	251	24/1/69	
19977	N258US	Northwest	251	14/2/69	
19978	N259US	Northwest	251	21/2/69	

Boeing 727

C/n	Current Marks	Current Owner/operator	Model Series	Initial Delivery	Remarks
19979	N260US	Northwest	251	5/3/69	
19980	N261US	Northwest	251	28/3/69	
19981	N262US	Northwest	251	11/7/69	
19982	N263US	Northwest	251	15/7/69	
19983	N264US	Northwest	251	1/8/69	
19984	N265US	Northwest	251	5/8/69	
19985	N266US	Northwest	251	8/8/69	
19987	OO–STE	Sabena	29C	1/10/68	
19991	N460BN	Braniff	291	8/2/68	
19992	N407BN	Braniff	291	18/2/68	
19993	N498BN	Braniff	291	25/3/68	
19994	N1648	Northeast AL	291		Built as N7279F for Frontier. S to GATX/ Boothe as N1784B. L 1969
19995	N1649	Northeast AL	295	31/1/69	
20003	SX–CBA	Olympic AW	284	19/12/68	*Mount Olympus*
20004	SX–CBB	Olympic AW	284	16/1/69	*Queen Anna Maria*
20005	SX–CBC	Olympic AW	284	7/2/69	*Mount Parnassus*
20006	SX–CBD	Olympic AW	284	7/2/69	*Mount Helicon*
20037	N7643U	United AL	222	19/3/69	
20038	N7644U	United AL	222	14/5/69	
20039	N7645U	United AL	222	26/5/69	
20040	N7646U	United AL	222	18/6/69	
20041	N7647U	United AL	222	30/6/69	
20042	SE–DDC	Scanair	134C		D to Transair. To Scanair 1/10/69.*Polar Circle*
20044	N1969	American AL	23	24/6/68	
20045	N2913	American AL	23	9/7/68	
20046	N2914	American AL	23	23/7/68	
20047	N94314	TWA	231	3/2/69	
20048	N64315	TWA	231	11/2/69	
20049	N44316	TWA	231	27/2/69	
20050	N74317	TWA	231	7/3/69	
20051	N74318	TWA	231	16/4/69	
20052	N6431N	TWA	231	19/4/69	
20053	N64320	TWA	231	18/4/69	
20054	N64321	TWA	231	15/5/69	
20055	N64322	TWA	231	18/5/69	
20075	F–BPJJ	Air France	228	29/3/69	
20078	JA8327	JAL	46	31/1/69	
20098	N64323	TWA	231	20/6/69	
20099	N64324	TWA	231	2/7/69	
20111	B–1822	China AL	109C	28/2/69	
20112	N7890	TWA	31	1/5/69	
20113	N97891	TWA	31	7/5/69	
20114	N7892	TWA	31		
20115	N7893	TWA	31	7/7/69	
20139	N1645	Northeast AL	295	9/10/68	
20140	N1646	Northeast AL	295	28/10/68	
20141	N1647	Northeast AL	295	15/11/68	
20143	N8789R	Trans Caribbean	1A7C	16/8/68	
20144	N8825E	Eastern AL	225	22/8/69	
20145	N8826E	Eastern AL	225	29/8/69	
20146	N8827E	Eastern AL	225	10/9/69	
20147	N8828E	Eastern AL	225	31/10/69	
20148	N8829E	Eastern AL	225	7/11/69	
20149	N8830E	Eastern AL	225	12/11/69	
20150	N8831E	Eastern AL	225	14/11/69	
20151	N8832E	Eastern AL	225	21/11/69	
20152	N8833E	Eastern AL	225	26/11/69	
20153	N8834E	Eastern AL	225	12/12/69	
20154	N8835E	Eastern AL	225	16/12/69	
20161	N535PS	Pacific Southwest	214	17/4/69	

C/n	Current Marks	Current Owner/operator	Model Series	Initial Delivery	Remarks
20162	N409BN	Braniff	214	24/4/69	D to Pacific Southwest as N536PS S to Braniff DEC–1–71
20163	N537PS	Pacific Southwest	214	17/5/69	
20164	N538PS	Pacific Southwest	214	23/5/69	
20165	N539PS	Pacific Southwest	214	27/5/69	
20166	N540PS	Pacific Southwest	214	4/6/69	
20167	N541PS	Pacific Southwest	214	4/6/69	
20168	N542PS	Pacific Southwest	214	31/7/69	
20169	N545PS	Pacific Southwest	214	31/7/69	
20180	N6827	American Airlines	223	21/3/69	
20181	N6828	American Airlines	223	24/3/69	
20182	N6829	American Airlines	223	31/3/69	
20183	N6830	American Airlines	223	7/4/69	
20184	N6831	American Airlines	223	11/4/69	
20185	N6832	American Airlines	223	18/4/69	
20186	N6833	American Airlines	223	21/5/69	
20187	N6834	American Airlines	223	28/5/69	
20188	N6835	American Airlines	223	20/6/69	
20189	N6836	American Airlines	223	26/6/69	
20190	N6837	American Airlines	223	22/7/69	
20191	N6838	American Airlines	223	28/7/69	
20192	N6839	American Airlines	223	22/9/69	
20193	N6841	American Airlines	223	26/9/69	
20201	SX–CBE	Olympic Airways	284	24/10/69	*Mount Athos*
20202	F–BPJK	Air France	228	26/11/69	
20203	F–BPJL	Air France	228	5/12/69	
20204	F–BPJM	Air France	228	15/12/69	
20217	XA–SEW	Mexicana	116	24/7/70	FF as N1780B. L to Braniff. reg N304BN. S to Mexicana
20228	VH–TJE	TAA	76	30/10/69	
20232	N54325	TWA	231	3/2/70	
20233	N54326	TWA	231	5/2/70	
20234	N54327	TWA	231	17/2/70	
20240	N8790R	American Airlines	2A7	30/4/69	WO
20241	N8791R	American Airlines	2A7	27/5/69	L from GATX/Boothe
20243	N88714	Continental	224	24/4/69	FF as N1781B
20244	5A–DAH	Libyan Arab Airlines	224	9/1/71	WO
20245	5A–DAI	Libyan Arab Airlines	224	27/1/71	
20248	N1650	Northeast AL	295	10/10/69	
20249	N11651	Northeast AL	295	17/10/69	
20250	N547PS	Pacific Southwest	254	12/12/69	Intended for Mohawk as N7270Q
20251	N548PS	Pacific Southwest	254	29/12/69	Intended for Mohawk as N7271Q
20252	N549PS	Pacific Southwest	254	6/1/70	Intended for Mohawk as N7272Q
20263	N2801W	Western AL	247	16/10/69	
20264	N2802W	Western AL	247	16/10/69	
20265	N2803W	Western AL	247	16/10/69	
20266	N2804W	Western AL	247	14/11/69	
20267	N2805W	Western AL	247	14/11/69	
20268	N2806W	Western AL	247	14/11/69	
20278	VH–RMS	Ansett–ANA	77C	31/10/69	
20279	CP–861	LAB	1AO	17/2/70	
20285	JA8335	All-Nippon AW	281	16/8/71	
20286	JA8336	All-Nippon AW	281	10/5/72	
20289	N267US	Northwest AL	251	12/8/69	
20290	N268US	Northwest AL	251	15/8/69	
20291	N269US	Northwest AL	251	12/9/69	
20292	N270US	Northwest AL	251	22/9/69	
20293	N271US	Northwest AL	251	26/9/69	
20294	N272US	Northwest AL	251	3/10/69	
20295	N273US	Northwest AL	251	18/11/69	

Boeing 727

C/n	Current Marks	Current Owner/operator	Model Series	Initial Delivery	Remarks
20296	N274US	Northwest AL	251	10/12/69	
20302	N404BN	Braniff	2B7	28/5/70	D to Allegheny AL as N750VJ S to Braniff NOV–30–71
20303	N405BN	Braniff	2B7	17/5/70	D to Allegheny AL as N751VJ S to Braniff NOV–25–71
20304	CN–CCF	Royal Air Maroc	2B6	4/5/70	
20306	N54328	TWA	231	3/3/70	
20307	N54329	TWA	231	10/3/70	
20308	N54330	TWA	231	2/4/70	
20309	N54331	TWA	231	7/4/70	
20310	N54332	TWA	231	4/5/70	
20327	CF–CPN	CP Air	17	10/3/70	
20328	CF–CPK	CP Air	17	8/4/70	
20343	YA–FAU	Ariana	113C	15/1/70	
20366	N546PS	Pacific Southwest	214		In Storage.
20367	N544PS	Pacific Southwest	214	27/5/71	
20370	VH–RMT	Ansett–ANA	77C	9/7/70	
20371	VH–TJF	TAA	76	10/7/70	
20379	N8836E	Eastern AL	225	17/6/70	
20380	N8837E	Eastern AL	225	30/6/70	
20381	N8838E	Eastern AL	225	14/7/70	
20382	N8839E	Eastern AL	225	21/7/70	
20383	N8840E	Eastern AL	225	20/8/70	
20384	N88715	Continental AL	224	12/2/70	
20385	N32716	Continental AL	224	16/3/70	
20386	N32717	Continental AL	224	27/3/70	
20387	N32718	Continental AL	224	8/4/70	
20388	N32719	Continental AL	224	15/4/70	
20392	N401BN	Braniff	227	30/6/70	
20393	N402BN	Braniff	227	30/6/70	
20394	N403BN	Braniff	227	30/6/70	
20409	F–BPJN	Air France	228	7/12/70	
20410	F–BPJO	Air France	228	11/12/70	
20411	F–BPJP	Air France	228	22/12/70	
20415	N8841E	Eastern AL	225	1/9/70	
20416	N8842E	Eastern AL	225	1/9/70	
20418	PP–CJE	Cruzeiro	C3	29/1/71	
20419	PP–CJF	Cruzeiro	C3	29/1/71	
20420	PP–CJG	Cruzeiro	C3	29/1/71	
20421	9N–ABD	Royal Nepal AL	1F8	1/8/72	
20422	PP–VLF	Varig	41	10/10/70	
20423	PP–VLG	Varig	41	10/10/70	
20424	PP–VLH	Varig	41	16/10/70	
20425	PP–VLD	Varig	41	23/10/70	
20426	HI–212	Dominican Republic	1J1	31/5/72	Built originally as Srs 45 for VASP as PP–VLE. Order cancelled.
20430	D–ABCI	Lufthansa	230	27/1/71	*Karlsruhe*
20431	D–ABDI	Lufthansa	230	9/3/71	*Lübeck*
20432	XA–TAA	Mexicana	264	17/10/70	
20433	XA–TAB	Mexicana	264	26/10/70	
20434	XA–TAC	Mexicana	264	9/11/70	
20435	JA8328	All-Nippon AW	281	22/2/71	
20436	JA8329	All-Nippon AW	281	12/3/71	WO
20437	N384PS	Pacific Southwest	254	17/3/70	L to All-Nippon AW
20438	N536PS	Pacific Southwest	254	9/4/70	L to All-Nippon AW
20441	N8843E	Eastern AL	225	4/9/70	
20442	N8844E	Eastern AL	225	28/9/70	
20443	N8845E	Eastern AL	225	10/11/70	
20444	N8846E	Eastern AL	225	16/11/70	
20445	N8847E	Eastern AL	225	18/11/70	
20446	N8848E	Eastern AL	225	19/11/70	
20447	N8849E	Eastern AL	225	20/11/70	

C/n	Current Marks	Current Owner/operator	Model Series	Initial Delivery	Remarks
20448	N8850E	Eastern AL	225	23/11/70	
20460	N54333	TWA	231	31/3/71	
20461	N54334	TWA	231	5/4/71	
20462	N54335	TWA	231	1/5/71	
20463	N32721	Continental AL	2F2	7/3/72	
20464	N32722	Continental AL	2F2	3/3/72	
20465	N32723	Continental AL	2F2	3/3/72	
20466	JA8332	All-Nippon AW	281	15/6/71	
20467	JA8333	All-Nippon AW	281	25/6/71	
20468	JA8330	All-Nippon AW	281	3/5/71	
20469	JA8331	All-Nippon AW	281	10/5/71	
20470	F–BPJQ	Air France	228	12/3/71	
20471	CN–CCG	Royal Air Maroc	286	1/2/71	
20472	7T–VEA	Air Algerie	2D6	12/2/71	
20473	7T–VEB	Air Algerie	2D6	12/3/71	
20475	ZS–SBH	SAA	44C	9/2/71	
20476	ZS–SBI	SAA	44C	9/3/71	
20489	CS–TBP	TAP–Portugal	82	4/3/71	*Cabo Verde*
20490	N54336	TWA	231	11/5/71	
20491	N54337	TWA	231	26/5/71	
20509	JA8334	All-Nippon AW	281	15/7/71	
20510	JA8337	All-Nippon AW	281	24/5/72	
20512	CF–CUR	CP Air	17	11/3/71	
20513	CF–CUS	CP Air	17	11/4/71	
20525	D–ABFI	Lufthansa	230	13/12/71	*Münster*
20526	D–ABGI	Lufthansa	230	26/2/72	*Leverkusen*
20533	N320HG		1H2	3/11/71	
20538	F–BPJR	Air France	228	14/2/72	
20539	F–BPJS	Air France	228	18/1/72	
20540	F–BPJT	Air France	228	13/3/72	
20545	TS–JHN	Tunis Air	2H3	14/2/72	
20548	VH–RMU	Ansett–ANA	277	19/2/73	
20549	VH–RMV	Ansett–ANA	277		
20550	VH–RMW	Ansett–ANA	277		
20551	VH–RMX	Ansett–ANA	277		
20552	VH–TBG	TAA	276	11/5/73	
20553	VH–TBH	TAA	276		
20554	VH–TBI	TAA	276		
20555	VH–TBJ	TAA	276		
20560	D–ABHI	Lufthansa	230	22/5/72	*Mönchengladbach*
20568	JA8338	All-Nippon AW	281	17/4/72	
20569	JA8339	All-Nippon AW	281	24/3/72	
20570	JA8340	All-Nippon AW	281	10/3/72	
20571	JA8341	All-Nippon AW	281	28/4/72	
20572	JA8343	All-Nippon AW	281	30/6/72	
20573	JA8344	All-Nippon AW	281	23/6/72	
20579	N2807W	Western AL	247	12/5/72	
20580	N2808W	Western AL	247	13/6/72	
20581	N2809W	Western AL	247	16/6/72	
20592	EC–CAI	Iberia AL	256	28/4/72	*Castilla la Neuva*
20593	EC–CAJ	Iberia AL	256	21/4/72	*Cataluña*
20594	EC–CAK	Iberia AL	256	6/5/72	*Aragon*
20595	EC–CBA	Iberia AL	256	11/5/73	*Andalucia*
20596	EC–CBB	Iberia AL	256	1/5/73	*Asturias*
20597	EC–CBC	Iberia AL	256		*Baleares*
20598	EC–CBD	Iberia AL	256		*Extremadura*
20599	EC–CBE	Iberia AL	256		*Galicia*
20600	EC–CBF	Iberia AL	256		*Gran Canaria*
20601	EC–CBG	Iberia AL	256		*Leon*
20602	EC–CBH	Iberia AL	256	5/1/73	*Murcia*
20603	EC–CBI	Iberia AL	256	2/2/73	*Navarra*
20604	EC–CBJ	Iberia AL	256	17/1/73	*Tenerife*
20605	EC–CBK	Iberia AL	256	14/2/73	*Valencia*
20606	EC–CBL	Iberia AL	256	20/4/73	*Vascongadas*

Boeing 727

C/n	Current Marks	Current Owner/operator	Model Series	Initial Delivery	Remarks
20607	EC–CBM	Iberia AL	256	21/5/73	*Castilla la Vieja*
20608	N410BN	Braniff	227	3/7/72	
20609	N411BN	Braniff	227	11/7/72	
20610	N412BN	Braniff	227	19/7/72	
20611	N413BN	Braniff	227	1/8/72	
20612	N414BN	Braniff	227	13/3/73	
20613	N415BN	Braniff	227	14/3/73	
20614	N8851E	Eastern AL	225	26/9/72	
20615	N8852E	Eastern AL	225	26/9/72	
20616	N8853E	Eastern AL	225	5/10/72	
20617	N8855E	Eastern AL	225	10/10/72	
20618	N8856E	Eastern AL	225	16/10/72	
20619	N8857E	Eastern AL	225	18/10/72	
20620	N8858E	Eastern AL	225	18/10/72	
20621	N8859E	Eastern AL	225	3/11/72	
20622	N8860E	Eastern AL	225	6/4/73	
20623	N8861E	Eastern AL	225	1/5/73	
20624	N8862E	Eastern AL	225	4/5/73	
20625	N8863E	Eastern AL	225	8/5/73	
20626	N8864E	Eastern AL	225	30/5/73	
20627	N8865E	Eastern AL	225	5/6/73	
20628	N8866E	Eastern AL	225	6/6/73	
20634	N452DA	Northeast AL	232	25/1/73	D as N461DA
20635	N453DA	Northeast AL	232	26/1/73	D as N462DA
20636	N454DA	Northeast AL	232	2/2/73	D as N463DA
20637	N455DA	Northeast AL	232	6/2/73	D as N464DA
20638	N456DA	Northeast AL	232	12/4/73	D as N465DA
20639	N457DA	Northeast AL	232	4/4/73	D as N466DA
20640	N458DA	Northeast AL	232	2/5/73	D as N467DA
20641	N459DA	Northeast AL	232	11/5/73	D as N468DA
20642	N460DA	Northeast AL	232	1/6/73	D as N469DA
20643	N461DA	Northeast AL	232	23/6/73	D as N470DA
20644	N462DA	Northeast AL	232	27/7/73	D as N471DA
20645	N463DA	Northeast AL	232	27/7/73	D as N472DA
20646	N464DA	Northeast AL	232	16/8/73	D as N473DA
20647	N465DA	Northeast AL	232	31/8/73	D as N474DA
20648	N2810W	Western AL	247	4/8/72	
20649	N2811W	Western AL	247	16/8/72	
20654	N32724	Continental AL	224	28/3/73	
20655	N32725	Continental AL	224	10/4/73	
20656	N66726	Continental AL	224	27/4/73	
20657	N24728	Continental AL	224	7/9/73	
20658	N25729	Continental AL	224	8/10/73	
20659	N25730	Continental AL	224	12/10/73	
20660	N66731	Continental AL	224		
20661	N66732	Continental AL	224		
20662	N66733	Continental AL	224		
20663	N66734	Continental AL	224		
20673	D–ABKI	Lufthansa	230	14/2/73	*Bremerhaven*
20674	D–ABLI	Lufthansa	230	22/2/73	*Ludwigshafen*
20675	D–ABMI	Lufthansa	230	2/3/73	L to Condor
20676	D–ABNI	Lufthansa	230	5/3/73	L to Condor
20677	D–ABPI	Lufthansa	230	2/4/73	L to Condor
20678	N550PS	Pacific Southwest	214	30/3/73	
20679	N551PS	Pacific Southwest	214	11/5/73	
20705	CN–CCH	Royal Air Maroc	2B6	18/5/73	
20706	N552PS	National Aircraft Leasing	2J7	14/6/73	L to Pacific Southwest
20707	N553PS	National Aircraft Leasing	2J7	21/6/73	L to Pacific Southwest
20709	XA–CUB	Mexicana	264	18/6/73	
20710	XA–CUE	Mexicana	264	25/9/73	
20724	JA8345	All-Nippon AW	281	6/7/73	
20725	JA8346	All-Nippon AW	281	16/7/73	
20726	JA8347	All-Nippon AW	281	9/8/73	

C/n	Current Marks	Current Owner/operator	Model Series	Initial Delivery	Remarks
20727	JA8348	All-Nippon AW	281	23/8/73	
20728	JA8349	All-Nippon AW	281	7/9/73	
20729	N416BN	Braniff	227	10/7/73	
20730	N417BN	Braniff	227	12/7/73	
20731	N418BN	Braniff	227	16/7/73	
20732	N419BN	Braniff	227	10/8/73	
20733	N420BN	Braniff	227	16/8/73	
20734	N421BN	Braniff	227	21/8/73	
20735	N422BN	Braniff	227	19/9/73	
20736	N423BN	Braniff	227	24/9/73	
20737	N424BN	Braniff	227	29/8/73	
20738	N425BN	Braniff	227	5/10/73	
20739	TS–JHO	Tunis Air	2H3	25/6/73	
20743	N466DA	Northwest AL	232	6/9/73	
20744	N467DA	Northwest AL	232	14/9/73	
20745	N468DA	Northwest AL	232	9/10/73	
20746	N469DA	Northwest AL	232		
20747	N470DA	Northwest AL	232		
20748	N471DA	Northwest AL	232		
20749	N472DA	Northwest AL	232		
20750	N473DA	Northwest AL	232		
20751	N474DA	Northwest AL	232		
20752	N475DA	Northwest AL	232		
20753	N476DA	Northwest AL	232		
20754	N477DA	Northwest AL	232		
20755	N478DA	Northwest AL	232		
20756	N479DA	Northwest AL	232		
20757	D–ABQI	Lufthansa	230		
20764	OY–SAU	Sterling Airways	2J4		
20765	OY–SAS	Sterling Airways	2J4		
20766	OY–SAT	Sterling Airways	2J4		
20772	N426BN	Braniff	227		
20773	N427BN	Braniff	227		
20774	N428BN	Braniff	227		
20775	N429BN	Braniff	227		
20780	XA–CUN	Mexicana	264		
20787	XA–DAT	Mexicana	264		
20788	D–ABRI	Lufthansa	230		
20789	D–ABSI	Lufthansa	230		
20790	D–ABTI	Lufthansa	230		For L to Condor
20791	D–ABVI	Lufthansa	230		For L to Condor
20792	D–ABWI	Lufthansa	230		For L to Condor
20811	EC–CFA	Iberia	256		
20812	EC–CFB	Iberia	256		
20813	EC–CFC	Iberia	256		
20814	EC–CFD	Iberia	256		
20815	EC–CFE	Iberia	256		
20816	EC–CFF	Iberia	256		
20817	EC–CFG	Iberia	256		
20818	EC–CFH	Iberia	256		
20819	EC–CFI	Iberia	256		
20820	EC–CFJ	Iberia	256		
20821	EC–CFK	Iberia	256		
20822	TS–JHP	Tunis Air	2H3		
20823	N8867E	Eastern AL	225		
20824	N8869E	Eastern AL	225		
20832	N431BN	Braniff	227		
20837	N430BN	Braniff	227		
20838	N432BN	Braniff	227		
20840	N433BN	Braniff	227		
20843	N54338	TWA	231		
20844	N64339	TWA	231		
20845	N54340	TWA	231		
20846	N54341	TWA	231		
20847	N54342	TWA	231		
20848	N24343	TWA	231		

Boeing 727

C/n	Current Marks	Current Owner/operator	Model Series	Initial Delivery	Remarks
20849	N54344	TWA	231		
20850	N54345	TWA	231		
20851	N64346	TWA	231		
20852	N64347	TWA	231		
20853	N54348	TWA	231		
20854	N54349	TWA	231		
20855	N54350	TWA	231		
20856	N54351	TWA	231		
20857	N54352	TWA	231		
20858	N54353	TWA	231		
20859	N54354	TWA	231		
20860	N480DA	Northwest AL	232		
20861	N481DA	Northwest AL	232		
20862	N482DA	Northwest AL	232		
20863	N483DA	Northwest AL	232		
20864	N484DA	Northwest AL	232		
20865	N485DA	Northwest AL	232		
20866	N486DA	Northwest AL	232		
20867	N487DA	Northwest AL	232		
20868	N2812W	Western AL	247		
20869	N2813W	Western AL	247		
20870	N2814W	Western AL	247		
20871	N2815W	Western AL	247		
20872	N2816W	Western AL	247		
20873	N2817W	Western AL	247		
20874	N2818W	Western AL	247		
20875	N554PS	Pacific Southwest	214		
20876	–	All-Nippon AW	281		
20877	–	All-Nippon AW	281		
20878	–	All-Nippon AW	281		
20879	–	National Aircraft Leasing	2J7		
20880	–	National Aircraft Leasing	2J7		
20894	–	Mexicana	264		
20895	–	Mexicana	264		
20896	–	Mexicana	264		
20899	–	Lufthansa	230		
20900	–	Lufthansa	230		
20901	–	Lufthansa	230		
20902	–	Lufthansa	230		

Boeing 737

C/n	Current Marks	Current Owner/operator	Model Series	Initial Delivery	Remarks
19013	D–ABEA	Lufthansa	130	28/12/67	Tested as N2282C *Coburg*
19014	D–ABEB	Lufthansa	130	28/12/67	Tested as N2286C *Regensburg*
19015	D–ABEC	Lufthansa	130	28/12/67	Tested as N2289C *Osnabrück*
19016	D–ABED	Lufthansa	130	2/2/68	*Flensburg*
19017	D–ABEF	Lufthansa	130	28/2/68	*Kempten*
19018	D–ABEG	Lufthansa	130	12/3/68	*Offenbach*
19019	D–ABEH	Lufthansa	130	25/4/68	*Solingen*
19020	D–ABEI	Lufthansa	130	14/4/68	*Oldenburg*
19021	D–ABEK	Lufthansa	130	4/4/68	D to Lufthansa at *Baden-Baden.* L to Condor 1969. Rtd to Lufthansa 1970 *Konstanz*
19022	D–ABEL	Condor	130	5/4/68	D to Lufthansa as *Osnabrück.* L to Condor 1969. *Mülheim*
19023	D–ABEM	Condor	130	29/4/68	D to Lufthansa as *Marburg.* L to Condor 1969. *Wolfsburg*
19024	D–ABEN	Lufthansa	130	19/5/68	*Tubingen*
19025	D–ABEO	Lufthansa	130	10/6/68	*Göttingen*
19026	D–ABEP	Lufthansa	130	24/6/68	*Wilhelmshaven*
19027	D–ABEQ	Lufthansa	130	1/8/68	*Koblenz*
19028	D–ABER	Lufthansa	130	15/11/68	*Goslar*
19029	D–ABES	Lufthansa	130	14/12/68	*Friedrichshafen*
19030	D–ABET	Lufthansa	130	1/1/69	*Baden-Baden*
19031	D–ABEU	Lufthansa	130	9/1/69	*Heilbronn*
19032	D–ABEV	Lufthansa	130	14/1/69	*Marburg*
19033	D–ABEW	Lufthansa	130	24/1/69	*Bayreuth*
19039	N9001U	United AL	222		
19040	N9002U	United AL	222	29/12/67	
19041	N9003U	United AL	222	23/2/68	
19042	N9004U	United AL	222	2/3/68	
19043	N9005U	United AL	222	16/3/68	WO
19044	N9006U	United AL	222	25/3/68	
19045	N9007U	United AL	222	28/4/68	
19046	N9008U	United AL	222	3/5/68	
19047	N9009U	United AL	222	10/5/68	
19048	N9010U	United AL	222	15/5/68	
19049	N9011U	United AL	222	24/5/68	
19050	N9012U	United AL	222	26/5/68	
19051	N9013U	United AL	222	29/5/68	
19052	N9014U	United AL	222	26/6/68	
19053	N9015U	United AL	222	10/6/68	
19054	N9016U	United AL	222	23/6/68	
19055	N9017U	United AL	222	26/6/68	
19056	N9018U	United AL	222	13/7/68	
19057	N9019U	United AL	222	27/7/68	
19058	N9020U	United AL	222	2/8/68	
19059	N9021U	United AL	222	31/7/68	
19060	N9022U	United AL	222	16/8/68	
19061	N9023U	United AL	222	27/8/68	
19062	N9024U	United AL	222	26/8/68	
19063	N9025U	United AL	222	4/9/68	
19064	N9026U	United AL	222	5/9/68	
19065	N9027U	United AL	222	14/9/68	
19066	N9028U	United AL	222	23/9/68	
19067	N2029U	United AL	222	23/9/68	
19068	N9030U	United AL	222	3/10/68	
19069	N9031U	United AL	222	30/9/68	WO DEC–8–72
19070	N9032U	United AL	222	8/10/68	

Boeing 737

C/n	Current Marks	Current Owner/operator	Model Series	Initial Delivery	Remarks
19071	N9033U	United AL	222	23/10/68	
19072	N9034U	United AL	222	28/10/68	
19073	N752N	Piedmont	222	4/11/68	D to UAL as N9035U. S to Piedmont JUN–8–73
19074	G–AZNZ	Britannia Airways	222	23/11/68	D to UAL as N9036U. S to Britannia AW MAR–1–72
19075	N7383F	Frontier Airlines	222	24/11/68	D to UAL as N9037U. S to Frontier AL JUN–19–73
19076	N9038U	United AL	222	27/11/68	
19077	N9039U	United AL	222	6/12/68	
19078	N9040U	United AL	222	13/12/68	
19306	N461GB	GATX/Boothe	293		Built for Pacific AL as N831PC. S to GATX/ Boothe. L to Wien Consolidated 1968
19307	N462GB	GATX/Boothe	293		Built for Pacific AL as N832PC. S to GATX/ Boothe. L to Air California
19308	N463GB	GATX/Boothe	293		Built for Pacific AL as N833PC. S to GATX/ Boothe. L to Air California from JUL–10–68
19309	N464GB	GATX/Boothe	293		Built for Pacific AL as N834PC. S to GATX/ Boothe. L to Air California from JUL–31–68
19408	LN–SUS	Braathens	205	2/1/69	*Hakon IV*
19409	LN–SUP	Braathens	205	31/1/69	*Hakon V*
19418	N734N	Piedmont	201	3/5/68	*Piedmont Pacemaker*
19419	N735N	Piedmont	201	3/7/68	*Appalachian Pacemaker*
19420	N736N	Piedmont	201	15/7/68	
19421	N737N	Piedmont	201	8/8/68	*Chesapeake Pacemaker*
19422	N738N	Piedmont	201	29/8/68	
19423	N740N	Piedmont	201	16/9/68	*Peninsular Pacemaker*
19424	EI–ASA	Aer Lingus	248	2/4/69	Originally allocated EI-APP *St. Jarlath.* L to Air Algerie from JUN–70
19425	EI–ASB	Aer Lingus	248	17/4/69	Originally allocated EI-APS *St. Albert.* L to Air Algerie DEC–14–69 to MAR–71
19426	N2711R	Wien Consolidated	202C	30/10/68	D to Wien Alaska
19437	N73700	Boeing Co	130		Prototype FF APL–9–67
19547	N749N	Piedmont	222	30/12/68	D to UAL as N9041U. S to Piedmont NOV–11–72
19548	N751N	Piedmont	222	31/12/68	D to UAL as N9042U. S to Piedmont OCT–30–72
19549	N9043U	United AL	222	13/1/69	
19550	N9044U	United AL	222	22/1/69	
19551	N9045U	United AL	222	23/1/69	
19552	N9046U	United AL	222	3/3/69	
19553	N9047U	United AL	222	10/2/69	
19554	N9048U	United AL	222	17/2/69	
19555	N9049U	United AL	222	14/2/69	
19556	N9050U	United AL	222	25/2/69	
19591	N	Lake Central AL	215C		Cancelled
19592	N	Lake Central AL	215C		Cancelled
19593	N	Lake Central AL	215C		Cancelled
19594	N4907	Wien Consolidated	210C	5/12/68	D to Northern Consolidated
19598	N4501W	Western AL	247	11/6/68	
19599	N4502W	Western AL	247	2/7/68	
19600	N4503W	Western AL	247	13/7/68	
19601	—	Air France	247	18/7/68	D to Western AL as N4504W. S to Air France
19602	N4505W	Western AL	247	22/7/68	

C/n	Current Marks	Current Owner/operator	Model Series	Initial Delivery	Remarks
19603	N4506W	Western AL	247	31/7/68	
19604	N4507W	Western AL	247	16/8/68	
19605	N4508W	Western AL	247	20/8/68	
19606	N4509W	Western AL	247	9/9/68	
19607	N4510W	Western AL	247	19/9/68	
19608	N4511W	Western AL	247	30/9/68	
19609	N4512W	Western AL	247	16/10/68	
19610	N4513W	Western AL	247	18/10/68	
19611	N4514W	Western AL	247	7/11/68	
19612	N4515W	Western AL	247	16/11/68	
19613	N4516W	Western AL	247	9/12/68	
19614	N4517W	Western AL	247	10/12/68	
19615	N4518W	Western AL	247	28/1/69	
19616	N4519W	Western AL	247	29/1/69	
19617	N4520W	Western AL	247	15/2/69	
19679	N73715	Aloha Airlines	159	15/11/68	D to Avianca as HK-1403 Returned to Boeing. S to Aloha MAR–16–73
19680	–	Aloha Airlines	159	15/11/68	D to Avianca as HK-1404 Returned to Boeing. S to Aloha MAR–73
19681	N7380F	Frontier Airlines	214	20/9/68	D to Pacific Southwest as N378PS. S to Frontier MAR–13–72
19682	N379PS	PSA	214	5/10/68	
19707	ZS–SBL	SAA	244	8/11/68	D as ZS–EUY *Pongola*
19708	ZS–SBM	SAA	244	8/11/68	D as ZS–EUZ *Gamtoos*
19709	G–AVRL	Britannia AW	204	8/7/68	L to Aerolineas Argentinas JAN–70
19710	G–AVRM	Britannia AW	204	10/8/68	
19711	G–AVRN	Britannia AW	204	9/4/69	
19712	G–AVRO	Britannia AW	204	26/4/69	
19713	N465GB	GATX/Boothe	293	14/10/68	Built for Pacific AL as N835PC. S to GATX/ Boothe. L to Air California from OCT–14–68
19714	N467GB	GATX/boothe	293	31/10/68	Built for Pacific AL as N836PC. S to GATX/ Boothe. L to Air California from OCT–31–68
19742	CF–PWD	Pacific Western	275	26/11/68	
19743	CF–PWE	Pacific Western	275C		
19758	–	NZNAC	222		Was Boeing-owned demonstrator reg N737Q. S to NZNAC for D during 1974.
19759	LN–	Braathens	205		Initial allocation cancelled
19768	9V–BFD	Malaysian	112	29/7/69	D as 9M-AOU
19769	9V–BBC	Malaysian	112	5/8/69	
19770	9V–BFE	Malaysian	112	6/9/69	D as 9M-AOV
19771	9V–BBE	Malaysian	112	12/10/69	
19772	9V–BFF	Malaysian	112	2/11/69	D as 9M-AOW
19794	D–ABEY	Lufthansa	130	6/2/69	*Worms*
19795	D–ABEZ	Lufthansa	130		Cancelled
19796	D–ABEJ	Lufthansa	130		Cancelled
19847	CF–NAB	Nordair	242C	28/11/68	N6241 before delivery
19848	CF–NAH	Nordair	242C		L to EPA 1969
19849	CF–	Nordair	242C		Initial allocation cancelled
19884	CF–CPB	CP Air	217	21/10/68	
19885	CF–CPC	CP Air	217	9/11/68	
19886	CF–CPD	CP Air	217	1/12/68	
19887	CF–CPE	CP Air	217	20/12/68	
19888	CF–CPU	CP Air	217	9/11/68	
19889	CF–CPV	CP Air	217		Initial allocation cancelled

Boeing 737

C/n	Current Marks	Current Owner/operator	Model Series	Initial Delivery	Remarks
19920	N380PS	PSA	214	25/11/68	
19921	CF–PWM	GATX/Boothe	214	17/12/68	D to Pacific Southwest as N381PS. S to GATX/ Boothe JUL–17–69 Pacific Western.
19929	ZK–NAC	NZNAC	219	30/8/68	
19930	ZK–NAD	NZNAC	219	12/9/68	
19931	ZK–NAE	NZNAC	219	7/10/68	
19932	N9051U	United AL	222	10/3/69	
19933	N9052U	United AL	222	7/3/69	
19934	N9053U	United AL	222	11/3/69	
19935	N9054U	United AL	222	31/3/69	
19936	N9055U	United AL	222	2/4/69	
19937	N9056U	United AL	222	9/4/69	
19938	N9057U	United AL	222	7/5/69	L to Nordair
19939	N9058U	United AL	222	5/5/69	
19940	N9059U	United AL	222	27/5/69	
19941	N9060U	United AL	222	29/5/69	
19942	N9061U	United AL	222	11/6/69	
19943	N9062U	United AL	222	19/6/69	
19944	N9063U	United AL	222	30/6/69	
19945	N9064U	United AL	222	8/7/69	
19946	N9065U	United AL	222	9/7/69	L to Nordair
19947	N9066U	United AL	222	15/7/69	L to Nordair
19948	N9067U	United AL	222	28/7/69	
19949	N9068U	United AL	222	12/8/69	
19950	N9069U	United AL	222	20/8/69	
19951	N9070U	United AL	222	28/8/69	
19952	N9071U	United AL	222	2/9/69	
19953	N9072U	United AL	222	12/9/69	
19954	N9073U	United AL	222	22/9/69	
19955	N9074U	United AL	222	7/10/69	
19956	N9075U	United AL	222	10/10/69	
20070	N7378F	GATX/Boothe	2C0		Built for Frontier AL as N7371F. D to GATX/ Boothe as N570GB. L to Frontier AL
20071	N7379F	GATX/Boothe	2C0		Built for Frontier AL as N7372F. D to GATX/ Boothe as N571GB. L to Frontier AL
20072	N7372F	GATX/Boothe	2C0		D to GATX/Boothe as N572 GB. L to Frontier AL
20073	N7370F	GATX/Boothe	2C0		Built for Frontier AL as N7374F. D to GATX/ Boothe as N573GB. L to Frontier AL
20074	N7371F	GATX/Boothe	2C0		D to GATX/Boothe as N574GB. L to Frontier AL
20092	PP–SMA	VASP	2A1	25/7/69	
20093	PP–SMB	VASP	2A1	25/7/69	
20094	PP–SMC	VASP	2A1	25/7/69	
20095	PP–SMD	VASP	2A1	25/7/69	
20096	PP–SME	VASP	2A1		
20125	N4521W	Western AL	247	18/2/69	
20126	–	Air France	247	4/3/69	D to Western AL as N4522W. S to Air France
20127	N4523W	Western AL	247	17/3/69	
20128	N4524W	Western AL	247	17/3/69	
20129	N4525W	Western AL	247	14/4/69	
20130	N4526W	Western AL	247	15/4/69	
20131	N4527W	Western AL	247	12/5/69	
20132	N4528W	Western AL	247	20/5/69	
20133	N4529W	Western AL	247	9/6/69	
20134	N4530W	Western AL	247	16/6/69	
20138	N4906	Wien Consolidated	210C		

C/n	Current Marks	Current Owner/operator	Model Series	Initial Delivery	Remarks
20142	CF–PWC	Pacific Western	275	1/5/70	
20155	N382PS	Pacific Southwest	214		
20156	ZK–NAK	NZNAC	214	18/6/69	D to Pacific Southwest as N983PS. S to NZNAC SEP–15–73
20157	N984PS	Pacific Southwest	214		
20158	N985PS	Pacific Southwest	214		
20159	N986PS	Pacific Southwest	214		
20160	N987PS	Pacific Southwest	214		
20194	VR–BEH	Maritime Investment and Shipping Co	2A6	25/8/69	D to LTV as N520L. S to Maritime APL–27–72
20195	N1288	Essex International	2A6		
20196	CF–CPV	CP Air	217	24/3/69	
20197	CF–CPZ	CP Air	217	28/3/69	
20205	CF–TAO	Transair	2A9C	13/3/70	
20206	CF–TAN	Transair	2A9C	14/4/70	
20209	N73711	Aloha AL	297		L from GATX/Boothe
20210	N73712	Aloha AL	297		L from GATX/Boothe *King Kahekiu*
20211	N741N	Piedmont	201	3/3/69	*Research Triangle*
20212	N743N	Piedmont	201	24/4/69	*Garden State*
20213	N744N	Piedmont	201	29/4/69	*Tarheel*
20214	N745N	Piedmont	201	29/5/69	*Blue Ridge*
20215	N746N	Piedmont	201	19/9/69	*Great Lakes*
20216	N747N	Piedmont	201	15/10/69	*Outer Banks*
20218	EI–ASC	Aer Lingus	248C	10/9/69	*St. Macartan*
20219	EI–ASD	Aer Lingus	248C	26/10/69	*St. Ide*
20220	EI–ASE	Aer Lingus	248C	27/11/69	*St. Fachtna*
20221	EI–ASF	Aer Lingus	248	15/1/70	*St. Nathy*
20222	EI–ASG	Aer Lingus	248	22/2/70	*St. Cormac*
20223	EI–ASH	Aer Lingus	248	25/4/70	*St. Eugene*
20226	JA8401	All Nippon	281		
20227	JA8402	All Nippon	281		
20229	ZS–SBN	SAA	244	27/10/69	Initial allocation ZS-FKH *Molopo*
20231	5R–MFA	Air Madagascar	2B2		
20236	G–AWSY	Britannia AW	204	12/5/69	
20242	N73713	Aloha AL	297		L from GATX/Boothe
20253	D–ABBE	Lufthansa	230C	17/12/69	*Remscheid*
20254	D–ABCE	Lufthansa	230C	24/1/70	*Landshut*
20255	D–ABDE	Lufthansa	230C	29/1/70	*Bamberg*
20256	D–ABFE	Lufthansa	230C	14/2/70	*Trier*
20257	D–ABGE	Lufthansa	230C		*Erlangen*
20258	D–ABHE	Lufthansa	230C		*Darmstadt*
20276	JA8403	All Nippon	281	15/1/70	
20277	JA8405	All Nippon	281	30/1/70	
20280	CR–BAA	DETA	2B1		
20281	CR–BAB	DETA	2B1		
20282	G–AXNA	Britannia AW	204C	18/3/70	
20299	CX–BHM	Iberia	2A3		First flown as N1787B, later N1797B. L to Pluna
20300	CF–EPO	Eastern Provincial	2A3	17/7/70	First flown as N1788B, later N1733B
20329	ZS–SBO	SAA	244	20/4/70	*Gouritz*
20330	ZS–SBP	SAA	244	27/5/70	*Nossop*
20331	ZS–SBR	SAA	244	29/6/70	*Umkomaas*
20334	N468AC	Air California	293		
20335	N469AC	Air California	293		
20336	N22SW	Southwest AL	2H4	15/6/71	
20344	ZK–NAJ	NZNAC	297	16/7/71	
20345	N21SW	Southwest AL	2H4	10/6/71	
20346	N23SW	Southwest AL	2H4C	29/9/71	
20361	N7373F	Frontier AL	291		L from GATX/Boothe
20362	N7374F	Frontier AL	291		L from GATX/Boothe

C/n	Current Marks	Current Owner/operator	Model Series	Initial Delivery	Remarks
20363	N7375F	Frontier AL	291		L from GATX/Boothe
20364	N7376F	Frontier AL	291	14/11/69	
20365	N7377F	Frontier AL	291	5/12/69	
20368	N988PS	PSA	214		
20369	N7381F	Frontier AL	2H4	2/6/71	D to Southwest AL as N20SW. S to Frontier JUN–23–72
20389	G–AXNB	Britannia AW	204C	18/4/70	
20396	CF–EPL	Eastern Provincial	2E1	25/11/69	First flown as N1785B
20397	CF–EPR	Eastern Provincial	2E1	15/12/69	First flown as N1786B
20403	LV–JMW	Aerolineas	287	27/2/70	
20404	LV–JMX	Aerolineas	287	25/3/70	
20405	LV–JMY	Aerolineas	287	9/4/70	
20406	LV–JMZ	Aerolineas	287	31/7/70	
20407	LV–JND	Aerolineas	287C	4/9/70	
20408	LV–JNE	Aerolineas	287C	2/10/70	
20412	LN–SUG	Braathens	2A6	3/8/71	*Harald Harfagre*
20413	JA8406	All-Nippon AL	281	20/2/70	
20414	JA8407	All-Nippon AL	281	10/3/70	
20417	G–AXNC	Britannia AW	204	12/5/70	
20440	N4902W	Wien Consolidated	210C	15/5/70	Leased from GATX/Boothe
20449	JA8408	All-Nippon AW	281	22/6/70	
20450	JA8409	All-Nippon AW	281	27/7/70	
20451	JA8410	All-Nippon AW	281	22/9/70	
20452	JA8411	All-Nippon AW	281	16/11/70	
20453	LN–MTC		2H5	3/9/71	
20454	LN–MTD		2H5	28/10/71	
20455	CF–NAQ	Nordair	242C	13/5/70	
20458	LN–SUA	Braathens	205C	17/3/71	*Halvdan Svarte*
20480	VT–EAG	Indian Airlines	2A8	9/11/70	
20481	VT–EAH	Indian Airlines	2A8	3/12/70	
20482	VT–EAI	Indian Airlines	2A8	21/12/70	
20483	VT–EAJ	Indian Airlines	2A8	12/1/71	
20484	VT–EAK	Indian Airlines	2A8	8/2/71	
20485	VT–EAL	Indian Airlines	2A8	9/3/71	
20486	VT–EAM	Indian Airlines	2A8	5/4/71	WO
20492	N7382F	Frontier AL	212	2/6/71	D to Singapore AL as 9V-BCR. S to Frontier DEC–18–73
20496	CF–NAP	Nordair	242C	16/6/71	
20498	EP–IRF	Iranair	286	2/7/71	
20499	EP–IRG	Iranair	286	16/7/71	
20500	EP–IRH	Iranair	286	1/9/71	
20506	JA8412	All-Nippon AW	281	20/5/71	
20507	JA8413	All-Nippon AW	281	4/6/71	
20508	JA8414	All-Nippon AW	281	4/10/71	
20521	CF–NAW	Nordair	212	18/11/71	D to Singapore AL as 9M-ACQ. S to Nordair MAY–1–73
20523	LV–JTD	Aerolineas	287	9/10/71	
20536	CR–BAC	DETA	2B1C	29/10/71	
20537	LV–JTO	Aerolineas	287	24/12/71	
20544	7T–YEC	Air Algerie	2D6	1/12/71	
20561	JA8415	All-Nippon AW	281	12/3/72	
20562	JA8416	All-Nippon AW	281	12/4/72	
20563	JA8417	All-Nippon AW	281	3/4/72	
20574	HZ–AGA	Saudi Arabian AL	268C	14/3/72	
20575	HZ–AGB	Saudi Arabian AL	268C	7/4/72	
20576	HZ–AGC	Saudi Arabian AL	268	5/5/72	
20577	HZ–AGD	Suadi Arabian AL	268	19/5/72	
20578	HZ–AGE	Saudi Arabian AL	268	26/5/72	
20582	9M–AQL	Malaysian Airlines System	2H6	2/10/72	
20583	9M–AQM	Malaysian Airlines System	2H6	7/8/72	

C/n	Current Marks	Current Owner/operator	Model Series	Initial Delivery	Remarks
20584	9M–AQN	Malaysian Airlines System	2H6	31/7/72	
20585	9M–AQO	Malaysian Airlines System	2H6	20/9/72	
20586	9M–AQP	Malaysian Airlines System	2H6	1/9/72	
20587	9M–AQQ	Malaysian Airlines System	2H6	12/9/72	
20588	CF–PWP	Pacific Western	275	28/4/72	
20589	PP–SMF	VASP	2A1	28/6/72	
20590	TJ–CBA	Cameroon AL	2H7C	7/7/72	
20591	TJ–CBB	Cameroon AL	2H7C	28/9/72	
20631	9M–ARG	Malaysian Airlines System	2H6	16/10/72	
20632	G–BADP	Britannia AW	204	10/1/73	
20633	G–BADR	Britannia AW	204	23/2/73	
20650	7T–VED	Air Algerie	2D6C	10/11/72	
20670	CF–PWW	Pacific Western	275	22/12/72	
20671	5N–ANC	Nigerian Airways	2F9	13/11/72	
20672	5N–AND	Nigerian Airways	2F9	29/11/72	
20680	5R–MFB	Air Madagascar	2B2	13/12/72	
20681	CF–EPP	Lineas Aeras Paraguayos	2E1	12/3/73	
20685	71–1403	USAF	T43A	31/7/73	
20686	71–1404	USAF	T43A	28/9/73	
20687	71–1405	USAF	T43A		
20688	71–1406	USAF	T43A		
20689	72–282	USAF	T43A		
20690	72–283	USAF	T43A		
20691	72–284	USAF	T43A		
20692	72–285	USAF	T43A		
20693	72–286	USAF	T43A		
20694	72–287	USAF	T43A		
20695	72–288	USAF	T43A		
20696	7301149	USAF	T43A		
20697	7301150	USAF	T43A		
20698	7301151	USAF	T43A		
20699	7301152	USAF	T43A		
20700	7301153	USAF	T43A		
20701	7301154	USAF	T43A		
20702	7301155	USAF	T43A		
20703	7301156	USAF	T43A		
20711	LN–SUD	Braathens	205	10/4/73	*Olav Trygvason*
20740	EP–IRI	Iranair	286C	1/5/73	
20758	7T–VEE	Air Algerie	2D6C	25/5/73	
20759	7T–VEF	Air Algerie	2D6		
20768	LV–LEB	Aerolineas	287		
20776	CF–EPU	Lineas Areas Paraguayos	2E1		
20777	PP–SMG	VASP	2A1	10/7/73	
20778	PP–SMH	VASP	2A1	17/8/73	
20779	PP–SMP	VASP	2A1	21/9/73	
20785	CF–PWB	Pacific Western	275		
20786	CR–BAD	DETA	2B1		
20793	9Q–CNI	Air Zaire	298C	20/11/73	
20794	9Q–CNJ	Air Zaire	298C		
20795	9Q–CNK	Air Zaire	298C		
20806	G–BAZG	Britannia AW	204		
20807	G–BAZH	Britannia AW	204		
20808	G–BAZI	Britannia AW	204		
20836	PH–TVC	Transavia	2K2C		
20882	HZ–AGF	Saudi Arabian AL	268		
20883	HZ–AGG	Saudi Arabian AL	268		
20884	7T–VEG	Air Algerie	2D6		
20892	–	Iraqi AL	200C		

Boeing 737

C/n	Current Marks	Current Owner/operator	Model Series	Initial Delivery	Remarks
20893	–	Iraqi AL	200C		
20907	–	Sabena	229		
20908	–	Sabena	229		
20909	–	Sabena	229		
20910	–	Sabena	229		
20911	–	Sabena	229		
20912	–	Sabena	229		
20917	N4905W	Wien Consolidated	210C		

Boeing 747

C/n	Current Marks	Current Owner/operator	Model Series	Initial Delivery	Remarks
19637	N731PA	PAA	121	11/7/70	*Bostonian*
19638	N732PA	PAA	121	13/7/70	*Storm King*
19639	N747PA	PAA	121		*America*
19640	N733PA	PAA	121	13/12/69	*Young America*
19641	N734PA	PAA	121	19/12/69	*Flying Cloud*
19642	N735PA	PAA	121	9/1/70	*Constitution*
19643	N736PA	PAA	121	20/1/70	*Victor*
19644	N737PA	PAA	121	21/1/70	*Red Jacket*
19645	N738PA	PAA	121	5/2/70	*Defender*
19646	N739PA	PAA	121	15/2/70	*Morning Light*
19647	N740PA	PAA	121	24/2/70	L to American AL 1970 *Rival*
19648	N741PA	PAA	121	28/2/70	*Kit Carson*
19649	N742PA	PAA	121	2/3/70	*Rainbow*
19650	N743PA	PAA	121	28/3/70	L to American AL 1970 *Derby*
19651	N744PA	PAA	121	21/3/70	*Star of the Union*
19652	N748PA	PAA	121	31/3/70	*Hornet*
19653	N749PA	PAA	121	10/4/70	*Intrepid*
19654	N750PA	PAA	121	26/4/70	*Rambler*
19655	N751PA	PAA	121	24/4/70	*Midnight Sun*
19656	N752PA	PAA	121	2/5/70	*Fortune.* WO
19657	N753PA	PAA	121	29/4/70	*Westwind*
19658	N754PA	PAA	121	26/5/70	*Ocean Rover*
19659	N755PA	PAA	121	31/5/70	*Sovereign of the Seas*
19660	N770PA	PAA	121	31/5/70	*Great Republic*
19661	N771PA	PAA	121	4/8/70	*Donald McKay*
19667	N93101	TWA	131	18/8/70	
19668	N93102	TWA	131	31/12/69	
19669	N93103	TWA	131	31/12/69	
19670	N93104	TWA	131	20/2/70	
19671	N93105	TWA	131	9/3/70	
19672	N93106	TWA	131	3/4/70	
19673	N93107	TWA	131	29/4/70	
19674	N93108	TWA	131	7/5/70	
19675	N93109	TWA	131	23/5/70	
19676	N53110	TWA	131	10/8/70	
19677	N53111	TWA	131	26/8/70	
19678	N53112	TWA	131	11/9/70	
19725	JA8101	JAL	146	22/4/70	
19726	JA8102	JAL	146	28/5/70	
19727	JA8103	JAL	146	27/6/70	
19729	I–DEMA	Alitalia	143	13/5/70	*Neil Armstrong*
19730	I–DEME	Alitalia	143	1/7/70	N1796B before D *Arturo Ferrarin*
19731	I–DEMO	Alitalia	243B	15/3/71	*Francesco de Pinedo*
19732	I–DEMU	Alitalia	243B	27/5/71	*Geo Chavez*
19733	N26861	Continental AL	124	18/5/70	
19734	N26862	Continental AL	124	13/7/70	
19735	N26863	Continental AL	124	12/8/70	
19744	HS–VGB	Aer Lingus-Irish	148	15/12/70	D to Aer Lingus as EI-ASI L to Air Siam
19745	EI–ASJ	Aer Lingus-Irish	148	18/3/71	*St Patrick*
19746	D–ABYA	Lufthansa	130	10/3/70	FF as N1800B. *Nordrhein-Westfalen*
19747	D–ABYB	Lufthansa	130	13/4/70	*Hessen*
19748	D–ABYC	Lufthansa	130	23/5/70	*Bayern*
19749	F–BPVA	Air France	128	20/3/70	
19750	F–BPVB	Air France	128	25/3/70	
19751	F–BPVC	Air France	128	12/5/70	
19752	F–BPVD	Air France	128	14/7/70	
19753	N4703U	United AL	122	30/6/70	*William M Allen*

Boeing 747

C/n	Current Marks	Current Owner/operator	Model Series	Initial Delivery	Remarks
19754	N4704U	United AL	122	4/8/70	
19755	N4710U	United AL	122	8/8/70	
19756	N4711U	United AL	122	28/8/70	
19757	N4712U	United AL	122	31/8/70	
19761	G–AWNA	British Airways	136	23/5/70	FF as N1799B
19762	G–AWNB	British Airways	136	24/5/70	D to BOAC, now British Airways
19763	G–AWNC	British Airways	136	30/6/70	D to BOAC, now British Airways
19764	G–AWND	British Airways	136	13/2/71	D to BOAC, now British Airways
19765	G–AWNE	British Airways	136	19/2/71	D to BOAC, now British Airways
19766	G–AWNF	British Airways	136	28/2/71	D to BOAC, now British Airways
19778	N601US	Northwest AL	151	30/4/70	
19779	N602US	Northwest AL	151	11/5/70	
19780	N603US	Northwest AL	151	22/5/70	
19781	N604US	Northwest AL	151	24/6/70	
19782	N605US	Northwest AL	151	24/7/70	
19783	N606US	Northwest AL	151	30/8/70	
19784	N607US	Northwest AL	151	9/9/70	
19785	N608US	Northwest AL	151	18/9/70	
19786	N609US	Northwest AL	151	28/10/70	
19787	N610US	Northwest AL	151	11/11/70	
19790	N	World AW	273C		Cancelled
19791	N	World AW	273C		Cancelled
19792	N	World AW	273C		Cancelled
19823	JA8104	JAL	246B	11/2/71	
19824	JA8105	JAL	246B	1/3/71	
19825	JA8106	JAL	246B	14/5/71	
19875	N4713U	United AL	122	3/11/70	
19876	N4714U	United AL	122	28/11/70	
19877	N4716U	United AL	122	11/12/70	
19878	N4717U	United AL	122	28/12/70	
19879	N4718U	United AL	122	27/5/71	
19880	N4719U	United AL	122	26/6/71	
19881	N4720U	United AL	122	23/7/71	
19882	N4723U	United AL	122	6/1/72	
19883	N4727U	United AL	122	27/6/72	
19896	N9896	Delta AL	132	25/9/70	
19897	N9897	Delta AL	132	22/10/70	
19898	N9898	Delta AL	132	18/11/70	
19918	N77772	National AL	135	8/9/70	
19919	N77773	National AL	135	20/10/70	
19922	PH–BUA	KLM	206	15/1/71	*Mississippi*
19923	PH–BUB	KLM	206	5/3/71	*The Danube*
19924	PH–BUC	KLM	206	21/5/71	*Amazon*
19925	N4728U	United AL	122	27/4/73	
19926	N4729U	United AL	122	20/4/73	
19927	N4732U	United AL	122	21/3/73	
19928	N4735U	United AL	122	30/5/73	
19957	EC–BRO	Iberia	156	2/10/70	*Cervantes*
19958	EC–BRP	Iberia	156	10/11/70	*Lope de Vega*
19959	VT–EBD	Air India	237B	22/3/71	*Emperor Ashoka*
19960	VT–EBE	Air India	237B	20/4/71	*Emperor Shahjehan*
20007	N	Alaska AL	90		Cancelled
20009	VH–EBA	Quantas	238B	16/8/71	*City of Canberra*
20010	VH–EBB	Quantas	238B	29/8/71	*City of Melbourne*
20011	VH–EBC	Quantas	238B	24/10/71	*City of Sydney*
20012	VH–EBD	Quantas	238B	12/12/71	*City of Perth*
20013	CF–TOA	Air Canada	133	11/2/71	
20014	CF–TOB	Air Canada	133	16/3/71	
20015	CF–TOC	Air Canada	133	24/6/71	
20080	N93113	TWA	125	22/10/70	
20081	N93114	TWA	125	2/11/70	

C/n	Current Marks	Current Owner/operator	Model Series	Initial Delivery	Remarks
20082	N93118	TWA	125	2/9/71	
20083	N93119	TWA	125	27/10/71	
20100	N9661	American AL	123	18/6/70	
20101	N9662	American AL	123	16/7/70	
20102	N9663	American AL	123	30/7/70	
20103	N9664	American AL	123	27/8/70	
20104	N9665	American Airlines	123	18/9/70	
20105	N9666	American Airlines	123	2/10/70	
20106	N9667	American Airlines	123	8/10/70	
20107	N9668	American Airlines	123	29/10/70	
20108	N9669	American Airlines	123	27/11/70	
20109	N9670	American Airlines	123	29/12/70	
20116	HB–IGA	Swissair	257B	29/1/71	*Geneve*
20117	HB–IGB	Swissair	257B	25/3/71	*Zurich*
20120	SE–DDL	SAS	283B	22/2/71	*Huge Viking*
20121	OY–KHA	SAS	283B	12/11/71	*Ivar Viking*
20135	4X–AXA	El Al	258B	26/5/71	
20137	EC–BRQ	Iberia	256B	4/1/72	*Calderon de la Barca*
20207	N601BN	Braniff	127	5/1/71	
20208	CF–DJC	Wardair	1D1		*Phil Garratt*
20237	ZS–SAL	SAA	244B		*Tefelburg*
20238	ZS–SAM	SAA	244B		*Drakensburg*
20239	ZS–SAN	SAA	244B		*Lebombo*
20246	N9899	Delta	132	30/9/71	
20247	N9900	Delta	132	11/11/71	
20269	G–AWNG	British Airways	136	8/9/71	D to BOAC, now British Airways
20270	G–AWNH	British Airways	136	23/11/71	D to BOAC, now British Airways
20271	G–AWNI	British Airways	136	7/1/72	D to BOAC, now British Airways
20272	G–AWNJ	British Airways	136	21/3/72	D to BOAC, now British Airways
20273	G–AWNK	British Airways	136	24/3/72	D to BOAC, now British Airways
20274	4X–AXB	El Al	258B		
20284	G–AWNL	British Airways	136	19/3/72	D to BOAC, now British Airways
20305	N26864	Continental AL	124	25/6/71	
20320	N93115	TWA	131	20/5/71	
20321	N53116	TWA	131	21/5/71	
20322	N93117	TWA	131	24/5/71	
20323	N9671	American Airlines	123	26/2/71	
20324	N9672	American Airlines	123	16/4/71	
20325	N9673	American Airlines	123	20/4/71	
20326	N9674	American Airlines	123	26/5/71	
20332	JA8107	JAL	246B	28/10/71	
20333	JA8108	JAL	246B	30/11/71	
20347	N652PA	PAA	121	25/4/71	*Clipper Pacific Trader*
20348	N653PA	PAA	121	8/4/71	*Clipper Unity*
20349	N654PA	PAA	121	28/4/71	*Clipper White Wing*
20350	N655PA	PAA	121	29/5/71	*Clipper Wild Fire*
20351	N656PA	PAA	121	18/6/71	*Clipper Live Yankee*
20352	N657PA	PAA	121	19/6/71	*Clipper Arctic*
20353	N658PA	PAA	121		*Clipper High Flyer*
20354	N659PA	PAA	121		*Clipper Plymouth Rock*
20355	F–BPVE	Air France	128	16/3/71	
20356	N611US	Northwest	251B		
20357	N612US	Northwest	251B		
20358	N613US	Northwest	251B		
20359	N614US	Northwest	251B		
20360	N615US	Northwest	251B		
20372	D–ABYD	Lufthansa	230B	3/5/71	*Baden-Württemburg*
20373	D–ABYE	Lufthansa	230F	9/3/72	
20376	F–BPVF	Air France	128		
20377	F–BPVG	Air France	128		

Boeing 747

C/n	Current Marks	Current Owner/operator	Model Series	Initial Delivery	Remarks
20378	F–BPVH	Air France	128		
20390	N9675	American Airlines	123	26/5/71	
20391	N9676	American Airlines	123	21/5/71	
20398	PH–BUD	KLM	206B		*The Nile*
20399	PH–BUE	KLM	206B		*Rio de la Plata*
20400	PH–BUF	KLM	206B		*The Rhine*
20401	OO–SGA	Sabena	129	9/9/70	
20402	OO–SGB	Sabena	129	4/12/70	
20427	PH–BUG	KLM	206B		*Orinoco*
20459	VT–EBN	Air India	237B		*Emperor Rajendra Chola*
20493	D–ABYF	Lufthansa	230B	2/4/71	L to Condor
20501	CS–TJA	TAP-Portugal	282B		*Portugal*
20502	CS–TJB	TAP-Portugal	282B		*Brasil*
20503	JA8109	JAL	246B	2/3/72	WO
20504	JA8110	JAL	246B	13/3/72	
20505	JA8111	JAL	246B	21/3/72	
20520	I–DEMB	Alitalia	243B	26/5/72	*Carlo del Prete*
20527	D–ABYG	Lufthansa	230B	25/2/72	*Niedersachsen*
20528	JA8112	JAL	146	14/7/72	
20529	JA8113	JAL	246B	30/6/72	
20530	JA8114	JAL	246B	3/11/72	
20531	JA8115	JAL	146	4/10/72	
20532	JA8116	JAL	146	8/12/72	
20534	VH–EBE	Quantas	238B		*City of Brisbane*
20535	VH–EBF	Quantas	238B	1/8/73	*City of Adelaide*
20541	F–BPVI	Air France	128		FF as N28903 before D
20542	F–BPVJ	Air France	128		FF as N28888 before D
20543	F–BPVK	Air France	128		FF as N28889 before D
20556	ZS–SAO	SAA	244B	7/8/72	*Magaliesberg*
20557	ZS–SAP	SAA	244B	29/9/72	*Swartberg*
20558	VT–EBO	Air India	237B	1/6/72	*Emperor Vikramaditya*
20559	D–ABYH	Lufthansa	230B		L to Condor
20651	N747WA	World Airways	273C	30/4/73	
20652	N748WA	World Airways	273C	25/5/73	
20653	N749WA	World Airways	273C		
20682	7301676	USAF	E4A		Advanced Airborne Command Post
20683	7301677	USAF	E4A		Advanced Airborne Command Post
20684	–	USAF	E4A		Advanced Airborne Command Post
20704	4X–AXC	El Al	258B		
20708	G–AWNM	British Airways	136		
20712	9V–SIA	Singapore International	212B	31/7/73	
20713	9V–SIB	Singapore International	212B	29/8/73	
20742	SX–OAA	Olympic Airways	284B		*Olympic Zeus*
20767	CF–TOD	Air Canada	133		
20770	HL–7410	Korean Air Lines	2B5B		
20771	HL–7411	Korean Air Lines	2B5B	12/7/73	FF as N1796B
20781	JA8117	JAL	SR-46	26/9/73	FF as N1795B
20782	JA8118	JAL	SR-46		
20783	JA8119	JAL	SR-46		
20784	JA8120	JAL	SR-46		
20798	F–BPVL	Air France	128		
20799	F–BPVM	Air France	128		
20800	F–BPVN	Air France	128		
20801	C–FCRA	CP Air	217B		*Empress of Asia*
20802	C–FCRB	CP Air	217B		
20809	G–AWNN	British Airways	136		
20810	G–AWNO	British Airways	136		
20825	SX–OAB	Olympic Airways	284B	3/12/73	*Olympic Eagle*
20826	N701SW	Seaboard World AL	245F		
20827	N702SW	Seaboard World AL	245F		

C/n	Current Marks	Current Owner/operator	Model Series	Initial Delivery	Remarks
20828	N703SW	Seaboard World AL	245F		
20841	VH–EBG	Quantas	238B		*City of Hobart*
20842	VH–EBH	Quantas	238B		*City of Newcastle*
20881	CF–TOE	Air Canada	133		
20923	JA8121	JAL	SR-46		
20924	JA8122	JAL	246B		
20928	CS–TJC	TAP	282B		

Bristol Britannia

C/n	Current Marks	Current Owner/operator	Model Series	Initial Delivery	Remarks
12873	G–ALBO	BAC/Mos	101		Prototype, FF AUG–16–52. To RAF St Athan as 7708M
12874	G–ALRX	BAC/Mos	101		FF NOV–23–53 WO FEB–4–54
12902	G–ANBA	Britannia AW	102	12/8/57	L from BOAC MAR–65. Sc 1970
12903	G–ANBB	Britannia AW	102	10/6/57	L from BOAC NOV–64. WO Ljubljana SEP–1–66
12904	G–ANBC	BOAC	102	30/12/55	WO NOV–11–66
12905	G–ANBD	BKS AT	102	30/12/55	L from BOAC JAN–65; L to Britannia AW, 1968. Sc 1970
12906	G–ANBE	Britannia AW	102	2/3/56	L from BOAC by Malayan AW 1963; L from BOAC by Britannia AW from FEB–66. S to Britannia MAR–70. Scrapped DEC–6–70
12907	G–ANBF	Britannia AW	102	14/3/56	L from BOAC FEB–65. Sc 1970
12908	G–APLL	BKS AT	102	8/8/56	Was G–ANBG. L from BOAC DEC–65. Scrapped FEB–69
12909	G–ANBH	BKS AT	102	24/7/57	L from BOAC MAR–65. Scrapped NOV–68
12910	G–ANBI	Britannia AW	102	29/6/56	L from BOAC APL–66. Sc FEB–70
12911	G–ANBJ	Britannia AW	102	22/11/56	L from BOAC MAR–66. Sc OCT–14–70
12912	G–ANBK	BKS AT	102	28/11/56	L from BOAC MAR–64. S to BKS APR–70. Sc DEC–31–71
12913	G–ANBL	Britannia AW	102	2/3/57	D to BOAC as G–ANBL. To Britannia AW JUL–65. L to Southern Cross International JUN–5–70. Scrapped DEC–29–70
12914	PK–ICA	Indonesian Angkasa	102	11/3/57	D to BOAC as G–ANBM. To Laker AW MAR–66; L to Treffield Aviation JUN–5–67. S FEB–69. Scrapped DEC–71
12915	PK–ICB	Indonesian Angkasa	102	4/5/57	D to BOAC as G–ANBN. To Laker AW APL–66; L to Monarch AL 1968. L to Britannia 1968. S FEB–69. Scrapped DEC–71
12916	G–ANBO	Britannia AW	102	31/5/57	L from BOAC by Malayan AW 1962. L from BOAC by Britannia AW from JAN–65. S to Britannia MAR–70. Scrapped OCT–16–70
12917	G–ANCA	BAC/Mos	301		Prototype long fuselage WO Filton NOV–6–67
12918	XA–MEC	Aeronaves Mexico	302	5/11/57	Built as G–ANCB, FF as G–18–1. *Tenochtitlan* later *Acapulco*. WO Tijuana APL–66

C/n	Current Marks	Current Owner/operator	Model Series	Initial Delivery	Remarks
12919	G–ANCC	African Air Safaris	302	15/12/57	Built as G–ANCC, FF as G–18–2. D to Aeronaves as XA–MED *Tzintzuntzan.* S to Transglobe AW. S 1968 (not used by AAS). Scrapped 1970
12920	G–ANCD	International Aviation Services	307F	17/7/58	Built as N6595C (Northeast); FF as G–18–3; L by El Al as 4X–AGE 1958-59; S to Air Charter (later BUA) MAR–24–59. S JAN–17–69. S International Aviation Services
12921	G–ANCE	International Aviation Services	307F	12/9/58	Built as N6596C (Northeast). S to Air Charter (later BUA) SEP–12–58. S FEB–17–69. S International Aviation Services
12922	G–ANCF	Monarch AL	308F	16/12/59	Built as N6597C (Northeast). FF as G–18–14, D Transcontinental SA as LV–PPJ later LV–GJB; S to British Eagle JAN–64 *New Frontier.* S DEC–11–68
12923	G–ANCG	British Eagle	308	17/12/59	Built as N6598C (Northeast). D. Transcontinental SA as LV–PPL, later LV–GJC. S FEB–64, *Trojan.* Cvtd to 308F. WO APL–4–67 Manston
12924	G–ANCH	Monarch AL	309	27/7/60	Built as N6599C (Northeast). FF as G–ANCH; L Ghana AW as 9G–AAG. S JUN–65 to BUA. S to British Eagle 1968. L to Ghana AW MAR–68. S SEP–28–68. Positioned at Biggin Hill for reduction to spares
12925	G–AOVH	Monarch AL	312	11/2/58	D BOAC; L by British Eagle 1964; *Crusader.* L by Caledonian MAR–65 to JAN–68. Scrapped NOV–16–71
12926	G–AOVI	Monarch AL	312	10/4/58	D BOAC; L by BUA 1961-64. L by Caledonian DEC–64 to JAN–68 *County of Argyll.* Scrapped JAN–10–72
13207	G–AOVA	Caledonian	319	8/11/60	FF as G–AOVA, Srs 311 development acft; S Ghana AW as 9G–AAH *Osagyefo;* S to BAC JAN–1–64; L BUA FEB–64; L British Eagle from APL–25–64 *Justice.* S to Caledonian APL–18–69 *County of Fife.* Scrapped APL–71

Bristol Britannia

C/n	Current Marks	Current Owner/operator	Model Series	Initial Delivery	Remarks
13230	LV–JNL	Aerotransportes Entre Rios	312F	10/9/57	D to BOAC as G–AOVB. L to British Eagle OCT–63. *Endeavour* S to Argentina OCT–3–69 and D as LV–PNJ. WO JUL–12–70 Buenos Aires
13231	G–AOVC	Donaldson	312	15/11/57	D to BOAC; L to British Eagle MAY–64 *Sovereign* S to Donaldson MAY–20–69 *Midado.* Scrapped 1970
13232	HB–ITB	Globe-Air	313	12/9/57	D El Al as 4X–AGA. L BUA 1963 as G–ASFV. WO Cyprus APL–20–67
13233	EC–BFL	Air Spain	313	19/10/57	D El Al as 4X–AGB. L BUA 1962-65 as G–ARWZ *Cantabrico.* Scrapped DEC–72
13234	4X–AGC	–	313	28/11/57	D El Al as 4X–AGC. L BUA 1962-65. S British Eagle as G–ARXA MAY–66 *Talisman* and *Renown.* Reverted to Israel marks OCT–68. Scrapped MAR–70
13235	G–AOVD	BOAC	312	6/12/57	WO Near Hurn DEC–24–58
13236	EC–BFK	Air Spain	312	21/12/57	D BOAC as G–AOVE; L BUA 1961-1964; L MEA 1964; L British Eagle 1964-1966 *Perseverance* and *Renown;* S DEC–29–66 *Mediterraneo.* Scrapped SEP–1971
13237	G–AOVF	International Aviation Services	312F	2/1/58	D to BOAC; L to British Eagle MAR–64 *Friendship.* To Donaldson MAY–70 *Nike.* S to International Aviation Services
13238	G–AOVG	Monarch	312	19/5/58	D to BOAC; L to British Eagle MAR–64 *Bounteous.* S to Monarch 1969
13393	5Y–ALP	African Air Safari	314	9/4/58	D to CPAL as CF–CZA *Buenos Aires* later *Hong Kong;* to Air Links MAY–65. S to Trans-globe as G–ATGD. S to African Air Safari as 5X–UVT, re-registered APR–70. Scrapped DEC–70
13394	CF–CZB	CPAL	314	29/4/58	*Vancouver* WO JUL–22–62, Honolulu
13395	G–ATLE	African Air Safari	314	20/5/58	D to CPAL as CF–CZC *Madrid* later *Tokyo;* to Air Links JUN–65. S to Trans-globe. L to Trek 1968-69. S 1968 (not used by AAS) Scrapped JUN–70
13396	G–ATNZ	Caledonian AW	314	27/6/58	D to CPAL as CF–CZD *Santiago* later *Winnipeg;* to Caledonian JAN–66 *Inverness.* Scrapped MAR–71
13397	XL635	RAF SC	253	29/1/60	*Bellatrix*
13398	XL636	RAF SC	253	4/6/59	*Argo* C Mk 1

C/n	Current Marks	Current Owner/operator	Model Series	Initial Delivery	Remarks
13399	XL637	RAF SC	253	26/6/59	*Vecia* C Mk 1
13400	XL638	RAF SC	253	5/8/59	*Sirius* C Mk 1. WO OCT–14–67, Khormaksar
13418	G–AOVJ	Caledonian AW	312	13/3/58	D to BOAC; L Caledonian APL–65 *Aberdeen.* S to Caledonian NOV–12–69. Scrapped NOV–70
13419	G–AOVK	Caledonian AW	312	5/58	D to BOAC; L British Eagle from AUG–65 *Concord.* S to Caledonian OCT–68 and Sc
13420	G–AOVL	Monarch AL	312	5/58	D to BOAC; L British Eagle JUL–65 *Resolution.* S FEB–17–69. Scrapped NOV–70
13421	XX367	MoD A & AEE	312F	10/6/58	D to BOAC as G–AOVM. L British Eagle MAR–64 *Team Spirit.* S DEC–7–69. S MoD
13422	G–AOVN	Monarch AL	312	4/7/58	D to BOAC; L British Eagle JUN–64 *Prospect.* S AUG–20–69. Scrapped NOV–73
13423	G–AOVO	British Eagle	312	4/9/58	D to BOAC; L British Eagle JAN–64 *Bonaventure* WO Austrian Alps FEB–29–64
13424	G–AOVP	International Aviation Services	312F	31/7/58	D to BOAC; L Lloyd APL–65. S Lloyd JAN–17–69. S International Aviation Services
13425	G–APNA	Donaldson	317	11/12/58	D to Hunting Clan (later BUA) S to Lloyd OCT–67 *Juno.* S to Donaldson MAY–69. Scrapped APL–30–72
13426	G–APNB	Donaldson	317	2/12/58	D to Hunting Clan (later BUA) S to Donaldson JAN–69 *Carillon.* Scrapped MAR–71
13427	G–AOVT	Monarch AL	312	1/1/59	D to BOAC; L British Eagle SEP–63 *Enterprise* later *Ajax.* S MAY–9–69
13428	5Y–ANS	African Air Safari	314	3/8/58	D to CPAL as CF–CZX *Santa Maria* later *Canada;* S to Caledonian NOV–65 *Midlothian,* reg G–ATMA. S to AAS. Scrapped MAY–73
13429		International Aviation Services	312	3/10/58	D to BOAC as G–AOVR; L British Eagle MAR–65 *Talisman;* to Air Spain as EC–BFJ OCT–66 *Atlantico* later *Islas Canarias.* Positioned at Biggin Hill for reduction to spares
13430	G–AOVS	International Aviation Services	312F	29/10/58	D to BOAC; L Lloyd AUG–65. S Lloyd JAN–17–69. S to International Aviation Services
13431	5Y–ALT	African Air Safari	313	7/3/59	D to El Al as 4X–AGD; L BUA 1963 as G–ASFU; S to Globe-Air as HB–ITC. S 1968 as 5X–UVH, re-registered 1970
13432	CU–T–668	Cubana	318	15/12/58	CU–P–668 before delivery. *Liberated.* L Cunard Eagle 1960-61 as G–APYY. L CSA as OK–MBA

Bristol Britannia

C/n	Current Marks	Current Owner/operator	Model Series	Initial Delivery	Remarks
13433	CU--T--669	Cubana	318	6/2/59	CU–P–669 before delivery
13434	XM489	RAF SC	253	4/5/60	*Denebola* C Mk 1
13435	XM490	RAF SC	253	8/6/60	*Aldebaran* C Mk 1
13436	XM491	RAF SC	253	6/7/60	*Procyon* C Mk 1
13437	CU–T–670	Cubana	318/2	15/5/59	D to Cubana as CU–P–670. L by CSA 1963
13448	XL639	RAF SC	253	7/10/59	*Atria* C Mk 1
13449	XL640	RAF SC	253	30/10/59	*Antares* C Mk 1
13450	XN392	RAF SC	252	10/10/59	*Accruse* C Mk 2. FF as G–APPE
13451	XN398	RAF SC	252	19/3/59	*Altair* C Mk 2. FF as G–APPF
13452	XN404	RAF SC	252	8/4/59	*Canopus* C Mk 2. FF as G–APPG
13453	G–ASTF	Caledonian AW	314	7/8/58	D to CPAL as CF–CZW *Edmonton* later *Toronto* later *Rome.* L British Eagle 1964 as G–ASTF; to Caledonian JAN–66 *Bonnie Scotland* later *Perth.* Scrapped DEC–69
13454	XL657	RAF SC	253	23/12/59	*Rigel* C Mk 1
13455	XL658	RAF SC	253	4/2/60	*Adhara* C Mk 1
13456	XL659	RAF SC	253	4/3/60	*Polaris* C Mk 1
13457	XL660	RAF SC	253	23/4/60	*Alphard* C Mk 1
13508	XM496	RAF SC	253	17/9/60	*Regulus* C Mk 1
13509	XM497	RAF SC	253	2/12/60	*Schedar* C Mk 1
13510	XM498	RAF SC	253	17/10/60	*Hadar* C Mk 1
13511	XM517	RAF SC	253	12/59	*Avior* C Mk 1
13512	XM518	RAF SC	253	19/12/59	*Spica* C Mk 1
13513	XM519	RAF SC	253	5/2/56	*Capella* C Mk 1
13514	XM520	RAF SC	253	19/3/60	*Arcturus* C Mk 1
13515	CU–T–671	Cubana	318/2	22/8/59	D to Cubana as CU–T–671. L by CSA as OK–MBB 1962-69
13516	G–ARKA	CCT Leasing	324	16/10/59	D to CPAL as CF–CPO *Amsterdam.* S Cunard Eagle MAR–8–61 *Good Fortune.* S to Caledonian. L by Tellair 1969 as HB–ITF. Scrapped APL–71
13517	G–ARKB	CCT Leasing	324	13/11/59	D to CPAL as CF–CPE *Mexico City.* S Cunard Eagle MAY–2–61 *Endeavour* later *Resolution.* S to Caledonian. L by Tellair 1969 as HB–ITG. Scrapped APL–71

Canadair CL-44

C/n	Current Marks	Current Owner/operator	Model Series	Initial Delivery	Remarks
1	–	UNI-AIR-France	CC-106		Prototype. FF NOV–15–59. as 15501. D to RCAF, subsequently reg 15555 and 15921. S to UNI-AIR
2	–	Air-Zaire	CC-106		D to RCAF as 16666, later reg 15922. S to Air-Zaire.
3	CF–CHC	Beaver Enterprises	CC-106		D to RCAF as 15923. S to Canhelas, now Beaver Enterprises
4	LV–	ATER-Argentine	CC-106		D to RCAF as 15924. S to ATER
5	LV–JSY	ATER-Argentine	CC-106		D to RCAF as 15925. S to ATER
6	LV–	ATER-Argentine	CC-106		D to RCAF as 15926. S to ATER
7	LV–JYF	ATER-Argentine	CC-106		D to RCAF as 15927. S to ATER. WO Santiago JUL–20–72
8	LV–JSB	ATER-Argentine	CC-106		D to RCAF as 15928, subsequently reg 106928. S to ATER
9	TF–LLH	Loftleidir	CL-44J		Civil demonstrator FF NOV–16–60 as CF-MKP-X *Gudridur Thorbajnardottir.*
10	–	Beaver Enterprises	CC-106		D to RCAF as 15555, subsequently reg 15929 VIP version. S to Beaver.
11	–	Air-Zaire	CC-106		D to RCAF as 15930. S to Air-Zaire
12	–	UNI-AIR-France	CC-106		D to RCAF as 15931. Ferried to Montreal under reg CF-DSY. S to UNI-AIR
13	–	Beaver Enterprises	CC-106		D to RCAF as 16666, subsequently reg 15932. VIP version. S to Beaver.
14	TF–CLA	Loftleidir	CL-44 D4-1	20/6/61	D to Canadair as CF-MYO. L to FTL. Reg G-AWVD for Transglobe but not D. L to TMA, reg N124SW. S to Loftleidir
15	N446T	Conroy Aircraft	CL-44 D4-2	3/3/62	D to FTL. S. DEC–68. L to Mobil Oil. WO Anchorage MAY–1–69
16	N447T	Trans Meridian	CL-44-0	31/5/61	D to FTL. S to Conroy Aircraft and cvtd to CL-44-0 "Guppy". L to Trans Meridian *Skymaster*
17	G–AWWB	Trans Meridian	CL-44 D4-2	16/3/62	D to FTL as N448T. S DEC–68 *African Trader*
18	G–AXAA	Trans Meridian	CL-44 D4-2	10/4/62	D to FTL as N449T. S FEB–69 *Pacific Trader*
19	G–AZIN	Trans Meridian	CL-44 D4-2	10/7/61	D to FTL as N450T. S to Trans Meridian
20	TF–LLJ	Loftleidir	CL-44 D4-2	1/6/61	D to FTL as N451T. S APR–30–68. *Porvaldur Eriksson Salenia*
21	G–ATZH	Trans Meridian	CL-44 D4-2	23/3/61	D to FTL as N452T. S to Trans Meridian
22	N453T	FTL	CL-44 D4-2	30/11/61	WO NAS Norfolk MAR–21–66

Canadair CL-44

C/n	Current Marks	Current Owner/operator	Model Series	Initial Delivery	Remarks
23	G–AWDK	Tradewinds AW	CL-44 D4-1	7/7/61	D to Seaboard as N125SW. S to Trans Globe. S to Tradewinds AW.
24	G–AXUL	Trans Meridian	CL-44 D4-2	25/1/61	D to FTL as N454T. S DEC–69
25	G–ATZI	Trans Meridian	CL-44 D4-2	20/7/61	D to FTL as N455T. S APR–70
26	G–AWSC	Tradewinds AW	CL-44 D4-1	30/9/61	D to Seaboard as N126SW. L to FTL. S to Tradewinds
27	G–AWGS	Tradewinds AW	CL-44 D4-1	30/9/61	D to Seaboard as N127SW. S 1968
28	N602SA	Slick AW	CL-44 D4-6	17/1/62	Civil demonstrator FF as CF–NYL–X. D to Slick. L to Airlift Int
29	N603SA	Bluebell Manufacturing Co	CL-44 D4-6	2/2/62	D to Slick AW. L to Airlift Int. S to Bluebell JUL–73
30	G–AWGT	Tradewinds AW	CL-44 D4-1	5/4/62	D to Seaboard as N123SW. S 1968
31	N228SW	Seaboard	CL-44 D4-1	15/6/62	L to BOAC. L to FTL. WO Wa Nang DEC–24–66
32	G–AWOV	Tradewinds AW	CL-44 D4-1	12/6/62	D to Seaboard as N229SW. L to FTL. S OCT–19–68
33	LV-JZM	ATER-Argentine	CL-44 D4-6	24/9/62	D to Slick AW as N604SA. L to Airlift Int. S to ATER
34	LV–JZN	ATER-Argentine	CL-44 D4-6	10/62	D to Slick AW as N605SA. L to Airlift Int. S to ATER
35	TF–LLF	Loftleidir	CL-44J		FF as CF–PBG. Cvtd from CL-44D4. *Leifur Eiriksson*
36	TF–LLG	Loftleidir	CL-44J		Cvtd from CL-44D4. *Salenia Vihjalmur Stefansson* WO Dacca DEC–2–70
37	G–AZKJ	Trans Meridian	CL-44 D4-8	1/1/65	FF as CF–PZZ. D to FTL as N1001T. S to Trans Meridian
38	G–AZML	Trans Meridian	CL-44 D4-8	14/1/65	D to FTL as N1002T. S to Trans Meridian
39	TF–LLI	Loftleidir	CL-44J		Prototype Canadair 400. FF NOV–8–65 as CF-SEE-X. Cvtd from CL-44D4. *Bjarni Herjolfsson.*

Convair 540/Canadair 540

C/n	Current Marks	Current Owner/operator	Model Series	Initial Delivery	Remarks
153	N271L	Arkansas Aviation	540	7/59	Prototype Eland-engine conversion by Napier in England. Ex-N8458H, FF as G–ANVP FEB–9–55. L to Allegheny. S to Arkansas Aviation

Convair 580

C/n	Current Marks	Current Owner/operator	Model Series	Initial Delivery	Remarks
410	N5802	Allegheny AL	580	6/4/65	Ex-N4827C. WO Bradford DEC–24–68
110	N5803	Allegheny AL	580	8/4/65	Ex-N1846D
155	N5804	Allegheny AL	580	11/6/65	Ex-N130B
19	N5805	Allegheny AL	580	15/10/65	Ex-N8425H. Previously CV–540 N541Z
168	N5806	Allegheny AL	580	11/12/65	Ex-N8427H. Previously CV–540 N543Z
154	N5807	Allegheny AL	580	21/1/66	Ex-N8426H. Previously CV–540 N542Z
348	N5808	Allegheny AL	580	3/2/66	Ex-N2043
17	N5809	Allegheny AL	580	16/2/66	Ex-N8428H
29	N5810	Allegheny AL	580	24/3/66	Ex-N8424H
459	N5811	Allegheny AL	580	28/4/66	Ex-N8420H
135	N5812	Allegheny AL	580	7/4/62	D to Eastern Canada Stevedoring as CF–ECS. S to Union as N7600. S 1966
130	N5813	Allegheny AL	580	27/7/66	Ex-N8419H
129	N5814	Allegheny AL	580	1/9/66	Ex-N8418H
78	N5815	Allegheny AL	580	29/9/66	Ex-N3424C
126	N5816	Allegheny AL	580	25/10/66	Ex-N8416H
81	N5817	Allegheny AL	580	29/11/66	Ex-N3426
128	N5818	Allegheny AL	580	17/12/67	Ex-N8425H
453	N5819	Allegheny AL	580	29/12/67	Ex-N3437
62	N5820	Allegheny AL	580	8/2/67	Ex-N3419
65	N5821	Allegheny AL	580	20/2/67	Ex-N3421
141	N5822	Allegheny AL	580	31/3/67	Ex-N144E
151	N5823	Allegheny AL	580	18/4/67	Ex-N11151
121	N5824	Allegheny AL	580	2/5/67	Ex-PH–TGH, PH–CGH and N4408
386	N5825	Allegheny AL	580	3/6/67	Ex-N3436. WO Bradford 6/1/69
385	N5826	Allegheny AL	580	22/6/67	Ex-N3435
46	N5827	Allegheny AL	580	27/7/67	Ex-N3415
375	N5828	Allegheny AL	580	4/8/67	Ex-N3432
458	N5829	Allegheny AL	580	23/8/67	Ex-N8421H
376	N5831	Allegheny AL	580	13/9/67	Ex-N3433
384	N5832	Allegheny AL	580	28/9/67	Ex-N3434
115	N5833	Allegheny AL	580	10/11/67	Ex-N8413H and 8436H
24	N5834	Allegheny AL	580	3/12/67	Ex-N5506K and N8423H
465	N5835	Allegheny AL	580	20/1/68	Ex-VH–BZM and N8422H
169	N5836	Allegheny AL	580	20/1/67	D to United Airlines as N7361. Later Lake Central
127	N5837	Allegheny AL	580	20/9/67	D to United Airlines as N73142. Later Lake Central
147	N5838	Allegheny AL	580	23/11/66	D to Union as N7600. S to Esso Tankers as N100A. S to Butterworth as N200A. S to Lake Central as N73158
114	N5839	Allegheny AL	580	12/8/67	Ex-PH–TGF, PH–CGF, N4406 and N73159
28	N5840	Allegheny AL	580	4/8/66	D to United Airlines as N73118. Later Lake Central
68	N5841	Allegheny AL	580	4/1/68	D to United Airlines as N73131. Later Lake Central
42	N5843	Allegheny AL	580	23/5/67	D to United Airlines as N73123. Later Lake Central

C/n	Current Marks	Current Owner/operator	Model Series	Initial Delivery	Remarks
43	N5844	Allegheny AL	580	5/11/67	D to United Airlines as N73124. Later Lake Central
52	N5845	Allegheny AL	580	10/12/66	D to United Airlines as N73125. Later Lake Central
89	N5846	Allegheny AL	580	17/3/67	D to United Airlines as N73138. Later Lake Central
163	N5847	Allegheny AL	580		D to United Airlines as N73149. Later Lake Central
15	YV–C–EVS	Avensa	580	15/7/64	Previously N540Z (CV–540)
161	YV–C–AVA	Avensa	580	8/10/64	Previously N544Z (CV–540)
445	YV–C–AVZ	Avensa	580	24/5/65	Previously N440EL (CV–540)
485	YV–C–EVD	Avensa	580	18/12/64	Ex-PH–CGO and PJ–CVM
454	YV–C–AVP	Avensa	580	20/8/67	Ex-N13328 and 11162 (CV–540)
157	YV–C–AVG	Avensa	580	28/5/66	D to Humble Oil as N73147
80	N73301	Frontier AL	580	2/4/66	D to Braniff, S to Frontier AL
2	N73102	Frontier AL	580	8/11/66	D to UAL, S to Frontier AL
7	N73106	Frontier AL	580	10/3/65	D to UAL, S to Frontier AL
8	N73107	Frontier AL	580	22/3/68	D to UAL, S to Frontier AL
11	N73108	Frontier AL	580	27/4/67	D to UAL, S to Frontier AL
16	N73112	Frontier AL	580	1/7/65	D to UAL, S to Frontier AL
25	N73117	Frontier AL	580	17/6/66	D to UAL, S to Frontier AL
34	N73120	Frontier AL	580	30/12/64	D to UAL, S to Frontier AL
35	N73121	Frontier AL	580	25/10/64	D to UAL, S to Frontier AL
41	N73122	Frontier AL	580	28/9/67	D to UAL, S to Frontier AL
53	N73126	Frontier AL	580	30/4/64	D to UAL, S to Frontier AL
54	N73127	Frontier AL	580	26/5/64	D to UAL, S to Frontier AL
57	N73129	Frontier AL	580	29/8/64	D to UAL, S to Frontier AL
69	N73132	Frontier AL	580	30/12/65	D to UAL, S to Frontier AL
86	N73136	Frontier AL	580	6/5/66	D to UAL, S to Frontier AL
94	N73140	Frontier AL	580	10/11/65	D to UAL, S to Frontier AL
132	N73143	Frontier AL	580	9/8/65	D to UAL, S to Frontier AL
145	N73145	Frontier AL	580	23/5/67	D to UAL as N73145. S to National Cash Register, reg N10CR. S to Frontier AL
170	N73152	Frontier AL	580	29/5/65	D to UAL, S to Frontier AL
179	N73153	Frontier AL	580	24/9/65	D to UAL, S to Frontier AL
119	N73155	Frontier AL	580	2/2/65	Ex-PJ–CVA and PH–CGL
186	N73156	Frontier AL	580	17/4/65	D to UAL, S to Frontier AL
312	N73157	Frontier AL	580	24/6/67	D to Cities Service as N1000. S to Gulf Oil, reg N109G. S to General Motors, reg N1092. S to Frontier AL
336	N73160	Frontier AL	580	13/4/68	D to Sabena as OO–SCL. S Frontier
354	N73161	Frontier AL	580	10/5/68	D to Sabena as OO–SCM. S Frontier
361	N73162	Frontier AL	580	26/2/68	D to Sabena as OO–SCN. S Frontier
366	N73163	Frontier AL	580	28/3/68	D to Sabena as OO–SCO. S Frontier
367	N73164	Frontier AL	580	4/6/68	D to Sabena as OO–SCP. S Frontier
368	N73165	Frontier AL	580	/68	D to Sabena as OO–SCQ. S Frontier
374	N73166	Frontier AL	580	10/7/68	D to Sabena as OO–SCS. S Frontier
381	N73167	Frontier AL	580	/68	D to Sabena as OO–SCT. S Frontier
382	N73168	Frontier AL	580	/68	D to Sabena as OO–SCV. S Frontier

Convair 580

C/n	Current Marks	Current Owner/operator	Model Series	Initial Delivery	Remarks
22	N90852	North Central AL	580	19/7/68	D to Continental AL. S to North Central
49	N90854	North Central AL	580	17/5/68	D to Continental AL. S to North Central
50	N90855	North Central AL	580	2/11/68	D to Continental AL. S to North Central
82	N90857	North Central AL	580	2/2/68	D to Continental AL. S to North Central
83	N90858	North Central AL	580	31/1/69	WO Appleton JUN–29–72
160	N9067R	North Central AL	580	7/6/68	D to LACSA as TI–1015C. S to North Central
100	N4810C	North Central AL	580	1/8/69	D to Delta AL. S to North Central
60	N4805C	North Central AL	580	12/12/67	D to Delta AL. S to North Central
30	N4801C	North Central AL	580	29/8/69	D to Delta AL. S to North Central
101	N4811C	North Central AL	580	10/1/69	D to Delta AL. S to North Central
39	N4803C	North Central AL	580	10/4/69	D to Delta AL. S to North Central
38	N4802C	North Central AL	580	8/5/69	D to Delta AL. S to North Central
51	N4804C	North Central AL	580	20/3/69	D to Delta AL. S to North Central
176	N4634S	North Central AL	580	15/5/67	D to LACSA as TI–1016C. S to North Central
67	N2728R	North Central AL	580	2/7/69	D to Continental AL as N90856. S to Minnesota Mining, reg N3M. S to North Central
150	N2729R	North Central AL	580	30/8/68	D to PAA as N11150. Since operated by National AL, Lockheed Corp, Allegheny AL. S to Minnesota Mining, reg NG3M. S to North Central
55	N3430	North Central AL	580	31/12/69	D to Braniff. S Alaskan Airlines. S North Central
13	N7517U	North Central AL	580	14/8/67	D to Texaco Inc as N1621. Trans to Texaco Canada, reg CF–TCL. S to North Central
137	N7528U	North Central AL	580	17/12/68	D to PAA as N11137. S to LAN-Chile, reg CC–CBH. S North Central
116	N7530U	North Central AL	580	26/2/69	D to National AL as N8414H. S to LAN-Chile, reg CC–CBJ. S to North Central
109	N3429	North Central AL	580	23/3/67	D to Braniff. S to North Central
					D to National AL as N8414H. S to LAN-Chile, reg CC–CBJ. S to North Central
					D to Braniff. S to North Central
61	N3418	North Central AL	580	15/3/68	D to Braniff. S to North Central
77	N3423	North Central AL	580	7/3/68	D to Braniff. S to North Central
334	N2041	North Central AL	580	27/6/68	D to National AL. S to North Central
347	N2042	North Central AL	580	20/9/68	D to National AL. S to North Central

C/n	Current Marks	Current Owner/operator	Model Series	Initial Delivery	Remarks
352	N2044	North Central AL	580	26/4/68	D to National AL. S to North Central
369	N0245	North Central AL	580	10/7/68	WO DEC–27–68 Chicago
370	N2046	North Central AL	580	10/11/68	D to National AL. S to North Central
377	N4822C	North Central AL	580	7/1/68	D to Delta AL. S to North Central
390	N7743U	North Central AL	580	22/11/68	D to Union Carbide as N424. S to Shell Investments, reg CF–KQ1. S to North Central
327A	N8444H	North Central AL	580	29/5/69	D to Union Producing Co. S to North Central
380	N4825C	North Central AL	580	24/2/67	D to Delta AL. S to North Central
379	N4824C	North Central AL	580	15/9/67	D to Delta AL. S to North Central
462	N968N	North Central AL	580	12/6/67	Previously CV–440 reg CF–MKO. Cvtd to CV–540 S to RCAF, reg 11163 as CC–109. Cvtd to CV–580 S to General Motors, reg N968N. S to North Central
475	N969N	North Central AL	580	18/7/67	Previously CV–440 reg CF–LMN. Cvtd to CV–540. S to RCAF, reg 11161 as CC–109. Cvtd to CV–580 S to General Motors, reg N969N. S to North Central
217	54–2815	USAF	C–131H	4/2/66	C–131D converted for SAM
220	54–2816	USAF	C–131H	26/4/66	C–131D converted for SAM
221	54–2817	USAF	C–131H	15/9/66	C–131D converted for SAM
326	55–299	USAF	C–131H	25/10/65	C–131D converted for SAM
1	11151	RCAF	CC–109	15/12/66	Converted from Eland power
2	11152	RCAF	CC–109	13/12/66	Converted from Eland power
3	11153	RCAF	CC–109	23/12/66	Converted from Eland power
4	11154	RCAF	CC–109	10/4/67	Converted from Eland power
6	11156	RCAF	CC–109	9/1/67	Converted from Eland power
7	11157	RCAF	CC–109	9/2/67	Converted from Eland power
9	11159	RCAF	CC–109	2/3/67	Converted from Eland power
10	11160	RCAF	CC–109	20/10/67	Converted from Eland power
479	N103	FAA	C–131B	9/6/61	
480	N104	FAA	C–131B	16/6/61	
478	N102	FAA	C–131B	18/7/61	
343	N105	FAA	C–131B	23/8/61	
477	N101	FAA	C–131B	4/10/61	
56	HR–SA	SAHSA-Honduras	580	11/6/60	D to General Motors as N5120. S to SAHSA–Honduras
489	N5121	General Motors	580	23/6/60	
500	N5122	General Motors	580	6/5/60	
501	N5123	General Motors	580	21/5/60	
507	N5124	General Motors	580	18/8/60	
508	N5125	General Motors	580	3/9/60	
496	N5126	General Motors	580	13/11/60	
33		SAHSA-Honduras	580	2/9/61	First CV–580 conversion, as N5100. D to General Motors as N5127. S to SAHSA–Honduras
79	N5128H	Rather Productions	580	1/11/61	Initially N3431 as PAC/Allison demonstrator. D to General Motors as N5128. S to Rather Productions
430	N5129	General Motors	580	25/6/64	
111	N5119	General Motors	580	11/4/65	D to Mead Johnson N158MJ

Convair 580

C/n	Current Marks	Current Owner/operator	Model Series	Initial Delivery	Remarks
318	N300K	Ford	580	26/5/60	
387	N321K	Ford	580	19/10/62	
18	N2004	Esso-Libya	580	24/2/61	D to Esso-Tankers as N200A. S to Butterworth as N2004
399	N98G	Gulf Oil	580	4/11/61	
372	N108G	Moncrief Drilling	580	31/3/62	D to Gulf Oil. S to Moncrief Drilling
509	N8860	Wolfe Industries	580	10/6/62	D to Scaife Inc. S to Wolfe Industries
202	N60FM	Forbes Magazine	580	20/2/63	D to Engelhard as N270E. S 1969. *Capitalist Tool*, reg N331G. Re-reg 1970
72	CF–BGY	Great Lakes Paper	580	14/10/63	D to Johnson & Johnson as N400J. S to Great Lakes Paper
473		National Research Council of Canada	580	13/9/64	D to Bethlehem Corp as N920BS. S to NRC of Canada
455	N910BS	Bethlehem	580	20/2/65	
214	N76Y	Great Lakes Carbon	580	7/11/64	
510	N440M	Allied Chemical	580	22/5/65	
383	N4479	Fram Corporation	580	11/9/65	D to Fairways as N4E. S to Fram Corp
466	N21466	Aero Spacelines	580	12/6/68	Ex-PP–CEN. Cvtd to TIFS 1969
70	N73133	North Dakota Farmers Union	580		D to Aero Spacelines Inc. S to North Dakota FU
85	N73135	Tex Johnston Inc	580		For TIFS conversion. Cvtd to
245	53–7793	USAF	NC–131H		Cvtd to TIFS by Cornell and FF JUL–24–70
4	N73104	Tex Johnston Inc			For TIFS conversion
180	N14278	Armstrong Cork			D to Tex Johnston Inc as N73154 intended for TIFS conversion. S to Armstrong Cork
12	N73109	Tex Johnston Inc			For TIFS conversion
98	N25278	Armstrong Cork			D to Tex Johnston Inc as N73141 intended for TIFS conversion. S to Armstrong Cork

Convair 600

C/n	Current Marks	Current Owner/operator	Model Series	Initial Delivery	Remarks
74	N74850	Frontier AL		1/8/66	Previously Central AL. Ex N94237
118	N74851	Frontier AL		14/9/66	Previously Central AL. Ex N94257
136		Mandala AW		1/7/66	Ex-N94263. D to Central (Frontier) as N74852. S 1970
164		Mandala AW		30/6/66	Ex-1-N94275. D to Central (Frontier) as N74853. L to Texas International 1969. S 1970
51	N74954	Frontier AL		17/11/66	Previously Central AL. L to Texas International 1969. Ex-N94227
46	N74855	Frontier AL			
170	N74856	Frontier AL		1/6/66	Ex-ET–AAW. Previously Central AL
168	N74857	Frontier AL		14/5/66	Ex-ET–AAV. Previously Central AL
171		Mandala AW		1/12/65	Ex-PK–GCA, N94295. D to Central (Frontier). S 1970
178	N74859	Frontier AL		22/12/65	Ex-PK–GCI. Prototype Dart-engined conversion by Convair as N94294. FF MAY–20–65. Previously Central AL
173	N74860	Frontier AL		25/1/66	Ex-PK–GCC. Previously Central AL
10	N94205	Texas International		24/4/66	
13	N94207	Texas International			
15	N94208	Texas International			
26	N94215	Texas International		1/7/66	
28	N94216	Texas International			
43	N94223	Texas International		28/2/67	
45	N94224	Texas International			
48	N94226	Texas International		31/3/67	
56	N94230	Texas International			WO Mena, Arkansas SEP–27–73
57	N94231	Texas International			
63	N94233	Texas International			
66	N94234	Texas International			
68	N94235	Texas International			
69	N94236	Texas International			
80	N94239	Texas International			
81	N94240	Texas International			
102	N94246	Texas International			
105	N94248	Texas International			
106	N94249	Texas International			
107	N94250	Texas International			
114	N94253	Texas International			
117	N94256	Texas International			
119	N94258	Texas International			
122	N94261	Texas International			
137	N94264	Texas International			
138	N94265	Texas International			
163	N94278	Texas International			
101	N94279	Texas International			
32	N278E	East Coast Leasing			D to Thunderbird AW as N331G - S to East Coast Leasing. WO Martinsburg AUG–22–68

Convair 640

C/n	Current Marks	Current Owner/operator	Model Series	Initial Delivery	Remarks
20	N3407	Caribair		23/12/65	WO NOV–66
21	N3408	Zantop Airways		20/5/66	D to Caribair. WO San Juan JAN–23–67. Rebuilt and S to Zantop
26	N3409	Zantop Airways			D to Caribair. S to Zantop
27	N3410	Zantop Airways		19/8/66	D to Caribair. S to Zantop
31	N3411	Zantop Airways		13/6/66	WO 1966. Rebuilt and S to Zantop.
32	N3412	Zantop Airways		23/3/66	D to Caribair. S to Zantop
48	N3417	Zantop Airways		21/4/66	D to Caribair. S to Zantop
64	N3420	Zantop Airways		15/1/66	D to Caribair. S to Zantop
463	CF–PWO	Pacific Western			D to Hawaiian AL as N4405. S to Pacific Western. Aft cargo door installed.
66	N5509K	Zantop Ariways		1/3/66	D to Hawaiian AL. S to Zantop
76	N5510K	Zantop Airways		18/11/66	D to Hawaiian AL. S to Zantop
171	N5511K	Zantop Airways		27/6/66	Ex-VH-BZE. D to Hawaiian AL. S to Zantop
133	N5515K	Zantop Airways		9/12/65	Ex-PH-CGN. D to Hawaiian AL. S to Zantop
134	N5512K	Zantop Airways		2/2/66	Ex-PH-CGM. D to Hawaiian AL. S to Zantop
58	N7529U	Zantop Airways			Ex-N5508K and CC-CBI. D to Hawaiian AL. S to Zantop
88	N73137	Zantop Airways			D to Hawaiian AL. S to Zantop
104	N111TA	Tuseey and Associates			Ex-PH-TGD *Pieter Breughel.* S to Martins Air Charter, reg PH-CGD. S to Tuseey.
332	–	Zantop Airways		6/2/67	Ex-HB–IMC. S to Martins Air Charter, reg PH-MAL. S to Zantop.
440	CF–PWR	Pacific Western		19/3/67	Ex-Caribair (L) as N45003. WO Campbell River, BC, SEP–17–69
441	CF–PWS	Pacific Western			Ex-JA5055. D after cvn to Hawaiian AL as N45004. S to Pacific Western.
9	CF–PWT	Pacific Western			Prototype Dart-engined cvn by Scottish Aviation as N7262. FF SEP–16–66. D to ARAMCO as N726A. Returned to General Dynamics as N7262. S to Pacific Western.
10	CF–PWU	Pacific Western		4/67	D to ARAMCO as N727A. Returned to General Dynamics as N7273. S to Pacific Western.
108	CF–PWY	Pacific Western			Ex-N8412H. D after cvn to Hawaiian AL as N5514K. S to Pacific Western.
408	7T–VAH	Air Algerie		1969	Formerly D-ACIB
409	7T–VAO	Air Algerie		1969	Formerly D-ACEX
451	7T–VAR	Air Algerie		1969	Formerly D-ACAP
460	7T–VAY	Air Algerie		1969	Formerly D-ACUM
412	HB–IMM	SATA			D to Swissair. D to SATA JUN–6–68. At present out of service after damage at Tromso, Norway JUL–73

Douglas DC-8

C/n	Current Marks	Current Owner/operator	Model Series	Initial Delivery	Remarks
45252	N808D	Delta AL	51	22/6/62	Prototype, FF MAY–30–58 as N8008D Srs 10; cvtd to Srs 50 prototype and FF DEC–20–60; L National AL in OCT–61. L to CPAL 1966 as CF-CPN *Santiago.* S to Delta OCT–1–67
45253	PP–PEA	Varig	33	2/6/61	D as N800PA for PAA *Flying Cloud;* L to Panair do Brasil SEP–26–62 *Garcia D'Avila.* To Varig JUL–65. WO Monrovia MAR–5–67
45254	N8016A	Delta AL	33	8/4/61	D to PAA as N801PA. *Queen of the Pacific.* S SEP–17–69
45255	N8027A	Delta AL	33	15/2/61	N8068D before D to PAA as N802PA *Cathy.* S AUG–25–69
45256	N8038A	Delta AL	32	7/2/60	D to PAA as N803PA *Mandarin.* S DEC–30–68
45257	N8240U	United AL	32	17/3/60	D to PAA as N804A *Pacific Trader.* S OCT–11–68
45258	N8243U	United AL	32	20/3/60	D to PAA as N805PA *Great Republic.* S OCT–18–68
45259	N8245U	United AL	32	7/5/60	D to PAA as N806PA *Northern Light* S SEP–27–68
45260	N8209U	United AL	32	3/6/60	D to PAA as N807PA *Polynesia.* S OCT–5–67
45261	N8215U	United AL	32	10/6/60	D to PAA as N808PA *Gauntlet.* S OCT–27–67
45262	N8246U	United AL	32	22/6/60	D to PAA as N809PA *Nightingale.* S SEP–20–68
45263	N8217U	United AL	32	16/7/60	D to PAA as N810PA *Intrepid.* S NOV–3–67
45264	N8252U	United AL	32	23/8/60	D to PAA as N811PA *Midnight Sun.* S OCT–11–68
45265	OO–TPC	Pomair Ostend	32	10/9/60	D to PAA as N812PA *Blue Jacket.* S MAY–13–71
45266	9Q–CLE	Air Zaire	32	13/10/60	D to PAA as N813PA *Bostonian,* later *Bill Findlow.* S JUN–10–69 *Majulah Singapura*
45267	N8148A	Delta AL	32	18/10/60	D to PAA as N814PA *Caroline.* S DEC–31–68
45268	9Q–CLF	Air Zaire	32	7/11/60	D to PAA as N815PA. S JUN–11–69
45269	N8166A	Delta AL	32	10/11/60	D to PAA as N816PA *East Indian.* S DEC–30–68
45270	N8170A	Delta AL	33	15/12/60	D to PAA as N817A *Derby.* S DEC–31–68
45271	N8184A	Delta AL	33	22/12/60	D to PAA as N818PA *Rambler* L Panair do Brasil, reg PP-PEF. S to Delta DEC–30–68
45272	PP–PDS	Varig	33	21/5/61	D to Panair do Brasil MAR–21–61. *Manoel de Borba Gato.* S JUL–65

Douglas DC-8

C/n	Current Marks	Current Owner/operator	Model Series	Initial Delivery	Remarks
45273	PP–PDT	Panair do Brasil	33	22/3/61	*Bras Cubas.* WO AUG–20–62, Rio de Janeiro
45274	N4901C	Capitol	31	6/4/60	D to Panagra as N8274H. S to Braniff FEB–66. S to Capitol NOV–10–67 as N1800 L to National AL as N4901C DEC–8–69 to DEC–1–72
45275	N8207U	United AL	31	25/5/60	D to PAA as N8275H *Fortune.* Trsfd to Panagra MAY–10–64. S to Braniff as N8275 FEB–1–67. S SEP–5–67
45276	N4902C	Capitol	31	29/6/60	D to Panagra as N8276H. S to Braniff FEB–1–67. S to Capitol OCT–10–67 as N1801. L to Air Congo 1967-68
45277	N1802	Capitol	31	30/6/60	D to Panagra as N8277H. S to Braniff FEB–67 as N8277. S NOV–14–67. Reservation as N4903C before WO Atlantic City APR–28–68
45278	N8001U	United AL	21	1/11/60	Prototype Series 20 FF NOV–29–58 as N8081D *Warren Burke*
45279	N8002U	United AL	21	11/5/61	Was N8028D. Cvtd from Srs 11/12
45280	N8003U	United AL	21	16/6/61	Was N8038D. Cvtd. from Srs 11/12 *Capt Ralph J. Johnson*
45281	N8004U	United AL	21	29/5/59	Cvtd from Srs 11/12 *Capt R. T. Freng*
45282	N8005U	United AL	21	27/6/59	Srs 11/12 cvtd *Capt W. D. Williams*
45283	N8006U	United AL	21	19/8/59	Srs 11/12 cvtd *Capt R. L. Dobie*
45284	N8007U	United AL	51	25/8/59	Srs 11/12 cvtd *Harry Huking*
45285	N8008U	United AL	51	3/9/59	Srs 11/12 cvtd *Capt R. L. Wagner*
45286	N8009U	United AL	51	14/9/59	Srs 11/12 cvtd *Capt George Douglass*
45287	N8010U	United AL	51	29/9/59	Srs 11/12 cvtd *Donald Douglas Sr*
45288	N8011U	United AL	51	22/10/59	Srs 11/12 cvtd
45289	N8012U	United AL	21	18/12/59	Srs 11/12 cvtd *J. A. Herlihy*
45290	N8013U	United AL	11/12	22/12/59	*Will Rogers.* WO Brooklyn DEC–16–60
45291	N8018U	United AL	21	28/2/60	*William A. Patterson*
45292	N8023U	United AL	21	26/2/60	*Hana-Maui*
45293	N8024U	United AL	21	6/4/60	*Hilo*
45294	N8025U	United AL	21	12/4/60	*Annie E. Johnson*
45295	N8026U	United AL	21	17/5/60	*Oahu*
45296	N8027U	United AL	21	25/5/60	*Kauai*
45297	N8028U	United AL	21	8/6/60	*Waipahu*
45298	N8029U	United AL	21	17/8/60	*James H. Doolittle*
45299	N8031U	United AL	21	11/9/60	
45300	N8033U	United AL	21	13/10/60	
45301	ZK–NZG	Air New Zealand	52	30/4/61	D to UAL as N8034U. S OCT–29–71
45302	N8035U	United AL	52	18/5/61	L to Air NZ NOV–13–67 to JAN–5–68
45303	ZK–NZF	Air New Zealand	52	8/6/61	D to UAL as N8036U. S JUN–2–71

C/n	Current Marks	Current Owner/operator	Model Series	Initial Delivery	Remarks
45304	N8037U	United AL	21	25/1/61	Srs 12 cvtd
45305	N8038U	United AL	21	8/2/61	Srs 12 cvtd
45306	N8039U	United AL	21	11/4/61	Srs 12 cvtd
45307	N8040U	United AL	12	16/6/61	WO Denver JUL–11–61
45376	OO–AMI	BIAS	32	19/3/60	D to KLM as PH-DCA *Albert Plesman.* S to Belgium International MAR–17–72. L to Panair Ostend. *Ville de Bruxelles.* Merger with Panair MAY–73
45377	YV–C–VIE	VIASA	32	17/4/60	*Daniel Bernoulli.* Joint operation with Garuda from MAR–24–69 *Bali* S to VIASA SEP–27–72
45378	PI–C827	PAL	32	9/5/60	D to KLM as PH-DCC *Sir Frank Whittle*
45379	PH–DCD	Martinair	32	4/7/60	D to KLM. *Nickolaus Otto.* S NOV–20–67
45380	PI–C829	PAL	32	19/8/60	D to KLM as PH-DCE *Thomas Alva Edison*
45381	YV–C–VIF	VIASA	32		D to KLM as PH-DCF *Anthony Fokker.* L to Martinair 1967-68. Joint operation with Garuda from SEP–69 *Java* Tsfd to VIASA
45382	OO–CMB	BIAS	32	26/10/60	D to KLM PH-DCG *Guglielmo Marconi.* S to Belgium International MAR–7–72. L to Pomair Ostend. Merger with Pomair MAY–73
45383	PH–DCH	KLM	53	13/7/61	N9603Z before delivery. *Orville Wright.* WO Schiphol JUN–29–68
45384	HS–TGT	Thai AW International	32	31/5/60	D to SAS as OY-KTA *Dan Viking.* S to Thai Airways SEP–27–71
45385	HS–TGS	Thai AW International	32	4/5/60	D to SAS as LN-MOA *Haakon Viking.* S to Thai AW DEC–28–70
45386	HS–TGO	THAI International	32	11/5/60	D to SAS as SE-DBA. *Rurik Viking.* L by Scanair 1969. S to THAI 1970
45387	N8258U	United AL	33	13/7/60	D to SAS as OY-KTB *Bue Viking.* S DEC–1–68. Srs 32 cvtd
45388	N8266U	United AL	33	31/8/60	D to SAS as LN-MOT *Olav Viking.* S NOV–3–68. Srs 32 cvtd
45389	HS–TGR	Thai AW International	32		*Ottar Viking.* D to SAS as SE-DBB. L to Scanair. S to Thai AW SEP–29–70
45390	HS–TGP	THAI International	32	11/11/60	D to SAS as SE-DBB *Visbur Viking.* L by THAI 1970
45391	N6571C	Pan Aero International	21	7/2/60	D to National AL. S to Pan Aero Int. JUN–28–73
45392	N6572C	Pegasus International Flying Club	21	7/3/60	D to National AL. S to Pegasus MAY–5–73
45393	N6573C	National AL	21	9/12/60	
45408	N801E	Delta	51	21/7/59	Srs 11/12 cvtd *Westward Ho*
45409	N802E	Delta	51	14/9/59	Srs 11/12 cvtd WO New Orleans MAR–30–67

Douglas DC-8

C/n	Current Marks	Current Owner/operator	Model Series	Initial Delivery	Remarks
45410	N803E	Delta	51	10/10/59	Srs 11/12 cvtd
45411	N804E	Delta	51	27/10/59	Srs 11/12 cvtd
45412	N805E	Delta	51	4/11/59	Srs 11/12 cvtd
45413	N806E	Delta	51	11/11/59	Srs 11/12 cvtd
45416	HS–TGW	Thai AW International	32	22/4/60	D to Swissair as HB-IDA *Geneve.* L to Sudflug and Atlantis AW. S APL–16–73
45417	HB–IDB	Swissair	53	19/6/60	*Basel-Stadt* Srs 32 cvtd
45418	JA8001	JAL	32	16/7/60	*Fuji*
45419	JA8002	JAL	32	29/7/60	*Nikko*
45420	JA8008	JAL	53	13/9/60	D as JA8003 *Matsushima* Srs 32; WO Tokyo APR–24–61 and rebuilt as Srs 53 *Hakkone*
45421	JA8005	JAL	33	23/11/60	*Miyajima*
45422	EC–BXR	Air Spain	21	3/1/60	D to Eastern AL as N8601. S JAN–7–71 *Isla de Mallorca*
45423	EC–CAD	Air Spain	21	22/1/60	D to Eastern AL as N8602. S APL–11–72 *Isla de Ibiza*
45424	EC–CDA	Air Spain	21	14/2/60	D to Eastern AL as N8603. S MAY–19–73 *Isla de Menorca*
45425	N8604	Eastern AL	21	19/2/60	
45426	EC–BZQ	Air Spain	21	9/4/60	D to Eastern AL as N8605. S DEC–1–71 *Gran Canaria*
45427	EC–CAM	Air Spain	21	26/4/60	D to Eastern AL as N8606. S JUN–1–72 *Isle de Tenerife*
45428	N8607	Eastern AL	21	22/5/60	WO Lake Pontchartrain FEB–25–64
45429	EC–CDB	Air Spain	21	8/8/60	D to Eastern AL as N8608. S APL–11–73 *Isla de Lanzarote*
45430	N8609	Eastern AL	21	9/10/60	
45431	N8610	Eastern AL	21	23/10/60	
45432	XA–SAS	Aeronaves Mexico	21	28/11/60	*20 de Noviembre* WO New York JAN–19–61
45433	N8612	Eastern AL	21	15/11/60	
45434	N8613	Eastern AL	21	28/7/61	
45435	N8614	Overseas National	21	15/8/61	D to Eastern AL. S JUN–20–73
45436	N8615	Eastern AL	21	6/9/61	
45437	N8617	Eastern AL	21	23/10/61	
45442	CF–TJA	Air Canada	41	25/5/60	Was N6577C before delivery
45443	CF–TJB	Air Canada	41	25/5/60	Was N6578C before delivery
45444	CF–TJC	Air Canada	41	27/5/60	
45445	CF–TJD	Air Canada	41	7/2/60	
45526	HS–TGU	Thai AW International	32	29/8/60	D to Swissair as HB-IDC *Zurich.* L to Sudflug and Atlantis. S FEB–26–73 WO Katmandu MAY–10–73
45565	CF–TJE	Air Canada	42	17/11/60	
45566	CF–TJF	Air Canada	42	14/12/60	
45567	EC–CDC	Transportes Aero	32	26/6/60	N9601Z before D to UTA as F-BJLA. L from JUN–1–73
45568	F–BJLB	UTA	53	5/8/60	Srs 32 cvtd
45569	EC–CCN	Transportes Aero	33	31/7/60	D to UTA as F-BIUY. L from MAR–23–73
45570	F–BIUZ	UTA	33	28/2/61	
45588	N8014U	United AL	21	18/11/59	Srs 11/12 cvtd
45589	N8015U	United AL	21	21/11/59	Srs 11/12 cvtd

C/n	Current Marks	Current Owner/operator	Model Series	Initial Delivery	Remarks
45590	N8016U	United AL	21	2/12/59	Cvtd from Srs 11/12 in APL–66
45591	N8017U	United AL	21	5/12/59	Srs 11/12 cvtd
45592	N8019U	United AL	21	30/12/59	Srs 11/12 cvtd *W. E. Rhoades*
45593	N8020U	United AL	21	14/1/60	Srs 11/12 cvtd
45594	N8021U	United AL	21	21/1/60	*W. C. Mentzer*
45595	N8022U	United AL	21	17/2/60	
45596	N8030U	United AL	21	27/8/60	
45597	N8032U	United AL	21	29/9/60	
45598	I–DIWA	Alitalia	42	28/4/60	*Amerigo Vespucci*
45599	9J–ABR	Zambia AW	42	5/7/60	D to Alitalia as I-DIWE *Cristoforo Columbo.* S FEB–28–70
45600	I–DIWI	Alitalia	42	27/7/60	*Giovanni Da Verrazzano*
45601	I–DIWO	Alitalia	42	2/11/60	*Marco Polo*
45602	OH–SOB	Spear-Air	32	18/5/60	D to Northwest as N801US. S SEP–15–63, reg N7181C. S DEC–8–72. *Harman Mimmi*
45603	N7182C	Pan Aero International	32	3/7/60	D to Northwest as N802US. S to National AL OCT–14–63, reg N7182C. S JUN–18–73
45604	4R–ACQ	Air Ceylon	53	11/8/60	D to Northwest as Srs 32 N803US. S to UTA as F-BLLC OCT–5–63. L by Air Afrique as TU-TBX. S to Air Ceylon MAR–30–72
45605	N7183C	National AL	32	22/9/60	D to Northwest as N804US. S OCT–28–63
45606	OH–SOA	Spear-Air	32	5/1/61	D to Northwest as N805US. S JUL–1–64, reg N7184C. S OCT–1–72. *Harman Jatka*
45607	PI–C804	PAL	53	8/8/62	Was N9607Z before delivery to KLM as PH-DCR *Gerard Mercator.* S DEC–19–67. *Ilang Ilang*
45608	PI–C801	PAL	53	26/4/62	Was N9608Z and PH-DCP before delivery. *Sampaguita*
45609	CF–TJG	Air Canada	42	22/12/60	
45610	CF–TJH	Air Canada	42	13/1/61	
45611	CF–TJI	Air Canada	43	2/2/61	
45612	CF–TJJ	Air Canada	43	22/3/61	
45613	PH–DCI	KLM	53	3/4/61	N9604Z before D *Sir Isaac Newton*
45614	PH–DCK	KLM	53	1/5/61	N9605Z before delivery *Admiral Richard E Byrd*
45615	PH–DCL	KLM	53	1/5/61	WO Lisbon MAY–30–61
45616	PH–DCM	KLM	53	24/6/61	*Henri Dunant*
45617	EC–ARA	Iberia	52	22/5/61	*Velazquez* WO Las Palmas JUL–6–72
45618	EC–ARB	Iberia	52	27/5/61	*El Greco*
45619	EC–ARC	Iberia	52	19/6/61	D to Iberia as EC-ARC. *Goya.* L MAR–31–69 to Aerolines Peruanes as OBR-931. Rtd. to Iberia JUN–17–71
45620	CF–CPF	CP Air	43	22/2/61	*Vancouver,* later *Rome*
45621	CF–CPH	CP Air	43	1/4/61	*Winnipeg,* later *Tokyo,* later *Lima*
45622	CF–CPI	CP Air	43	20/5/61	*Calgary,* later *Amsterdam*

Douglas DC-8

C/n	Current Marks	Current Owner/operator	Model Series	Initial Delivery	Remarks
45623	CF–CPG	CP Air	43	15/11/61	N9604Z before delivery *Montreal,* later *Buenos Aires*
45624	I–DIWU	Alitalia	43	28/4/61	*Giovanni Caboto*
45625	I–DIWB	Alitalia	43	31/5/61	*Antonia Pigafetta* WO Palermo MAY–5–72
45626	JA8006	JAL	33	4/5/61	*Kamakura*
45627	TU–TCD	Air Afrique	33	3/6/61	D to UTA as F-BJUV. L by Air Afrique from OCT–31–67 as TU-TCD *Dakar.* Transferred to Air Afrique
45628	OH–KDM	Kar-Air	51	6/11/61	D Trans-Caribbean as N8708R *James Roy.* S to Eastern AL as N8780 JAN–31–65. S NOV–6–72
45629	PH–DCN	KLM	53	1/1/62	L to Garuda. *Bali*
45630	I–DIWF	Alitalia	43	28/2/62	*Antoniotto Usodimare.* WO AUG–2–68 Nr Milan
45631	I–DIWD	Alitalia	43	24/3/62	WO near Junnar, India JUL–6–62
45632	PH–DCO	KLM	53	26/6/62	L to Garuda. *Java*
45633	XA–NUS	Aeronaves Mexico	51	10/5/62	*Chapoltepec* WO Mexico City DEC–24–66
45634	N774C	National AL	51	23/2/62	
45635	N875C	National AL	51	6/4/62	
45636	I–DIWP	Alitalia	43	3/11/61	*Alvise di la' da Mosto*
45637	I–DIWR	Alitalia	43	1/2/62	*Nicolose da Recca.* L to Zambia AW 1969
45638	CF–TJK	Air Canada	43	16/12/61	
45640	CF–TJL	Air Canada	54F	24/4/63	Was N9609Z before delivery
45641	N276C	National AL	51	25/5/62	
45642	N877C	Braniff	51	25/9/62	D to National AL. S JUN–15–73
45643	N278C	National AL	51	23/10/62	L to Air Jamaica from DEC–15–72
45644	N779C	National AL	51	24/11/62	
45645	N807E	Delta AL	51	27/4/62	
45646	N808E	Delta AL	51	15/5/62	
45647	JA8007	JAL	53	27/3/62	*Yoshino*
45648	6Y–JGE	Air Jamaica	51	6/7/62	D Trans-Caribbean as N8781R *Barbara Henry.* S to Eastern AL as N8781 APL–30–64. S to Air Jamaica MAY–8–72
45649	N809E	Delta AL	51	20/6/62	
45650	N810E	Delta AL	51	12/12/62	
45651	JA8010	JAL	53	31/1/64	*Kirishima*
45652	XA–PEI	Aeronaves Mexico	51	24/11/62	WO Acapulco AUG–13–66
45653	CF–TJM	Air Canada	54F	30/1/63	Was N9612Z before delivery. WO MAY–19–67 Ottawa
45654	CF–TJN	Air Canada	54F	8/2/63	WO Ste Therese NOV–29–63
45655	CF–TJO	Air Canada	54F	27/2/63	
45656	HB–IDD	Swissair	53	29/10/63	*Nid walden.* WO SEP–12–70 Dawsons Field
45657	EC–AUM	Iberia	52	28/8/63	*Zurbaran*
45658	EC–ATP	Iberia	52	29/3/63	*Sorolla*
45659	EC–ASN	Iberia	52	4/10/62	*Murillo*
45660	I–DIWG	Alitalia	43	21/5/63	*Luca Tarigo*
45661	CF–CPJ	CP Air	43	3/5/63	*Toronto,* later *Mexico City*
45662	JA8009	JAL	53	16/6/63	*Shima*
45663	N108RD	Airlift Int	54F	20/9/63	L to National from JUL–1–69
45664	JA8011	JAL	53	15/6/64	*Towada*

C/n	Current Marks	Current Owner/operator	Model Series	Initial Delivery	Remarks
45665	I–DIWS	Alitalia	43	12/12/63	*Leone Pancaldo*
45666	I–DIWT	Alitalia	43	14/4/64	*Emanuele Pessagno*
45667	N8782R	Trans Caribbean	54F	21/6/63	*Katy Leigh II* L to Seaboard from JUN–1–72
45668	N4904C	Capitol	54F	13/9/63	L to Eastern as N8740 DEC–12–67 to APR–29–68
45669	N8008F	Trans International	54F	26/4/63	L to Saturn OCT–27–68
45670	TU–TCA	Air Afrique	53	19/10/63	*Abidjan*
45671	TU–TCB	Air Afrique	53	10/1/64	*Brazzaville.* L by UTA as F-BJCB, NOV–29–67 to JUN–13–68
45672	N811E	Delta AL	51	14/11/63	
45673	N812E	Delta AL	51	4/12/63	
45674	N109RD	Airlift Int	54F	14/4/64	L to Sudflug 1967. L to JAL from MAY–68. L to National from NOV–15–69
45675	N8041U	United AL	54F	28/3/64	
45676	N8042U	United AL	54F	30/1/64	
45677	N8043U	United AL	54F	14/2/64	
45678	JA8014	JAL	55F	5/3/65	*Asama*
45679	CF–TJP	Air Canada	54F	25/3/64	
45680	JA8012	JAL	53	20/11/64	*Akan* WO Delhi JUN–14–72
45681	JA8013	JAL	53	14/1/65	*Haruna* WO Bombay SEP–23–72
45682	I–DIWL	Alitalia	43	21/3/65	*Nicola Zeno*
45683	PH–DCS	KLM	55F	25/7/65	*Alfred Nobel*
45684	N8783R	Trans Caribbean	54F	16/12/63	*Peter Jonathan II.* L by Sabena AUG–1–68 to SEP–30–68
45685	XA–PIK	Aeronaves Mexico	51	30/4/64	
45686	CF–TJQ	Air Canada	54F	27/8/64	
45687	N814E	Delta AL	51	28/10/64	
45688	N813E	Delta AL	51	15/5/64	
45689	N815E	Delta AL	51	5/11/64	
45690	N816E	Delta AL	51	24/3/65	
45691	PH–DCT	KLM	55F	15/8/64	*Pierre de Baron Coubertin.*
45692	F–RAFB	French Air Force	55F	17/6/64	D to Seaboard World as N801SW. S to UTA as F-BOLI APL–5–69. S to AUG–69
45693	N8060U	United AL	52	17/4/65	
45694	N8061U	United AL	52	7/5/65	
45750	ZK–NZA	Air New Zealand	52	13/2/65	Was N9683Z before delivery. L to KLM as PH-ADA MAY–27–69 to SEP–20–69
45751	ZK–NZB	Air New Zealand	52	10/8/65	WO Auckland JUL–4–66
45752	ZK–NZC	Air New Zealand	52	17/9/65	
45753	SE–DBD	SAS	55	27/4/65	*Folke Viking* L to Swissair NOV–69 to MAR–70, L to Scanair
45754	F–BOLI	UTA	55F	18/5/69	D to Trans International as N3325T. L to Saturn APL–1–69. S 1970
45755	I–DIWM	Alitalia	43	15/4/65	*Ugolino Vivaldi*
45756	N8065U	United AL	52	29/7/65	
45757	N8062U	United AL	52	15/6/65	
45758	N8063U	United AL	52	2/7/65	
45759	N8064U	United AL	52	10/7/65	
45760	6Y–JGD	Air Jamaica	51	30/12/64	D to Eastern AL as N8779R. S OCT–12–71
45761	CF–CPK	CP Air	43	14/10/65	WO Tokyo MAR–4–66

Douglas DC-8

C/n	Current Marks	Current Owner/operator	Model Series	Initial Delivery	Remarks
45762	PH–DCW	KLM	55	25/8/65	D to PAL as PI-C802 *Mabuhay*. To KLM *Gerard Mercator* on DEC–19–67
45763	JA8015	JAL	55	10/11/65	*Seto*
45764	JA8016	JAL	55	14/2/66	*Shikotsu*
45765	PK–GJD	Garuda	55	13/6/66	D to Garuda as PK-GJD *Siliwangi*. L to ONA 1968 as N2310B. To KLM MAR–24–69 *Anthony Fokker* L MAY–22–73
45766	PH–DCV	KLM	55	19/8/66	*Bali* later *Daniel Bernoulli*
45767	LN–MOH	SAS	55	8/2/66	*Harold Viking* L to Scanair
45768	YV–C–VID	VIASA	53	4/11/65	
45769	N8784R	Trans Caribbean	54F	11/12/64	WO Miami NOV–24–65
45800	N8044U	United AL	54F	10/9/65	
45801	N8045U	United AL	54F	28/9/65	*City of Philadelphia*
45802	N8046U	United AL	54F	3/1/66	
45803	F–BOLK	UTA	54F	15/7/65	D to Trans Caribbean as N8785R. L to Air Centrafrique as TL-AAK. S to UTA JUL–17–72
45804	PH–DCZ	KLM	55F	19/3/66	D to SAS as OY-KTC *Gorm*. S APL–29–70 *Hans Christian Andersen*
45805	N4905C	Capitol	55F	30/11/65	L by Eastern AL DEC–65 to APL–66
45806	N819E	Delta AL	51	12/12/65	
45807	N817E	Delta AL	51	28/10/65	
45808	N818E	Delta AL	51	23/11/65	
45809	CF–CPM	CP Air	53	30/5/66	*Lisbon*
45810	N8070U	United AL	61	7/5/67	
45811	N8071U	United AL	61	13/8/67	
45812	N8072U	United AL	61	17/2/68	
45813	N8073U	United AL	61	26/1/67	
45814	EC–BAV	Iberia	52	21/4/66	*Romero de Torres*
45815	N820E	Delta AL	51	21/1/66	
45816	YV–C–VIM	Trans Carga	55F	29/9/65	L from FTL by Seaboard SEP–29–65 to DEC–22–68. L to VIASA for use by Trans Carga
45817	HB–IDU	Balair	55F	12/1/66	L from FTL by Seaboard as N805SW JAN–12–66 to APL–5–69. S APL–5–69 to Universal as N805U. S JAN–8–71
45818	TF–LLK	Icelandic AL	55F	13/11/65	D to Seaboard N802SW. L to Air Bahamas. S to Icelandic AL NOV–1–71
45819	F–RAFC	French Air Force	55F	5/11/65	L to Air Afrique as TU-TXG MAR–APL–66 and TU-TXK FEB–24–67 to APL–5–67. L French AF as F-RCFA. S JUN–29–72
45820	F–RAFA	French Air Force	55F	31/12/65	D as F-BLKX
45821	N803SW	Affretair	55F	17/3/66	D to Seaboard. S OCT–9–72
45822	LN–MOO	SAS	62	20/6/67	TF as N1501U *Sverre*. WO JAN–13–69 Los Angeles
45823	SE–DBE	SAS	62	4/5/67	TF as N1502U *Anund*. WO APL–19–70 Rome
45824	PH–MAS	Martinair	55F	22/6/66	D to ONA as N851F *Resurgence*. S NOV–22–68 *Hong Kong*
45848	JA8050	JAL	61	23/2/67	D to Eastern AL as N8778. S JUN–11–71

C/n	Current Marks	Current Owner/operator	Model Series	Initial Delivery	Remarks
45849	N8074U	United AL	61	30/4/67	
45850	N8066U	United AL	52	1/4/66	
45851	N8067U	United AL	52	5/5/66	
45852	N8068U	United AL	52	18/5/66	
45853	N8069U	United AL	53	16/6/66	
45854	JA8017	JAL	55	27/9/66	*Bandai*
45855	XA–SIB	Aeronaves Mexico	51	31/10/66	*Jalisco*
45856	PH–MAU	Martinair	55F	7/7/66	D to ONA as N852F *Contender.* S JAN–70 *Toronto*
45857	TU–TCC	Air Afrique	55F	2/8/66	*Cotonou*
45858	CF–CPT	CP Air	55F	2/9/66	D to Panagra. S to Braniff as N1509U. S NOV–17–67 *Santiago*
45859	PH–DCU	KLM	55F	27/2/66	*Sir Winston Churchill*
45860	CF–TJR	Air Canada	54F	26/3/66	
45861	CF–TJS	Air Canada	54F	7/4/66	
45862	N4906C	Capitol	55F	26/4/66	L by Seaboard JAN–3–67 to APL–3–67
45877	N821E	Delta AL	51	25/8/66	
45878	XA–SIA	Aeronaves Mexico	51	14/10/66	FF as N8954U *Puebla*
45879	YV–C–VIC	VIASA	53	1/7/66	
45880	N8047U	United AL	54F	9/9/66	
45881	N8048U	United AL	54F	28/9/66	
45882	JA8018	JAL	55F	16/10/66	*Ise*
45883	N806SW	Seaboard World	55F	20/10/67	L to Inex Adria APL–20–72 to OCT–8–72
45884	N8050U	United AL	54F	12/3/68	
45885	N8051U	United AL	54F	19/3/68	
45886	N8049U	United AL	54F	11/11/66	
45887	JA8049	JAL	61	27/3/67	D to Eastern AL as N8777. S MAY–24–71
45888	JA8060	JAL	61	16/5/67	D to Eastern AL as N8776. S JUN–30–73
45889	JA8061	JAL	61	28/5/67	D to Eastern AL as N8775. S JUN–29–73
45890	CF–TJT	Air Canada	61	13/9/67	
45891	CF–TJU	Air Canada	61	4/10/67	
45892	CF–TJV	Air Canada	61	14/10/67	
45893	CF–TJW	Air Canada	61	4/11/67	
45894	N8774	Eastern AL	61	6/8/67	
45895	N1803	Braniff	62	22/8/67	
45896	N1804	Braniff	62	20/9/67	
45897	EC–CCF	Spantax	61F	6/12/67	D to Trans Caribbean as N8786R. *Barbara Henry II.* S FEB–12–73
45898	EC–CCG	Spantax	61F	29/12/67	D to Trans Caribbean as N8787R. *Claire Roy.* S FEB–21–73
45899	N1805	Braniff	62	29/9/67	
45900	N8962T	Trans International	61F	1/12/67	L to Seaboard. Sub-L to Icelandic AL
45901	PH–DEB	KLM	63	15/7/67	TF as N1503U. *Christopher Columbus*
45902	N8961T	Trans International	61F	16/6/67	L to Sabre Air NOV–12–71 to JAN–7–73
45903	PH–DEA	KLM	63	8/11/67	TF as N1504U *Amerigo Vespucci*
45904	N1807	Braniff	62F	11/11/67	
45905	SE–DBF	SAS	62	8/8/67	*Ingvar*
45906	OY–KTD	SAS	62	29/8/67	*Knud*
45907	N822E	Delta AL	61	9/4/67	
45908	N45090	National AL	61	6/8/67	
45909	I–DIWN	Alitalia	62	28/10/67	TF as N1505U. *Giuseppe Verdi*

Douglas DC-8

C/n	Current Marks	Current Owner/operator	Model Series	Initial Delivery	Remarks
45910	I–DIWV	Alitalia	62	16/11/67	*Gioacchino Rossini*
45911	N1806	Braniff	62	19/12/67	
45912	N8771	Eastern AL	61	9/12/67	
45913	N8770	Eastern AL	61	19/1/68	
45914	N823E	Delta AL	61	16/5/67	
45915	N824E	Delta AL	61	19/7/67	
45916	JA8019	JAL	55	18/9/67	*Aso*
45917	F–BNLE	UTA	62	23/2/68	
45918	F–BOLF	UTA	62	27/4/68	
45919	HB–IDE	Swissair	62	24/11/67	*Uri*
45920	HB–IDF	Swissair	62	1/1/68	*Schwyz*
45921	SE–DBG	SAS	62	11/1/68	*Jorund*
45922	OY–KTE	SAS	62	29/2/68	*Skjold*
45923	LN–MOU	SAS	63	16/8/68	*Leif*
45924	SE–DBH	SAS	62	18/9/68	*Ring*
45925	HB–IDG	Swissair	62	25/2/68	*Neuchatel*
45926	CF–CPO	CP Air	63	17/1/68	*Tokyo*
45927	CF–CPP	CP Air	63	31/1/68	*Honolulu.* L as N198 before D
45928	CF–CPQ	CP Air	63	24/2/68	*Hong Kong.* L by FTL as N625FT JUL–2–68 to DEC–30–68
45929	CF–CPS	CP Air	63	16/6/68	*Madrid.* L by FTL as N624FT, JUN–16–68. N19B before D
45930	EC–BMX	Iberia	63	6/8/68	*El Espanoleto*
45931	EC–BMY	Iberia	63	18/9/68	*Rosales*
45932	ZK–NZD	Air New Zealand	52	27/1/68	
45933	CF–TIH	Air Canada	53	13/8/68	
45934	CF–TII	Air Canada	53	30/8/68	
45935	XA–SID	Aeronaves Mexico	51	7/2/68	*Guanajuato*
45936	N8631	Seaboard World	63F	21/6/68	L by Loftleidir 1970. L to Icelandic AL.
45937	PI–C803	PAL	53	27/1/68	*Champaca*
45938	N8960T	Trans International	61F	2/2/68	L to Seaboard. Sub-L to Icelandic AL
45939	N801U	Overseas National AW	61F	18/4/68	L to Capitol APL–18–68 to SEP–30–68 Tsfd to ONA MAY–1–72. L to Capitol AW APL–16–73
45940	N8075U	United AL	61	8/12/67	
45941	N8076U	United AL	61	23/12/67	
45942	JA8058	JAL	61	12/4/68	D to Eastern AL as N8773. S SEP–25–72
45943	JA8059	JAL	61	18/5/68	D to Eastern AL as N8772. S SEP–27–72
45944	N825E	Delta	61	24/1/68	
45945	N8077U	United AL	61	5/3/68	
45946	N8078U	United AL	61	14/3/68	
45947	N8079U	United AL	61	20/3/68	
45948	N8955U	Saturn AW	61F	28/12/67	
45949	N8956U	Saturn AW	61F	30/1/68	
45950	N802U	Universal AL	61F	26/4/68	L to Capitol APL–26–68 to SEP–30–68 Trsfd to ONA. L to Seaboard MAR–22–73 Sub-L to Icelandic AL
45951	N4863T	Trans International	63F	22/11/68	WO SEP–8–70 New York
45952	N8788R	Trans Caribbean	61F	29/2/68	*Bennet C* L to Saturn AW MAY–1–72
45953	JA–8031	JAL	62	19/4/68	*Awaji*
45954	JA–8032	JAL	62	27/5/68	*Hidaka*
45955	JA–8033	JAL	62	10/6/68	*Amakusa*
45956	JA–8034	JAL	62	19/7/68	*Daisen*
45960	I–DIWC	Alitalia	62F	10/4/68	*Titano*
45961	I–DIWQ	Alitalia	62F	30/6/68	*Ciclope.* N8964U before D

C/n	Current Marks	Current Owner/operator	Model Series	Initial Delivery	Remarks
45962	CF–TIJ	Air Canada	53	16/10/68	WO Toronto JUN–21–73
45963	6Y–JGC	Air Jamaica	61	29/4/68	D to Air Canada as CF-TJX L MAR–25–69
45964	CF–TJY	Air Canada	61	30/5/68	
45965	EC–BMV	Iberia	55F	31/3/58	*Pedro Berruguete*
45966	N8632	Seaboard World	63F	16/9/68	
45967	N4907C	Capitol	63F	20/8/68	
45968	N4908C	Capitol	63F	29/8/68	
45969	N6161A	Airlift	63F	25/9/68	Ordered for Lloyd AL
45970	N8080U	United AL	61	29/3/68	
45971	N8081U	United AL	61	12/5/68	
45972	N8082U	United AL	61	22/5/68	
45973	N8083U	United AL	61	20/5/68	
45974	N8084U	United AL	61	21/6/68	
45975	N8085U	United AL	61	25/6/68	
45976	N8086U	United AL	61	10/7/68	
45977	N8087U	United AL	61	16/7/68	
45978	N8088U	United AL	61	31/7/68	
45979	N826E	Delta	61	30/5/68	
45980	CF–TJZ	Air Canada	61	13/7/68	
45981	N45091	National AL	61	23/4/68	
45982	JA8057	JAL	61	29/3/68	D to Eastern AL as N8769. S SEP–25–72
45983	N8768	Eastern AL	61	19/4/68	L to JAL JUL–6–70
45984	HB–IDH	Swissair	62F	11/7/68	*Piz Bernina*
45985	ZK–NZE	Air New Zealand	52	27/2/68	
45986	I–DIWJ	Alitalia	62	26/7/68	*Antonio Vivaldi*
45987	F–BOLG	UTA	62	14/6/68	
45988	EC–BMZ	Iberia	63F	16/12/68	*Los Madrazo*
45989	N779FT	Flying Tiger	63F	28/6/68	
45990	N780FT	Flying Tiger	63F	17/7/68	
45991	N781FT	Flying Tiger	63F	26/7/68	
45992	N8767	Eastern AL	61	21/5/68	L to JAL APL–5–71
45993	N8089U	United AL	61	6/8/68	
45994	N8090U	United AL	61	27/8/68	
45995	N8091U	United AL	61	4/9/68	
45996	N8092U	United AL	61	1/10/68	
45997	N8093U	United AL	61	8/10/68	
45998	N8094U	United AL	61	22/10/68	
45999	PH–DEC	KLM	63	21/7/68	*Marco Polo*
46000	PH–DED	KLM	63	25/8/68	*Leifur Eriksson*
46001	N863F	Overseas National	63F	23/9/68	*Triumphant* L to *Air Siam* MAR–28–71 to JAN–31–72
46002	N782FT	Flying Tiger	63F	17/9/68	
46003	N783FT	Flying Tiger	63F	22/10/68	
46004	N784FT	Flying Tiger	63F	25/10/68	
46005	N785FT	Flying Tiger	63F	25/11/68	WO JUL–26–70 Okinawa
46006	N786FT	Flying Tiger	63F	3/12/68	
46007	N787FT	Flying Tiger	63F	3/1/69	
46008	N788FT	Flying Tiger	63F	6/1/69	
46009	N8052U	United AL	54F	31/10/68	
46010	N8053U	United AL	54F	7/11/68	
46011	N8054U	United AL	54F	11/11/68	
46012	N8055U	United AL	54F	23/11/68	
46013	OH–LFT	Finnair	62F	27/1/69	*Paavo Nurmi,* D as OH-LFR
46014	N1300L	Delta AL	61	18/10/68	
46015	N8766	Eastern AL	61	7/11/68	L to JAL OCT–16–72
46016	N8765	Eastern AL	61	15/11/68	L to JAL NOV–21–72
46017	N8764	Eastern AL	61	17/12/68	
46018	N1301L	Delta AL	61	19/12/68	
46019	PH–DEE	KLM	63	27/11/68	*Abel Tasman*
46020	N8633	Seaboard World	63F	27/11/68	
46021	N8634	Seaboard World	63F	9/1/69	WO Stockton OCT–16–69

Douglas DC-8

C/n	Current Marks	Current Owner/operator	Model Series	Initial Delivery	Remarks
46022	JA8036	JAL	62F	13/12/68	*Wakasa*
46023	JA8035	JAL	62	11/11/68	*Taisetsu*
46024	JA8037	JAL	62	27/1/69	*Yashima*
46026	I–DIWZ	Alitalia	62	30/4/69	*Gaetano Donizetti.* WO SEP–15–70 New York
46027	I–DIWY	Alitalia	62	25/2/69	*Vincenzo Bellini*
46028	F–BOLH	UTA	62	24/5/69	
46029	N1302L	Delta AL	61	16/1/69	
46030	N1303L	Delta AL	61	22/1/69	
46031	JA8038	JAL	61	20/2/69	*Izu*
46032	JA8039	JAL	61	25/2/69	*Tukuba*
46033	CF–TIK	Air Canada	63	15/2/69	
46034	CF–TIL	Air Canada	63	16/2/69	
46035	CF–TIM	Air Canada	63	27/2/69	
46036	CF–TIN	Air Canada	63	27/3/69	
46037	N8763	Eastern AL	61	19/12/68	L to JAL SEP–25–72
46038	N8762	Eastern AL	61	3/2/69	
46039	N8095U	United AL	61	14/5/69	
46040	N8096U	United AL	61	14/5/69	
46041	OY–KTF	SAS	63	28/2/69	*Frode*
46042	YV–C–VIA	VIASA	63	22/12/68	
46043	OH–LFV	Finnair	62F	22/3/69	*Jean Sibelius.* D as OH-LFS
46044	N790FT	Flying Tiger	63F	28/2/69	
46045	N791FT	Flying Tiger	63F	17/3/69	L by American Flyers from MAY–1–69 to APL–30–70
46046	N792FT	Flying Tiger	63F	21/3/69	L by American Flyers from MAY–26–69 to MAY–21–70
46047	N793FT	Flying Tiger	63F	31/3/69	L by Overseas National from APL–4–69 to SEP–30–70
46048	N1304L	Delta AL	61	24/4/69	
46049	N8639	Seaboard World	63F	8/8/69	L to Loftleider 1970. L to Icelandic AL
46050	N8635	Seaboard World	63F	30/1/69	L to Korean AL JAN–13–73
46051	N8636	Seaboard World	63F	28/2/69	L to Korean AL DEC–13–72
46052	N8637	Seaboard World	63F	11/3/69	L to Korean AL MAR–11–73
46053	N8638	Seaboard World	63F	28/3/69	L to Korean AL APL–11–73
46054	LN–MOY	SAS	63	26/4/69	*Eirik*
46055	N1306L	Delta AL	61	5/11/69	
46056	N1307L	Delta AL	61	6/11/69	
46057	JA8040	JAL	62	18/7/69	*Hida* WO Moscow NOV–28–71
46058	N8759	Eastern AL	63	24/2/69	
46059	N4864T	Trans International	63F	25/4/69	
46060	N4909C	Capitol	63F	2/7/69	WO NOV–27–70 Anchorage
46061	N6162A	Airlift	63F	20/8/69	
46062	N6163A	Airlift	63F	15/9/69	
46063	YV–C–VIB	VIASA	63	9/5/69	
46064	N8097U	United AL	61	23/5/69	
46065	N8098U	United AL	61	4/6/69	
46066	N8099U	United AL	61	16/6/69	
46067	N8966U	United AL	62	22/6/69	
46068	N8967U	United AL	62	15/6/69	
46069	N8968U	United AL	62	8/7/69	
46070	N8969U	United AL	62	16/7/69	
46071	N8970U	United AL	62	28/7/69	
46072	N1305L	Delta AL	61	8/8/69	
46073	N4865T	Trans International	63F	22/8/69	L to Aeromexico from MAR–17–71

C/n	Current Marks	Current Owner/operator	Model Series	Initial Delivery	Remarks
46074	HB–IDZ	Balair	63	21/6/69	D to Eastern AL as N8760. S MAY–1–72
46075	PH–DEH	KLM	63	29/8/69	*Vasco da Gama*
46076	CF–TIO	Air Canada	63	19/4/69	
46077	HB–IDI	Swissair	62	5/7/69	*Solothurn*
46078	HB–IDK	Swissair	62F	6/8/69	*Matterhorn*
46079	EC–BQS	Iberia	63	2/8/69	*Claudio Coello*
46080	PH–DEF	KLM	63	20/6/69	*Henry Hudson*
46081	N8971U	United AL	62	11/8/69	
46082	I–DIWK	Alitalia	62	14/5/69	*Giacomo Puccini*
46084	N8972U	United AL	62	19/8/69	
46085	N8973U	United AL	62	4/9/69	
46086	N794FT	Flying Tiger	63	4/8/69	
46087	N864F	Overseas National	63F	28/4/69	*Serene*
46088	N865F	Overseas National	63F	29/5/69	*Superb*
46089	N4866T	Trans International	63F	29/12/69	L to Aeromexico from MAR–13–71
46090	N4867T	Trans International	63F	29/12/69	
46091	N4868T	Trans International	63F	4/4/70	
46092	PH–DEG	KLM	63	23/12/69	*Jan van Riebeek*
46093	OY–KTG	SAS	63	6/11/69	D to Eastern AL as N8758. S MAR–19–73
46094	N4910C	Capitol	63F	15/8/69	
46095	CF–CPL	CP Air	63	15/11/69	D to Eastern AL as N8757. S to CP Air SEP–26–72 *Athens*
46096	N8756	UTA	63	21/11/69	D to Eastern AL as N8756. S APL–30–73
46097	N8755	Eastern AL	63	14/12/69	
46098	I–DIWW	Alitalia	62		*Arcangelo Corelli*
46099	JA8041	JAL	61	15/1/70	
46100	CF–TIP	Air Canada	63	11/12/69	
46101	N8630	Seaboard World	63F	25/9/69	L to Air Bahama Int from MAY–21–70
46102	LN–MOG	SAS	62	1/2/70	L to Swissair OCT–25–71 to MAY–1–72 *Odd Viking*
46103	N795FT	Flying Tiger	62	29/8/69	
46104	N796FT	Flying Tiger	63	3/10/69	
46105	N1808	Braniff	62	23/10/69	
46106	N8641	Seaboard World	63F	2/10/69	L to Loftleidir, 1970. L to Icelandic AL
46107	N1809	Braniff	62	17/11/69	
46108	N798FT	Flying Tiger Line	63	23/4/70	D to American Flyers as N123AF S JUNE–4–71
46109	N8642	Seaboard World	63F	23/10/69	
46110	N8974U	United AL	62	23/9/69	
46111	N8975U	United AL	62	14/10/69	
46112	N866F	Overseas National	63F	7/4/70	
46113	CF–TIU	Air Canada	63	12/3/70	
46114	CF–TIW	Air Canada	63	30/4/70	WO Toronto JUL–5–70
46115	CF–TIX	Air Canada	63	23/5/70	
46116	EC–BSD	Iberia	63	23/12/70	*Ribalta*
46117	N4869T	Trans International	63	15/5/70	
46118	N8717U	United AL	63F		
46119	N8724U	United AL	63F		
46121	PH–DEK	KLM	63	28/11/69	*David Livingstone* L to PAL MAY–1–73
46122	PH–DEL	KLM	63	30/12/69	L to PAL APL–1–73
46123	CF–TIQ	Air Canada	63	24/2/70	
46124	CF–TIR	Air Canada	63	5/2/70	
46125	CF–TIS	Air Canada	63	27/2/70	
46126	CF–TIV	Air Canada	63	1/4/70	
46127	JA8042	JAL	61	2/2/70	
46128	JA8043	JAL	61	24/2/70	

Douglas DC-8

C/n	Current Marks	Current Owner/operator	Model Series	Initial Delivery	Remarks
46129	SE–DBI	SAS	62F	5/4/70	*Torgny Viking*
46130	OH–LFY	Finnair	62CF	29/12/70	
46131	LN–MOW	SAS	62	25/2/70	*Roald Viking*
46132	I–DIWH	Alitalia	62	24/7/70	*Giovanni Pierluigi da Palestrina*
46133	N801WA	World Airways	63CF	19/3/71	
46134	HB–IDL	Swissair	62F	7/2/70	*Aargau*
46135	TU–TCF	Air Afrique	63	28/5/70	*Fort Lamy*
46136	SE–DBK	SAS	63	14/1/70	*Edmund Viking*
46137	N801WA	World Airways	63F	29/4/70	D to Atlantic as D–ADIX. S JAN–3–73 to Booth Leasing. L to World Airways
46138	OY–KTG	SAS	63		*Torodd Viking*
46139	JA8044	JAL	62AF	14/9/70	*Izumo*
46140	N797FT	Flying Tiger Line	63CF	19/5/70	D to American Flyers as N124AF. S JUN–4–71. L to Trans International JUN–1–72
46141	PH–DEM	KLM	63	22/6/70	*James Cook*
46142	I–DIWX	Alitalia	62	12/3/71	*Luigi Cherubini*
46143	N804WA	World Airways	63CF	15/4/71	D to Atlantis as D–ADIY. S JAN–3–73. L to World Airways
46144	N6164A	Airlift International	63CF	26/6/70	
46145	N805WA	World Airways	63CF	26/5/71	D to Atlantis as D–ADIZ. S JAN–3–73. L to World Airways
46146	N806WA	World Airways	63CF	12/3/71	
46147	9Q–CLH	Air Zaire	63CF	19/7/71	
46148	JA8054	JAL	62AF	10/1/72	
46149	N803WA	World Airways	63CF	29/3/71	
46150	LN–MOC	SAS	62AF	22/10/70	*Kettil Viking*
46151	9Q–CLG	Air Zaire	63CF	9/11/70	
46152	JA8051	JAL	62	23/8/71	
46153	JA8052	JAL	62	5/10/71	
46154	JA8055	JAL	62AF	17/2/72	
46155	EC–BSE	Iberia	63	23/12/70	*Alonso Cano*
46157	JA8045	JAL	61	4/12/70	*Noto*
46158	JA8046	JAL	61	10/1/71	*Hiei*
46159	JA8047	JAL	61	18/2/71	*Asabi*
46160	JA8048	JAL	61	12/3/71	*Hidaka*
46161	JA8053	JAL	62	18/11/71	
46162	JA8056	JAL	62AF	21/3/72	
46163	SE–DBL	SAS	63	13/5/72	*Tord Viking*

Douglas DC-9

C/n	Current Marks	Current Owner/operator	Model Series	Initial Delivery	Remarks
45695	N1301T	Texas International	14	1/10/66	Prototype FF FEB–25–65 as N9DC. Leased
45696	N3301L	Delta AL	14	20/7/66	
45697	N3302L	Southern AW	14	10/6/66	D to Delta AL. S JUL–26–73
45698	N3303L	Southern AW	14	4/12/65	D to Delta AL. S FEB–20–73
45699	N3304L	Southern AW	14	18/9/65	D to Delta AL. S MAR–28–73
45700	N3305L	Delta AL	14	27/11/65	WO Fort Worth Texas MAY–30–72
45701	N3306L	Southern AW	14	29/11/65	D to Delta AL. S MAY–29–73
45702	N3307L	Southern AW	14	11/1/66	D to Delta AL. S FEB–28–73
45703	N3308L	Southern AW	14	17/3/66	D to Delta AL. S APL–19–73
45704	N3309L	Southern AW	14	29/4/66	D to Delta AL. S MAY–16–73
45705	N3310L	Southern AW	14	24/9/66	D to Delta AL. S AUG–17–73
45706	N3311L	Delta AL	14	25/10/66	
45707	N3312L	Southern AW	14	23/11/66	D to Delta AL. S JUL–12–73
45708	N3313L	Southern AW	14	30/12/66	D to Delta AL. S AUG–30–73
45709	N3314L	Southern AW	14	12/1/67	D to Delta AL. S JUN–15–73
45710	N3315L	Delta AL	32	8/4/67	
45711	OH–LYC	Finnair	14	12/4/66	Was N9684Z before delivery to Air Canada as CF–TLB. Retnd to Douglas DEC–3–68, reg N13694. S MAR–11–71
45712	OH–LYB	Finnair	14	6/1/66	D to Air Canada as CF–TLC. Retnd to Douglas SEP–17–68 L to Trans-Texas from OCT–1–68. L to Southern DEC–22–69. S FEB–13–71
45713	OH–LYA	Finnair	14	10/2/66	D to Air Canada as CF–TLD. Retnd to Douglas SEP–24–68. L to Southern NOV–17–68 to APL–30–69. S to Finnair
45714	N1051T	TWA	14	26/3/66	
45715	N1052T	TWA	14	11/2/66	
45716	N1054T	TWA	14	20/2/66	
45717	I–TIGE	Itavia	15	12/3/66	Returned to Douglas SEP–27–71. S to Itavia DEC–8–71
45718	PH–DNA	KLM	15	25/3/66	*Amsterdam*
45719	PH–DNB	KLM	15	3/4/66	*Brussels*
45720	PH–DNC	KLM	15	2/5/66	*Luxembourg*
45721	PJ–DNC	ALM	15	17/8/66	D to KLM as PH–DND *Hamburg.* S OCT–1–70
45722	PJ–DNA	ALM	15	10/10/66	D to KLM as PH–DNE *Rome.* S NOV–1–68 *Aruba*
45723	PJ–DNB	ALM	15	16/11/66	D to KLM as PH–DNF *Paris.* S NOV–1–68 *Bonaire*
45724	I–TIGI	Itavia	15	29/3/66	Returned to Douglas JAN–7–72. S to Itavia FEB–27–72

Douglas DC-9

C/n	Current Marks	Current Owner/operator	Model Series	Initial Delivery	Remarks
45725	OH–LYD	Finnair	14	22/2/66	D to Air Canada as CF–TLE. Retnd to Douglas SEP–25–68. L to Texas Intnl NOV–10–68. L to Southern NOV–69. S to Finnair
45726	N5726	Texas International	14	17/6/66	D to Air Canada as CF–TLF. Retnd to Douglas and L to Texas Intnl NOV–11–68
45727	N5728	Texas International	14	31/7/66	D to Air Canada as CF–TLG. Retnd to Douglas and L to Texas Intnl NOV–18–68
45728	I–TIGA	Itavia	11	19/12/65	D to Bonanza AL. Retnd to Douglas as N945L MAY–28–69. S OCT–12–71
45729	OH–LYE	Finnair	11	17/1/66	D to Bonanza AL. Retnd to Douglas as N946L MAY–14–69. S to Southern AW FEB–27–70. S JUL–24–71
45730	OH–LYG	Finnair	11	1/7/68	D to Bonanza as N947L. Returned to Douglas JUN–4–69. S to Southern AW FEB–28–70. S OCT–5–71
45731	N8500	Douglas	15	20/7/66	D to Swissair as HB–IFA *Graubunden.* Rtd to Douglas SEP–17–68. S to Dominicana DEC–16–68. Rtd to Douglas JAN–22–70
45732	N199	FAA	15	15/8/66	D to Swissair as HB–IFB *Obwalden.* S to FAA AUG–16–68
45733	N8916E	Eastern AL	31	20/10/67	First long-fuselage Srs 30 FF AUG–1–66
45734	N8917E	Eastern AL	31	23/3/67	
45735	N1054T	TWA	14	21/4/66	
45736	N1055T	TWA	14	26/8/66	
45737	N1056T	TWA	14	12/9/66	
45738	N1057T	TWA	15	11/10/66	
45739	N1058T	TWA	15	28/10/66	
45740	N1059T	TWA	15	16/11/66	
45741	N1060T	TWA	15	29/11/66	
45742	N8901E	Eastern AL	14	26/4/66	
45743	N8902E	Eastern AL	14	13/5/66	L to Texas International MAY–2–72
45744	N8903E	Southern AW	14	19/5/66	D to Eastern AL. S to Southern AW MAY–19–70
45745	N8904E	Southern AW	14	31/5/66	D to Eastern AL. S to Southern AW MAY–26–70
45746	N8905E	Southern AW	14	2/7/66	D to Eastern AL. S to Southern AW JUL–1–70
45747	N8906E	Southern AW	14	19/7/66	D to Eastern AL. S to Southern AW AUG–29–70
45748	N8907E	Southern AW	14	29/8/66	D to Eastern AL. S to Southern AW AUG–31–70
45749	N8908E	Eastern AL	14	11/9/66	
45770	N8909E	Eastern AL	14	7/11/66	
45771	N8910E	Eastern AL	14	27/10/66	
45772	N970Z	Ozark AL	15	25/5/66	
45773	N971Z	Ozark AL	15	10/7/66	

C/n	Current Marks	Current Owner/operator	Model Series	Initial Delivery	Remarks
45774	TC–JAB	THY	32	9/7/69	*Bogazici*
45775	N1061T	TWA	15	20/12/66	
45776	N1062T	TWA	15	22/12/66	
45777	N1063T	TWA	15	19/1/67	WO nr Urbana, Ohio MAR–9–67
45778	N1064T	TWA	15	2/2/67	
45779	N1065T	TWA	15	11/3/67	
45780	N1066T	TWA	15	1/4/67	
45781	N1067T	TWA	15	11/4/67	
45782	N1068T	TWA	15	30/5/67	
45783	N1069T	TWA	15	1/7/67	
45784	N1070T	TWA	15	19/8/67	
45785	XA–SOJ	Aeromexico	15	30/11/66	D to Swissair as HB–IFC *Appenzell A. Rh.* Rtd to Douglas SEP–68 as N1790U. L to Texas Intnl 1969. L to Hawaiian AW 1969. S AUG–70
45786	N968E	Ozark AL	15	11/3/67	D to Swissair as HB–IFD *Glarus.* Rtd to Douglas SEP–68 as N1791U. To Air Panama JUL–8–69 as HP–SOS. S DEC–7–72
45787	N1793U	Air West	15	26/1/67	D to Swissair as HB–IFE *Ticino.* Rtd to Douglas SEP–8–68. L to German-air as D–AMOR *Lovebird.* S to Korean AL JUN–1–70, reg HL–7205. S to Air West DEC–14–72
45788	HB–IFF	Swissair	32	21/10/67	*Fribourg*
45789	HB–IFG	Swissair	32	23/12/67	*Valais*
45790	HB–IFH	Swissair	32	1/3/68	*Opfikon*
45791	HB–IFI	Swissair	32	28/7/68	*Zug*
45792	HB–IFK	Swissair	32	11/9/68	*Kloten*
45793	HB–IFL	Swissair	32	28/9/68	*Appenzell I Rhein*
45794	N9101	West Coast AW	14	16/9/66	WO Portland, Oregon OCT–1–66
45795	N9102	Air West	14	4/11/66	D to West Coast AW
45796	N9103	Air West	14	14/12/66	D to West Coast AW
45797	N8860	Richard M. Scaife	15	29/12/66	Allocated EC–BAX before completion. Leased to Northeast AL as N8953U to mid-67. L to Delta JUL–13–67. S OCT–28–71
45798	N490SA	Ozark AL	15	3/11/66	D to Standard. L by Ozark from OCT–1–68
45799	N491SA	Ozark AL	15	30/11/66	D to Standard. L by Ozark from OCT–1–68 *City of Las Vegas*
45825	N8911E	Eastern AL	14	24/11/66	
45826	CF–TON	Air Canada	15F	7/3/67	D to Continental as N8901. S APL–5–72
45827	N9347	Air West	32	19/7/67	D to Korean AL as HL–7201. S FEB–2–73
45828	N8918	Continental AL	15F	19/1/68	
45829	N8912E	Eastern AL	14	30/11/66	
45830	N8913E	Eastern AL	14	23/12/66	
45831	N8914E	Eastern AL	14	29/12/66	
45832	N8915E	Eastern AL	14	30/12/66	
45833	N8918E	Eastern AL	31	27/1/67	
45834	N8919E	Eastern AL	31	22/2/67	
45835	N8920E	Eastern AL	31	29/3/67	
45836	N8921E	Eastern AL	31	22/3/67	

Douglas DC-9

C/n	Current Marks	Current Owner/operator	Model Series	Initial Delivery	Remarks
45837	N8922E	Eastern AL	31	13/4/67	
45838	N8923E	Eastern AL	31	18/4/67	
45839	N8924E	Eastern AL	31	29/5/67	
45840	N8925E	Eastern AL	31	29/7/67	
45841	N972Z	Ozark AL	15	24/8/66	
45842	N8961	Texas Intnl	14	4/3/66	D to Continental as N8961. Rtd to Douglas JAN–4–68. L to Air California MAR–6–68. S to GATX/Boothe SEP–68. L to TI from MAY–1–69
45843	N8962	Texas Intnl	14	1/5/66	D to Continental as N8962. Rtd to Douglas JAN–7–68. L to Air California MAR–6–68. S to GATX/Boothe SEP–68. L to TI from MAY–69
45844	N949L	Texas Intnl	14	2/6/66	L by Continental from Douglas to 1967 as N8963. D to Bonanza as N949L OCT–31–67. Returned to Douglas MAY–14–72. S MAY–16–72
45845	CF–TLH	Air Canada	32	7/3/67	
45846	CF–TLI	Air Canada	32	12/5/67	
45847	HB–IFM	Swissair	32	17/10/68	*Thurgau*
45863	N8926E	Eastern AL	31	21/6/67	
45864	N8927E	Eastern AL	31	1/7/67	
45865	N8928E	Eastern AL	31	27/7/67	
45866	N8929E	Eastern AL	31	29/7/67	
45867	N8952E	Eastern AL	31	28/3/68	
45868	N8953E	Eastern AL	31	11/4/68	
45869	N8960E	Eastern AL	31	25/6/68	
45870	N8961E	Eastern AL	31	22/6/68	WO Fort Lauderdale, Texas MAY–18–72
45871	N8962E	Eastern AL	31	19/7/68	
45872	N8963E	Eastern AL	31	26/7/68	
45873	N8964E	Eastern AL	31	2/8/68	
45874	N8965E	Eastern AL	31	1/8/68	
45875	N8968E	Eastern AL	31	24/8/68	
45876	N8969E	Eastern AL	31	28/8/68	
47000	YV–C–ANP	LAV	15	8/2/67	D to Saudi Arabian AL as HZ–AEA. S JUN–16–72
47001	N969Z	Ozark AL	15	30/3/67	D to Saudi Arabian AL as HZ–AEB. S JUL–3–72
47002	YV–C–ANV	LAV	15	29/4/67	D to Saudi Arabian AL as HZ–AEC. S JUL–21–72
47003	VH–CZA	Ansett–ANA	31	24/4/67	
47004	VH–CZB	Ansett–ANA	31	11/4/67	
47005	VH–CZC	Ansett–ANA	31	29/8/67	
47006	YV–LEV	LAV	31	23/3/67	D to Pacific Southwest as N981PS. S JAN–28–70
47007	VH–TJJ	TAA	31	18/3/67	*Edmund Kennedy*
47008	VH–TJK	TAA	31	3/5/67	*Douglas Mawson*
47009	VH–TJL	TAA	31	20/8/67	*Angus McMillan*
47010	CF–TOO	Air Canada	15F	11/4/67	D to Continental as N8902. S APL–18–72
47011	CF–TOP	Air Canada	15F	25/4/67	D to Continental as N8903. S MAY–9–72
47012	CF–TOQ	Air Canada	15F	23/5/67	D to Continental as N8904. S JUL–28–72
47013	CF–TOR	Air Canada	15F	26/6/67	D to Continental as N8905. S SEP–22–72
47014	CF–TOS	Air Canada	15F	23/7/67	D to Continental as N8906. S DEC–4–72

C/n	Current Marks	Current Owner/operator	Model Series	Initial Delivery	Remarks
47015	CF–TOT	Air Canada	15F	29/8/67	D to Continental as N8907. S APL–24–73
47016	N9349	Air West	15F	22/9/67	D to Continental as N8909. S APL–16–73
47017	N8911	Continental AL	15F	28/10/67	
47018	N8913	Continental AL	15F	22/11/67	
47019	CF–TLJ	Air Canada	32	21/5/67	
47020	CF–TLK	Air Canada	32	30/5/67	
47021	CF–TLL	Air Canada	32	7/7/67	
47022	CF–TLM	Air Canada	32	27/7/67	
47023	CF–TLN	Air Canada	32	30/8/67	
47024	CF–TLO	Air Canada	32	31/8/67	
47025	N3316L	Delta AL	32	2/5/67	
47026	N3317L	Delta AL	32	14/6/67	
47027	N3318L	Delta AL	32	10/7/67	
47028	N3319L	Delta AL	32	2/8/67	
47029	N3320L	Delta AL	32	1/9/67	
47030	N3321L	Delta AL	32	3/10/67	
47031	N3322L	Delta AL	32	31/10/67	
47032	N3323L	Delta AL	32	30/11/67	
47033	N973Z	Ozark AL	15	31/7/67	
47034	N974Z	Ozark AL	15	1/9/67	L by Air West to OCT–16–68. WO DEC–27–68 Sioux City
47035	N975Z	Ozark AL	15	10/10/67	
47036	N8973E	Eastern AL	31	13/9/68	
47037	EC–BIG	Iberia	32	30/6/67	*Emilio Arrietta,* later *Villa de Madrid*
47038	I–DIKA	Alitalia	32	8/8/67	*Isola di Capri*
47039	I–DIKE	Alitalia	32	1/9/67	*Isola d'Elba*
47040	N931F	Overseas National	32F	10/10/67	*Pioneer*
47041	CF–TMN	Air Canada	32F	7/11/67	D to Overseas National as N932F. S MAY–25–73
47042	N89S	Southern AL	31	29/4/69	
47043	N1302T	Texas Intnl	14	2/2/67	
47044	OH–LYH	Finnair	15F	28/9/67	D to Texas International as N1303T. S MAY–72
47045	OH–LYI	Finnair	15F	9/11/67	D to Texas International as N1304T. S MAY–72
47046	I–DIKI	Alitalia	32	25/9/67	*Isola di Murano*
47047	I–DIKO	Alitalia	32	31/10/67	*Isola di Pantelleria*
47048	XA–DEV	Aeromexico	15	3/7/66	D to Continental AL on L from Douglas as N8964 to JUL–67. L to THY AUG–15–67 *Topkapi.* Returned to Douglas L MAY–1–73
47049	N948L	Air West	14	29/6/66	D to Allegheny on L as N6140A. S to Bonanza JUN–29–67
47050	N970VJ	Allegheny AL	31	2/6/67	
47051	N971VJ	Allegheny AL	31	26/6/67	
47052	N972VJ	Allegheny AL	31	28/7/67	
47053	N970NE	Delta AL	31	5/5/67	D to Northeast, trsfd to Delta
47054	N971NE	Delta AL	31	8/5/67	D to Northeast, trsfd to Delta
47055	N1305T	Texas International	15F	22/11/67	
47056	YV–C–AVM	Avensa	12	28/2/67	L by KLM 1967
47057	N972NE	Delta AL	31	14/6/67	D to Northeast, trsfd to Delta
47058	N973NE	Delta AL	31	16/6/67	D to Northeast, trsfd to Delta
47059	XA–SOA	Aeronaves Mexico	15	30/5/67	*Baja California Star*
47060	YV–C–AVR	LAV	14	10/5/67	D to Avensa. L to VIASA and to PAISA/ALM/Dominicana for pooled ops
47061	N1306T	Texas International	15C	22/12/67	
47062	N1307T	Texas International	15C	26/1/68	
47063	N91S	Southern AW	15	8/5/67	L by Bonanza/Air West

Douglas DC-9

C/n	Current Marks	Current Owner/operator	Model Series	Initial Delivery	Remarks
47064	N925	Southern AW	15	9/6/67	
47065	VH–CZD	Ansett-ANA	31	12/3/68	
47066	N974E	Delta AL	31	14/8/67	D to Northeast, trsfd to Delta
47067	N951N	North Central	31	21/7/67	
47068	CF–TLP	Air Canada	32	31/8/67	
47069	CF–TLQ	Air Canada	32	30/9/67	
47070	CF–TLR	Air Canada	32	30/9/67	
47071	CF–TLS	Air Canada	32	2/11/67	
47072	VH–TJM	TAA	31	8/3/68	*John Roe* later *Robert Towns*
47073	N952N	North Central	31	1/9/67	
47074	N8974E	Eastern AL	31	14/9/68	
47075	N975E	Delta AL	31	25/9/67	D to Northeast, trsfd to Delta
47076	EC–BIH	Iberia	32	19/7/67	*Ciudad de Barcelona*
47077	EC–BII	Iberia	32	14/8/67	*Ciudad de Sevilla* WO La Trauche, France MAR–5–73
47078	N93S	Southern AW	15	28/7/67	
47079	EC–BIJ	Iberia	32	15/9/67	*Santa Cruz de Tenerife*
47080	EC–BIK	Iberia	32	14/9/67	*Las Palmas de Gran Canaria*
47081	N9104	Air West	14	23/8/67	D to West Coast AL
47082	N976E	Delta AL	31	19/10/67	D to Northeast, trsfd to Delta
47083	N953N	North Central	31	5/10/67	
47084	EC–BIL	Iberia	32	11/10/67	*Ciudad de Zaragoza*
47085	XA–SOB	Aeronaves Mexico	15	19/7/67	*Sinaloa*
47086	N8915	Continental AL	15F	1/12/67	
47087	N8917	Continental AL	15F	9/1/68	
47088	EC–BIM	Iberia	32	28/10/67	*Ciudad de Santander*
47089	EC–BIN	Iberia	32	6/11/67	*Palma de Mallorca*
47090	EC–BIO	Iberia	32	7/11/67	*Villa de Bilbao*
47091	EC–BIP	Iberia	32	5/12/67	*Santiago de Compostela*
47092	EC–BIQ	Iberia	32	20/12/67	*Ciudad de Málaga*
47093	EC–BIR	Iberia	32	12/1/68	*Ciudad de Valencia*
47094	HB–IFN	Swissair	32	12/9/67	D to SAS (on L) as SE–DBZ *Keltil.* To Swissair MAY–1–68 *Obwalden*
47095	N977E	Delta AL	31	3/11/67	D to Northeast, trsfd to Delta
47096	N978E	Delta AL	31	4/11/67	D to Northeast, trsfd to Delta
47097	N979E	Delta AL	31	6/11/67	D to Northeast, trsfd to Delta
47098	N8988E	Eastern AL	31	1/6/67	D to Overseas National as N938PR. L to Caribair. S OCT–14–68
47099	N973VJ	Allegheny AL	31	14/11/67	
47100	XA–SOC	Aeronaves Mexico	15	25/8/67	WO Puerta Vallarta JUN–20–73
47101	I–DIKU	Alitalia	32	24/11/67	*Isola d'Ischia*
47102	PH–DNG	KLM	32	21/11/67	*Rotterdam*
47103	N3324L	Delta AL	32	29/11/67	
47104	N3325L	Delta AL	32	19/12/67	
47105	N3326L	Delta AL	32	20/12/67	
47106	N3327L	Delta AL	32	13/1/68	
47107	N3328L	Delta AL	32	12/1/68	
47108	N3329L	Delta AL	32	1/2/68	
47109	N3330L	Delta AL	32	6/2/68	
47110	HB–IFO	Swissair	32	6/10/67	D to SAS (on L) as OY–KGU *Gaut.* To Swissair on AUG–9–68 *Appenzell A. Rhein*
47111	HB–IFP	Swissair	32	7/11/67	D to SAS (on L) as LN–RLS *Lodin.* To Swissair on AUG–20–68 *Glarus*
47112	HB–IFR	Swissair	32	6/12/67	D to SAS (on L) as SE–DBY *Yngve.* To Swissair on AUG–29–68 *Ticino*

C/n	Current Marks	Current Owner/operator	Model Series	Initial Delivery	Remarks
47113	HB–IFS	Swissair	32	20/12/67	D to SAS (on L) as OY–KGW *Ossur.* To Swissair on SEP–6–68 *Grisons* later *Winterthur*
47114	SE–DBX	SAS	41	23/5/68	N8960U before D. *Arnljot*
47115	OY–KGA	SAS	41	28/2/68	*Heming*
47116	LN–RLK	SAS	41	14/5/68	*Erling*
47117	SE–DBW	SAS	41	28/5/68	*Adils Viking*
47118	I–DIKB	Alitalia	32	30/11/67	*Isola di Caprera*
47119	N8975E	Eastern AL	31	19/9/68	
47120	N8990E	Eastern AL	31	12/12/67	D to Caribair as N939PR. S MAY–15–73
47121	N8989E	Eastern AL	31	23/3/68	D to Caribair as N946PR. S MAY–15–73
47122	XA–SOD	Aeronaves Mexico	15	20/12/67	
47123	XA–SOE	Aeronaves Mexico	15	9/2/68	
47124	XA–SOF	Aeronaves Mexico	15	8/2/68	
47125	XA–SOG	Aeronaves Mexico	15	9/10/68	
47126	XA–SOH	Aeronaves Mexico	15	8/11/68	
47127	XA–SOI	Aeronaves Mexico	15	27/11/68	
47128	I–DIKC	Alitalia	32	11/12/67	*Isola di Penza*
47129	I–DIKD	Alitalia	32	25/12/67	*Isola del Giglio*
47130	N974VJ	Allegheny AL	31	8/12/67	
47131	PH–DNH	KLM	32	17/12/67	*Zurich*
47132	PH–DNI	KLM	32	3/1/68	*Istanbul*
47133	PH–DNK	KLM	32	15/1/68	*Copenhagen*
47134	N980NE	Delta AL	31	15/12/67	D to Northeast, trsfd to Delta
47135	N981NE	Delta AL	31	15/1/68	D to Northeast, trsfd to Delta
47136	N982NE	Delta AL	31	24/1/68	D to Northeast, trsfd to Delta
47137	N983NE	Delta AL	31	23/2/68	D to Northeast, trsfd to Delta
47138	N9330	Air West	31	27/5/68	Built as N9105 for West Coast
47139	N8930E	Eastern AL	31	4/10/67	
47140	N8931E	Eastern AL	31	7/12/67	
47141	N8932E	Eastern AL	31	23/12/67	
47142	N8933E	Eastern AL	31	30/12/67	
47143	N8934E	Eastern AL	31	17/1/68	
47144	N8935E	Eastern AL	31	15/1/68	
47145	N8936E	Eastern AL	31	30/1/68	
47146	N975VJ	Allegheny AL	31	28/12/68	
47147	N933F	Overseas National	32F	14/12/67	*Calypso Queen*
47148	N934F	Hawaiian AL	32F	25/1/68	D to ONA. S JUN–13–72
47149	N903H	Hawaiian AL	31	22/11/67	
47150	N905H	Hawaiian AL	31	4/4/68	
47151	N228Z	American Capital Aviation	15	21/4/68	D to Tracinda Investment Corp. S SEP–15–72
47152	CF–TOU	Air Canada	15F	22/9/67	D to Continental as N8908. S MAY–1–73
47153	N8910	Air West	15F	18/10/67	D to Continental as N8910. S JUN–7–73
47154	N8912	Continental AL	15F	28/11/67	
47155	N8914	Continental AL	15F	12/12/67	
47156	N8916	Continental AL	15F	29/12/67	
47157	N8959E	Eastern AL	31	8/6/68	
47158	N8937E	Eastern AL	31	31/1/68	
47159	N954N	North Central	31	2/1/68	WO Chicago DEC–20–72
47160	N955N	North Central	31	16/1/68	
47161	N8938E	Eastern AL	31	2/2/68	
47162	N8939E	Eastern AL	31	17/2/68	
47163	N8940E	Eastern AL	31	15/2/68	
47164	N8941E	Eastern AL	31	19/2/68	
47165	N8942E	Eastern AL	31	22/2/68	
47166	N8943E	Eastern AL	31	25/2/68	
47167	N8944E	Eastern AL	31	27/2/68	
47168	PH–DNS	KLM	32	14/12/68	*Arnhem*

C/n	Current Marks	Current Owner/operator	Model Series	Initial Delivery	Remarks
47169	PH–DNT	KLM	32	16/12/68	*Lisbon*
47170	PH–DNV	KLM	32	19/12/68	*Warsaw*
47171	N906H	Hawaiian AL	31	28/3/69	
47172	N3331L	Delta AL	32	29/2/68	
47173	N3332L	Delta AL	32	18/3/68	
47174	N3333L	Delta AL	32	7/4/68	
47175	N3334L	Delta AL	32	28/4/68	
47176	N3335L	Delta AL	32	25/5/68	
47177	N3336L	Delta AL	32	21/6/68	
47178	OY–KGB	SAS	41	10/6/68	*Toste*
47179	LN–RLC	SAS	41	29/6/68	*Gunnar*
47180	SE–DBU	SAS	41	27/7/68	*Hjalmar*
47181	N8945E	Eastern AL	31	29/2/68	
47182	N8946E	Eastern AL	31	8/3/68	
47183	N8947E	Eastern AL	31	14/3/68	
47184	N8948E	Eastern AL	31	22/3/68	
47185	N8949E	Eastern AL	31	16/3/68	
47186	N8950E	Eastern AL	31	20/3/68	
47187	N8951E	Eastern AL	31	26/3/68	
47188	N8954E	Eastern AL	31	11/4/68	
47189	N8955E	Eastern AL	31	4/5/68	
47190	PH–DNL	KLM	32	24/1/68	*London*
47191	PH–DNM	KLM	33F	30/4/68	*Madrid*
47192	PH–DNN	KLM	33F	17/4/68	N8963U before D. *Vienna*
47193	PH–DNO	KLM	33F	21/5/68	*Oslo*
47194	PH–DNP	KLM	33F	12/6/68	*Athens*
47195	CF–TLT	Air Canada	32	22/3/68	
47196	CT–TLU	Air Canada	32	7/4/68	
47197	CF–TLV	Air Canada	32	7/4/68	
47198	CF–TLW	Air Canada	32	30/4/68	
47199	CF–TLX	Air Canada	32	31/5/68	
47200	CF–TLY	Air Canada	32	11/7/68	
47201	PH–DNW	KLM	32	22/2/69	*Moscow*
47202	VH–CZE	Ansett–ANA	31	2/11/68	
47203	VH–TJN	TAA	31	31/10/68	*Paul Strzelecki*
47204	N94S	Southern AW	15	9/2/68	
47205	N95S	Southern AW	15	9/2/68	
47206	N96S	Southern AW	15	17/6/68	
47207	N984VJ	Allegheny AL	31	17/4/68	
47208	N985VJ	Allegheny AL	31	10/5/68	
47209	N986VJ	Allegheny AL	31	14/6/68	
47210	N987VJ	Allegheny AL	31	12/7/68	
47211	N988VJ	Allegheny AL	31	9/8/68	WO SEP–9–69 Indianapolis
47212	N989VJ	Allegheny AL	31	29/8/68	
47213	TC–JAC	THY	32	13/8/68	*Marmara* WO Adana JAN–21–72
47214	N8956E	Eastern AL	31	10/5/68	
47215	N8957E	Eastern AL	31	23/5/68	
47216	N8958E	Eastern AL	31	25/5/68	
47217	N8966E	Eastern AL	31	16/8/68	
47218	HB–IFX	Swissair	32	21/5/68	D to Sudflug as D–ACEB. S OCT–20–68 *Lausanne*
47219	HB–IFY	Swissair	32	13/6/68	D to Sudflug as D–ACEC. S OCT–22–68 *Bellinzona*
47220	I–DIKF	Alitalia	32F	3/5/68	*Atlante*
47221	N938F	Overseas National	32F	9/5/68	D to Alitalia as I–DIKG *Anteo.* L FEB–10–72
47222	I–DIKJ	Alitalia	32	3/5/68	*Isola di Lipari*
47223	I–DIKL	Alitalia	32	30/4/68	*Isola di Panarea*
47224	I–DIKM	Alitalia	32	25/5/68	*Isola di Tavolara*
47225	I–DIKN	Alitalia	32	27/5/68	*Isola di Nisida*
47226	I–DIKP	Alitalia	32	28/6/68	*Isola di Marettimo*
47227	I–DIKQ	Alitalia	32	29/6/68	*Isola di Stromboli*
47228	I–DIKR	Alitalia	32	9/8/68	*Isola di Torcello*
47229	I–DIKS	Alitalia	32	8/8/68	*Isola di Filicudi*

C/n	Current Marks	Current Owner/operator	Model Series	Initial Delivery	Remarks
47230	I–DIKT	Alitalia	32	18/10/68	*Isola di Ustica*
47231	I–DIKV	Alitalia	32	19/10/68	*Isola di Vulcano*
47232	I–DIKY	Alitalia	32	18/12/68	*Isola d'Alicudi.* L by JAT 1969
47233	I–DIBC	Alitalia	32	19/12/68	*Isola di Lampedusa*
47234	I–DIBD	Alitalia	32	4/1/69	*Isola di Montecristo*
47235	I–DIBJ	Alitalia	32	9/1/69	*Isola di Capraia*
47236	I–DIBQ	Alitalia	32	4/2/69	*Isola di Pianosa*
47237	I–DIBO	Alitalia	32	6/2/69	*Isola di Procida*
47238	I–DIZA	Alitalia	32	14/3/69	*Isola di Palmarola*
47239	YU–AHJ	Inex Adria	32	25/4/69	*Ljubljana.* Built as I–DIZE *Isola di Basiluzzo* for Alitalia
47240	N8919	Continental AL	15F	20/7/68	
47241	67–22583	USAF	32F	13/9/68	USAF C–9A
47242	67–22584	USAF	32F	8/8/68	USAF C–9A
47243	YV–C–AVD	VIASA	32	27/2/69	L from Avensa. WO MAR–16–69, Maracaibo
47244	N90S	Southern AW	31	23/5/69	
47245	N97S	Southern AW	31	20/6/69	WO NOV–15–70 Huntington
47246	N9333	Air West	31	24/6/68	Built as N950L for Bonanza
47247	N9334	Air West	31	17/7/68	
47248	N976Z	Ozark AL	31	26/2/68	
47249	N977Z	Ozark AL	31	19/4/68	
47250	N978Z	Ozark AL	31	10/5/68	
47251	N982PS	Ozark AL	31	24/1/68	D to Pacific Southwest as N982PS. S JUL–14–69
47252	N956N	North Central AL	31	15/4/68	
47253	N957N	North Central AL	31	19/4/68	
47254	N958N	North Central AL	31	30/4/68	
47255	N959N	North Central AL	31	13/5/68	
47256	N960N	North Central AL	31	17/6/68	
47257	N1262L	Delta AL	32	4/10/68	
47258	N1263L	Delta AL	32	10/10/68	
47259	N1264L	Delta AL	32	15/11/68	
47260	N1265L	Delta AL	32	21/11/68	
47261	N1266L	Delta AL	32	19/11/68	
47262	N1267L	Delta,AL	32	23/11/68	
47263	N9331	Air West	31	4/6/68	Built as N9106 for West Coast
47264	N9332	Air West	31	20/6/68	Built as N9107 for West Coast
47265	CF–TLZ	Air Canada	32	10/7/68	
47266	CF–TMA	Air Canada	32	27/7/68	
47267	N8967E	Eastern AL	31	17/8/68	
47268	N8970E	Eastern AL	31	4/9/68	
47269	N8971E	Eastern AL	31	6/9/68	
47270	N8972E	Eastern AL	31	11/9/68	
47271	N8976E	Eastern AL	31	9/10/68	
47272	N8977E	Eastern AL	31	9/10/68	
47273	N3337L	Delta AL	32	25/7/68	
47274	N3338L	Delta AL	32	27/7/68	
47275	N3339L	Delta AL	32	22/8/68	
47276	N3340L	Delta AL	32	14/9/68	
47277	N5341L	Delta AL	32	25/9/68	
47278	N5342L	Delta AL	32	26/9/68	
47279	PH–DNR	KLM	33F	5/7/68	*Stockholm*
47280	N1334U	Southern AW	31	29/6/71	
47281	HB–IFT	Swissair	32	19/12/68	*Rümlang*
47282	HB–IFU	Swissair	32	31/1/69	*Chur*
47283	I–DIKW	Alitalia	32	24/10/68	*Isola di Giannutri*
47284	N1268L	Delta AL	32	26/11/68	
47285	N1269L	Delta AL	32	7/12/68	
47286	OY–KGC	SAS	41	17/8/68	*Helge*

Douglas DC-9

C/n	Current Marks	Current Owner/operator	Model Series	Initial Delivery	Remarks
47287	LN–RLJ	SAS	41	24/8/68	*Stein*
47288	SE–DBT	SAS	41	28/8/68	*Agne*
47289	CF–TMB	Air Canada	32	29/7/68	
47290	CF–TMC	Air Canada	32	29/8/68	
47291	PH–MAN	Martinair	32F	21/7/68	*Karel de Grote*
47292	CF–TMD	Air Canada	32	28/9/68	
47293	CF–TME	Air Canada	32	26/9/68	
47294	CF–TMF	Air Canada	32	4/11/68	
47295	67–22585	USAF	32F	21/8/68	USAF C–9A
47296	67–22586	USAF	32F	24/9/68	USAF C–9A WO Scott AFB, Illinois SEP–16–71
47297	68–8932	USAF	32F	14/10/68	USAF C–9A
47298	68–8933	USAF	32F	27/11/68	USAF C–9A
47299	68–8934	USAF	32F	18/12/68	USAF C–9A
47300	68–8935	USAF	32F	6/2/69	USAF C–9A
47301	LN–RLL	SAS	21	22/3/69	*Guttorm*
47302	OY–KGD	SAS	21	11/12/68	*Ubbe*
47303	SE–DBS	SAS	21	6/1/69	*Svipdag*
47304	LN–RLM	SAS	21	30/1/69	*Reidar.* N1794U before D. Retired from service JAN–30–73
47305	OY–KGE	SAS	21	22/1/69	*Orvar*
47306	SE–DBR	SAS	21	27/2/69	*Skate*
47307	LN–RLO	SAS	21	6/3/69	*Gunder*
47308	OY–KGF	SAS	21	31/3/69	*Rolf*
47309	YV–C–AAA	LAV	14	23/10/68	
47310	N991VJ	Allegheny	31	5/2/69	
47311	I–DIKZ	Alitalia	32	21/10/68	*Isola di Linosa*
47312	EC–BIS	Iberia	32	24/2/68	*Ciudad de Alicante*
47313	EC–BIT	Iberia	32	8/3/68	*Ciudad de San Sebastian*
47314	EC–BIU	Iberia	32	28/3/68	*Ciudad de Oviedo*
47315	N1308T	Texas International	31	10/1/69	
47316	N1309T	Texas International	31	23/1/69	
47317	N1261L	Delta AL	32	9/10/68	
47318	N1270L	Delta AL	32	14/12/68	
47319	N1271L	Delta AL	32	6/2/69	
47320	N1272L	Delta AL	32	19/2/69	
47321	N1273L	Delta AL	32	28/2/69	
47322	N1274L	Delta AL	32	26/2/69	
47323	N1275L	Delta AL	32	3/4/69	
47324	N1276L	Delta AL	32	16/4/69	
47325	VH–CZF	Ansett-ANA	31	10/7/69	
47326	VH–TJO	TAA	31	11/7/69	*William Wentworth*
47327	N8978E	Eastern AL	31	15/10/68	
47328	N8979E	Eastern AL	31	17/10/68	
47329	N8980E	Eastern AL	31	9/11/68	
47330	N8981E	Eastern AL	31	9/11/68	
47331	N8982E	Eastern AL	31	15/11/68	
47332	N993VJ	Allegheny AL	31	27/2/69	
47333	N994VJ	Allegheny AL	31	11/4/69	
47334	N995VJ	Allegheny AL	31	12/5/69	
47335	N996VJ	Allegheny AL	31	14/5/69	
47336	N997VJ	Allegheny AL	31	27/5/69	
47337	N9335	Allegheny AL	31	27/11/68	D to Air West. S MAR–15–73
47338	N9336	Air West	31	26/11/68	
47339	I–DIBN	Alitalia	32	11/1/69	*Isola di Palmaria*
47340	CF–TMG	Air Canada	32	7/11/68	
47341	CF–TMH	Air Canada	32	7/11/68	
47342	CF–TMI	Air Canada	32	27/11/68	
47343	N979Z	Ozark AL	31	25/2/69	
47344	N980Z	Ozark AL	31	27/3/69	
47345	N981Z	Ozark AL	31	21/4/69	
47346	N9337	Air West	31	6/3/69	
47347	N9338	Air West	31	10/4/69	

C/n	Current Marks	Current Owner/operator	Model Series	Initial Delivery	Remarks
47348	CF–TMJ	Air Canada	32	18/12/68	
47349	CF–TMK	Air Canada	32	7/12/68	
47350	CF–TML	Air Canada	32	29/12/68	
47351	6Y–JGA	Air Jamaica	32	23/1/69	D to Air Canada as CF–TMM. L to Air Jamaica MAR–7–69
47352	6Y–JGB	Air Jamaica	32	18/2/69	D to Air Canada as CF–TMN. L to Air Jamaica MAR–7–69
47353	CF–TMO	Air Canada	32	26/3/69	
47354	CF–TMP	Air Canada	32	17/4/69	
47355	I–DIBK	Alitalia	32F	12/2/69	*Ercole*
47356	N1277L	Delta AL	32	18/4/69	
47357	N1278L	Delta AL	32	8/5/69	
47358	N1279L	Delta AL	32	7/5/69	
47359	N1280L	Delta AL	32	23/5/69	
47360	SE–DBP	SAS	21	12/4/69	*Rane*
47361	SE–DBO	SAS	21	1/5/69	*Siger*
47362	N907H	Hawaiian AL	31	9/5/69	
47363	PH–MAO	Martinair	33F	9/2/69	*Desiderius Erasmus*
47364	EC–BPF	Iberia	32	17/4/69	*Ciudad de Almeria*
47365	EC–BPG	Iberia	32	7/6/69	*Ciudad de Vigo*
47366	68–10958	USAF	32F	30/9/69	USAF C–9A
47367	68–10959	USAF	32F	7/11/69	USAF C–9A
47368	EC–BPH	Iberia	31	7/6/69	*Ciudad de Gerona*
47369	N1798U	Hawaiian AL	31	31/10/69	
47370	N1799U	Hawaiian AL	31	30/9/71	L to Allegheny AL, returned JUN–30–73
47371	N978VJ	Allegheny AL	31	12/6/69	
47372	N979VJ	Allegheny AL	31	1/7/69	
47373	N964VJ	Allegheny AL	31	9/9/69	
47374	N965VJ	Allegheny AL	31	9/9/69	
47375	N967VJ	Allegheny AL	31	16/9/69	
47376	N9346	Air West	32	22/7/69	D to Purdue AL as N394PA. S JUL–14–71
47377	N1281L	Delta AL	32	27/5/69	
47378	N1282L	Delta AL	32	2/7/69	
47379	N1283L	Delta AL	32	10/7/69	
47380	N1284L	Delta AL	32	8/8/69	
47381	N1285L	Delta AL	32	3/9/69	
47382	N9339	Air West	31	11/4/69	L by Purdue AL from APL–23–69 to APL–4–71
47383	HB–IFV	Swissair	32	15/10/69	*Bülach*
47384	HB–IFW	Swissair	33F	22/10/69	*Payerne*
47385	PK–GJE	Garuda	32	15/10/69	*Barito*
47386	PK–GJF	Garuda	32	15/11/69	*Kapuas*
47389	N9340	Air West	31	25/4/69	
47390	N9341	Air West	31	13/5/69	
47391	N9342	Air West	31	13/6/69	L to Allegheny AL, returned JUN–28–72
47392	YU–AJB	Inex Adria	32	3/2/69	D to Purdue AL as N393PA. S MAY–18–71
47393	N1335U	Southern AW	31	29/6/71	
47394	N950PB	"Playboy"	32	24/2/69	L to Ozark AL for maintenance and operation
47395	OY–KGG	SAS	41	23/11/69	D to SAS as OY–KGG. L to THAI from JAN–29–70 to OCT–71
47396	LN–RLD	SAS	41	21/12/69	D to SAS as LN–RLR. L to THAI from JAN–27–70 to APL–1–72 *Torleif Viking*
47397	TC–JAK	THY	32	18/8/71	
47399	N8983E	Eastern AL	31	24/1/69	

C/n	Current Marks	Current Owner/operator	Model Series	Initial Delivery	Remarks
47400	N8984E	Eastern AL	31	30/1/69	
47401	N8985E	Eastern AL	31	21/3/69	
47402	N8986E	Eastern AL	31	8/5/69	
47403	N8987E	Eastern AL	31	11/7/69	
47404	N1332U	Hawaiian AL	31	5/11/71	L to Allegheny AL, returned JUN–2–73
47405	N961N	North Central	31	9/5/69	
47406	N962N	North Central	31	23/5/69	
47407	N935F	Overseas National	33F	7/3/69	Initially allocated N915U for Universal AL. L to ALM and WO MAY–2–70, near St Croix
47408	N936F	Overseas National	33F	14/3/69	Initially allocated for Universal AL *Carib Queen*
47409	N937F	Overseas National	33F	23/5/69	*Mistress*
47410	PH–MAR	Martinair	33F	19/4/69	*Jean Monnet*
47411	N983Z	Ozark AL	31	8/12/69	
47412	N984Z	Ozark AL	31	11/12/69	
47413	SE–DBN	SAS	33F	31/7/69	*Sigtrygg*
47414	LN–RLW	SAS	33F	3/10/69	*Rand*
47415	N963N	North Central	31	15/9/69	
47416	N964N	North Central	31	15/9/69	
47417	N965N	North Central	31	31/7/70	
47418	VH–TJP	TAA	31	8/2/70	*Charles Kingsford Smith*
47419	VH–TJQ	TAA	31	20/8/70	
47420	N966VJ	Allegheny AL	31	5/12/69	
47421	N969VJ	Allegheny AL	31	30/3/70	
47422	CF–TMQ	Air Canada	32	28/2/70	
47423	CF–TMR	Air Canada	32	9/4/70	
47424	CF–TMS	Air Canada	32	8/4/70	
47425	YU–AHL	JAT	32	8/5/70	
47426	N1286L	Delta AL	32	19/2/70	
47427	N1287L	Delta AL	32	25/2/70	
47428	EC–BYK	Iberia	33RC	8/8/72	*Ciudad de Badajoz*
47429	N968VJ	Allegheny AL	31	16/9/69	
47430	SH–MOI	East African AW	32	9/12/70	
47431	I–ATIA	ATI	32	24/7/69	
47432	I–DIZI	Alitalia	32	28/8/69	*Isola di Basiluzzo*
47433	I–DIZU	Alitalia	32	15/8/69	*Isola di Bergeggi*
47434	I–DIZB	ATI	32	26/9/69	*Isola di Maddalena* Initially allocated to Alitalia
47435	I–DIZC	ATI	32	15/10/69	*Isola di Meloria.* Initially allocated to Alitalia
47436	I–ATIE	ATI	32	8/10/69	Initially allocated as Alitalia I–DIZF
47437	I–ATIO	ATI	32	27/10/69	Initially allocated as Alitalia I–DIZG
47438	I–ATIU	ATI	32	7/11/69	Initially allocated as Alitalia I–DIZL
47439	N9343	Air West	31	4/5/69	
47440	N9344	Air West	31	4/6/69	
47441	N9345	Air West	31	4/6/69	WO Duarte, California JUN–6–71
47442	TC–JAG	THY	31	24/8/70	
47443	N1288L	Delta	32	10/4/70	FF as N1795U
47444	N1289L	Delta	32	9/4/70	
47445	N1290L	Delta	32	6/5/70	
47446	EC–BQT	Iberia	32	24/12/69	*Villa de Murcia*
47447	EC–BQU	Iberia	32	8/1/70	*Ciudad de la Coruna*
47448	68–10960	USAF	32F	1/12/69	USAF C–9A
47449	68–10961	USAF	32F	31/12/69	USAF C–9A
47450	N941N	North Central AL	31	23/2/70	FF as N179U. D to Atlantis AW as D–ADIT. S JAN–5–73
47451	TC–JAF	THY	32	7/8/70	
47452	EC–BYI	Iberia	32	10/5/72	*Ciudad de Vitoria*

C/n	Current Marks	Current Owner/operator	Model Series	Initial Delivery	Remarks
47453	EC–BQV	Iberia	32	8/1/70	*Ciudad de Ibiza*
47454	EC–BQX	Iberia	32	24/1/70	*Ciudad de Valladolid*
47455	EC–BQY	Iberia	32	18/3/70	*Ciudad de Cordoba*
47456	EC–BQZ	Iberia	32	26/3/70	*Santa Cruz de la Palma*
47457	YU–AJO	Inex Adria	32	1/4/71	D to Atlantis AW as D–ADIN S MAR–13–73
47458	OE–LDF	Austrian Airlines	32	2/12/71	*Salzburg*
47459	N942N	North Central AL	32	15/1/70	D to Atlantis AW as D–ADIS S JAN–2–73
47460	YU–AHV	JAT	32	14/5/71	
47461	EC–BYJ	Iberia	32	9/6/72	*Ciudad de Salamanca*
47462	PH–DNY	KLM	32	17/1/70	*City of Paris*
47463	PK–GJH	Garuda AW	32	5/1/72	
47464	SE–DAN	SAS	41	3/9/70	*Alf Viking*
47465	HB–IDN	Balair	33CF	17/4/70	
47466	N1291L	Delta Airlines	32	14/4/71	
47467	71–874	USAF	32F	17/12/71	USAF C–9A
47468	5Y–ALR	East African AW	32	19/2/71	
47469	YU–AHM	JAT	32	13/5/70	
47470	YU–AHN	JAT	32	15/5/70	
47471	71-875	USAF	32F	10/2/72	USAF C–9A
47472	YU–AHO	JAT	32	8/6/70	
47473	YU–AHP	JAT	32	18/6/70	
47474	I–ATIX	ATI	32	4/12/70	
47475	71-876	USAF	32F	3/3/72	USAF C–9A
47476	PH–DNZ	KLM	33	6/2/70	*City of Rome*
47477	I–ATIK	ATI	32	26/2/71	
47478	5X–UVY	East African AW	32	24/2/71	
47479	HB–IFZ	Swissair	32	18/9/70	*Dubendorf*
47480	HB–IDO	Swissair	32	20/8/70	*Bointrin*
47481	PK–GJG	Garuda AW	32	4/2/71	
47482	UY–AHT	JAT	32	2/2/71	WO near Prague JAN-26-72
47484	OE–LDG	Austrian Airlines	32	11/11/71	*Tirol*
47485	CF–TMX	Air Canada	32	6/7/72	
47486	N1293L	Delta Airlines	32	11/11/71	
47487	N1310T	Texas International	31	19/11/69	
47488	TC–JAD	THY	32	27/8/69	
47489	TC–JAE	THY	32	27/8/69	
47490	N1311T	Texas International	31	17/12/69	
47491	N985Z	Ozark AL	31	25/7/70	
47492	SE–DAK	SAS	41	9/1/70	*Ragnvold Viking*
47493	OY–KGH	SAS	41	16/1/70	*Eiliv Viking*
47494	OY–KGI	SAS	41	15/9/70	*Bent Viking*
47495	71-877	USAF	22F	31/3/72	USAF C–9A
47496	EC–BYM	Iberia	32	19/9/72	*Cangas de Onis*
47497	LN–RLB	SAS	41	1/10/70	*Arne Viking*
47498	SE–DAL	SAS	41	25/1/70	*Algot Viking*
47499	SE–DAM	SAS	41	18/2/70	*Starkad Viking*
47500	HI–177	Dominicana	32	16/12/69	WO Santo Domingo FEB-15-70
47501	VH–CZG	Ansett-ANA	31	13/2/70	
47502	I–DIZE	Alitalia	32	20/2/70	*Isola della Meloria*
47503	YU–AHR	Inex Adria	32	27/4/70	WO near Aden MAR–19–72
47504	EC–BYE	Iberia	32	4/2/72	*Ciudad de Mahon*
47505	N960VJ	Allegheny Airlines	31	11/6/71	
47506	N961VJ	Allegheny Airlines	31	18/11/70	
47507	N962VJ	Allegheny Airlines	31	22/11/70	
47508	N963VJ	Allegheny Airlines	31	14/6/71	
47509	SE–DAO	SAS	41	2/12/71	*Asgant Viking*
47510	OY–KGK	SAS	41	9/12/71	*Ebbe Viking*
47511	LN–RLU	SAS	41	1/12/72	*Eivind Viking*
47512	SE–DAP	SAS	41	5/12/72	*Torgils Viking*
47513	LN–RLX	SAS	41	15/12/72	*Sote Viking*
47514	PH–MAX	Martinair	32	24/2/71	*Europa*
47516	N1294L	Delta Airlines	32	24/6/71	
47517	N908H	Hawaiian Airlines	31	28/4/70	

Douglas DC-9

C/n	Current Marks	Current Owner/operator	Model Series	Initial Delivery	Remarks
47518	I–DIZO	Alitalia	32	16/2/71	*Isola del Tino*
47519	I–DIZF	Alitalia	32	18/2/71	*Isola di Shargi*
47520	OE–LDC	Austrian Airlines	32	10/8/71	*Karnten*
47521	OE–LDA	Austrian Airlines	32	10/6/71	*Niederosterreich*
47522	EC–BYD	Iberia	32	11/6/71	*Arrecife de Lanzarate*
47523	HB–IDP	Swissair	32	20/11/70	*Basel-Land*
47524	OE–LDB	Austrian Airlines	32	8/7/71	*Burgenland*
47525	N1295L	Delta Airlines	32	8/7/71	
47526	VH–CZH	Ansett-ANA	31	28/8/70	
47527	VH–CZI	Ansett-ANA	31	17/2/71	
47528	VH–TJR	TAA	31	5/2/71	
47529	N1292L	Delta Airlines	32	12/5/71	
47530	YU–AHW	Inex Adria	33CF	22/4/71	
47531	OE–LDE	Austrian Airlines	32	9/9/71	*Oberosterreich*
47532	YU–AHU	JAT	32	7/5/71	
47533	I–ATIW	ATI	32	2/12/71	
47534	TC–JAL	THY	32	9/11/71	
47535	HB–IDR	Swissair	32	22/12/70	*Baden*
47536	71–878	USAF	32F	5/5/72	USAF C–9A
47537	71–879	USAF	32F	24/5/72	USAF C–9A
47538	71–880	USAF	32F	30/6/72	USAF C–9A
47539	OE–LDD	Austrian Airlines	32	26/8/71	*Steiermark*
47540	71–881	USAF	32F	27/7/72	USAF C–9A
47541	71–882	USAF	32F	18/8/72	USAF C–9A
47542	EC–BYF	Iberia	32	21/2/72	*Ciudad de Granada*
47543	EC–BYG	Iberia	32	29/2/72	*Ciudad de Pamplona*
47544	I–ATIJ	ATI	32	18/10/72	
47545	EC–BYL	Iberia	eeRC	29/8/72	*Ciudad de Albacete*
47546	CF–TMT	Air Canada	32	21/3/72	
47547	VH–CZJ	Ansett-ANA	31	29/3/71	
47548	VH–CZK	Ansett-ANA	31	19/7/71	
47549	VH–CZL	Ansett-ANA	31	17/11/71	
47550	VH–TJS	TAA	31	1/4/71	
47551	VH–TJT	TAA	31	27/7/71	
47552	VH–TJU	TAA	31	14/10/71	
47553	I–ATIH	ATI	32	9/12/71	
47554	CF–TMU	Air Canada	32	20/4/72	
47555	OE–LDH	Austrian Airlines	32	17/7/72	*Vorarlberg*
47556	EC–BYH	Iberia	32	10/4/72	*Ciudad de Cadiz*
47557	CF–TMV	Air Canada	32	17/5/72	
47559	OE–LDI	Austrian Airlines	32	30/8/72	*Wien*
47560	CF–TMW	Air Canada	32	14/6/72	
47561	PK–GJI	Garuda AW	32	21/9/72	
47562	YU–AJH	JAT	32	12/2/73	
47563	YU–AJI	JAT	32	28/2/73	
47564	N950VJ	Allegheny AL	31	6/2/73	
47565	EC–BYN	Iberia	33RC	7/10/72	*Ciudad de Caceres*
47466	N949N	North Central AL	31	10/4/72	
47567	YU–AJJ	JAT	32	19/3/73	
47568	YU–AJK	JAT	32	6/4/73	
47569	PK–GJJ	Garuda AW	32	16/1/73	
47570	YU–AJF	Pan Adria	32	16/5/73	
47571	YU–AJL	JAT	32	21/5/73	
47573	N967N	North Central AL	31	15/5/73	
47574	N952VJ	Allegheny Airlines	31	17/4/73	
47575	I–ATIY	ATI	32	13/12/72	
47576	N951VJ	Allegheny Airlines	31	22/1/73	
47577	159113	USN	32F	8/5/73	USN C–9B
47578	159119	USN	32F	17/8/73	USN C–9B
47579	YU–AJN	Inex Adria	32	10/5/73	
47581	159117	USN	32F	8/5/73	USN C–9B
47582	YU–AJM	JAT	32	31/7/73	
47583	N953VJ	Allegheny Airlines	31	20/6/73	
47584	159114	USN	32F	13/6/73	USN C–9B
47585	159118	USN	32F	3/7/73	USN C–9B

C/n	Current Marks	Current Owner/operator	Model Series	Initial Delivery	Remarks
47587	159115	USN	32F	26/7/73	USN C–9B
47590	N954VJ	Allegheny Airlines	31	24/8/73	

Douglas DC-10

C/n	Current Marks	Current Owner/operator	Model Series	Initial Delivery	Remarks
46500	N101AA	American Airlines	10	8/12/72	
46502	N102AA	American Airlines	10	27/6/72	
46503	N103AA	American Airlines	10	29/7/71	
46504	N104AA	American Airlines	10	17/9/71	
46505	N105AA	American Airlines	10	9/11/71	
46506	N106AA	American Airlines	10	10/12/71	
46507	N107AA	American Airlines	10	15/12/71	
46508	N108AA	American Airlines	10	31/1/72	
46509	N109AA	American Airlines	10	21/1/72	
46510	N110AA	American Airlines	10	28/2/71	
46511	N111AA	American Airlines	10	15/3/72	
46512	N112AA	American Airlines	10	30/3/72	
46513	N113AA	American Airlines	10	20/4/72	
46514	N114AA	American Airlines	10	17/5/72	
46515	N115AA	American Airlines	10	26/5/72	
46516	N116AA	American Airlines	10	14/7/72	
46517	N117AA	American Airlines	10	21/7/72	
46518	N118AA	American Airlines	10	30/7/72	
46519	N119AA	American Airlines	10	12/8/72	
46520	N120AA	American Airlines	10	25/8/72	
46521	N121AA	American Airlines	10	1/9/72	
46522	N122AA	American Airlines	10	18/9/72	
46523	N123AA	American Airlines	10	20/10/72	
46524	N124AA	American Airlines	10	17/11/72	
46525	N125AA	American Airlines	10	19/12/72	
46550	PH–DTA	KLM	30		*Johann Sebastian Bach*
46551	PH–DTB	KLM	30	3/12/72	*Ludwig von Beethoven*
46552	PH–DTC	KLM	30	6/2/73	*Frederic Francais Chopin* L to Garuda
46553	PH–DTD	KLM	30	28/2/73	*Maurice Ravel*
46554	PH–DTE	KLM	30	9/3/73	*Wolfgang Amadeus Mozart*
46555	PH–DTF	KLM	30	13/4/73	*Giueseffe Verdi*
46575	HB–IHA	Swissair	30	30/11/72	*St Gallen*
46576	HB–IHB	Swissair	30	5/2/73	*Schaffhansen*
46577	HB–IHC	Swissair	30	11/9/73	*Luzern*
46600	N1801U	United Airlines	10	25/5/72	
46601	N1802U	United Airlines	10	29/7/71	
46602	N1803U	United Airlines	10	3/6/72	
46603	N1804U	United Airlines	10	27/9/71	
46604	N1805U	United Airlines	10	29/10/71	
46605	N1806U	United Airlines	10	23/12/71	
46606	N1807U	United Airlines	10	20/12/71	
46607	N1808U	United Airlines	10	27/2/72	
46608	N1809U	United Airlines	10	5/3/72	
46609	N1810U	United Airlines	10	20/4/72	
46610	N1811U	United Airlines	10	25/4/72	
46611	N1812U	United Airlines	10	27/4/72	
46612	N1813U	United Airlines	10	27/5/72	
46613	N1814U	United Airlines	10	24/6/72	
46614	N1815U	United Airlines	10	7/7/72	
46615	N1816U	United Airlines	10	30/1/73	
46616	N1817U	United Airlines	10	22/3/73	
46617	N1818U	United Airlines	10	9/4/73	
46700	N60NA	National Airlines	10	1/11/71	
46701	N61NA	National Airlines	10	19/11/71	
46702	N62NA	National Airlines	10	21/12/71	
46703	N63NA	National Airlines	10	12/1/72	
46704	TC–JAV	THY	10	10/12/72	
46705	TC–JAU	THY	10	1/12/72	
46706	N64NA	National Airlines	10	10/5/72	
46707	N65NA	National Airlines	10	13/10/72	
46708	N66NA	National Airlines	10	30/11/72	
46709	N67NA	National Airlines	10	12/12/72	

C/n	Current Marks	Current Owner/operator	Model Series	Initial Delivery	Remarks
46710	N68NA	National Airlines	10	12/12/72	
46711	N80NA	National Airlines	30	11/6/73	*Tammy*
46712	N81NA	National Airlines	30	18/6/73	*Renee*
46750	N141US	Northwest Airlines	40	13/6/73	
46751	N142US	Northwest Airlines	40	19/2/73	
46752	N143US	Northwest Airlines	40	10/11/72	
46753	N144US	Northwest Airlines	40	12/12/72	
46754	N145US	Northwest Airlines	40	31/1/73	
46755	N146US	Northwest Airlines	40	9/5/73	
46756	N147US	Northwest Airlines	40	2/6/73	
46757	N148US	Northwest Airlines	40	6/7/73	
46758	N149US	Northwest Airlines	40	25/7/73	
46759	N150US	Northwest Airlines	40	31/7/73	
46801	N102TV	Trans International	30CF	10/5/73	
46802	N103TV	Trans International	30CF	6/7/73	
46806	N101TV	Trans International	30CF	27/4/73	
46825	N1031F	Overseas National AL	30CF	1/5/73	*Holidayliner America*
46826	N1032F	Overseas National AL	30CF	30/6/73	*Holidayliner Freedom*
46850	F–BTDB	UTA	30	18/2/73	
46851	F–BTDC	UTA	30	19/2/73	
46852		UTA	30	1/5/73	FF as N54629
46890	TU–TAL	Air Afrique	30	29/2/73	
46900	N68041	Continental Airlines	10	14/4/72	
46901	N68042	Continental Airlines	10	22/5/72	
46902	N68043	Continental Airlines	10	19/5/72	
46903	N68044	Continental Airlines	10	9/6/72	
46904	N68045	Continental Airlines	10	23/6/72	
46905	G–AZZC	Laker Airways	10	26/10/72	
46906	G–AZZD	Laker Airways	10	16/11/72	
46907	TC–JAY	THY	10	26/2/73	
46908	N901WA	Western Airlines	10	27/4/73	
46925	EC–CBN	Iberia	30	20/3/73	*Costa Brava*
46926	EC–CBO	Iberia	30	19/5/73	*Costa del Sol*
46927	EC–CBP	Iberia	30	29/5/73	*Costa Dorada*
46928	N902WA	Western Airlines	10	12/6/73	
46929	N903WA	Western Airlines	10	27/6/73	
46930	N904WA	Western Airlines	10	25/7/73	
47800	N68046	Continental Airlines	10	12/4/73	
47801	N68047	Continental Airlines	10	10/5/73	
47802	N68048	Continental Airlines	10	23/5/73	
47846	ZK–NZL	Air New Zealand	30	11/1/73	
47847	ZK–NZM	Air New Zealand	30	14/9/73	
47861	I–DYNA	Alitalia	30	6/2/73	*Galileo Galilei*
47862	I–DYNE	Alitalia	30	21/3/73	*Dante Alighieri*
47683	I–DYNI	Alitalia	30	20/4/73	*Michelangelo Buonarroti*
47886	–	Air Zaire	30	12/6/73	
47906	OO–SLA	Sabena	30CF	18/9/73	
47965	N601DA	Delta Airlines	10	10/10/72	
47966	N602DA	Delta Airlines	10	10/11/72	
47967	N603DA	Delta Airlines	10	28/11/72	
47968	N604DA	Delta Airlines	10	6/1/73	
47969	N605DA	Delta Airlines	10	16/2/73	
–	OO–SLB	Sabena	30CF	–	
–	PH–MBG	Martinair	30CF	–	*Kohoutek*
–	PH–DTG	KLM	30	–	To be L to VIASA
–	PH–DTH	KLM	30	–	To be L to VIASA
–	PP–VMA	Varig	30	–	
–	PP–VMB	Varig	30	–	
–	SE–DEA	SAS	30	–	
–	SE–DEB	SAS	30	–	
–	LN–RKA	SAS	30	–	
–	LN–RKB	SAS	30	–	
–	D–ADAO	Lufthansa	30	11/12/73	
–	D–ADBO	Lufthansa	30	–	
–	D–ADCO	Lufthansa	30	–	
–	D–ADDO	Lufthansa	30	–	

Douglas DC-10

C/n	Current Marks	Current Owner/operator	Model Series	Initial Delivery	Remarks
–	D–ADFO	Lufthansa	30	–	
–	D–ADGO	Lufthansa	30	–	
–	D–ADHO	Lufthansa	30	–	
–	D–ADJO	Lufthansa	30	–	
–	D–ADKO	Lufthansa	30	–	
–	I–DYNO	Alitalia	30	–	*Benvenuto Cellini*
–	I–DINB	Alitalia	30	–	*Giotto di Bondone*
–	I–DINU	Alitalia	30	–	*Gugliemo Marconi*
–	HB–IHD	Swissair	30	–	*Bern*
–	HB–IHE	Swissair	30	–	*Vaud*
–	HB–IHF	Swissair	30	–	*Nidwalden*

Fairchild F-27

C/n	Current Marks	Current Owner/operator	Model Series	Initial Delivery	Remarks
1	HC–ADV	AREA	F–27	26/6/59	Proto, FF APR–12–58 as N1027. WO in AREA service NOV–7–60 nr Quito
2	N4303F	Omni Aircraft Sales	F–27	10/4/59	FF as N2027. D to Trans Mar de Cortes as XA–MOT. S. to Ozark AL. S OCT–12–67
3	N2701	Air West	F–27	24/7/58	D to West Coast AL
4	PI–C–892	Air Manila	F–27	10/6/58	D to Piedmont as N2700R *Peninsula.* S to Fairchild Hiller JUL–3–67. S 1970
5	N2702	John Erickson Associates	F–27	8/11/58	D to West Coast AL later Air West, S MAY–20–70 to Southeast AL. S to J. Erickson
6	N2703	West Coast AL	F–27	8/8/58	WO Great Salt Lake JAN–17–73
7	N2704	John Erickson Associates	F–27	14/8/58	D to West Coast AL later Air West. S MAY–20–70 to Southeast AL. S to J. Erickson
8	PI–C–873	Air Manila	F–27	1/10/58	D to Piedmont as N2701R *Old Dominion.* S AUG–28–67
9	PI–C–872	Air Manila	F–27	6/10/58	D to Piedmont as N2702R *Cape Fear.* S JUN–9–67
10	PI–C–875	Air Manila	F–27	20/10/58	D to Piedmont as N2703R *Catawba.* S DEC–1–67
11	CF–QBA	Quebecair	F–27	17/9/58	
12	YV–C–EVH	Avensa	F–27	18/9/58	WO Margarita Is. FEB–25–62
13	N4304F	Mountain West AL	F–27	25/9/58	D to Avensa as YV–C–EVK. S to Ozark AL as N4304F. S SEPT–21–67 to Carco. S to Mountain West NOV–30–72
14	CF–QBZ	Quebecair	F–27	6/10/58	
15	N4903	Wien Consolidated	F–27B	28/10/58	D to Northern Consolidated *Carl Ben Eielson*
16	N2705	Air West	F–27	23/10/58	D to West Coast AL
17	PI–C–874	Air Manila	F–27	31/10/58	D to Piedmont *Palmetto.* S. MAY–4–67
18	PI–C–871	Air Manila	F–27	31/10/58	D to Piedmont as N2705R *Kitty Hawk*. S NOV–3–67 WO Panay Is MAR–9–68
19	PI–C–870	Air Manila	F–27	26/11/58	D to Piedmont as N2706R *Cumberland.* S 1967
20	PI–C–893	Air Manila	F–27	26/11/58	D to Piedmont as N2707R *James River.* S to Fairchild Hiller OCT–20–67. S 1969
21	N4904	Wien Consolidated	F–27B	26/11/58	D to Northern Consolidated
22	N2706	Air West	F–27	12/12/58	D to West Coast AL
23	N5G	General Tire & Rubber	F–27A	29/11/58	Cvtd to F–27F
24	N2708	Air West	F–27	5/12/58	D to Avensa as YV–C–EVS. S 1963 to West Coast AL
25	N4305F	Omni Aircraft Sales	F–27	3/12/58	D to Avensa as YV–C–EVP. S 1963 to Ozark as N4305F. S to Fairchild Hiller AUG–29–67. S to Omni

Fairchild F-27

C/n	Current Marks	Current Owner/operator	Model Series	Initial Delivery	Remarks
26	N2709	Mouldings Inc	F–27	5/12/58	D to Avensa as YV–C–EVQ. S 1963 to West Coast AL S to Mouldings Inc.
27	CF–QBD	Quebecair	F–27	30/12/58	D to Reynolds Metal as N994. S to Yale University, then to Frdk. Ayer
28	N2740	Air West	F–27A	13/1/59	D to Continental Can as N1500. S to Miami Avn as N15001. L to Aspen AL.L to West Coast 1966. L to Pacific AL 1967
29	N745L	Bonanza AL	F–27A	16/1/59	D as N145L. WO NOV–15–64
30	N781R	Bank of Nevada	F–27A	17/1/59	D to Bank of Mexico as XC–CAT; changed to APO–203. *Insurgente* for presidential use. S to Bonanza as N781R; L to Sudflug MAR–29–66 to 1967 as D–BFOK. L to Pacific AL as N781R, 1967. L to Carco Air Service. Returned to Bank of Nevada
31	N1924	Ideal Cement	F–27A	13/1/59	Cvtd to F–27F *Keva III*
32	N2707	West Coast AL	F–27	8/5/59	D H. K. Porter as N3027. S to WCA 1962; WO AUG–24–63
33	N44R	Ross Aviation	F–27A	10/4/59	D Butler; S Pepsi Cola, Cvtd to F–27F S to Carco, reg. N1004. S. Ross Aviation
34	N65A	Noland Co	F–27F	4/2/59	Cvtd to F–27F JUL–1973
35	N768RL	Lawrence Radiation Laboratory	F–27	5/2/59	Was N1000L. Cvtd to F–27F S to Westinghouse Electric as N291WX. S to LPI Leasing Corp 1968. To Wells Fargo Bank 1968 S to Lawrence
36	N2770R	Pacific AL	F–27A	19/2/59	WO MAY–7–64
37	N746L	Air West	F–27A	17/2/59	D to Bonanza as N146L, later reregistered
38	N747L	Air West	F–27A	26/2/59	D to Bonanza as N147L, later reregistered
39	N2708R	Wien Alaska AW	F–27A	22/5/59	
40	N3225	Fred B. Ayer Associates	F–27	15/5/59	D to Aloha as N5095A. L West Coast 1964. S 1968 to Quebecair as CF–QBE. S 1969 S to F.B. Ayer
41	N200KC	Kimberley-Clark Corp	F–27A	13/3/59	Cvtd to F–27F
42	N184K	Indiana University	F–27A	25/3/59	Cvtd to F–27F S to Champion Spark Plug, reg. N1823A. S to Indiana U.
43	N2771R	Air West	F–27A	2/4/59	D to Pacific AL
44	N2772R	Air West	F–27A	18/4/59	D to Pacific AL. L to Bonanza 1964
45	N2HB	Hubbard Broadcasting	F–27A	23/4/59	D to Johns Manville Corp, reg. N25JM. S to Hubbard
46	PI–C–895	Air Manila	F–27	17/4/59	D to Aloha as N5093A. S DEC–13–63 to West Coast AL, reg N2710 S to Air Manila. WO Manila SEP–1973
47	CF–QBL	Quebecair	F–27	27/7/59	

C/n	Current Marks	Current Owner/operator	Model Series	Initial Delivery	Remarks
48	N753L	Air West	F–27	2/6/61	Was demonstrator N2712. S to Bonanza as N753L. S to Southeast AL. S to Air West MAY–17–70
49	N4905	Wien Consolidated	F–27B	30/4/59	D to Northern Consolidated WO DEC–2–68, Fox Lake
50	PI–C–894	Air Manila	F–27	8/5/59	D to Aloha as N5094A. S NOV–22–63 to West Coast AL, reg N2711. S to Air Manila
51	N2773R	Norcanair	F–27A	28/5/59	D to Pacific AL S to Air West. S to Norcanair
52	N2774R	Air West	F–27A	11/6/59	D to Pacific AL
53	N2775R	Air West	F–27A	24/6/59	D to Pacific AL
54	N757L	Bonanza AL	F–27A	22/6/59	D toRaytheon as N200R. S. Bonanza as N157L and re-numbered WO APR–18–65
55	N2710R	Wien Alaska	F–27A	30/6/59	
56	N42N	Forke Brothers	F–27A	21/7/59	D as N42N to Union Carbide Re-reg. N42NL S to Forke Bros.
57	N46K	Koppers Co	F–27A	20/1/60	D as N27C to Murray Corp
58	N4300F	Universal Resources Co	F–27	16/7/59	D to Ozark. S NOV–30–66 to Fairchild Hiller. L to Interior 1968 S to Universal
59	N49UC	Union Camp	F–27	13/8/59	D to Ozark. S OCT–30–67. L by Air West 1969, reg. N4301F. S to Union Camp
60	N4302F	Cavanaugh Committees Corp	F–27	12/8/59	D to Ozark. S SEP–28–67 S Omni Aircraft Sales. S Cavanaugh
61	N2742R	Qualitron Aero	F–27	13/8/59	Was N27R D to Reynolds Tobacco. S to Qualitron
62	N748L	Air West	F–27A	17/8/59	D to Bonanza as N148L, later reregistered
63	N749L	Air West	F–27A	17/8/59	D to Bonanza as N149L, later reregistered
64	N270VR	John Whitney	F–27A	3/10/59	Cvtd to F–27F
65	N750L	Air West	F–27A	15/10/59	D to Bonanza as N150L, later reregistered
66	N42Q	Union Carbide	F–27A	12/11/59	Cvtd to F–27F
67	YV–P–APZ	Orinoco Mining Co	F–27A	19/11/59	Cvtd to F–27F D to US Steel reg N12500 S to Orinoco
68	N276AB	Alton Box Board Co	F–27A	1/12/59	D to Reynolds Metal. Cvtd to F–27F S to Lockheed, reg. N5503L. S to Alton
69	N31LG	Landis-Gardner	F–27A	7/1/61	Was demonstrator N1027. Cvtd to F–27F
70	N758L	Air West	F–27A	8/4/60	D as N1X to Olin Mathieson. Was N620M then N6200S before S to Bonanza DEC–8–64
71	N906L	Westinghouse Electric	F–27A	30/1/60	Was N1100L. Cvtd to F–27F as N292WX
72	CF–LWN	Abitibi Aviation	F–27	4/2/60	
73	N2712	West Coast AL	F–27	16/2/60	D as N5096A to Aloha. WO Klamath Falls, Or, MAR–10–67
74	N2614	Mobil Oil Corp	F–27A	7/3/60	D to Union Carbine as N38N, later N3802, S. 1969
75	HL–5205	Korean AL	F–27	14/3/60	D to Aloha AL as N5097A. S 1970 WO

Fairchild F-27

C/n	Current Marks	Current Owner/operator	Model Series	Initial Delivery	Remarks
76	N2709R	Wien Alaska	F–27A	16/6/61	D as N2X to Olin Mathieson; re-numbered N630M. S to Fairchild Hiller, Cvtd to F–27F. L to Wien Alaska 1966 as N6301. S to Wien Alaska 1967
77	N751L	Air West	F–27A	6/5/60	D to Bonanza as N151L, later reregistered
78	N752L	Air West	F–27A	14/5/60	D to Bonanza as N152L, later reregistered
79	N1911B	Gates Rubber	F–27F	13/3/61	
80	HL–5203	Korean AL	F–27	26/5/60	D to Aloha AL as N5098A. S 1970
81	TC–KOC	THY	F–27	1/7/60	
82	TC–KOD	THY	F–27	19/7/60	
83	TC–KOP	THY	F–27	26/7/60	WO Mt. Medetsiz, MAR–8–62
84	CF–POH	Quebec Provincial Government	F–27F	29/3/61	D to IBM. S 1970 to Omni Investment, reg N1410 S to Quebec Provincial Govt.
85	N172C	Brown and Root Inc	F–27F	12/4/61	D to Cameron Iron Works
86	TC–KOR	THY	F–27	3/7/61	
87	TC–KOZ	THY	F–27	12/7/61	
88	N9090	W. E. Walker Stores	F–27F	14/11/61	D to IBM. S 1970
89	CF–SHA	Shell Canada	F–27F	31/10/62	Was demonstrator N27C. S to Champion Oil & Refining Co. S to Scott Paper, reg N472SP. S to Shell Canada
90	APO204	Bank of Mexico	F–27F	20/2/62	FF as N2719R
91	N754L	Air West	F–27A	5/4/62	D to Bonanza as N154L, later reregistered
92	N755L	Air West	F–27A	1/5/62	D to Bonanza as N155L, later re-registered
93	N16R	National Convenience Stores	F–27F	29/5/62	Was N2720R before delivery to Reynolds Tobacco as N16R. S to Eastex. S to National Convenience Stores
94	CF–BNX	Mackenzie Air Ltd	F–27F	7/7/62	D to Norfolk & Western Rlwy as N227W. S 1967 to Greyhound Leasing & Financial as CF-BNX. S to Mackenzie Air
95	N44R	Rockwell Mfg Corp	F–27F	18/10/62	
96	N228X	AFLC Inc	F–27F	20/9/63	Was N227K. S to Kratter Corps. S to W R Grace
97	N20W	AFLC Inc	F–27F	3/7/63	D to Cluett Peabody as N2724R. S to C J Langen-felder & Sons Inc. S 1968
98	N756L	Air West	F–27F	8/5/63	Was N2725R. D to Bonanza as N156L, later reregistered
99	N630TL	Time & Life	F–27F	21/1/64	D to Wayfarer-Ketch, reg. N2726R. S to Time & Life
100	N471SP	Scott Paper	F–27F	12/3/64	Was N2727R
101	N3M	3M Co	F–27F	2/12/63	FF as N2728R
102	N63M	3M Co	F–27F	12/12/63	FF as N2729R
103	N2776R	Air West	F–27A	16/3/64	FF as N2730R. D to Pacific AL
104	N2777R	Air West	F–27A	4/3/64	FF as N2731R. D to Pacific AL

C/n	Current Marks	Current Owner/operator	Model Series	Initial Delivery	Remarks
105	N2778R	Air West	F–27A	4/3/64	FF as N2732R. D to Pacific AL
106	N2779R	Air West	F–27A	23/3/64	FF as N2733R. D to Pacific AL
107	N1782	Air West	F–27	25/10/63	N2734R before D to Ozark as N4306F. S NOV–9–67 to Pacific AL as N1782
108	N759L	Air West	F–27A	25/5/65	D to Bonanza
109	CF–IOG	Imperial Oil Co	F–27F	4/6/65	
110	N966P	Phillips Petroleum	F–27F	5/6/65	
111	N2701J	Allegheny AL	F–27J	30/10/65	
112	N1823G	Champion Spark Plug	F–27J	31/7/65	
113	CF–GND	Great Northern AW	F–27J	30/10/65	D to Allegheny as N2702J. L to GKA 1968. WO 1968 Inuvik, NWT
114	N2703J	Allegheny AL	F–27J	5/11/65	L to Great Northern as CF–GNG from JUL–12–68 WO DEC–1969
115	N2704J	Allegheny AL	F–27J	24/11/65	
116	N2705J	Allegheny AL	F–27J	30/11/65	
117	N2706J	Allegheny AL	F–27J	8/12/65	
118	N2707J	Allegheny AL	F–27J	23/12/65	D to Allegheny as N2707J. L to GNA 1970 Returned to Allegheny 1973
119	N2708J	Allegheny AL	F–27J	12/1/66	
120	N2709J	Allegheny AL	F–27J	31/12/65	
121	N2710J	Allegheny AL	F–27J	8/2/66	
122	N994	Reynolds Metal Co	F–27F	23/2/66	
123	NI–	Eastex	F–27F		WO 1968
124	N516T	Tenneco	F–27J		
125	CF–PAP	Stanair	F–27J		WO FEB–1969
126	N517T	Commonwealth Plan Inc	F–27J		
127	CP–862	LAB	F–27M		FF as N2736R
128	CP–863	LAB	F–27M		

Fairchild FH-227

C/n	Current Marks	Current Owner/operator	Model Series	Initial Delivery	Remarks
501	N2227L	Fairchild-Hiller	FH-227		Prototype. FF JAN-27-66
502	N2227F	Tenneco Inc.	FH-227		Executive demonstrator. S to ERA. S to Zapata Morness. S to Tenneco
503	N7801M	World Aviation Services	FH-227		D to Mohawk as N7801M *Albany*. Rtd to Fairchild S World Aviation
504	N374NE	Delta AL	FH-227C	13/7/66	D to Northeast AL. Now merged with Delta
505	CF–NAI	Nordair	FH-227C	13/7/66	D to Mohawk as N7802M. Rtd to Fairchild and L to Paraense 1967, as PP-BUK S to Nordair
506	N375NE	Delta AL	FH-227C	31/8/66	S to Nordair
507	N376NE	Delta AL	FH-227	14/9/66	S to Nordair
508	CF–NAJ	Nordair	FH-227	28/6/66	D to Mohawk as N7803M *Syracuse*. Rtd to Fairchild SEP–14–67. S to Nordair.
509	N7804M	Bahamais Air Holdings	FH-227	5/8/66	D to Mohawk as N7804M *Watertown*. Rtd to Fairchild APR-12-67 and L to Northeast JUN-11-68 to SEP-69. S to Bahamais
510	N377NE	Delta AL	FH-227C	15/10/66	D to Northeast AL. Now merged with Delta.
511	HC–AYM	Texaco Petroleum Co	FH-227	30/8/66	D to Mohawk as N7805M *Glen Falls*. Rtd to Fairchild OCT-26-67. S to Texaco.
512	N378NE	Delta AL	FH-227C	2/11/66	WO JUL-1973
513	N4215	Ozark AL	FH-227B	5/8/66	WO JUL-1973
514	N4216	Ozark AL	FH-227B	24/8/66	
515	N7806M	Allegheny AL	GH-227B	30/9/66	*Plattsburg* D to Mohawk AL.Now merged with Allegheny
516	N379NE	Delta AL	FH-227B	2/12/66	D to Northeast AL. Now merged with Delta
517	N380NE	Delta AL	FH-227B	23/12/66	WO Lebanon OCT-25-68
518	N7807M	Allegheny AL	FH-227B	29/10/66	*Ithaca*. D to Mohawk AL. Now merged with Allegheny.
519	CF–NAK	Nordair	FH-227B		S to Nordair
520	N4217	Ozark AL	FH-227B	6/10/66	
521	N4218	Ozark AL	FH-227B	30/11/66	
522	VP–BDL	Bahamas Air	FH-227B	19/11/66	*Saranac Lake*. L to Bahamais
523	N702U	Piedmont AL	FH-227B	4/11/66	*Buckeye*
524	N701U	Piedmont AL	FH-227B	30/11/66	*Appomatox*
525	N7809M	Allegheny AL	FH-227B	12/12/66	D to Mohawk AL. Now merged with Allegheny.
526	N4219	Ozark AL	FH-227B	20/12/66	
527	N4221	Ozark AL	FH-227B	1/1/67	
528	N7810M	Allegheny AL	FH-227B	22/12/66	*Ogdensburg*. D to Mohawk AL. Now merged with Allegheny.
529	N4220	Ozark AL	FH-227B	29/12/66	
530	N703U	Piedmont AL	FH-227B	19/1/67	*Peninsula*.
531	N7811M	Mohawk AL	FH-227B	14/1/67	*Burlington*. WO NOV-19-69 Mt Pilot Knob
532	N7812M	Allegheny AL	FH-227B	30/1/67	D to Mohawk AL. Now merged with Allegheny

C/n	Current Marks	Current Owner/operator	Model Series	Initial Delivery	Remarks
533	N7813M	Allegheny AL	FH-227B	18/2/67	*Erie* D to Mohawk AL. Now merged with Allegheny.
534	N7814M	Allegheny AL	FH-227B	2/3/67	D to Mohawk AL. Now merged with Allegheny.
535	N4222	Ozark AL	FH-227B	10/2/67	
536	N7815M	Allegheny AL	FH-227B	23/3/67	*Utica* D to Mohawk AL. Now merged with Allegheny
537	N7816M	Allegheny AL	FH-227B		*Worcester* D to Mohawk AL. Now merged with Allegheny
538	N4223	Ozark AL	FH-227B	10/3/67	
539	N7817M	Allegheny AL	FH-227B		D to Mohawk AL. Now merged with Allegheny.
540	N704U	Piedmont AL	FH-227B	21/3/67	*Old Dominion*
541	N7818M	Allegheny AL	FH-227B		*Keene* WO Albany MAR-4-72
542	N7819M	Allegheny AL	FH-227B		*Albany* D to Mohawk AL. Now merged with Allegheny
543	N4224	Ozark AL	FH-227B		
544	N4225	Ozark AL	FH-227B		
545	N705U	Piedmont AL	FH-227B	5/5/67	*Palmetto*
546	N4226	Ozark AL	FH-227B		
547	N4227	Ozark AL	FH-227B	2/6/67	
548	N4228	Ozark AL	FH-227B	9/6/67	
549	N708U	Piedmont AL	FH-227B	9/6/67	*Catawba*
550	N4229	Ozark AL	FH-227B	28/6/67	
551	N4230	Ozark AL	FH-227B	6/7/67	
552	N709U	Piedmont AL	GH-227B	3/7/67	*Kittyhawk*
553	N4231	Ozark AL	FH-227B	21/7/67	Built as N710U for Piedmont
554	N710U	Piedmont AL	FH-227B	25/7/67	*Cumberland*
555	N4232	Ozark AL	FH-227B	28/7/67	
556	PP–BUF	Paraense	FH-227B		WO MAR-14-70, Belem
557	N712U	Piedmont AL	FH-227B	28/8/67	*James River.* WO Charleston AUG-10-68
558	N7820M	Allegheny AL	FH-227B	14/9/67	*Elmira* D to Mohawk AL. Now merged Allegheny
559	N4233	Ozark AL	FH-227B	17/8/67	
560	N7821M	Allegheny AL	FH-227B	26/10/67	D to Mohawk AL. Now merged Allegheny
561	N4234	Ozark AL	FH-227B	14/9/67	
562	N7822M	Allegheny AL	FH-227B	21/11/67	*Watertown.* D to Mohawk AL Now merged Allegheny.
563	N7823M	Caribbean United AL	FH-227B	21/12/67	S to Caribbean United
564	N435	Ozark AL	FH-227B	29/9/67	
565	PP–BUG	Varig	FH-227B		FF as N2738R
566	N706U	Piedmont AL	FH-227B	20/10/67	*Cape Fear*
567	PP–BUH	Varig	FH-227B		FF as N2739R
568	PP–BUT	Varig	FH-227B		FF as N2742R
569	PP–BUJ	Varig	FH-227B		FF as N2740R
570	N227V	Chesapeake & Ohio	FH-227B		
571	570	Fuerza Aerea Uruguaya	227D	8/71	
572	571	Fuerza Aerea Uruguaya	227D	8/71	WO OCT-1972
573	N2784R	Atomic Energy Commission	227D	6/73	
574	572	Fuerza Aerea Uruguaya	227D	8/73	
575	HK–1411W	Texas Petroleum Company	227D	11/71	
576	XC–XOP	Secretaria De Obras Publicas	227D	11/71	
577	XC–FII	Secretaria De Recursos Hidroulicas	227D	11/71	
578	XB–DOU	Secretaria De Obras Publicas	227D	12/72	

Fokker F-27

C/n	Current Marks	Current Owner/operator	Model Series	Initial Delivery	Remarks
10101	PH–NIV	Fokker	100		Prototype, FF NOV–24–55. Sc DEC–10–62
10102	D–BAKI	LTU Interregional	100		Second prototype, FF JAN–31–57 as PH–NVF. L by LTU 1961. L by Luxair 1962. S to LTU 1963 *Wibbel*
10103		Fokker	100		Static test airframe
10104		Fokker	100		Fatigue test airframe
10105	ZK–NAH	ZNAC	100	19/11/58	FF as PH–FAA D Aer Lingus as EI-AKA *Fionntan.* S to Fokker 1966 as PH-FSF. S JUN–15–66 *Kawatere*
10106	EC–BNJ	Aviaco	100	19/11/58	FF as PH–FAB D Aer Lingus as EI–AKB *Fearghal.* S. JAN–17–66 to PAL as PI–C–530. S to Fokker MAR–20–67 as PH–FSH. L to Alia APR–21–67 to JUL–67 as JY–ADO. To Spantax NOV–3–67 L APR–1972
10107	EC–BFV	Aviaco	100	11/12/58	FF as PH–FAC D Aer Lingus as EI–AKC *Fionnbharr.* S to Schreiner as PH–SAP, MAR–18–66. To Fokker OCT–31–66. L to Spantax NOV–18–66 *Islas Canarias* L APR–1972
10108	EC–BPJ	Aviaco	100	20/12/58	FF as PH–FAD. D to Braathens as LN–SUN. S NOV–1–68 to Spantax as EC–BPJ. L. APR–1972
10109	EC–BRN	Aviaco	200	23/1/59	FF as PH–FAE. D Aer Lingus EI–AKD *Flannan.* S to Fokker as PH–YFF 1966. S to LTU as D–BAKA MAR–1966. S JUN–9–69 to Spantax as EC–BRN. Cvtd to Srs. 200 L APR–1972
10110	ZK–NAF	NZNAC	100	4/2/59	FF as PH–FAF. D Aer Lingus as EI–AKE *Feidhlim.* S to Fokker 1966 as PH–FSE. S JUN–10–66 *Korimako*
10111	VH–TFA	AL New Guinea	200	13/6/59	FF as PH–FAG. D to TAA *Dirk Hartog,* later *Charles Todd* Cvtd to Srs 200. Transferred to TAA's New Guinea division
10112	VH–TFB	TAA	100	6/4/59	FF as PH–FAH *Abel Tasman* WO Mackay JUN–10–60
10113	VH–TFC	TAA	200	18/6/59	FF as PH–FAI *Arthur Phillip.* Cvtd to Srs 200
10114	VH–TFD	TAA	100	5/5/59	FF as PH–FAK *George Evans* later *William Landsborough*
10115	59–0259	Philippine AF	200	2/9/59	FF as PH–FAM. Cvtd to Srs 200
10116	EC–BPK	Aviaco	100	24/4/59	FF as PH–FAL. D to Braathens as LN–SUO. S NOV–11–68 to Spantax as EC–BPK. L APR–72

C/n	Current Marks	Current Owner/operator	Model Series	Initial Delivery	Remarks
10118	ZK–NAA	NZNAC	100	6/5/59	FF as PH–FAN. D to Aer Lingus as EI–AKF *Finghin* S to Fokker 1966 as PH–FSA. S JAN–4–66 *Kohihi*
10119	ZK–NAB	NZNAC	100	12/5/59	FF as PH–FAO. D to Aer Lingus as EI–AKG *Fiachra* S 1966 as PH–FSB. S JAN–4–66 *Koreke*
10120	VH–TFE	Australian DCA	100	6/6/59	FF as PH–FAP. D to TAA *Angus McMillan,* later *Robert Burke*
10121	VH–TFF	TAA	100	24/6/59	FF as PH–FAR *Allan Cunningham*
10122	VH–TFG	TAA	100	13/7/59	FF as PH–FAS *Charles Todd,* later *Dirk Hartog*
10123	TC–TEZ	THY	100	27/10/60	FF as PH–FAT
10124	TC–TON	THY	100	27/10/60	FF as PH–FAU
10125	TC–TOY	THY	100	27/10/60	FF as PH–FAV
10126	EP–MRP	Shah of Iran	200	12/9/59	FF as PH–FAW. Cvtd to Srs 200. WO OCT–10–62
10127	VH–EWA	East-West AL	100	29/7/59	FF as PH–FAX Was TAA VH–TFH. *City of Tamworth*
10131	VH–CAV	Australian DCA	100	19/9/59	FF as PH–FAY
10132	VH–CAT	Australian DCA	100	28/9/59	FF as PH–FAZ
10133	VH–FNA	Ansett–ANA	200	5/10/59	FF as PH–FBA. Used by MMA APR–27–69 to SEP–28–69
10134	VH–TFI	AL New Guinea	200	5/10/59	FF as PH–FBB. D to TAA *Fránk Hann.* Later *Port Moresby*
10135	VH–TFJ	AL New Guinea	200	21/10/59	FF as PH–FBC. D to TAA *Fred Brockman.* Later *Rabaul*
10136	VH–FNB	Ansett–ANA	200	30/10/59	FF as PH–FBD
10137	F–BRHL	Europe Air Charter	200	30/12/59	FF as PH–FBE. D Horten GmbH as D–BATU. S to Fokker 1965 as PH-FSD. L to ATI 1966. L to KLA to MAY–1–67. L to Air Inter JUL–1–67. To Euralair NOV–22–68 as F–BRHL. To Europe Air Charter
10138	VH–TFK	AL of New Guinea	200	30/11/59	FF as PH–FBF. D to TAA *Charles Throsby.* L to Associated Airlines of Australia *Silver Friendship.* Later *Kieta*
10139	VH–MMS	MacRobertson Miller AL	200	7/12/59	FF as PH–FBG Was TAA VH–TFL *Swan*
10140	–	Trans National AL	100	11/1/60	D to Iranian Oil as PH–IOK *Pazanun* S OCT–1973
10141	HB–AAI	Balair	200	22/1/60	FF as PH–IOP D to Iranian Oil *Kharg.* Cvtd to Srs 200 S to Balair APR–2–64 WO SEP–12–64
10142	PK–KFR	Nusantara Merpati	100	13/5/60	D to Netherlands Royal Flight as PH–PBF *Gerben Sonderman* S MAR–1973
10143	VH–FNC	Ansett–ANA	200	4/2/60	FF as PH–FBH. For Airlines of NSW
10144	VH–FND	Ansett–ANA	200	12/2/60	FF as PH–FBI. For Airlines of NSW

Fokker F-27

C/n	Current Marks	Current Owner/operator	Model Series	Initial Delivery	Remarks
10145	VH–FNE	Ansett–ANA	200	25/2/60	FF as PH–FBK. For Queensland. AL *Sir Henry Abel Smith.* Used by MMA MAR–12–69 to AUG–31–69
10146	VH–MMO	MacRobertson Miller AL	200	10/3/60	FF as PH–FBL. D to Ansett–ANA as VH–FNF *Ord*
10147	PI–C–501	PAL	100	23/2/60	FF as PH–FBM WO Mactan FEB–28–67
10148	10148	Philippine AF	100	9/3/60	FF as PH–FBN D to PAL as PI–C–502 S to Philippine AF
10149	C–2	Neth AF	100	6/7/60	FF as PH–FBO L to UN JUN–67
10150	C–3	Neth AF	100	6/8/60	FF as PH–FBP
10151	–	Iranian National AL	300	11/5/60	D to KLM as PH–IOS, *Shemiran,* later *Shiraz.* L to Iranian Oil, then S to company JUL–1962 S OCT–1973
10152	C–1	Neth AF	100	23/8/60	FF as PH–FBR
10153	–	Iranian National AL	300	31/5/60	D to KLM as PH–IOT *Tehran* L to Iranian Oil, then S to company JUL–1962 S OCT–1973
10154	C–4	Neth AF	300	6/10/60	FF as PH–FBS. L to UN AUG–67
10155	C–5	Neth AF	300	30/9/60	FF as PH–FBT
10156	C–6	Neth AF	300	7/12/60	FF as PH–FBU. Reg PH–FSC 1963 as demonstrator
10157	C–7	Neth AF	300	29/12/60	FF as PH–FBV
10158	C–8	Neth AF	300	28/12/60	FF as PH–FBW. L to Fokker PH–FSC. Cvtd to NASARR trainer
10159	PH–KFA	NLM	300	4/1/61	FF as PH–FBX. D to Neth AF as C–9. L to NLM *Jan Dellaert*
10160	C–10	Neth AF	300	17/1/61	FF as PH–FBY
10161	C–11	Neth AF	300	2/2/61	FF as PH–FBZ. D to Neth AF as C–11. L to NLM *Willem Versteegh* as PH–KFB
10162	C–12	Neth AF	300	28/4/61	FF as PH–FCA
10163	AP–ALM	PIA	200	3/1/61	FF as PH–FCB. WO AUG–6–70
10164	AP–ALN	PIA	200	19/1/61	FF as PH–FCC
10165	AP–ALO	PIA	200	6/2/61	FF as PH–FCD WO JUN–25–64
10166	ZK–BXA	NZNAC	100	26/11/60	FF as PH–FCE *Kuaka*
10167	ZK–BXB	NZNAC	100	9/2/61	FF as PH–FCF *Kotuku*
10168	ZK–BXC	NZNAC	100	24/2/61	FF as PH–FCG *Koweka*
10169	ZK–BXD	NZNAC	100	3/3/61	FF as PH–FCH *Korere*
10170	VH–FNG	Ansett–ANA	200	17/3/61	FF as PH–FCI For Airlines of NSW
10171	VT–DMA	IAC	100	5/4/61	FF as PH–FCK *Ganga*
10172	VT–DMB	IAC	100	7/4/61	FF as PH–FCL *Jamuna*
10173	VT–DMC	IAC	100	27/4/61	FF as PH–FCM *Sutlej*
10174	VT–DMD	IAC	100	28/4/61	FF as PH–FCN *Brahmaputra*
10175	VT–DME	IAC	100	4/5/61	FF as PH–FCO *Narbada*
10176	D–BEKU	LTU	700	18/5/61	FF as PH–FCP. D to Braathens as LN–SUG. Resold to Fokker as PH–FCP and cvtd to Srs 700. S DEC–30–69 to TAA, reg. VH–TFH, *George Bass* Returned to Fokker. S MAR–1972

C/n	Current Marks	Current Owner/operator	Model Series	Initial Delivery	Remarks
10177	PK–PFW	Pertamina	200	30/5/61	FF as PH–FCR D to All-Nippon AW as JA8601. S NOV–1972
10178	PK–PFX	Pertamina	200	14/6/61	FF as PH–FCS D to All-Nippon AW as JA8602. S DEC–1972
10179	JA8603	All-Nippon AW	200	20/6/61	FF as PH–FCT
10180	VH–FNH	Ansett–ANA	200	11/7/61	FF as PH–FCU WO MAR–17–65
10181	VH–FNI	Ansett–ANA	200	14/7/61	FF as PH–FCV. Used by Airlines of S Australia *City of Whyallo*
10182	TC–TAY	THY	100	30/8/61	FF as PH–FCW WO. Ankara SEP–23–61
10183	TC–TEK	THY	100	30/8/61	FF as PH–FCX
10184	ZK–BXE	NZNAC	100	30/8/61	FF as PH–FCY *Kahu*
10185	ZK–BXF	NZNAC	100	12/9/61	FF as PH–FCZ *Koparu*
10186	VH–MMB	East-West AL	300	16/11/61	FF as PH–FDA. D to LTU *Jan Wellem.* Rtd to Fokker DEC–28–66 as PH–FSG. L to Luxair to SEP–30–67 L to Sobelair 1968. L to LTU as D–BAKU 1969. Rtd. to Fokker MAY–1969 S to Ansett-ANA AUG–1970, reg. VH–MBB S MAR–1971
10187	AP–ALW	PIA	400	19/10/61	FF as PH–FDB
10188	AP–ALX	PIA	200	6/11/61	FF as PH–FDC
10189	ZK–BXG	NZNAC	100	17/11/61	FF as PH–FDD *Kea*
10190	ZK–BXH	NZNAC	100	30/11/61	FF as PH–FDE *Koropio* L to East West AL 1963–1965 as VH–EWH
10191	PI–C–503	PAL	100	14/12/61	FF as PH-FDF WO Manila OCT–12–62
10192	ST–AAA	Sudan AW	200	23/1/62	FF as PH–FDG
10193	ST–AAR	Sudan AW	200	2/2/62	FF as PH–FDH
10194	ST–AAS	Sudan AW	200	20/2/62	FF as PH–FDI
10195	PK–PFR	Pertamina	200	20/2/62	FF as PH–FDK D to All-Nippon AW as JA8605 S to Pertamina
10196	PK–PFS	Pertamina	200	5/5/62	FF as PH–FDL D to All-Nippon AW as JA8606. S to Pertamina
10197	PK–PFT	Pertamina	200	23/3/62	FF as PH–FDM D to All-Nippon AW as JA8607 S to Pertamina
10198	PH–LIP	Philips	100	7/4/62	
10199	560	Fuerza Aerea Uraguaya	100	5/62	FF as PH–FDN. D to Braathens as LN–SUW. Resold to Fokker and S on FEB–10–70
10200	PH–KFC	NLM Dutch AL	200	20/8/62	FF as PH–FDO. Intended as LV–PMP. D to LTU as D–BAKE *Schneider Wibbel.* Cvtd to Srs 200 and S to Balair as HB–AAU MAR–1965. L to NLM MAR–1972
10201	PH–OGA	Limburg AL	200	8/10/62	FF as PH–DPF! Intended as LV–PMR D to All-Nippon AW as JA8615. S to Limburg

Fokker F-27

C/n	Current Marks	Current Owner/operator	Model Series	Initial Delivery	Remarks
10202	561	Fuerza Aereas Uraguaya	100	/62	FF as PH–FDR. Intended as LV–PMŞ. D to Braathens as LN–SUA. S to Fokker JUN–69, reg PH–FDR. L to Spantax JUL–69. S MAR–70
10203	PK–PFU	Pertamina	200	27/7/62	FF as PH–FDS. Intended as LV–PMT. D to Fujita AW. To All-Nippon AW as JA8608. S NOV–71
10204	CR–AIA	DETA	200	6/7/62	FF as PH–FDT *Lourenco Marques*
10205	CR–AIB	DETA	200		FF as PH–FDU *Beira.* WO MAR–28–70 near Lourenco Marques
10206	CR–AIC	DETA	200		FF as PH–FDV *Qelimane*
10207	CR–LEO	DTA	200		FF as PH–FDW
10208	CR–LEP	DTA	200		FF as PH–FDX
10209	PI–C–504	PAL	100		FF as PH–FDY. WO JUL–1–70 Dumaquete
10210		Philippine AF	100		FF as PH–FDZ.D to PAL as PI–C–506. To Philippine AF
10211	5Y–AAB	EAA	200		FF as PH–FEA.D as VP–KSA
10212	5Y–AAC	EAA	200		FF as PH–FEB.D as VP–KSB
10213	5H–AAI	EAA	200		FF as PH–FEC.D as VP–KSC
10214	VT–DOJ	IAC	100		FF as PH–FED *Tapti.* WO APR–21–69, Khulna
10215	VT–DOK	IAC	100		FF as PH–FEE *Mahanadi*
10216	5N–AAV	Nigeria AW	200	22/1/63	FF as PH–FEF.WO OCT–7–67, Biafra
10217	5N–AAW	Nigeria AW	200	2/63	FF as PH–FEG
10218	5N–AAX	Nigeria AW	200	2/63	FF as PH–FEH
10219	VT–DOL	IAC	100		FF as PH–FEI *Godavari.* WO OCT–15–64
10220	VT–DOM	IAC	100		FF as PH–FEK *Krishna*
10221	VT–DON	IAC	100	23/3/63	FF as PH–FEL *Kaveri*
10222	N–AAY	Nigerian AW	200	24/4/63	FF as PH–FEM
10223	5N–AAZ	Nigerian AW	200	1/5/63	FF as PH–FEN. L to Ghana AW AUG–1–68
10224	LX–LGA	Luxair	100	7/5/63	FF as PH–FEO *Prince Henri*
10225	G–BAUR	Air Anglia	200	6/5/63	FF as PH–FEP.D to Malayan AW as 9M–AMI. To MSA as 9V–BAP. S to Fokker DEC–71. S APR–73
10226	PK–JFK	Sempati	200	24/5/63	FF as PH–FER.D to Malayan AW as 9M–AMJ. To MSA same reg. S MAY–72
10227	F–OCSH	Air Polynésie	200	31/5/63	FF as PH–FES. D to All-Nippon AW as JA8616. S to Air Polynésie
10228	F–BUFU	Touraine Air Transport	200	19/6/63	FF as PH–FET.D to All-Nippon AW as JA8617. S to Touraine AT
10229	F–BUTA	Touraine Air Transport	200	4/7/63	FF as PH–FEU.D to All-Nippon AW as JA8618. S to Touraine AT
10230	F–OCSI	Air Polynésie	200	25/7/63	FF as PH–FEV.D to All-Nippon AW as JA8619. S to Air Polynésie
10231	PK–KFG	Nusantara AL	200	8/8/63	FF as PH–FEW.D to Malayan AW as 9M–AML. To MSA as 9V–BAQ. S to Fokker JUN–72. S JUN–72

C/n	Current Marks	Current Owner/operator	Model Series	Initial Delivery	Remarks
10232	S2–ABK	Bangladesh Biman	200	28/8/63	FF as PH–FEX.D to Malayan AW as 9M–AMM. To MSA same reg. S to Fokker, re-reg PH–FEX. S APR–73
10233	S2–ABL	Bangladesh Biman	200	12/9/63	FF as PH–FEY.D to Malayan AW as 9M–AMN. To MSA as 9V–BAR. S to Fokker, re-reg PH–FEY. S MAY–73
10234	PH–OGB	Limburg AL	200	2/10/63	FF as PH–FEZ.D to Fujita AW then All-Nippon AW as JA8621. S JUN–73
10235	XY–ADK	Union of Burma AW	200	10/10/63	FF as PH–FFA
10236	XY–ADL	Union of Burma AW	200	26/10/63	FF as PH–FFB
10237	XY–ADM	Union of Burma AW	200	18/11/63	FF as PH–FFC
10238	ST–AAY	Sudan AW	200	3/12/63	FF as PH–FFD
10239	HL5201	Korean AL	200	20/12/63	FF as PH–FFE
10240	HL5202	Korean AL	200	3/1/64	FF as PH–FFF
10241	SX–AAP	EAA	200	16/1/64	FF as PH–FFG D as VP–KTK
10242	F–BUFA	Touraine Air Transport	200	19/2/64	FF as PH–FFH. D to All-Nippon AW as JA8622 S FEB–1973
10243	F–BUFB	Touraine Air Transport	200	26/2/64	FF as PH–FFI D to All-Nippon AW as JA8623 S MAR–1973
10244	PK–PFV	Pertamina	200	6/3/64	FF as PH–FFK. D to All-Nippon AW as JA8624 S OCT–1972
10245	LN–SUE	Braathens	100	3/64	FF as PH–FFL. D to Braathens. Re sold to Fokker JUN–27–69 L. To Braathens *Harald Gille*
10246	10246	Philippines AF	100	23/3/64	FF as PH–FFM. D to PAL as PI–C–507 Trans to Philippine AF
10247	I–SARK	Alisarda	100	7/4/64	FF as PH–FFN D to PAL as PI–C–508 S MAY–1971
10248	LN–SUL	Braathens	100	10/4/64	FF as PH–FFO L by Schreiner as PH–SAF in 1964 *Sigurd Munn*
10249	I–ATIM	ATI	200	6/5/64	FF as PH–FFP L by KLA to 1969
10250	AP–ATO	PIA	200	9/64	FF as PH–FFR
10251	I–ATIP	ATI	200	25/5/64	FF as PH–FFS
10252	VH–FNV	Ansett–ANA	200	3/6/64	FF as PH–FFT. D to All-Nippon AW as JA8630 S OCT–1971
10253	VH–TFW	TAA	200	17/6/64	FF as PH–FFU. D to All-Nippon AW as JA8631 S MAY–1972
10254	VH–FNW	Ansett–ANA	200	1/7/64	FF as PH–FFV. D to All-Nippon AW as JA8632 S NOV–1971
10255	TF–FIN	Icelandair	200	15/7/64	FF as PH–FFW. D to All-Nippon AW as JA8633 S JUL–1972
10256	I–ATIS	ATI	200	22/7/64	FF as PH–FFX. L by KLA to 1969
10257	I–SARQ	Alisarda	100	17/8/64	FF as PH–FFY D to PAL as PI–C–509 S JAN–27–69

Fokker F-27

C/n	Current Marks	Current Owner/operator	Model Series	Initial Delivery	Remarks
10258	I–SARO	Alisarda	100	28/9/64	FF as PH–FFZ. D to PAL as PI–C–512 L by McRobertson Miller 1967 to NOV–68 as VH–MMU S JAN–27–69
10259	F–BUFC	Touraine Air Transport	200	18/9/64	FF as PH–FGA. D to All-Nippon AW as JA8634 S APR–1973
10260	TF–SYR	Icelandic Coast Guard	200	20/10/64	FF as PH–FGB D to All-Nippon AW as JA8635 S MAY–1972
10261	JA8636	All-Nippon AW	200	12/11/64	FF as PH–FGC
10262	ZK–DCG	DCA New Zealand	200	17/11/64	FF as PH–FGD D to All-Nippon AW as JA8637 S FEB–1972
10263	TF–FIM	Icelandair	200	1/12/64	FF as PH–FGE D to All-Nippon AW as JA8638 S MAY–1972
10264	VH–FNJ	AL of NSW	200	1/12/64	FF as PH–FGF
10265	10265	Philippine AF	100	10/2/65	FF as PH–FGG D to PAL as PI–C–514 S NOV–1971
10266	VH–EWG	East-West AL	100	20/1/65	FF as PH–FGH *City of Orange*
10267	10267	Philippine AF	100	10/2/65	FF as PH–FGI D to PAL as PI–C–516. S AUG–1971
10268	HB–AAZ	Balair	400		FF as PH–FGK. L by Condor as D–BARI. To Fokker as PH–ARI. L to Air Congo. S OCT–15–69 S to Euralair as F–BRQL. S JUN–1973
10269	LX–LGB	Luxair	100	10/2/65	FF as PH–FGL *Prince Jean*
10270	PH–ARO	Fokker–VFW	400		FF as PH–FGM. L by Condor as D–BARO. To Fokker as PH–ARO in JUN–69. L by Air Congo AUG–22–68 to MAY–8–69. L by ATI JUL–25–69 to NOV–26–69 L to Lina Congo. L to BIAS/Linair
10271	PH–SAB	Schreiner	200		FF as PH–FGN L to IAC WO Kashmir FEB–7–66
10272	PH–SAD	KLM	200	13/4/65	FF as PH–FGO. D to Schreiner. S to KLM (for NLM) NOV–1–67. *Evert van Dijk*
10273	833	Sudan AF	400		FF as PH–FGP
10274	TF–FIJ	Icelandair	100	14/5/65	FF as PH–FGR *Blikfaxi*
10275	N10625	Oasis Oil	400		FF as PH–FGS
10276	PH–KFD	NLM Dutch AL	200	1/6/65	FF as PH–FGT L from Swissair as HB–AAV L to NLM MAR–1972
10277	ST–ADY	Sudan AL	400		FF as PH–FGU D to Sudan AF, reg 844 S AUG–1970
10278	AP–ATU	PIA	200	9/8/65	FF as PH–FGV
10279	AP–ATT	PIA	400	9/8/65	FF as PH–FGW WO OCT–8–65
10280	VH–FNK	Ansett–ANA	200	2/9/65	FF as PH–FGX
10281	AP–ATW	Pakistan DCA	200	5/10/65	FF as PH–FGY
10282	ST–ADW	Sudan AL	400	5/10/65	FF as PH–FGZ D to Sudan AF, reg 888 S AUG–1970
10283	899	Sudan AF	400	3/11/65	FF as PH–FIA
10284	VH–TFL	TAA	200		FF as PH–FIB *William Lawson*
10285	PI–C–527	PAL	100		FF as PH–FIC. WO JUL–6–67 Nr Bacolod

C/n	Current Marks	Current Owner/operator	Model Series	Initial Delivery	Remarks
10286	ZK–BXI	NZNAC	100	11/65	FF as PH–FID *Kotare*
10287	VH–EWJ	East-West AL	100	18/11/65	FF as PH–FIE *City of Parkes*
10288	AP–AXB	PIA	200	14/12/65	FF as PH–FIF D to ATI as I–ATIG. S APR–1973
10289	I–ATIB	ATI	200	7/1/66	FF as PH–FIG. L by KLA 1968
10290	9N–AAR	R Nepal AL	200	21/1/66	FF as PH–FIH *Ganesh Himal.* WO JAN–25–70 Delhi
10291	VH–FNL	Ansett–ANA	200	4/1/66	FF as PH–FII L to Mac-Robertson Miller
10292	VH–FNM	Ansett–ANA	200	14/2/66	FF as PH–FIK
10293	G–BAKL	Air Anglia	200	2/2/66	FF as PH–FIL D to MSA as 9M–AOJ. S to Fokker, reg. PH–FIL L to Air Anglia. S DEC–1972
10294	N710A	Aramco	400	9/2/66	FF as PH–FIN
10295	N714A	Aramco	400	24/2/66	FF as PH–FIO
10296	10296	Philippine AF	100	28/3/66	FF as PH–FIP D to PAL as PI–C–528. S NOV–1971
10297	VH–FNN	Ansett–ANA	200	31/3/66	FF as PH–FIR. For Queens-land AL
10298	LN–SUF	Braathens	100	12/4/66	FF as PH–FIS L by Schreiner as PH–SAN 1966 *Magnus Lagaboter*
10299	PK–PFA	Permina	400	15/6/66	FF as PH–FIT *Rantau*
10300	TF–FIK	Icelandair	100	28/5/66	FF as PH–FIU *Snarfaxi*
10301	I–ATIR	ATI	200	30/4/66	FF as PH–FIV
10302	S2–ABF	Bangladesh Biman	200	2/7/66	FF as PH–FIW D to IAC as VT–DUT *Ravi* S MAR–1972
10303	VH–MMR	MacRobertson Miller AL	200	19/7/66	FF as PH–FIX *Rabe*
10304	VH–FNO	Ansett–ANA	400	5/8/66	FF as PH–FIY
10305	VH–FNP	Airlines of NSW Australia	200	23/6/66	FF as PH–FIZ *City of Whyalla,* Used by Airlines of S Australia until 1968
10306	PK–PFB	Permina	400	29/12/66	FF as PH–FKA *Sorong* WO Malaybalay APR–27–67
10307	AP–AUR	PIA	200	23/9/66	FF as PH–FKB
10308	S2–ABG	Bangladesh Biman	200	10/10/66	FF as PH–FKC D TO IAC as VT–DVF *Beas.* S MAR–1972
10309	VT–DVG	IAC	200	19/10/66	FF as PH–FKD *Sarju*
10310	10310	Philippine AF	100	8/12/66	FF as PH–FKE D to PAL as PI–C–531 S JUL–1971
10311	PI–C–532	PAL	100	12/1/67	FF as PH–FKF. WO MAY–9–70 Lligan
10312	XY–ADN	Union of Burma	400	5/12/66	FF as PH–FKG
10313	XY–ADO	Union of Burma	400	15/12/66	FF as PH–FKH
10314	AP–AUS	PIA	400	16/12/66	FF as PH–FKI
10315	VH–FNQ	Ansett–ANA	400	16/12/66	
10316	G–AVDN	Gulf Aviation	400	6/1/67	FF as PH–FKL
10317	VH–FNR	Ansett–MAL	400	17/1/67	FF as PH–FKM
10318	VH–FNS	Ansett–ANA	400	26/1/67	FF as PH–FKN
10319	VH–EWK	East-West AL	100	17/2/67	FF as PH–FKO *City of Armidale*
10320	I–ATID	ATI	200	30/1/67	FF as PH–FKP
10321	I–ATIF	ATI	200	22/2/67	FF as PH–FKR
10322	VH–FNT	Ansett–ANA	400	9/3/67	FF as PH–FKS
10323	G–AZFD	Gulf Aviation	400	23/3/67	FF as PH–FKT D to Swissair as HB–AAW. S OCT–1971
10324	I–ATIL	ATI	200	28/3/67	FF as PH–FKU

Fokker F-27

C/n	Current Marks	Current Owner/operator	Model Series	Initial Delivery	Remarks
10325	G–AWFU	Gulf Aviation	400	18/4/67	FF as PH–FKV. Built for Schreiner as PH–SAR. To KLM DEC–1–67. S to Gulf APR–7–68
10326	CR–LIJ	DTA	200	25/4/67	FF as PH–FKW
10327	10327	Philippine AF	100	27/7/67	FF as PH–FKX D to Swissair as HB–AAW. S OCT–1971
10328	10328	Philippine AF	100	4/9/67	FF AS PH–FKY D to PAL as PI–C–534 S JUL–1971
10329	VH–TFM	TAA	400	13/7/67	FF as PH–FKZ *John Oxley*
10330	AP–AUV	PIA	200	14/6/67	FF as PH–FLA
10331	AP–AUW	PIA	200	27/6/67	FF as PH–FLB WO Riseale-wola MAY–18–73
10332	EC–BMS	Iberia	400	29/9/67	FF as PH–FLC *Ebro*
10333	VT–EBJ	IAC	400	13/10/67	FF as PH–FLD. L to Air France as F–BOOC. L to Botswana from OCT–24–69 as AZ–ZEW *Chobe*. S JAN–1971
10334	VH–FNU	Ansett–ANA	600	10/10/67	FF as PH–FLE. L to Air France as F–BOOD 1967–69
10335	AP–AUX	PIA	400	17/8/67	FF as PH-FLF
10336	VT–DWT	IAC	400	29/8/67	FF as PH–FLG *Sabarmati*. WO AUG–28–70 Assam
10337	VT–DWU	IAC	400	7/9/67	FF as PH–FLH *Jehlum*
10338	LX–LGD	Luxair	400	30/9/67	FF as PH–FLI *Princess Margaretha*
10339	PK–PEC	Permina Oil	400	13/11/67	FF as PH–FLK *Klamono*
10340	OO–SBP	BIAS	400	25/4/68	FF as PH–FLL *Common Market Commuter* D to Sobelair/ Sabena. L to BIAS.
10341	OY–STO	Sterling AW	500	17/5/68	Prototype long Fuselage, FF NOV–15–67 as PH–FLM
10342	OY–DNF	BIAS (Lin Air)	400	29/11/67	FF as PH–FLN. L from Danish Aero Lease
10343	EC–BMT	Iberia	400		FF as PH–FLO *Tajo*
10344	VH–EWL	East West AL	100	11/11/67	FF as PH–FLP
10345	T–41	Fuerza Aerea Argentina	400	8/68	FF as PH–FLR. D as T–79
10346	T–42	Fuerza Aerea Argentina	500	8/68	FF as PH–FLS. D as T–80
10347	EC–BMU	Iberia	400	15/1/68	FF as PH–FLT *Guadalguivir*
10348	EC–BOA	Iberia	400	26/1/68	FF as PH–FLU *Duero*
10349	I–ATIC	ATI	400	25/1/68	FF as PH–FLV
10350	I–ATIN	ATI	400	25/1/69	FF as PH–FLW
10351	PH–KFE	NLM Dutch AL	400	31/1/68	FF as PH–FLX D to Swissair/ Belair as HB–AAX L to NLM FEB–1972
10352	EC–BOB	Iberia	400	29/2/68	FF as PH–FLY *Mino*
10353	EC–BOC	Iberia	400	15/3/68	FF as PH–FLZ *Rio Segura*
10354	OO–SCA	Sabena	400	2/3/68	FF as PH–FMA. L to Alia as JY–ADF. L to Nigeria AW as 5N–CLN from NOV–22–68
10355	VH–MMV	MacRobertson Miller AL	200	8/3/68	FF as PH–FMB *Victoria*
10356	TF–FIL	Icelandair	300	6/4/68	FF as PH–FMC. WO SEP–26–70 Mygganaes
10357	XY–ADP	Union of Burma AW	200	22/3/68	FF as PH–FMD
10358	CR–LMV	DTA	200	2/4/68	FF as PH–FME D to MSA as 9V–BMF. S to Fokker, reg PH–FME S NOV–1972

C/n	Current Marks	Current Owner/operator	Model Series	Initial Delivery	Remarks
10359	CR–LMU	DTA	200	11/4/68	FF as PH–FMF D to MSA as 9V–AOX. S to Fokker, reg. PH–FMF S NOV–1972
10360	EC–BOD	Iberia	400	10/5/68	FF as PH–FMG
10361	EC–BOE	Iberia	400	16/5/68	FF as PH–FMH *Rio Pisuerga*
10362	PK–CFD	Caltex	400	20/5/68	FF as PH–FMI *Riau*
10363	I–ATIT	ATI	400	21/5/68	FF as PH–FMK. WO MAY–24–69 Reggio Calabria
10364	ZK–NAN	NZNAC	500	4/6/68	FF as PH–FLM. D to ALM as PJ–FRE St. *Eustatius.* S. 1970
10365	ZK–NAO	NZNAC	500	17/6/68	FF as PH–FMM. Intended as PJ–ALB. D to ALM as PJ–FRM *St. Maarten.* S 1970 to MSA as 9V–BCN S to SIA. S JUL–1973
10366	F–BPNA	Air Inter	500		FF as PH–FMN
10367	F–BPNB	Air Inter	500	12/10/68	FF as PH–FMO
10368	N20XY	Occidental Oil	400	17/4/69	FF as PH–FMP. Intended as AP–AUY for PIA. L to NLM for one week APR–69
10369	F–BPUA	Air France/PT	500	7/10/68	FF as PH–FMR
10370	F–BPUB	Air France/PT	500	26/9/68	FF as PH–FMS
10371	F–BPNC	Air Inter	500	24/9/68	FF as PH–FMT
10372	F–BPND	Air Inter	500	25/9/68	FF as PH–FMU
10373	F–BPUC	Air France/PT	500	11/10/68	FF as PH–FMV
10374	F–BPUD	Air France/PT	500	21/10/69	FF as PH–FMW
10375	F–BPNE	Air Inter	500	29/10/68	FF as PH–FMX
10376	F–BPNF	Air Inter	500	1/11/68	FF as PH–FMY
10377	F–BPUE	Air France/PT	500	13/11/68	FF as PH–FMZ
10378	F–BPUF	Air France/PT	500	22/11/68	FF as PH–FNA
10379	F–BPUG	Air France/PT	500		FF as PH–FNB
10380	F–BPNG	Air Inter	500		FF as PH–FNC
10381	F–BPNH	Air Inter	500	10/1/69	FF as PH–FND
10382	F–BPUH	Air France/PT	500	24/1/69	FF as PH–FNE
10383	F–BPNI	Air Inter	500	1/7/69	FF as PH–FNF
10384	F–BPNJ	Air Inter	500	1/7/69	FF as PH–FNG
10385	VH–TQN	TAA	600	7/12/68	FF as PH–FNH *John Batman*
10386	VH–TQO	TAA	600	18/12/68	FF as PH–FNI *Augustus Gregory*
10387	VH–TQP	TAA	600	27/12/68	FF as PH–FNK *John McKinlay*
10388	VH–TQQ	TAA	600	8/1/69	FF as PH–FNL *David Collins*
10389	F–BPUI	Air France/PT	500	7/3/69	FF as PH–FNM
10390	F–BPUJ	Air France/PT	500	28/3/69	FF as PH–FNN
10391	9Q–CLK	Air Congo	600	20/2/69	FF as PH–FNO
10392	9Q–CLL	Air Congo	600	20/2/69	FF as PH–FNP
10393	9Q–CLM	Air Congo	600	12/3/69	FF as PH–FNR
10394	9Q–CLN	Air Zaire	600	17/3/69	FF as PH–FNS
10395	9Q–CLO	Air Zaire	600	1/4/69	FF as PH–FNT
10396	EC–CAU	Aviaco	600	25/4/69	FF as PH–FNU. L to Sabena and Linair in 1969 as OY–DHW. To Aviaco AUG–1972
10397	F–BPUK	Air France/PT	500	16/5/69	FF as PH–FNV
10398	F–BPUL	Air France/PT	500	10/7/69	FF as PH–FNW
10399	5N–ABA	Nigeria AW	600	22/8/69	FF as PH–FNX
10400	5N–ABB	Nigeria AW	600	29/7/69	FF as PH–FNY
10401	CR–AMD	DETA	600R		FF as PH–FNZ Series 600R prototype. L to Sabena 1970 as PH–FNZ. S JUL–1970
10402	9Q–CLP	Air Zaire	600	1/5/69	FF as PH–FOA

Fokker F-27

C/n	Current Marks	Current Owner/operator	Model Series	Initial Delivery	Remarks
10403	TC–71	Fuerza Aerea Argentina	400M	9/6/69	FF as PH–FOB
10404	TC–72	Fuerza Aerea Argentina	400M	18/6/69	FF as PH–FOC
10405	9Q–CLQ	Air Zaire	600	25/9/69	FF as PH–FOD
10406	9Q–CLR	Air Zaire	600	25/9/69	FF as PH–FOE
10407	TC–73	Fuerza Aerea Argentina	400M	24/7/69	FF as PH–FOF
10408	TC–74	Fuerza Aerea Argentina	400M	31/7/69	FF as PH–FOG
10409	PK–GFE	Garuda Indonesian	600	14/8/69	FF as PH–FOH *Kerintji*
10410	PK–JFF	Sempati	600	14/8/69	FF as PH–FOI D to Garuda as PK–GFF *Dempo.* S SEP–1971
10411	TC–75	Fuerza Aerea Argentina	400M	15/8/69	FF as PH–FOK. WO JUN–10–70 Peru
10412	TC–76	Fuerza Aerea Argentina	400M	26/8/69	FF as PH–FOL
10413	PK–GFG	Garula Indonesian	600	2/9/69	FF as PH–FOM *Merapi*
10414	HL–5209	Korean A/L	200	29/9/69	FF as PH–FON
10415	PK–GFH	Garuda Indonesian	600	25/9/69	FF as PH–FOO *Gede*
10416	TC–77	Fuerza Aerea Argentina	400M	29/9/69	FF as PH–FOP
10417	HL–5201	Korean A/L	500	2/10/69	FF as PH–FOR
10418	TC–78	Fuerza Aerea Argentina	400M	17/10/69	FF as PH–FOS
10419	I–ATIV	ATI	600	27/10/69	FF as PH–FOT
10420	I–ATIZ	ATI	600	11/11/69	FF as PH–FOU
10421	PK–GFI	Garuda Indonesian	600	12/11/69	FF as PH–FOV *Galunggung*
10422	PK–GFJ	Garuda Indonesian	600	14/11/69	FF as PH–FOW *Semaru*
10423	PK–GFK	Garuda Indonesian	600	21/11/69	FF as PH–FOX *Bromo*
10424	PK–GFL	Garuda Indonesian	600	10/12/69	FF as PH–FOY *Agung*
10425	OY–APA	Maersk Air	500	9/12/69	FF as PH–FOZ
10426	OY–APB	Maersk Air	500	17/12/69	FF as PH–FPA. WO DEC–27–69 Ronne
10427	HL–5211	Korean A/L	500	6/1/70	FF as PH–FPB.
10428	HL–5212	Korean A/L	500	22/1/70	FF as PH–FPC
10429	PK–FGM	Garuda Indonesian	600	2/2/70	FF as PH–FPD *Rindjani*
10430	PK–GFN	Garuda Indonesian	600	13/2/70	FF as PH–FPE *Salahutu*
10431	OY–APC	Maersk Air	500	14/2/70	FF as PH–FPF
10432	CN–CDA	Royal Air Inter	600	25/3/70	FF as PH–FPG
10433	CN–CDB	Royal Air Inter	600	24/4/70	FF as PH–FPH
10434	OY–STN	Sterling	500	10/6/70	FF as PH–FPI
10435	PK–GFO	Garuda	600	1/5/70	FF as PH–FPK *Locon*
10436	PH–FPL	Oasis Oil	600	10/7/70	FF as PH–FPL
10437	OY–APD	Maersk Air	600	4/8/70	FF as PH–FPM
10438	S2–ABH	Bangladesh Baiman	600	22/9/72	FF as PH–EXB, re-reg PH–FPN
10439	CR–LLD	DTA	200	7/7/70	FF as PH–FPO
10440	VH–TQR	TAA	600	29/7/70	FF as PH–EXB *William Hovell*
10441	VH–TQS	TAA	600	11/8/70	FF as PH–EXB
10442	S2–ABI	Bangladesh Baiman	600	23/11/73	FF as PH–EXA. L to Air Anglia. L to South West Aviation. S to Turavia as I–VANA, order cancelled
10443	OY–APE	Maersk Air	600	12/11/70	FF as PH–EXD
10444	ZK–DCA	NZNAC	200	18/3/71	FF as PH–EXE
10445	ZK–DCB	NZNAC	200	18/3/71	
10446	TN–ABZ	Lina Congo	600	28/12/71	
10447	F–BSUM	French Government	500	27/11/70	
10448	F–BSUN	French Government	500	14/1/71	

C/n	Current Marks	Current Owner/operator	Model Series	Initial Delivery	Remarks
10449	F–BSUO	French Government	500	11/2/71	
10450	TU–VAJ	Ivory Coast Government	600	22/12/70	
10451	T–43	Argentine AF	600	27/12/71	FF as PH–EXA
10452	XY–ADQ	Union of Burma AW	600	26/2/71	
10453	SZ–ABJ	Bangladesh Baiman	600	15/9/72	FF as PH–EXD, re-reg PH–FPU
10454	T–44	Argentine AF	600	27/12/71	FF as PH–EXB
10455	9M–ARI	Malayan Airlines System	500	31/3/71	FF as 9V-BCS
10456	9M–APU	Malayan Airlines System	500	15/4/71	
10457	CR–LMB	DTA	600	11/5/71	FF as PH–FPP
10458	VH–TQT	TAA	600	20/4/71	
10459	OY–APF	Maersk Air	500	1/11/71	FF as PH–EXD
10460	9M–ARJ	Malayan Airlines System	500	11/6/71	FF as 9V–BCT
10461	9M–APV	Malayan Airlines System	500	26/7/71	
10462	PK–GFP	Garuda	600	13/7/71	*Sibajak*
10463	9V–BCU	MSA	500	28/7/71	
10464	9M–APW	Malayan Airlines System	500	19/8/71	
10465		C/n not used			
10466		C/n not used			
10467	9M–ARK	Malayan Airlines System	500	22/9/71	FF as 9V–BCV
10468	9M–APX	Malayan Airlines System	500	6/10/71	
10469	TU–VAK	Ivory Coast Government	400	1/11/71	
10470	9M–ARL	Malayan Airlines System	500	4/11/71	FF as 9V–BCW
10471	9M–ARE	Malayan Airlines System	500	5/9/72	FF as PH–EXF
10472	9M–ASF	Malayan Airlines System	500	14/6/73	FF as PH–EXA, re-reg. PH–EXF
10473	NAF–901	Nigerian AF	600	31/1/72	
10474	5–201	Imperial Iranian AF	600	1/2/72	
10475	5–202	Imperial Iranian AF	600	16/2/72	
10476	NAF–902	Nigerian AF	600	25/3/72	
10477	S2–ABO	Bangladesh Baiman	600	30/10/73	FF as PH–EXB, re-reg. PH–EXC
10478	5–203	Imperial Iranian AF	400	2/3/72	
10479	5–204	Imperial Iranian AF	400	22/3/72	
10480	5–205	Imperial Iranian AF	400	10/4/70	
10481	5–206	Imperial Iranian AF	400	17/5/72	FF as PH–FPV
10482	5–207	Imperial Iranian AF	400	4/5/72	
10483	5–208	Imperial Iranian AF	400	7/7/72	
10484	5–209	Imperial Iranian AF	400	25/8/72	WO
10485	5–209	Imperial Iranian AF	400	19/7/72	FF as 5–210, re-reg 5–209
10486	5–210	Imperial Iranian AF	400	1/9/72	FF as 5–211, re-reg 5–210

Fokker F-27

C/n	Current Marks	Current Owner/operator	Model Series	Initial Delivery	Remarks
10487	NAF–903	Nigerian AF	400	8/8/72	
10488	NAF–904	Nigerian AF	400	5/2/73	FF as PH–EXE
10489	5–211	Imperial Iranian AF	400	20/9/72	FF as PH–EXA, re-reg PH–FPW, re-reg 5–212, re-reg 5–211
10490	NAF–905	Nigerian AF	400	15/2/73	FF as PH–EXC
10491	5–212	Imperial Iranian AF	400	10/11/72	FF as PH–EXA, re-reg 5–213 re-reg 5–212
10492	5–213	Imperial Iranian AF	400	2/1/73	FF as PH–EXF, re-reg 5–214 re-reg 5–213
10493	NAF–906	Nigerian AF	400	5/3/73	FF as PH–EXA
10494	7T–WAI	Air Algerie	400	19/4/73	FF as PH–EXB
10495	7T–WAK	Air Algerie	400	13/6/73	
10496	7T–WAL	Air Algerie	400	2/8/73	
10497	5–214	Imperial Iranian AF	400	17/10/73	FF as PH–EXW
10498	5–215	Imperial Iranian AF	600	21/11/73	FF as PH–EXX
10499	5–216	Imperial Iranian AF	400		
10500	5–217	Imperial Iranian AF	400		

Fokker F-28

C/n	Current Marks	Current Owner/operator	Model Series	Initial Delivery	Remarks
11001	PH–JHG	Fokker-VFW	6000		Prototype Srs 1000, FF MAY-9-67. Rebuilt as Srs 2000, FF APR-28-71. Rebuilt as Srs 6000, FF SEP-28-73.
11002	PH–WEV	Fokker-VFW	1000		Second prototype FF AUG-3-67.
11003	PH–MOL	Ghana Airways		26/4/69	FF as PH-MOL. L to Braathens 1970 as LN-SUM L to Ghana AW
11004	I–TIDU	Itavia	1000	24/2/69	FF as PH–ZAA. D to LTU as D-ABAQ. S APR-1973
11005	–	Fokker-VFW	–		Test aircraft
11006	I–TIBD	Itavia	1000	19/4/68	FF as PH–ZAB. D to LTU as D-ABAX. S APR-1973
11007	–	Fokker-VFW	–		Test aircraft
11008	PH–MAT	Martinair	1000	19/9/69	*Prinses Margriet*
11009	LN–SUC	Braathens	1000	3/3/69	FF as PH–ZAD. *Olar Kyrre*
11010	LN–SUX	Braathens	1000	27/3/69	FF as PH–ZAE. *Harald Hardrade.*
11011	LN–SUY	Braathens	1000	29/4/69	FF as PH–ZAF. *Sverre Sigurdson.* WO Oslo DEC-23-72
11012	LN–SUN	Braathens	1000	17/6/69	FF as PH–ZAG. *Hakon Sverreson*
11013	LN–SUO	Braathens	1000	19/6/69	FF as PH–ZAH L to Ansett-ANA as VH–MMJ, *RMA Pilbara* AUG-1969 to JUL-1970. *Magnus Barfet*
11014	I–TIDA	Itavia	1000	5/11/69	FF as PH–ZAI
11015	I–TIDE	Itavia	1000	28/2/70	FF as PH–ZAK
11016	N281FH	Eastex	1000	13/9/69	FF as PH–ZAL. D to Fairchild. S MAR-6-73
11017	EC-BYA	Iberia	1000	23/4/70	FF as PH–ZAM *Rio Arga*
11018	N282FH	Fairchild	1000	6/4/70	FF as PH–ZAN
11019	EC–BVB	Iberia	1000	27/5/70	FF as PH–ZAO *Rio Segre*
11020	N283FH	Fairchild	1000	6/7/70	FF as PH–ZAP
11021	VH–FKA	Ansett-ANA	1000	4/6/70	FF as PH–ZAS *RMA Pilbara II*
11022	VH–FKB	Ansett-ANA	1000	8/7/70	FF as PH–ZAT *RMA Kimberley*
11023	EC–BVC	Iberia	1000	14/8/70	FF as PH–EXA *Rio Jamara* WO Bilbao DEC-28-72
11024	N284FH	Fairchild	1000	24/10/70	FF as PH–EXC
11025	VH–FKC	Ansett-ANA	1000	16/10/70	FF as PH–EXF *RMA Arnhemland*
11026	VH–FKD	Ansett-ANA	1000	9/11/70	FF as PH-EXA *RMA Goldfields*
11027	PH–ZBG	Fokker-VFW	1000	25/2/71	FF as D-AHLA. D to Aviation. Returned to Fokker – VFW as PH-ZBG DEC-1973
11028	T–01	Argentine Government	1000	28/12/70	President's aircraft
11029	D–ABAN	LTU	1000	22/2/71	
11030	D–ABAM	LTU	1000	16/3/71	
11031	PH–ZBH	Fokker-VFW	1000	1/4/71	FF as D-AHLB. D to Aviation. L to Braathens, reg LN-HLB. Returned to Fokker-VFW as PH-ZBH DEC-1973

Fokker F-28

C/n	Current Marks	Current Owner/operator	Model Series	Initial Delivery	Remarks
11032	PH–ZAV	Fokker-VFW	1000		FF as I-VAGA for Turavia, order cancelled, L to Ghana AW, reg PH-ZAV. L to Braathens, reg LN-SUM L to SATCO, reg OB-R-390. Ret to Fokker-VFW. Used for silenced engine tests DEC-1973
11033	CF–TAV	Transair	1000	14/7/71	FF as N285FH. D toFairchild. S to Transair
11034	PH–ZBI	Fokker-VFW	1000	6/7/71	FF as D-AHLC. D to Aviation. Returned to Fokker-VFW after liquidation NOV-1973 L to Nigeria AW from JAN-1974.
11035	PK–GJZ	Garuda Airways	1000	19/8/71	FF as PH–EXF. Intended for Aerocoop. *Batanghari*
11036	PK–GJY	Garuda Airways	1000	4/10/71	Intended for Aerocoop. *Indragiri*
11037	PK–GJR	Garuda Airways	1000	25/9/73	FF as PH–EXE. Intended for Itavia as I–TIDO. Order cancelled. *Kampur.*
11038	CF–TAY	Transair	1000	23/2/72	FF as N286FH. D to Transair APR-15-73
11039	PK–GJX	Garuda Airways	1000	29/11/71	Intended for Aerocoop. *Mahakam*
11040	VH–FKE	Ansett-ANA	1000	21/9/71	*RMA Gascoyne*
11041	C2–RNI	Air Nauru	1000	18/1/72	FF as PH-EXF *Nauru Chief*
11042	PK–PJT	Pertamina AW	1000	10/12/71	*Pangkalan Susu*
11043	N287FH	Fairchild	1000	3/7/72	
11044	N288FH	Fairchild	1000	1/9/72	
11045	PH–PBX	Netherlands Government	1000	3/2/71	VIP aircraft
11046	D–AGAB	Bonn-Air/Germanair	1000	9/3/72	*Nürnberg*
11047	N289FH	Fairchild	1000	2/2/72	
11048	N280FH	Fairchild	1000	5/5/72	FF as PH-EXF
11049	5N–AGN	Nigerian Government	1000	14/2/72	FF as PH-EXD President's and VIP aircraft
11050	D–AGAC	Bonn-Air/Germanair	1000	25/4/72	*Bremen*
11051	D–AGAD	Bonn-Air/Germanair	1000	9/5/72	*Hannover*
11052	D–AGAE	Bonn-Air/Germanair	1000	29/5/72	*Saarbrücken*
11053	5N–ANB	Nigerian Airways	2000	6/1/73	First production Srs 2000. FF as PH-EXF. JUN-2-72
11054	PK–GJW	Garuda Airways	1000	31/7/72	*Bogowonto*
11055	PK–GJV	Garuda Airways	1000	24/8/72	*Mamberamo*
11056	PH–EXB	Fokker-VFW	1000	29/12/72	
11057	TC–JAO	THY	1000	29/12/72	FF as PH–ZBA *Van*
11058	TC–JAP	THY	1000	29/12/72	FF as PH–ZBB *Bursa*
11059	OB–R–1020	Aeroperu	1000	14/3/73	FF as PH–ZBD. D to SATCO as OB–R–397
11060	TC–JAR	THY	1000	19/1/73	FF as PH–ZBC *Sivas*
11061	PK–GJU	Garuda Airways	1000	10/11/72	*Tulang Bawang*
11062	PH–ZBE	Fokker-VFW	2000	--	
11063	PK–GJT	Garuda Airways	1000	26/2/73	FF as PH–EXE *Siak*
11064	PK–GJS	Garuda Airways	1000	19/3/73	FF as PH–EXD *Citanduy*
11065	OB–R–1018	Aeroperu	1000	30/5/73	FF as PH–EXN. D to SATCO as OB–R–398
11066	OB–R–1019	Aeroperu	1000	28/6/73	FF as PH–EXO D to SATCO as OB–R–399
11067	SE–DGA	Linjeflyg	1000	18/5/73	FF as PH–EXL
11068	SE–DGB	Linjeflyg	1000	24/4/73	FF as PH–EXI
11069	SE–DGC	Linjeflyg	1000	4/5/73	FF as PH–EXK
11070	TC–JAS	THY	1000	10/7/73	FF as PH–EXP. *Samsun*
11071	TC–JAT	THY	1000	6/8/73	FF as PH–EXR *Trabzon*
11072	PH–EXS	Fokker-VFW	1000	–	

C/n	Current Marks	Current Owner/operator	Model Series	Initial Delivery	Remarks
11073	PK–PJV	Pertamina Airways	1000	9/11/73	FF as PH–EXT VIP aircraft. *Pangkalan Brandon*
11074	–	Fokker-VFW	1000C	–	Cargo door prototype
11075	PK–GJQ	Garuda Airways	1000	9/11/73	FF as PH–EXV *Prago*
11076	PH–EXY	Fokker-VFW	1000	--	
11077	PH–EXU	Fokker-VFW	1000	–	
11078	PK–GJP	Garuda Airways	1000	1974	FF as PH–EXZ *Cimanuk*
11991	I–TIDI	Itavia	1000	28/4/70	FF as PH–ZAR
11992	FAC–001	Columbian AF	1000	15/2/71	FF as PH-EXA President's and VIP aircraft
11993	5N-ANA	Nigerian Airways	1000	16/8/72	FF as PH-EXE
11994	PH–FPT	Fokker-VFW	1000	31/1/72	FF as PH-EXA. L to Nigerian AW. WO SEP-19-72

General Dynamics (Convair) 880

C/n	Current Marks	Current Owner/operator	Model Series	Initial Delivery	Remarks
1	N871TW	TWA	22–1	29/10/65	Prototype FF JAN–27–59 as N801TW. Cvtd to 880M and FF OCT–3–60 as 8489H
2	N802TW	TWA	22–1	18/3/61	
3	N803TW	TWA	22–1	13/10/61	
4	N8801E	Delta	22–2	13/12/61	
5	N804TW	TWA	22–1	21/1/61	L by Northeast as N8478H to SEP–11–63
6	N805TW	TWA	22–1	10/8/61	
7	N8802E	Delta	22–2	31/1/60	
8	N806TW	TWA	22–1	30/1/61	L by Northeast as N8479H to SEP–12–63
9		LANICA-Nicaragua	22–1	10/9/63	D to Hughes Tool Co. as N8492H. L to Northeast S to LANICA JUL–1972
10	N808TW	TWA	22–1	18/5/60	
11	N8803E	Delta	22–2	5/5/60	
12	N809TW	TWA	22–1	14/12/60	L by Northeast as N8480H to JUL–29–63
13	N810TW	TWA	22–1	15/2/61	
14	N811TW	TWA	22–1	2/2/61	
15	N812TW	TWA	22–1	9/6/61	
16	N8804E	Delta	22–2	6/5/60	WO Atlanta MAY–23–60
17	N8805E	Delta	22–2	2/6/60	
18	N8493H	Hughes Tool Co	22–1	8/8/63	L by Northeast to JAN–24–68
19	N814TW	TWA	22–1	2/9/61	
20	N815TW	TWA	22–1	8/12/60	L by Northeast as N8481H to AUG–26–63
21	N8806E	Delta	22–2	4/7/60	
22	N816TW	TWA	22–1	5/12/60	L by Northeast as N8482H to SEP–13–63
23	N817TW	TWA	22–1	30/11/60	L by Northeast as N8483H to AUG–29–63
24	N818TW	TWA	22–1	5/1/61	
25	N819TW	TWA	22–1	12/1/61	
26	N820TW	TWA	22–1	20/3/61	WO at Kansas City SEP–13–65
27	N821TW	TWA	22–1	8/1/61	WO Cincinnati NOV–21–67
28	N822TW	TWA	22–1	6/1/61	
29	N8807E	Delta	22–2	4/8/60	WO Chicago DEC–20–72
30	N823TW	TWA	22–1	15/3/61	
31	N824TW	TWA	22–1	1/1/61	
32	N825TW	TWA	22–1	21/1/61	
33	N826TW	TWA	22–1	6/5/61	
34	N8494H	Hughes Tool Co	22–1	25/10/62	L by Northeast to FEB–24–68
35	N828TW	TWA	22–1	26/4/61	
36	N8808E	Delta	22–2	1/10/60	
37M	VR–HFX	Cathay Pacific	22M–3	19/4/63	D to VIASA as YV–C–VIC; used in joint VIASA/KLM colours. S 1966. WO Hong Kong NOV–5–67
38	N8809E	Delta	22–2	23/10/60	
39	N8495H	LANICA-Nicaragua	22–1	1/12/61	D to Hughes Tool Co. as N8495H. L to Northeast S to LANICA JUL–1972
40	N830TW	TWA	22–1	25/5/61	
41	N8810E	Delta	22–2	21/11/60	
42	N801TW	TWA	22–1	9/7/61	

C/n	Current Marks	Current Owner/operator	Model Series	Initial Delivery	Remarks
43M	VR–HFT	Cathay Pacific	22M–3		L by Swissair as HB–ICL; returned to GD as N94284. S to CPA OCT–15–64
44M	VR–HGA	Cathay Pacific	22M–4	6/6/61	FF as N8486H. D to CAT as B-1008. S MAR–68
45M	JA8030	JDA	22M–3		L by Swissair as HB–ICM; returned to GD as N94285. S to JDA JAN–4–65. *Gina* WO Tokyo AUG–26–66
46M		Aero America	22M–3	3/7/63	D to JAL as JA8026 *Yanagi.* S to Aero America
47M	VR–HFS	Cathay Pacific	22M–3	20/2/62	
48M	TF–	Air Viking	22M–3	1/3/63	D to JAL as JA8027 *Sumire.* S to Glenaire. D to Air Viking JUL–1973
49M	JA8028	JAL	22M–3		*Kikyo.* WO Moses Lake, Wash, JUN–24–69
50	N8811E	Delta	22–2	9/9/61	
51	N8812E	Delta	22–2	20/9/61	
52	N8813E	Delta	22–2	25/10/61	
53-62	N8814E	Delta	22–2	14/7/62	
54-63	N8815E	Delta	22–2	2/7/62	
55-64	N8816E	Delta	22–2	11/7/62	
56-65	N8817E	Delta	22–2	19/7/62	
7-1-53	VR–HFZ	Cathay Pacific	22M–21	1/8/61	D to VIASA as YV–C–VIA. S 1968 WO Vietnam JUN–1972
7-2-54	VR–HFY	Cathay Pacific	22M–21	31/7/61	D to Alaska AL as N8477H S NOV–5–66
7-3-55	N112	FAA	22M–21	13/8/61	
7-4-56	VR–HGC	Cathay Pacific	22M–21	28/9/61	D to VIASA as YV–C–VIB. and used in joint VIASA/KLM colours. S 1969
7-5-57	N5865	Vacation Corp of America	22M–22	21/7/61	D to JAL as JA8021 *Sakuru.* S to Vacation Corp.
7-6-58	VR–HGF	Cathay Pacific	22M–22	1/9/61	D to JAL as JA8022 *Matsu.* S JAN–1970
7-7-59	JA8023	JAL	22M–22	8/9/61	*Kaede.* WO FEB–27–65
7-8-60	VR–HGG	Cathay Pacific	22M–22	7/6/62	D to JAL as JA8024 *Kiku.* S JUN–1970
7-9-61	N8566	Aero Leasing	22M–22	2/7/62	D to JAL as JA8205 *Ayame.* S to Aero Leasing. L to FAA OCT–1971. L to Sun Seekers Air Travel Club. 1972

General Dynamics (Convair) 990

C/n	Current Marks	Current Owner/operator	Model Series	Initial Delivery	Remarks
1	N5601G	NASA	30–5	17/11/64	Prototype. FF JAN–24–61 as N5601G. Cvtd to 990A before delivery to NASA WO Moffett Field APR–12–73
2	OBR–765	APSA	30–5	8/7/64	Was N5602G. L from Garrett–AiResearch from FEB–1–65 In Storage at Tucson, Arizona
3	PK–GIA	Garuda	30–5	24/1/64	*Pajajaran* WO MAY–28–68 Bombay
4	N7876	Ports-of-Call Travel Club	30–5	21/10/63	D to Garuda as PK–GJB *Sriwijaja.* S to Ports-of-Call Travel Club. WO Guam SEP–1973
5	OBR–728	APSA	30–6	15/11/63	Was N8484H. L from UTC, initially as OB–OAG. In storage at Tucson, Arizona
6	HB–ICF	Swissair	30–6	6/2/64	Was N8485H
7	HB–ICA	Swissair	30–6	12/1/62	Was N8497H
8	HB–ICG	Swissair	30–6	23/2/62	*Grisons.* L by SAS 1962–1966 as SE–DAY
9	N5605	Modern AT	30–5	7/1/62	D to American AL. S MAR–13–67. L to Air France 1967–68
10	OD–AEX	Lebanese Intl AW	30–5	12/1/62	D to American AL as N5606. S 1966. WO DEC–28–68 Beirut
11	HB–ICB	Swissair	30–6	18/1/62	
12	HB–ICC	Swissair	30–6	25/1/62	(Original c/n 12 used by GD as N94280, not delivered; original c/n 38 re-numbered as second c/n 12)
13	N987AS	Alaska Intnl	30–8	1/3/63	D to Varig as PP–VJE. S to Alaska AL as N73675 MAY–67. L to AREA 1968. L to Modern AT as N5603, 1969 WO AUG–8–70 Acapulco
14	HB–ICE	Swissair	30–6	3/8/62	L Ghana AW 1964–65
15	HB–ICD	Swissair	30–6	3/2/62	*Basel-Land.* WO FEB–21–70 near Zurich
16	N5624	Modern AT	30–5	9/2/62	D to American AL. S 1967 and D as N5607
17	HB–ICH	Swissair	30–6	10/4/62	D to Swissair *St Gotthard.* L by SAS 1962–1966 as OY–KVA, later SE–DAZ *Ring Viking* and released to THAI as HS–TGE. To Swissair MAR–66. To Balair APR–1968. L to El Al 1968
18	EC–BZP	Spantax	30–5	5/3/62	D to American AL as N5608. S 1969 to MEA, reg. OD–AFF. S to Spantax
19	N5625	Modern Air	30–8	1/3/63	D to Varig as PP–VJF. S to Modern Air
20	N5623	Modern Air	30–8	1/3/63	D to Varig as PP–VJG. S to Modern Air
21	EC–BTE	Spantax	30–5	20/3/62	D to American AL as N5609. S to Modern AT 1967. S 1970

C/n	Current Marks	Current Owner/operator	Model Series	Initial Delivery	Remarks
22	EC–BJC	Spantax	30–5	4/4/62	D to American AL as N5610. S 1967. L to Iberia
23	EC–BJD	Spantax	30–5	4/4/62	D to American AL as N5611. S 1967.
24	N5612	Fredk B Ayer	30–5	9/4/62	D to American AL. S to Ayer 1967. L to Northeast AL 1967 to APR–30–68 *Rita*
25	EC–BZR	Spantax	30–5	8/5/62	D to American AL as N5613. L to Internord as OY–ANI JUN–23–67 to 1968. S to Spantax 1969 WO Teneriffe DEC–3–72
26	N5614	Modern Air	30–5	21/4/62	D to American AL as N5614. S 1969 to MEA, reg OD–AFK. S to Modern Air OCT–1970
27	N5615	Modern AT	30–5	11/5/62	D to American AL. S 1968. L to Nordair 1968
28	N5616	American AL	30–5	29/6/62	WO MAY–30–63
29	N5617	Modern AT	30–5	11/5/62	D to American AL. S 1968. *Berliner Bar*
30	EC–BZO	Spantax	30–5	5/6/62	D to American AL as N5618. S 1969 to MEA, reg OD–AFG. S to Spantax OCT–1971
31	OD–AEW	Lebanese Intl AW	30–5	23/6/62	D to American AL as N5619. WO DEC–28–68 Beirut
32	EC–BNM	Spantax	30–5	21/2/62	D to American AL as N5620. S FEB–68. WO JAN–5–70 Arlanda
33	N5601	Modern Air	30–5	18/1/63	D to American AL as N5601. S 1969 to MEA, reg OD–AFJ. S to Modern Air. 1970
34	EC–BQQ	Spantax	30–5	31/1/63	D to American AL as N5602. L to Internord as SS–DDK DEC–2–67. Rtd to American AL as N5606 1968. S 1969
35	EC–BXI	Spantax	30–5	8/2/63	D to American AL as N5603. S to MEA. S to Spantax
36	N5604	American AL	30–5	21/3/63	L to Internord as OY–ANL FEB-68 to DEC–68
37		NASA	30–5	3/9/63	D to Garuda as PK–GJC *Majapakit*. S to NASA AUG–1973

Handley Page Herald

C/n	Current Marks	Current Owner/operator	Model Series	Initial Delivery	Remarks
147	G–AODE	Handley Page Ltd			FF with Leonides (HPR 3) AUG–25–55; FF with Darts (HPR 7) MAR–11–58; WO AUG–30–58
148	G–ARTC	Handley Page Ltd			FF as HPR 3 G–AODF AUG–3–56; FF as HPR 7 Srs 100 DEC–17–58; FF as Srs 200 APR–8–61
149	G–APWA	Handley Page Ltd	100		L to Jersey AL 1961. L to Autair 1963. L to Sadia as PP–ASV SEP–64 to SEP–65 and as PP–SDM from NOV–18–66. L to BMA MAR to SEP–66
150	G–APWB	Autair	101	10/3/62	L to Jersey AL 1961. Bought by MOA for BEA. S to Autair 1966. WFS 1969
151	G–APWC	Autair	101	5/1/62	L to Jersey AL 1961. Bought by MOA for BEA. S to Autair 1966. WFS 1969
152	G–APWD	Autair	101	30/4/62	Bought by MOA for BEA. S to Autair 1966. WFS 1969
153	G–APWE	British Island AW	201	4/1/62	
154	G–APWF	British Island AW	201	9/4/62	
155	G–APWG	British Island AW	201	22/5/62	
156	G–APWH	British Island AW	201	6/6/62	
157	B–2009	Far East Air Transport	201	24/5/62	D to BU(CI) as G–APWI. S 1969. WO FEB–24–69, S Taiwan
158	G–APWJ	British Island AW	201	13/6/63	
159	CF–NAC	Eastern Provincial	202	13/2/62	D to Nordair
160	CF–NAF	Maritime Central	211	13/3/62	D to Nordair. WO MAR–17–65
161	G–ASKK	British Island AW	211		Built as CF–MCK for MCA; re-allocated as PI–C–910 for Cruz; L Autair as G–ASKK; L Sadia as PP–ASV. D to BMA as G–ASKK FEB–1–65. S 1967
162	B–2001	Far East Air Transport	210	4/5/63	Built as CF–MCM for MCA. D to Globe Air as HB–AAG *Herald of Bern.* Returned to HP as G–ATHB. S FEB–16–66
163	PI–C–869	Air Manila	204	26/11/62	D BUA (executive) as G–ASBP; L to Air Manilla as PI–C–869 before D on OCT–21–66
164	G–ASBG	British Island AW	203	12/4/63	FF as G–ASBG D to Itavia as I–TIVA. S JUL–1973
165	B--2011	Far East Air Transport	207	22/1/63	D as 109 to Royal Arab Air Force; trsfd to Alia as JY–ACR DEC–63; rtnd to HP and L to BMA as G–ATHE. D to Bavaria Flug as D–BOBO *Herald of the Alps* APR–4–66. Ret to HP as G–ATHE 1968. S FEB–19–69
166	CF–EPI	Eastern Provincial	206	13/2/63	
167	CF–EPC	Eastern Provincial	206	29/3/63	L Bahamas AW as VP–BCG FEB–MAY–64

C/n	Current Marks	Current Owner/operator	Model Series	Initial Delivery	Remarks
168	I–TIVE	Itavia	203	4/5/63	
169	G–AVEZ	British Island AW	210	16/8/63	D as HB–AAH to Globe Air *Herald of Zurich.* S DEC–15–66 L to Sadia 1967–68 as PP–AFW
170	JY–ACQ	Alia	207	12/7/63	D as 110 to Royal Arab Air force; trsfd to Alia DEC–63 and WO APR–10–65
171	FM1020	RMAF	401	1/11/63	
172	FM1021	RMAF	401	29/12/63	
173	F–BLOY	Europe Air Service	210	13/3/64	Built as HB–AAI; temp G–ASPJ for L to Alia. D to Globe Air as HB–AAK *Herald of Basle* MAR–13–64 S 1968 to Europe Air Service as F–OCLY
174	4X–AHS	Arkia	209	18/5/64	FF as G–8–2
175	FM1022	RMAF	401	17/1/64	
176	G–AVPN	Itavia	213	1/5/64	D Bavaria Fluggesellschaft as D–BIBI. S to HP 1967 G–AVPN. L Itavia 1967
177	G–ATIG	British Midland	214	18/9/65	FF as G–ATIG and L to Globe Air S to Sadia as PP–SDI. S. APR–28–73
178	FM1023	RMAF	401	8/2/64	
179	D–BEBE	Bavaria Flug	213	29/3/65	*Herald of Bavaria.* L to Arkia NOV–24–67. WFS 1970
180	FM1024	RMAF	401	28/9/64	
181	FM1025	RMAF	401	3/11/64	
182	FM1026	RMAF	401	8/12/64	
183	4X–AHR	Arkia	209	17/4/64	FF as G–8–1
184	I–TIVU	Itavia	203	29/5/64	
185	PP–SDG	Sadia	214	6/10/64	FF as G–8–3, then G–ASVO
186	PP–SDH	Sadia	214	26/1/65	
187	FM1027	RMAF	401	1/11/65	
188	F–BOIZ	Europe Air Service	210	18/5/65	D to Globe Air as HB–AAL *Herald of Interlaken.* S to Europe Air Service 1968, as F–OCLZ
189	4X-AHT	Arkia	209	28/7/66	FF as G–ATDS
190	PP–SDJ	Sadia	214	12/7/65	WO NOV–3–67 Curitiba
191	PP–SDL	Sadia	214	1/2/66	
192	PI–C–866	Air Manila	215	18/3/66	
194	G–BAVX	British Midland	214	11/1/68	D to Sadia as PP–SDN S APR–28–73
195	4X–AHQ	Arkia	209	10/4/68	
196	I–TIVI	Itavia	203	4/7/68	
197	4X–AHN	Arkia	209	15/8/68	

Hawker Siddeley AW650 Argosy

C/n	Current Marks	Current Owner/operator	Model Series	Initial Delivery	Remarks
6651	N896U	Duncan Aviation	102	19/12/61	Proto FF JAN–8–59 as G–AOZZ. S to BEA; re-sold to HSA JUL–27–65. S to Universal 1968, reg. N896U. S JUL–1973
6652	N890U	Shackleton Aviation	101	17/8/61	Was G–APRL. D to Riddle AL as N6507R. S to Zantop (later Universal) as N602Z re-reg N890U. S JUL–1973
6653	G–APRM	Rolls-Royce	102	23/11/61	D to BEA. Resold to HSA 1965. L to BEA 1966. S to Rolls-Royce 1970
6654	G–APRN	Air Bridge Carriers	102	6/11/61	D to BEA as G–APRN. Resold to HSA MAY–3–65 S 1968 to Universal AW, reg N897U. S to Sagittair and taken over by ABC when Sagittair ceased ops.
6655	N891U	Duncan Aviation	101	22/6/61	Was G–APVH. D to Riddle as N6504R. S to Capitol. S to Zantop (later Universal) and reg N891U. S MAY–1972
6656	G–APWW	Air Bridge Carriers	101	24/1/61	Was G–1–3 and G–APWW. D to Riddle as N6503R. S to Capitol. S to Zantop (later Universal) and reg N892U. S to Sagittair and taken over by ABC when Sagittair ceased ops.
6657	G–AZHN	Air Bridge Carriers	101	11/6/61	Was G–1–4. D to Riddle as N6505R. S to Zantop (later Universal) and reg N893U, later N6002. S to Sagittair and taken over by ABC when Sagittair ceased ops.
6658	N894U	Duncan Aviation	101	18/7/61	Was G–1–5. D to Riddle. S to Capitol. S to Zantop (later Universal) and reg. N6506R. S MAY–1972
6659	N601Z	Universal AW	101	18/12/60	Was G–1–6. D Riddle as N6501R. S to Zantop (later Universal) WO OCT–14–65
6660	G–	Air Bridge Carriers	101	7/1/61	Was G–1–7. D Riddle as N6502R. S to Capitol. S to Zantop (later Universal) reg. N895U S MAY–1972
6799	G–ASKZ	HSA	200	–	Proto Series 200. Scrapped 1966
6800	G–ASXL	BEA	222	28/1/65	WO Italy JUL–4–65
6801	CF–TAG	Transair	222	2/3/65	D to BEA as G–ASXM. S JUN–70 L to Aer Turas as EI–AVJ during 1972.
6802	CF–TAJ	Transair	222	26/3/65	D to BEA as G–ASXN. S 1970
6803	CF–TAX	Transair	222	28/4/65	D to BEA as G–ASXO. S 1970
6804	G–ASXP	BEA	222	16/6/65	WO Stanstead DEC–4–67
6805	CF–TAZ	Transair	222	21/11/66	D to BEA as G–ATTC. S APR–70

Hawker Siddeley/DH Comet

C/n	Current Marks	Current Owner/operator	Model Series	Initial Delivery	Remarks
06001	G–ALVG	MoS/DH			Proto. FF JUL–27–49 as G–5–1. Varied test programmes until broken up for structural tests at RAE end 1953
06002	G–ALZK	MoS/DH		2/4/51	2nd proto FF JUL–27–50 as G–5–2. Route proving and test programmes. Broken up Hatfield March 1957
06003	G–ALYP	BOAC	1	8/4/52	First production Srs 1 FF JAN –9–51. Flew world's first turbojet service MAY–2–52. WO Elba JAN–10–54
06004	G–ALYR	BOAC	1	17/5/52	Used for water tank test, RAE, JULY 55
06005	G–ALYS	BOAC	1	4/2/52	Used for jet buffet test, RAE, 1955
06006	G–ALYT	MoS/DH	2X	–	Proto Srs 2 FF FEB–16–52. Eventually to RAF Halton as 7610M Scrapped SEP–1967
06007	G–ALYU	BOAC	1	6/3/52	Used for ground trials 1955
06008	G–ALYV	BOAC	1	23/4/52	WO over Calcutta MAY–2–53
06009	G–ALYW	BOAC	1	14/6/52	Handed over to RAE 1955, to 71M.U.RAF 1972
06010	G–ALYX	BOAC	1	25/7/52	Static ground tests at RAE 1955–63
06011	G–ALYY	BOAC	1	23/9/52	WO over Naples APR–8–54
06012	G–ALYZ	BOAC	1	30/9/52	WO Rome OCT–26–52
06013	G–ANAV	BOAC	1A	1953	Laid down as G–ALZA; FF as CF–CUM for CPAL. Scrapped at RAE 1955
06014	CF–CUN	CPAL	1A	2/3/53	WO Karachi on delivery MAR–3–53
06015	F–BGSA	UAT	1A	11/12/52	WFS APR–12–54 and scrapped at Le Bourget
06016	F–BGSB	UAT	1A	19/2/53	WFS APR–12–54 and scrapped at Le Bourget
06017	5301	RCAF	1XB	18/3/53	Modified to Comet 1XB SEP–57. Scrapped 1965.
06018	N3735	R. C. Rose	1XB	13/4/53	D to RCAF as 5302. Modified to Comet 1XB SEP–57. S to Eldon Armstrong as CF–SVR 1965. S to B Dallas Airmotive
06019	F–BGSC	UAT	1A	30/4/53	WO Dakar JUN–25–53
06020	G–AOJT	MoS	1A	12/6/53	D Air France as F–BGNX returned to UK JUN–27–56 for RAE tests and then scrapped
06021	XM829	MoA	1XB	7/7/53	First Air France service AUG–26–53 as F–BGNY. returned to UK and mod to 1XB; BOAC crew training as G–AOJU At Stanstead FEB–20–64. S NOV–70.

Hawker Siddeley/DH Comet

C/n	Current Marks	Current Owner/operator	Model Series	Initial Delivery	Remarks
06022	XM823	MoA	1XB	22/7/53	Air France service as F–BGNZ; mod to 1XB in 1956 and used for tests as G–5–23 and G–APAS before becoming XM823 for Hawker Siddeley Dynamics. Last flight APR–8–68 to Shawbury for RAF Museum.
06023	XK655	RAF (Wyton)	2R	17/2/58	First production Srs 2 FF AUG–27–53 as G–AMXA. D to No. 51 Sqdn. Burnt 1969
06024	XK669	RAF	T2–C2	8/6/56	Built as G–AMXB for BOAC. *Taurus.* Grounded 1967 at Brize Norton.
06025	XK659	RAF (Wyton)	2R	12/7/57	Built as G–AMXC for BOAC. Radar trials with No. 51 Sqdn.
06026	XN453	Mintech (RAE)	2E	29/8/57	Built as G–AMXD and mod to Srs 2E (Avon RA29 trials) in APRIL 1957. Retired FEB–1973
06027	XK663	RAF (Wyton)	2R	19/4/57	Built as G–AMXE for BOAC. Radar trials with No. 51 Sqdn. WO
06028	XK670	RAF	T2–C2	7/6/56	Built as G–AMXF for BOAC. *Corvus*. Grounded 1967. RAF Lyneham as 7926M Burnt 1968
06029	XK671	RAF (Topcliffe)	C2	22/8/56	Built as G–AMXG for BOAC *Aquilla.* To No. 216 Sqdn, Later No. 51 Sqdn.
06030	XK695	RAF (Wyton)	C2–2R	14/9/56	Built as G–AXMH for BOAC *Perseus* To No. 216 Sqdn. later No. 51 Sqdn.
06031	XK696	RAF	C2	14/11/56	Built as G–AMXI for BOAC *Orion.* Grounded OCT–27–66 at RAF Watton Scrapped 1969
06032	XK697	RAF (Wyton)	C2	12/12/56	Built as G–AMXJ for BOAC *Cygnus* To No. 216 Sqdn, later No. 51 Sqdn. Retired 1973
06033	XV144	Mintech (RAE)	2F	26/8/57	First production Srs 2 F Built as G–AMXK and mod to Srs 2E Returned to Farnborough MAY–18–71
06034	XK698	RAF	C2	1/1/57	Built as G–AMXL for BOAC *Pegasus.* Grounded 1967, RAF Shawbury as 8031M Broken up at 19MU APR–1973
06035	XK699	RAF (Henlow)	C2	20/2/57	Built for BOAC. *Sagittarius.* To RAF Museum JUN–13–67 as 7971M
06036		MoA	2		Not flown; used for pressure tests
06037	XK715	RAF	C2	22/5/57	Built for BOAC. *Columba.* Grounded DEC–13–66, RAF Cosford
06038		MoA	2		Laid down for BOAC. Scrapped
06039		RAF	C2		Not flown – incomplete
06040		RAF	C2		Not flown – incomplete

C/n	Current Marks	Current Owner/operator	Model Series	Initial Delivery	Remarks
06041		MoA	2		Scrapped before completion
06042		MoA	2		Scrapped before completion
06043		MoA	2		Scrapped before completion
06044		MoA	2		Scrapped before completion
06045	XK716	RAF	C2	7/5/57	*Cepheus.* Grounded JUN–1967. To RAF Halton as 7958M. Scrapped 1973
06046		MoA	2		Scrapped before completion
06047		RAF	C2		Not flown–incomplete
06048		RAF	C2		Not flown–incomplete
06049		RAF	C2		Not flown–incomplete
06100	XP915	MoA (RAE)	3B	21/6/61	Prototype Srs 3 FF JUL–19–54 as G–ANLO; mod to Srs 3B and FF AUG–21–58 Retired MAR–29–72
6401	G–APDA	Dan-Air	4	24/2/59	D BOAC. S Malaysian as 9M–AOA, later 9V–BAS. S to Dan-Air NOV–69 scrapped SEP–1972
6402		HSA	4		Airframe for water tank test
6403	G–APDB	Dan-Air	4	30/9/58	D BOAC. L to MSA as 9M–AOB. S to Dan-Air OCT–69
6404	G–APDC	Dan-Air	4	30/9/58	D BOAC. S Malaysian as 9M–AOC, later 9V–BAT. To Dan-Air AUG–69
6405	G–APDD	Dan-Air	4	18/11/58	D BOAC. L to MSA as 9M–AOD. S to Dan-Air OCT–69
6406	G–APDE	Dan-Air	4	2/10/58	D BOAC. S Malaysian as 9M–AOE, later 9V–BAU. S to Dan-Air NOV–69. L to EAA as 5Y–ALF, 1970 Rtd to Dan–Air JAN–1971 WFS APR–2–73
6407	XV814	MinTech (RAE)	4	31/12/58	D BOAC as G–APDF. S1967
6408		Dan-Air	4	2/3/59	*Las Tres Marias* D as LV–PLM S to Aerolineas, reg. LV–AHN. S to Dan-Air OCT–1971. Scrapped 1972.
6409	G–APDH	BOAC	4	6/12/58	WO MAR–22–64 Singapore on L to Malaysian
6410	LV–AHO	Aerolineas	4	18/3/59	*Lucero de la Tarde* D as LV–PLO WO at Beunos Aires FEB–20–60
6411	LV–AHP	Aerolineas	4	2/5/59	*Lucero del Alba* D as LV–PLP WO AUG–27–59 Asuncion
6412	G–APDK	Dan-Air	4	12/2/59	D to BOAC. S NOV–66. L to EAA as 5Y–ALD 1969–70
6413	G–APDL	Dan-Air	4	6/5/59	D to BOAC. L by EAA as 5Y–ADD, OCT–65 to MAR–67. S JAN–69 WO OCT–7–70
6414	G–APDM	Dan-Air	4	16/4/59	D to BOAC. L to MEA as OD–AEV 1967. L to MSA as 9V–BBJ 1968. S JAN–1969 WO near Barcelona JUL–30–70
6415	G–APDN	Dan-Air	4	10/6/59	D to BOAC. S MAY–68.
6416	G–APDO	Dan-Air	4	14/5/59	D to BOAC. S MAY–66

Hawker Siddeley/DH Comet

C/n	Current Marks	Current Owner/operator	Model Series	Initial Delivery	Remarks
6417	XW944	RAE	4	11/6/59	D to BOAC. L to MSA as 9V–BBH NOV–30–67 to JAN–23–68. S JAN–69 to Dan-Air, reg G–APDP. To RAE for AEW
6418		Channel AW		20/7/59	D to BOAC as G–APDR. S to Mexicana 1965 as XA–NAP. S to Channel and sited at Stanstead Fire School JUN–1972
6419	XW626	MinTech	4	14/8/59	D to BOAC as G–APDS
6420	G–APDT	BOAC	4	19/10/59	D to BOAC. L to Mexicana as XA–NAB, later XA–POW, NOV–65 to DEC–19–69 and used for ground training on return.
6421	G–APMA	BEA	4B	20/12/59	WFS JAN–25–72 and scrapped
6422	G–APMB	Dan-Air	4B	9/11/59	D to BEA. S to Channel AW JUN–25–70. S to Dan-Air APR–72
6423	G–APMC	British Airways Airtours	4B	16/11/59	D to BEA. S MAR–12–70
6424	XA–NAR	Mexicana	4C	8/6/60	Was G–AOVU before delivery *Golden Aztec.* Retired 1971
6425	XA–NAS	Mexicana	4C	14/1/60	Was G–AOVV before delivery Retired 1971
6426	G–APMF	Dan-Air	4B	27/1/60	D to BEA. S APR–1–70 to BEA Airtours. S to Dan-Air APR–1973
6427	G–APDG	Dan-Air	4	28/11/59	D to BOAC as G–APDG. S 1966. S to Kuwait AW, reg 9K-ACI. L to MEA 1968–69. S DEC 1970
6428	HC–ALT	AREA	4	18/12/59	D to BOAC as G–APDI. S 1966
6429	G–APDJ	Dan-Air	4	11/1/60	D to BOAC. S MAY-67
6430	LV–AHR	Aerolineas	4	8/3/60	*Arco Iris* D as LV–POY. WO NOV–23–61 at Campinas
6431	5X–AAO	EAA	4	25/7/60	D as VP–KPJ re-reg 5X–AAO. S to Dan-Air NOV–1970. Scrapped 1972
6432	G–AZLW	Dan-Air	4	19/3/60	*Alborada.* D as LV–POZ re-reg. LV–AHS. S to Dan-Air NOV–1971 WFS MAR–2–73 and scrapped.
6433	–	Dan-Air	4	6/9/60	D as VP–KPK re-reg 5H–AAF. S to Dan-Air JAN–1971. Scrapped 1972
6434	G–AZIY	Dan-Air	4	26/7/60	*Centaurus.* D as LV–PPA Re-reg. LV–AHU. S to Dan-Air NOV–1971
6435	G–APMD	Dan-Air	4B	29/3/60	D to BEA. S MAR–31–70 to BEA Airtours S SEP–1972
6436	G–APME	Dan-Air	4B	10/5/60	L to BEA Airtours during 1970 S APR–1972
6437	G–APYC	Dan-Air	4B	26/4/60	D to Olympic AW as G–APYC later SX–DAK *Queen Frederica.* S JAN 70 to Channel AW. S APR–1972

C/n	Current Marks	Current Owner/operator	Model Series	Initial Delivery	Remarks
6438	G–APYD	Dan-Air	4B	14/5/60	D to Olympic AW as G–APYD later SX–DAL *Queen Olga*. S FEB–70 to Channel AW S APR–1972
6439	SU–ALC	Egyptair	4C	10/6/60	D to Misrair. Transferred JAN–2–71
6440	G–APZM	Dan-Air	4B	14/7/60	D to Olympia AW as G–APZM later SX–DAN *Queen Sophia.* S APR–70 to Channel AW S APR–1972
6441	SU–ALD	UAA	4C	29/6/60	WO Bombay JUL–28–63
6442	G–APMG	Dan-Air	4B	31/7/60	D to BEA. S MAR–16–70 to BEA Airtours. S APR–1973
6443	XA–NAT	Mexicana	4C	29/11/60	Was G–ARBB before delivery. Retired 1971
6444	SU–ALE	UAA	4C	23/12/60	WO FEB–9–70 Munich
6445	OD–ADR	MEA	4C	19/12/60	D to OD–ADK. WO Beirut DEC–28–68
6446	OD–ADQ	MEA	4C	15/2/61	Was G–ARJH before delivery. WO Beirut DEC–28–68
6447	G–ARDI	Channel AW	4B	25/3/61	D to OLYMPIC AW as G–ARDI later SX–DAO *Princess Sophia.* S MAY–70 Scrapped APR–1972
6448	OD–ADS	MEA	4C	14/3/61	WO Beirut DEC–28–68
6449	G–ARCO	BEA	4B	13/4/61	WO OCT–12–67 over Mediterranean. Destroyed by bomb in aircraft.
6450	–	Dan-Air	4C	18/3/61	D to MEA as OD–ADT. S OCT–3–73. Based at Lasham and being broken down for spares
6451	G–ARCP	British Airways Airtours	4B	19/4/61	D to BEA. S MAY–22–70
6452	G–ARJK	British Airways Airtours	4B	15/5/61	D to BEA. S MAR–5–70
6453	G–ARGM	British Airways Airtours	4B	6/5/61	Initially allocated G–AREI, marks not used. D to BEA. S MAR–31–70
6454	SU–ALL	Egyptair	4C	12/6/61	Formerly UAA
6455	G–ARJL	British Airways Airtours	4B	31/5/61	D to BEA. S MAR–1–70
6456	G–ARJM	BEA	4B	26/6/61	WO Ankara DEC–21–61
6457	ST–AAW	Sudan AW	4C	14/11/62	Was G–ASDZ before delivery, intended as XA–NAD
6458	SU–ALM	Egyptair	4C	15/7/61	Formerly UAA
6459	G–ARJN	Dan-Air	4B	4/8/61	D to BEA. S MAR–25–70 to BEA Airtours. S APR–1973
6460	G–AROV	Dan-Air	4C	27/4/62	G–AROV before D as LV–PTS to Aerolineas. Re-reg LV–AIB. S OCT–1971
6461	SA–R–7	King Saud	4C	15/6/62	WO Italian Alps MAR–20–63
6462	SU–AMV	Egyptair	4C	6/4/62	Formerly UAA
6463	ST–AAX	Sudan AW	4C	21/12/62	Intended as XA–NAE
6464	SU–AMW	UAA	4C	16/4/62	WO Nr Bangkok JUL–19–62
6465	G–AYWX	Dan-Air	4C	18/1/63	D to Kuwait AW as 9K–ACA L to MEA. S MAR–1971
6466	SU–ANC	Egyptair	4C	22/12/62	Formerly UAA
6467	XR395	RAF	C4	1/6/62	
6468	XR396	RAF	C4	12/3/62	

Hawker Siddeley/DH Comet

C/n	Current Marks	Current Owner/operator	Model Series	Initial Delivery	Remarks
6469	XR397	RAF	C4	15/2/62	
6470	XR398	RAF	C4	16/3/62	
6471	XR399	RAF	C4	26/4/62	
6472	–	Dan-Air	4	10/4/62	D as VP–KRL to EAA, re-reg 5Y–AAA. S FEB–1971. Scrapped 1972
6473	XS235	MoD (A & AEE)	4C	2/12/63	
6474	G–AYVS	Dan-Air	4C	2/2/64	D to Kuwait AW as 9K–ACE. L to MEA. S APR–1971
6475	SU–ANI	Egyptair	4C	26/2/64	Formerly UAA
6476	XV147	MoD	–	–	Built as Srs 4C and cvtd to HS801 Nimrod (Avon engines). FF OCT–25–65
6477	XV148	MoD	–	–	Built as Srs4C and ctvd to HS801 Nimrod (Spey engines). FF MAY–23–67

Hawker Siddeley HS748

C/n	Current Marks	Current Owner/operator	Model Series	Initial Delivery	Remarks
1534	G–APZV	Hawker Siddeley	100		FF JUN-24-60. Became HS748 MF prototype, re-registered G-ARRV (1548)
1535	G–ARAY	Dan-Air	200		2nd proto, FF APR-10-61 as G-ARAY; cvtd to Srs 2 proto and FF NOV-6-61 *Pride of Perth;* L LAV 1965 YV-C-AMC; L Varig 1965 PP-VJQ; L LIAT 1966 VP-LIO; L PAL as PI-C-784 1967. S AUG-4-67 to Falckair S to Maersk Air, reg OY-DFV. S to Skyways MAY-3-71. Taken over by Dan-Air APR-1972
1536	G–ARMV	Skyways	101	1/4/62	WO JULY-11-65 Lympne
1537	G–ARMW	Dan-Air	101	5/6/62	L LIAT 1966 VP-LII. L by BKS 1967/68. S to Skyways. Taken over by Dan-Air
1538	G–ARMX	Dan-Air	101	2/4/63	L by BKS 1967/68. S to Skyways. Taken over by Dan-Air
1539	LV–HGW	Aerolineas	105	18/1/62	D as LV-PIZ *Cuidad de Bahia Blanca.* WO FEB-2-70, Nr Corrientes
1540	LV–HHB	Yacimientos Petroliferos Fiscales	105	24/3/62	D as LV-PIA *Cuidad de Corrientes* to Aerolineas, re-reg LV-HHD. S MAR-28-73
1541	LV–HHC	Aerolineas	105	24/4/62	D as LV-PJR *Cuidad de Concordia*
1542	LV–HHD	Yacimientos Petroliferos Fiscales	105	7/5/62	D as LV-PUC *Cuidad de Salta* to Aerolineas, re-reg LV-HHD. S MAR-19-73
1543	LV–HHE	Aerolineas	105	5/6/62	D as LV-PUF *Cuidad de Resistencie to* Aerolineas, re-reg LV-HHG. S APR-12-73
1544	LV–HHF	Aerolineas	105	30/6/62	D as LV-POM. *Cuidad de San Juan*
1545	LV–HHG	Yacimientos Petroliferos Fiscales	105	7/7/62	D as LV-PUP *Cuidad de Mar del Plata* to Aerolineas, re-reg LV-HHG. S APR-12-73
1546	LV–HHH	Aerolineas	105	10/8/62	D as LV-PVH *Cuidad de Neuquen* WO JUL-31-71
1547	LV–HHI	Aerolineas	105	20/8/62	D as LV-PVF *Cuidad de Rio Gallegos.* WO NOV-27-69
1548	G–ARRV	Hawker Siddeley	MF		Proto G-APZV cvtd to 748 MF (Andover) aero-dynamic test vehicle and FF DEC-21-63. Grounded 1965
1549	G–ARRW	Dan-Air	106	23/4/63	D to BKS, AT. S MAR-13-67 L by BKS 1968 S to Skyways. Taken over by Dan-Air
1550	C–91–2500	Brazilian AF	204	17/11/62	First production Srs 2

Hawker Siddeley HS748

C/n	Current Marks	Current Owner/operator	Model Series	Initial Delivery	Remarks
1551	C–91–2501	Brazilian AF	205	26/2/63	
1552	C–91–2502	Brazilian AF	205	20/3/63	
1553	C–91–2503	Brazilian AF	205	18/4/63	
1554	C–91–2504	Brazilian AF	205	4/7/63	
1555	C–91–2505	Brazilian AF	205	28/9/63	
1556	LV–IDV	Aerolineas	105	31/8/63	D as LV-PXD *Cuidad de Montevideo*
1557	LV–IEE	Aerolineas	105	30/10/63	D as LV-PXH *Cuidad de Santa Fe*
1558	LV–IEV	Aerolineas	105	15/11/63	D as LV-PXP *Ciudad de Gualequay Chu.* WO JUL-15-69
1559	XW750	MinTech(RAE)	107	20/10/63	D to Smiths Aviation as G-ASJT S JAN-13-70
1560	G–ASPL	Dan-Air	108	14/4/64	D to BKS AT. S MAR-18-67 to Skyways. Taken over by Dan-Air
1561	XS789	RAF ASC	206	7/8/64	Andover CC Mk 2 Queen's Flight
1562	XS790	RAF ASC	206	10/7/64	Andover CC Mk 2 Queen's Flight
1563	XS791	RAF ASC	206	21/12/64	Andover CC Mk 2 VIP
1564	XS792	RAF ASC	206	8/2/56	Andover CC Mk 2 VIP
1565	XS793	RAF ASC	206	12/4/65	Andover CC Mk 2 Queen's Flight
1566	XS794	RAF ASC	206	9/9/65	Andover CC Mk 2 VIP
1567	HS–THA	Thai Airways	207	27/8/64	
1568	HS–THB	Thai Airways	207	7/10/64	
1569	HS–THC	Thai Airways	207	19/11/64	
1570	11–111	RTAF	208	31/12/65	D as HS-THF for Thai King's Flight
1571	4R–ACJ	Air Ceylon	212	22/10/64	
1572	XS594	RAF ASC	212	2/12/65	Andover C Mk 1 First production FF JUL-9-65
1573	XS595	RAF ASC	212	25/1/66	Andover C Mk 1
1574	XS596	RAF ASC	212	1/6/66	Andover C Mk 1
1575	XS597	RAF ASC	212	17/2/65	Andover C Mk 1
1576	TR–LQY	Transgabon	214	17/2/65	D to BKS AT as G-ATAM. L Aerotaxi Mexico 1966 to JAN-11-67 as XA-SEI. S to HSA JUL-12-67. L to PAL as PI-C-1020, FEB-68. L to Ghana AW as 9G-ABV APR to JUL-69. L to Maersk Air as OY-DFS JAN to FEB-70 L to Zambia AW MAR-70 as 9J-ABL L to SAA as ZS-HSA from SEP-1970 to FEB-1971. S AUG-1972
1577	YV–C–AME	LAV	215	15/5/65	*Paramagay*
1578	YV–C–AMI	LAV	215	2/7/65	
1579	YV–C–AMO	LAV	215	30/7/65	WO MAY-24-73
1580	YV–C–AMY	LAV	215	17/11/65	WO AUG-20-68, Maturin
1581	YV–C–AMF	LAV	215	4/2/66	
1582	YV–C–AMC	LAV	215	24/5/66	
1583	VP–LIK	LIAT	217	21/5/65	
1584	VP–LIP	LIAT	217	16/8/66	
1585	VP–LIW	LIAT	222	8/10/65	D to Channel AW as G-ATEH L COPA OCT-8-65 to MAY-25-66 as H P-416. S APR-68

C/n	Current Marks	Current Owner/operator	Model Series	Initial Delivery	Remarks
1586	PI–C–1029	PAL	222	2/12/65	D to Channel AW as G-ATEI. L LIAT DEC-4-65 to MAY 16-66 as VP-LIN. L to Transair as CF-TAX MAY-23-69. L to Rousseau Avn MAY to SEP-70
1587	CF–MAL	Transair	222	21/2/66	D to Channel AW as G-ATEJ S DEC-14-67 to Midwest, now Transair.
1588	VP–LIV	LIAT	222	28/3/66	D to Channel AW as G-ATEK S MAY-16-68
1589	G–AXVG	Dan-Air	226	30/4/66	D to Austrian AL as OE-LHS *Franz Lehar.* S NOV-15-69 to Skyways. Taken over by Dan-Air
1590	PI–C–1028	PAL	226	31/5/66	D as OE-LHT to Austrian AL. *Anton Bruckner* S SEP-1970
1591	0111	Venezuelan AF	223	8/1/66	
1592	VP–LIU	LIAT	225	30/3/66	D to Autair as G-ATMI. L LIAT NOV-13-67 to MAY-14-68 as VP-LIU. L to Skyways as G-ATMI MAY-14-68 to OCT-1-68 and MAR-15-69 to NOV-11-69. L to LIAT NOV-11-69 to APR-70. L to SATA MAY-70. S OCT-70 L to BAF APR-71 to NOV-71. L to LIAT.
1593	G–ATMJ	CAFU	225	20/4/66	D to Autair as G-ATMJ. L Jamaica AS as 6Y-JFJ JAN 15-68 to APL-2-69 L to SATA APL-30-69 L LIAT as VP-LAJ NOV-71 to APR-72, L Rousseau APR-72 to JUN-72. L LIAT JUL-72 to OCT-72 S OCT-72
1594	HP–432	COPA	227	29/7/66	*Chiriqui*
1595	A10–595	RAAF	229	19/3/67	
1596	A10–596	RAAF	229	4/5/67	
1597	T–02	Argentine AF	221	20/12/66	D as LV-PGG Re-reg JAN-1971. *Libertad*
1598	XA–SEV	SAESA	230	11/11/66	D to Aeromaya WO JAN-6-72
1599	XA–SEY	SAESA	230	2/1/67	D to Aeromaya *Palenque*
1600	AF601	Zambian AF	231	27/6/67	WO AUG–26–69
1601	A10–601	RAAF	228	7/9/68	G-AVZD before D
1602	A10–602	RAAF	228	3/10/68	
1603	A10–603	RAAF	228	30/10/68	
1604	A10–604	RAAF	228	15/12/68	
1605	A10–605	RAAF	228	2/2/69	
1606	A10–606	RAAF	228	15/5/69	
1607	A10–607	RAAF	228	27/6/69	
1608	A10–608	RAAF	228	29/7/69	
1609	PI–C–1027	PAL	232	22/12/66	D to Bahamas AW as VP-BCJ Bahamas AW ceased ops OCT-70 S JUL-1971 WO NOV-28-72
1610	PK–RHQ	Mandela AW	232	7/3/67	D to Bahamas AW as VP-BCK S JUN-1971
1611	CF–INE	Inexco Oil	232	13/4/67	D to Bahamas AW as VP-BCL. S FEB-1973
1612	G–AZSU	Dan-Air	232	23/4/67	D to Bahamas AW as VP-BCM. S APR-1972

Hawker Siddeley HS748

C/n	Current Marks	Current Owner/operator	Model Series	Initial Delivery	Remarks
1613	DQ–FAL	Air Pacific	233	11/9/67	D to Fiji AW as VQ-FAL. Company changed title and reg APR-1971
1614	CC–CEC	LAN–Chile	234	13/7/67	
1615	CC–CED	LAN–Chile	234	18/8/67	
1616	CC–CEE	LAN–Chile	234	5/10/67	
1617	CC–CEF	LAN–Chile	234	15/12/67	
1618	CC–CEG	LAN–Chile	235		
1619	CC–CEH	LAN–Chile	234	20/11/68	
1620	CC–CEI	LAN–Chile	234	22/1/69	
1621	CC–CEJ	LAN–Chile	234	18/6/69	
1622	CC–CEK	LAN–Chile	234	7/8/69	
1623	G–AVXI	BoT (CAFU)	238	15/7/69	
1624	G–AVXJ	BoT (CAFU)	238	4/9/69	
1625	PP–VDN	Varig	235	14/11/67	
1626	PP–VDO	Varig	235	3/1/68	
1627	PP–VDP	Varig	235	25/1/68	
1628	PP–VDQ	Varig	235	17/2/68	WO DEC-14-69
1629	PP–VDR	Varig	235	11/4/68	
1630	PP–VDS	Varig	235	16/5/68	
1631	PP–VDT	Varig	235	26/6/68	
1632	PP–VDU	Varig	235	18/7/68	WO FEB-9-72
1633	PP–VDV	Varig	235	21/8/68	
1634	PP–VDX	Varig	235	15/9/68	
1635	TR–LQJ	Transgabon	239		Demonstrator, Srs 2A, FF SEP-5-67. L to SATA FEB-69, L to Skways APR-69. L to Transair as CF-YQD, APR-69 to MAY-30-69. L to Air Cape as ZS-IGI DEC-69. L to Zambia AW as 9J-ABM MAR to APR-70. L to SAA as ZS-HSI MAY-1-70 to AUG-31-70 L to Merpati Nusantara JAN-71 to JUN-71. L to Trangabon OCT-71. S AUG-72.
1636	PI–C–1014	PAL	209	9/9/67	
1637	PI–C–1015	PAL	209	31/10/67	
1638	PI–C–1016	PAL	209	21/11/67	
1639	PI–C–1017	PAL	209	13/12/67	
1640	PI–C–1018	PAL	209	16/1/68	
1641	PI–C–1019	PAL	209	13/3/68	
1642	PI–C–1021	PAL	209	18/7/68	
1643	PI–C–1022	PAL	209	4/8/68	WO APR-21-70 Pantabangan
1644	HS–THD	Thai AW	243	5/10/68	
1645	HS–THE	Thai AW	243	7/11/68	
1646	HS–THF	Thai AW	243	29/11/68	
1647	ZK–CWJ	Mt. Cook AL	242	26/9/68	
1656	D–AFSD	BFS	244	12/2/69	
1657	HK–1408	Avianca	245	7/9/68	
1658	HK–1409	Avianca	245	25/10/68	
1659	PI–C–1023	PAL	209	3/3/69	
1660	PI–C–1024	PAL	209	26/3/69	
1661	DQ–FBH	Air Pacific	233	8/12/69	D to Fiji AW as VQ-FBH. Company changed title and reg APR-1971
1662	HP–484	COPA	227	10/5/69	
1663	PI–C–1025	PAL	209	28/5/69	L to Transair as CF-TAZ, MAY–28–69 to NOV–6–69
1664	PI–C–1026	PAL	209	25/6/69	L to Transair as CF–TAG, JUN–25–69 to NOV–29–69

C/n	Current Marks	Current Owner/operator	Model Series	Initial Delivery	Remarks
1665	DQ–FBK	Air Pacific	233	6/10/69	D to Fiji AW as VQ–FBK. Company changed title and reg APR–1971
1666	7Q–YKA	Air Malawi	256	6/12/69	
1667	7Q–YKB	Air Malawi	256	10/1/70	
1668	CF–MAK	Gateway Aviation	257	17/7/69	D to Midwest AL. S APR–1972
1669	CF–AMO	Amoco	258	21/8/69	
1670	VP–LAA	LIAT	217	8/10/69	Originally ordered as 9Y–TDH for BWIA
1671	9N–AAU	Royal Nepal AL	253	21/1/70	D as G–AXVZ for ferry flight
1672	9N–AAV	Royal Nepal AL	253	3/3/70	
1673	XA–SAB	SAESA	259	27/2/70	WO JUL–27–73
1674	XA–SAC	SAESA	259	25/3/70	
1675	XA–SAF	SAESA	259	17/4/70	
1676	9J–ABJ	Zambia AW	263	17/4/70	
1677	9J–ABK	Zambia AW	263	20/7/72	
1678	F–BSRA	Rousseau Avn	264	15/5/70	FF as G–11–2, later G–AYDH before D
1679	CF–CSE	Chevron Standard Oil	269	2/12/70	FF as G–11–1, later was G–AYFL before D
1980	9J–ABW	Zambia AW	263	2/9/70	FF as G–11–4
1681	F–BSRU	Rousseau Avn	264	27/10/70	FF as G–11–3, later G–AYIR before D L to SATA as CS–TAF OCT–14–70 to OCT–27–70
1682	FAE682	Ecuador AF	246	3/10/70	
1683	FAE683	Ecuador AF	246	23/10/70	
1684	FAE684	Ecuador AF	267	21/11/70	VIP aircraft
1685	9G–ABW	Ghana AW	254	10/12/70	WO JAN–22–71
1686	9G–ABX	Ghana AW	254	1/1/71	
1687	CS–TAG	SATA	270	21/10/70	FF as G–11–5, later G–AYIM before D L to SATA before S on APR–30–72
1688	AF–602	Zambia AF	265	17/2/71	VIP aircraft
1689	ZK–DES	Mount Cook AL	242	2/7/71	
1690	ZS–SBT	SAA	272	17/2/71	*Skukuza*
1691	ZS–SBU	SAA	272	29/1/71	*Umfolozi* L Botswana AW as A2–ZFT JAN–29–71 to MAY–15–71
1692	ZS–SBV	SAA	272	17/2/71	*Etosha*
1693	HS–THG	Thai Airways	243	9/12/70	
1694	AMDB–110	Brunei Government	273	20/1/71	Rolled out as AMB–110
1695	PK–MHM	Merpati Nusantara	274	16/6/71	Initially PK–MHD, then G–11–10 and G–AZAE. *Mandau*
1696	PK–MHR	Merpati Nusantara	274	15/12/71	*Rentjong*
1697	G–AYYG	HSA	275		Demonstrator FF as G–11–9 MAY–7–71
1698	G–AZJH	HSA	271		Demonstrator, large cargo door FF DEC–31–71
1699	CF–AGI	Air Gaspe	276	1/4/71	FF as G–11–6
1700	PK–IHD	Bouraq	216	3/1/73	FF as G–11–7 then G–AYVR
1701	5W–FAN	Polynesian AL	266	11/1/72	FF as G–11–8 then G–AYYH
1702	FAC–1101	SATENA	260	2/3/72	FF as G–11–1
1703	FAC–1102	SATENA	260	3/3/72	FF as G–11–2
1704	FAC–1103	SATENA	260	16/3/72	FF as G–11–3
1705	FAC–1104	SATENA	260	20/3/72	FF as G–11–4
1706	9J–ADM	Zambia AW	263	9/2/72	FF as G–11–5 L to Botswana AW as A2–ZGF *Okavango* FEB–9–72 to JUN–1972
1707	HS–THH	Thai Airways	243	21/1/72	FF as G–11–6
1708	HS–THI	Thai Airways	243	7/2/72	
1709	N15–709	R. Australian Navy	268	29/5/73	
1710	N15–710	R. Australian Navy	268	3/8/73	

Hawker Siddeley HS748

C/n	Current Marks	Current Owner/operator	Model Series	Initial Delivery	Remarks
1711	D–AFSE	BFS	244		FF as G–
1712	ZK–MCA	Mount Cook AL	242		FF as G–11–7
1713	HL–	Korean AL	280		FF as G–11–8
1714	5W–FAO	Polynesian AL	266	17/11/72	FF as G–11–10
1715	99–999	Royal Thai AF	208	26/1/73	King's Flight
1716	N748LL	Air Illinois	FAA		FF as G–11–3 then G–BAFY
1717	F–BUTR	Rousseau Aviation	264		FF as G–11–9 then G–BASZ
1718	HL–	Korean AL	280		FF as G–11–1 then G–BABZ
1719	CR–CAV	Cape Verde Air Transport	278		FF as G–11–2
1720	CR–CAX	Cape Verde Air Transport	278		FF as G–11–4
1721	CS–TAH	SATA	270		
1722	5H–	Tanzania Government	282		
1723	D–AFSF	BFS	244		
1724	D–AFSG	BFS	244		
1725	D–AFSH	BFS	244		
1726	D–AFSI	BFS	244		
1727	D–AFSJ	BFS	244		
1728					
1729					
1730					

Hawker Siddeley HS748 (India)

C/n	Current Marks	Current Owner/operator	Model Series	Initial Delivery	Remarks
501	BH572	IAF	103	17/4/64	First Indian, FF NOV–1–61
502	BH573	IAF	104	4/4/64	HS748 (India)
503	BH574	IAF	104	24/2/65	
504	BH1047	IAF	104	27/6/66	
505	BH1048	IAF	203	18/11/65	
506	BH1010	IAF	203	14/12/65	
507	VT–DUO	IAC	224	17/7/67	*Tajmahal*
508	BH1011	IAF	203	6/12/66	
509	BH1012	IAF	203	17/3/67	
510	BH1013	IAF	203	17/6/67	
511	H913	IAF	203	27/9/67	
512	VT–DXF	IAC	224	25/11/67	*Ajanta*
513	VT–DXG	IAC	224	1/1/68	*Sauchi*
514	VT–DXH	IAC	224	23/3/68	*Somnath*
515	VT–DXI	IAC	224	30/5/68	*Amber*
516	VT–DXJ	IAC	224	17/7/68	*Rameswaram*
517	H914	IAF	203	5/12/68	
518	H915	IAF	218	14/1/69	
519	VT–DXK	IAC	224	22/1/69	*Ellora*
520	VT–DXL	IAC	224	29/3/69	*Konark*
521	VT–DXM	IAC	225	28/4/69	*Khajuraho*
522	VT–DXN	IAC	224	17/6/69	
523	VT–DXO	IAC	224	9/8/69	
524	VT–DXP	IAC	224	3/12/69	
525	VT–DXQ	IAC	224	12/2/70	
526	VT–DXR	IAC	224	26/2/70	
527	–	IAF	219	21/10/70	
528	H–1031	IAF	219	12/1/71	
529	H–1032	IAF	219	30/1/71	
530	H–1033	IAF	219	23/3/71	
531	H–1034	IAF	219	30/3/71	
532	H–1386	IAF	220	17/5/72	
533	H–1176	IAF	219	30/3/71	Large cargo door
534	H–1177	IAF	218	4/3/71	
535	H–1178	IAF	218	30/3/71	
536	H–1179	IAF	218	9/7/71	
537	H–1180	IAF	220	31/3/72	
538	H–1181	IAF	220	1/2/72	
539	H–1182	IAF	220	17/2/72	
540	VT–EAT	IAC	224	21/4/72	
541	VT–EAU	IAC	224	30/5/72	WO MAR–15–73
542	VT–EAV	IAC	224	15/6/72	
543	VT–EAW	IAC	224		
544	VT–EAX	IAC	224		
545	VT–EAY	IAC	224		
546	VT–EAZ	IAC	224		
547	VT–EBA	IAC	224		
548	VT–EBB	IAC	224		
549	VT–EBC	IAC	224		
550					

Hawker Siddeley Trident

C/n	Current Marks	Current Owner/operator	Model Series	Initial Delivery	Remarks
2101	G–ARPA	British Airways	IC	8/8/65	FF JAN-9-62
2102	G–AEPB	British Airways	1C	30/6/61	Retained for Autoland development. To BEA DEC -6-67
2103	G–ARPC	British Airways	1C	9/9/64	D to BEA
2104	G–ARPD	British Airways	1C	8/1/65	D to BEA
2105	G–ARPE	British Airways	1C	10/7/64	D to BEA
2106	G–ARPF	British Airways	1C	19/12/63	D to BEA
2107	G–ARPG	British Airways	1C	19/2/64	D to BEA
2108	G–ARPH	British Airways	1C	25/3/64	D to BEA
2109	G–ARPI	British Airways	1C	2/5/64	D to BEA WO Staines JUN-18-72
2110	G–ARPJ	British Airways	1C	26/5/64	D to BEA
2111	G–ARPK	British Airways	1C	26/6/64	D to BEA
2112	G–ARPL	British Airways	1C	6/8/64	D to BEA
2113	G–ARPM	British Airways	1C	9/10/64	D to BEA
2114	5B–DAD	Cyprus AW	1C	18/3/66	FF NOV–2–64 as G–ASWU. FF full 1E standard MAR–5–66. S to Kuwait AW as 9K–ACF. S MAR–15–73
2115	G–ARPN	British Airways	1C	4/12/64	D to BEA
2116	G–ARPO	British Airways	1C	31/1/65	D to BEA
2117	G–ARPP	British Airways	1C	25/2/65	D to BEA
2118	9K–ACG	Kuwait AW	1E	27/5/66	FF as G-ASWV. WO Kuwait JUN-30-66
2119	G–ARPR	British Airways	1C	12/4/65	
2120	G–ARPS	BEA	1C	1/6/65	WO London Heathrow JUL-29-69
2121	G–ARPT	BEA	1C	9/7/65	WO London Heathrow JUL-3-68
2122	G–ARPU	British Airways	1C	25/8/65	D to BEA
2123	G–ARPW	British Airways	1C	15/10/65	D to BEA
2124	G–ARPX	British Airways	1C	25/5/66	D to BEA
2125	YI–AEA	Iraqi AW	1E		
2126	G–ARPY	HSA	1C		WO Felthorpe JUN-3-66 on first flight.
2127	YI–AEB	Iraqi AW	1E	5/3/66	
2128	G–ARPZ	British Airways	1C	1/7/66	D to BEA
2129	YI–AEC	Iraqi AW	1E	13/5/66	
2130		CAAC	1E	1/3/66	G-ATNA before delivery to PIA as AP-ATK. S 1970
2131		CAAC	1E	12/4/66	D to PIA as AP-ATL. S 1970
2132		CAAC	1E	17/6/66	D to PIA as AP-ATM. S 1970
2133		CAAC	1E	13/2/67	Temporarily in PAF colours before D to PIA as AP-AUG. S 1970
2134	5B–DAE	Cyprus Airways	1E	21/11/66	D to BEA as G-AZND. S Kuwait AW, reg 9K-ACH. S APR-6-73
2135	4R–ACN	Air Ceylon	1E	16/7/69	
2136	G–AVYB	Northeast Airlines	1E	31/5/68	FF FEB-13-68 as G-AVYA D to Channel AW as G-AVYB S FEB-20-72
2137	G–AVYC	Northeast Airlines	1E	9/4/69	D to BKS, now Northeast Airlines
2138	G–AVYD	Northeast Airlines	1E	28/3/69	D to BKS, now Northeast Airlines
2139	G–AVYE	British Airways	1E	14/6/68	D to Channel AW, S to BEA JAN-20-72
2140	G–AVFA	British Airways	2E	23/12/69	D to BEA
2141	5B–DAC	Cyprus Airways	2E	6/6/68	D to BEA. as G-AVFB. S JUN-19-72

C/n	Current Marks	Current Owner/operator	Model Series	Initial Delivery	Remarks
2142	G–AVFC	British Airways	2E	15/2/68	D to BEA
2143	G–AVFD	British Airways	2E	16/4/68	D to BEA
2144	G–AVFE	British Airways	2E	8/5/68	D to BEA
2145	G–AVFF	British Airways	2E	30/5/68	D to BEA
2146	G–AVFG	British Airways	2E	4/7/68	D to BEA
2147	G–AVFH	British Airways	2E	1/8/68	D to BEA
2148	G–AVFI	British Airways	2E	27/11/68	D to BEA
2149	G–AVFJ	British Airways	2E	21/12/68	D to BEA
2150	G–AVFK	British Airways	2E	17/1/69	D to BEA
2151	G–AVFL	British Airways	2E	18/2/69	D to BEA
2152	G–AVFM	British Airways	2E	25/4/69	D to BEA
2153	G–AVFN	British Airway	2E	23/5/69	D to BEA
2154	G–AZXM	British Airways	2E	19/9/69	D to Cyprus AW as 5B-DAA. Damaged MAR-15-72. S to BEA. Repaired and re-entered service JUN-28-72
2155	5B–DAB	Cyprus Airways	2E	1/5/70	
2156	G–AVFO	British Airways	2E	23/6/70	D to BEA
2157	240	CAAC	2E	19/11/72	FF as G-AZFT
2158	242	CAAC	2E	8/2/73	FF as G-AZFU
2159	244	CAAC	2E	17/6/73	FF as G-AZFY
2160	246	CAAC	2E	5/8/73	FF as G-AZFW
2161	G–AZFX	CAAC	2E		
2162	G–AZFY	CAAC	2E		
2163	G–BABP	CAAC	2E		
2164	G–BABR	CAAC	2E		
2165	G–BABS	CAAC	2E		
2166	G–BABT	CAAC	2E		
2167	G–BABU	CAAC	2E		
2168	G–BABV	CAAC	2E		
2169	G–BAJF	CAAC	2E		
2170	G–BAJG	CAAC	2E		
2171	G–BAJH	CAAC	2E		
2172	G–BAJI	CAAC	2E		
2173	G–BAJJ	CAAC	2E		
2174	G–BAJK	CAAC	2E		
301	G–AWYZ	British Airways	3B	23/3/72	FF DEC-11-69. D to BEA
302	G–AWZA	British Airways	3B	11/1/71	D to BEA
303	G–AWZB	British Airways	3B	24/2/71	D to BEA
304	G–AWZC	British Airways	3B	18/2/71	D to BEA
305	G–AWZD	British Airways	3B	26/3/71	D to BEA
306	G–AWZE	British Airways	3B	8/4/71	D to BEA
307	G–AWZF	British Airways	3B	11/5/71	D to BEA
308	G–AWZG	British Airways	3B	12/6/71	D to BEA
309	G–AWZH	British Airways	3B	15/7/71	D to BEA
310	G–AWZI	British Airways	3B	9/8/71	D to BEA
311	G–AWZJ	British Airways	3B	16/9/71	D to BEA
312	G–AWZK	British Airways	3B	16/10/71	D to BEA
313	G–AWZL	British Airways	3B	25/11/71	D to BEA
314	G–AWZM	British Airways	3B	16/12/71	D to BEA
315	G–AWZN	British Airways	3B	20/1/72	D to BEA
316	G–AWZO	British Airways	3B	16/2/72	D to BEA
317	G–AWZP	British Airways	3B	21/3/72	D to BEA
318	G–AWZR	British Airways	3B	13/4/72	
319	G–AWZS	British Airways	3B	5/5/72	
320	G–AWZT	British Airways	3B	6/6/72	
321	G–AWZU	British Airways	3B	10/7/72	
322	G–AWZV	British Airways	3B	9/8/72	
323	G–AWZW	British Airways	3B	29/11/72	
324	G–AWZX	British Airways	3B	23/3/73	
325	G–AWZY	British Airways	3B	14/3/73	
326	G–AWZZ	British Airways	3B	19/3/73	
327	G–BAJL	CAAC	3B–104		
328	G–BAJM	CAAC	3B–104		
329					
330					

Lockheed Electra

C/n	Current Marks	Current Owner/operator	Model Series	Initial Delivery	Remarks
1001	N974HA	Holiday AL	188A	19/4/61	Prototype FF DEC–6–57 as N1881. D to PSA as N174PS. S JUL–30–68
1002	HC–AMS	Cia Ecuatoriana	188A	29/6/59	FF as N1882. D to Cathay Pacific as VR–HFN. S MAR–22–67
1003	N927NA	NASA	188A		Demonstrator as N1883. Cvtd to YP3V–1 test vehicle. FF NOV–25–1959 D as 148276
1004	HC–ANQ	Cia Ecuatoriana	188A	1/4/59	FF as N1884. World demonstration tour as N7144C. S to Cathay Pacific as VR–HFO. S to Fdk. Ayer MAY–26–66 as N16816. L by Braniff OCT–12–66
1005	HK554	SA Medellin	188A	3/1/59	D to Eastern AL as N5501. S AUG–1–69
1006	N1006T	Intermountain	188A	10/7/58	D to General Motors as N5501V. S AUG–11–61 to Los Angeles Dodgers as N1R. S to Intermountain
1007	PI–C–1061	Air Manila	188A	8/10/58	D to Eastern AL as N5502. S to Air Manila
1008	PI–C–1062	Air Manila	188A	20/10/58	D to Eastern AL as N5503. S to Air Manila
1009	N5504	Eastern AL	188A	2/11/58	
1010	HK1274	SA Medellin	188A	10/11/58	D to Eastern AL as N5505. S to SA Medellin
1011	HP–579	COPA	188A	3/11/58	D to Eastern AL as N5506. S to COPA
1012	N5507	Eastern AL	188A	14/11/58	
1013	HK553	SA Medellin	188A	29/11/58	D to Eastern as N5509. S AUG–1–69
1014	HK557	SA Medellin	188A	13/1/59	D to Eastern as N5510. S AUG–1–69
1015	N6101A	American AL	188A	27/11/58	*New York* . WO FEB–3–59
1016	N5511	Eastern AL	188A	11/1/59	
1017	N5512	Eastern AL	188A	25/11/58	
1018	HR–SAW	SAHSA	188A	16/12/58	D to Eastern as N5513 S to Winner AL. S to SAHSA
1019	N6102A	American AL	188A	10/12/58	*Chicago* WO at Knoxville AUG–6–62
1020	N301FA	Fiesta AL	188A	13/2/59	D to Eastern AL as N5514. S to Fiesta AL
1021	PI–C–1060	Air Manila	188A	2/2/59	D to Eastern AL as N5515. S to Air Manila WO JAN–9–72
1022	N5516	Eastern AL	188A	19/1/59	
1023	N5517	Eastern AL	188A	18/1/59	
1024	PP–VJL	Varig	188A	4/1/59	D to American AL as N6103A *Detroit.* S AUG–31–62
1025	PP–VJM	Varig	188A	9/1/59	D to American AL as N6104A *Washington* S AUG–30–62
1026	N5518	Eastern AL	188A	14/2/59	
1027	N5016K	American Jet Industries	188A	23/1/59	D to American AL as N6105A *Boston*. S to National AL as N5016K NOV–1–62. S JAN–8–68 to Pan Aero Int. S to AJI

C/n	Current Marks	Current Owner/operator	Model Series	Initial Delivery	Remarks
1028	N6106A	McCulloch International	188A	27/1/59	D to American AL *Dallas.* S OCT–25–67 to Lake Havasau City. S to McCulloch
1029	HK–555	SA Medellin	188A	26/2/59	D to Eastern AL as N5519. S AUG–1–69
1030	HK1275	SA Medellin	188A	28/2/59	D to Eastern AL as N5520. S to SA Medellin
1031	N5017K	Adventurers Travel Club	188A	5/2/59	D to American AL as N6107A *Fort Worth.* S to National AL as N5017K NOV–30–62. S DEC–23–68
1032	ZP–CBX	LA Paraguayas	188A	12/3/59	D to Eastern AL as N5521. S OCT–4–68 to ONA. *Pegasus.* S DEC–1968
1033	N5522	Eastern AL	188A	3/2/59	
1034	N5523	Eastern AL	188A	25/2/59	
1035	CF–PWG	Pacific Western	188A	1/4/59	D to National AL S to Pan Aero DEC–23–68. S OCT–1969 to Trans Arctic as N5001K. S to Pacific West
1036	XA–FAM	Aero Carga	188A	26/2/59	D to Eastern AL as N5524. S to Aero Carga
1037	PP–VJN	Varig	188A	16/2/59	D to American AL as N6108A *Buffalo.* S SEP–1–62
1038	N5525	Eastern AL	188A	28/3/59	
1039	VH–RMA	Ansett-ANA	188A	27/2/59	
1040	N9701C	Ayer Associates	188A	29/4/59	D to Braniff. S to Boeing MAY 12–69. S OCT–1969
1041	PP–VJO	Varig	188A	27/2/59	D to American AL as N6109A *Toronto* S. SEP–30–62
1042	HC–AQF	Cia Ecuatoriana	188A	8/4/59	D to Eastern AL as N5526. S to Ecuatoriana Scrapped for spares SEP–10–73
1043	HK691	SA Medellin	188A	16/4/69	D to Eastern AL as N5527. S to SA Medellin
1044	VH–RMC	Ansett-ANA	188A	5/1/60	
1045	N5528	Eastern AL	188A	27/4/59	
1046	N7135C	Trans Continental AL	188A	20/5/59	D to Western AL. S to Trans Continental
1047	VH–RMB	Ansett-ANA	188A	1/4/59	
1048	N5529	Eastern AL	188A	7/5/59	
1049	PP–VJP	Varig	188A	1/4/59	D to American AL as N6110A *St. Louis* S OCT–11–62 Scrapped for spares FEB–5–70
1050	N278AC	Ayer Associates	188A	16/4/59	D to American AL as N6111A *Tulsa* S DEC–30–66 to Air California S to Aircraft Holdings, then to Ayer Assc.
1051	N6112A	Banco de Mexico	188A	22/4/59	D to American AL as N6112A *Philadelphia* S to BANCO de Mexico
1052	N9702C	Ayer Associates	188A	6/5/59	D to Braniff S to Boeing APR–25–69. S OCT–1969
1053	HK692	SA Medellin	188A	20/5/59	D to Eastern AL as N5530. S to SA Medellin
1054	N5015K	American Jet Industries	188A	30/4/59	D to American AL as N6113A *Syracuse* S to National AL NOV–27–62. S to Pan Aero Int as N5015K JAN–1–69 S to AJI
1055	N5531	Eastern AL	188A	26/5/59	
1056	N6114A	Dart Industries	188A	13/5/59	D to American AL as N6114A *Rochester* S to Dart Ind.

Lockheed Electra

C/n	Current Marks	Current Owner/operator	Model Series	Initial Delivery	Remarks
1057	N121US	Northwest AL	188C	19/7/59	WO Tell City MAR–17–60
1058	N278AC	WHARFCA	188A	18/5/59	D to American AL as N6115A *New York* S to WHARFCA
1059	N5002K	Fairbanks Air Service	188A	25/5/59	D to National AL. S to Pan Aero DEC–23–68. S to Trans Arctic OCT–1969. S to to Fairbanks AS
1060	HR–SAV	SAHSA	188A	2/6/59	D to Eastern AL as N5532 S AUG–18–69
1061	XW–PKA	Royal Air Laos	188A	15/6/59	D to TAA as VH–TLA *John Eyre.* S to Royal Air Laos
1062	N5533	Eastern AL	188A	8/6/59	WO at Boston OCT–4–60
1063	HK–1416	Aerocondor	188A	4/6/59	D to American AL as N6116A *Cincinatti* S to Aerocondor
1064	CF–PWK	Pacific Western	188A	12/6/59	D to National AL. S to Pan Aero JAN–1–69 S Oct–1969 to Trans Arctic as N5003K. S to Pacific Western
1065	N6117A	American AL	188A	17/6/59	D to American AL as N6117A *Louisville* S to McCulloch Int. Scrapped for spares 1971
1066	N5534	Eastern AL	188A	25/6/59	
1067	HR–TNN	TAN–Honduras	188A	22/6/59	D to Braniff S to Boeing MAY–8–69. S OCT–1969 to Ayer Ass. as N9703C. S to TAN
1068	N5535	Eastern AL	188A	9/7/59	
1069	XW–PKB	Royal Air Laos	188A	14/7/59	D to TAA as VH-TLB *John Gilbert* S to Royal Air Laos
1070	N7136C	Johnson Flying Services	188A	10/7/59	D to Western AL. S to Johnson FS
1071	N5536	Eastern AL	188C	27/7/59	
1072	N6118A	McCulloch International	188A	25/7/59	D to American AL as *Hartford.* S to Lake Havasau City. S to McCulloch Int.
1073	HK–775	Aerocondor	188A	1/8/59	D to American AL as N6119A *Cleveland.* S to Aerocondor
1074	N7137C	Johnson Flying Services	188A	29/7/59	D to Western AL. S to Johnson FS.
1075	N64405	Air Florida	188C	13/8/59	D to Eastern AL as N5537. S to Falconair AUG–8–69 reg SE–FEC S to Air Florida
1076	N280F	Overseas National AL	188A	6/8/59	D to National AL as N5004K. S MAR–7–68. *Resolute*
1077	N300GA	FM Productions	188C	29/7/59	D to Northwest as N122US. S to American Flyers JUN–16–66. S to King Resources JAN–23–70. S to FMP
1078	ZP–CBY	LA Paraguayas	188C	20/8/59	D to Eastern AL as N5538. S DEC–15–68
1079	N281F	Overseas National AL	188A	17/8/59	D to National AL as N5005K. S MAR–13–68. *Indomitable*
1080	ZP–CBZ	LA Paraguayas	188C	28/8/59	D to Eastern AL as N5539. S DEC–31–68
1081	HK–1415	Aerocondor	188A	17/8/59	D to American AL as N6120A *Newark*.S 1970
1082	N123US	Air California	188C	11/8/59	D to Northeast. S to Western Skyways MAR–3–69. S to Air California.

C/n	Current Marks	Current Owner/operator	Model Series	Initial Delivery	Remarks
1083	HK–774	Aerocondor	188A	23/8/59	D to American AL as N6121A *Providence* S NOV–9–69
1084	N282F	Overseas National AL	188A	30/8/59	D to National AL as N5006K. S MAR–7–68. *Pegasus*
1085	N124US	Vagabond Air Travel	188C	30/8/59	D to Northwest. S SEP–25–66
1086	OB–R–941	LANSA	188A	28/8/59	D to Braniff as N9704C. S to Boeing MAY–12–69.[To Ayer Associates OCT–69. S to LANSA. WO DEC–24–71
1087	N7318C	Boise Interagency Fire Center	188A	4/9/59	D to Western AL. S to Boise.
1088	N11VG	Voyager	188C	17/9/59	D to Eastern AL as N5540. S to International Aerodyne OCT–10–68. L to Falconair as SE–FGA. S to Voyager.
1089	N283F	Overseas National AL	188A	4/9/59	D to National AL as N5007K. S MAR–1968. *Rebel*
1090	N9705C	Braniff	188A	18/9/59	WO SEP–29–59
1091	N971HA	Holiday Airlines	188C	6/11/59	D to PSA as N171PS. S JUL–30–68
1092	N5008K	American Jet Industries	188A	22/9/59	D to National AL. S to Pan Aero International. S to AJI.
1093	PP–VLC	Varig	188A	23/9/59	D to American AL as N6122A *Albany* S APR–1970
1094	CF–IJY	Jet Air	188A	26/9/59	D to Western AL as N7193C. S to Jet Air
1095	OB–R–945	LANSA	188A	1/10/59	D to Braniff as N9706C. S to Boeing APR–28–69. S to Ayer Assc. S to LANSA
1096	N5009K	Voyager	188A	5/10/59	D to National AL. S to Voyager
1097	N5010K	American Jet Industries	188A	10/10/59	D to National AL. S to AJI.
1098	N12VG	Voyager	188C	14/10/59	D to Eastern AL as N5541. S to International Aerodyne. L to Falconair as SE–FGB. S to Voyager
1099	N9707C	Braniff	188A	17/10/59	WO Dawson. MAY–3–68
1100	N289AC	Ayer Associates	188A	22/10/59	D to American AL as N6123A *Nashville.* S to Air California JAN–13–67. S to GATX/Boothe. S to Ayer.
1101	N125US	Emerald Shillelagh	188C	22/10/59	D to Northwest. S NOV–15–66 to American Flyers S to Emerald
1102	N6124A	McCulloch International	188A	23/10/59	D to American AL as N6124A *El Paso* S to McCulloch Int.
1103	N111	FAA	188C	3/3/61	
1104	N284F	Overseas National AL	188A	13/11/59	D to National AL as N5011K S MAR–7–68 *Ranger*
1105	N126US	Airlines Aircraft Leasing	188C	14/11/59	D to Northwest. S JAN–19–67 to American Flyers S to AAL
1106	OB–R–939	LANSA	188A	17/11/59	D to Braniff as N9708C. S to Boeing MAY–15–69. To Ayer OCT–69 WO Cuzco AUG–9–70

Lockheed Electra

C/n	Current Marks	Current Owner/operator	Model Series	Initial Delivery	Remarks
1107	N285F	Overseas National AL	188A	24/11/59	D to National AL as N5012K. S MAR–7–68 *Ardent*
1108	CF–IJM	Jet Air	188C	25/11/59	D to Northwest. S NOV–17–69
1109	N172PS	Airlines Aircraft Leasing	188C	30/11/59	D to PSA MAR–10–69 S to Cal-Air. S to AAL.
1110	N289F	Overseas National AL	188C	9/12/59	D to PSA as N173PS, S MAY-10–68 to Universal AL as N862U. S to ONA
1111	N128US	Air Holiday	188C	10/12/59	D to Northwest. S to Air Holiday
1112	PT–DZK	Pignatari	188C	15/12/59	D to Northwest. S to International Skyways as N777DP. S to Pignatari.
1113	CF–NAY	Nordair	188C	30/12/59	D to Northwest as N 130 US. S to Nordair
1114	N9709C	Ayer Associates	188A	9/1/60	D to Braniff as N9709C. S to Boeing APR–30–69. To Ayer OCT–69
1115	HK–777	Aerocondor	188A	31/12/59	D to American AL as N6125A *Oklahoma City*. S JUL–16–69 WO AUG–27–73, near Bogota
1116	N6126A	McCulloch International	188A	13/1/60	D to American AL as N6126A *Tucson*. S FEB–17–70 to Lake Havasu City. S to McCulloch Int.
1117	N6127A	American AL	188A	21/1/60	WO La Guardia SEP–14–60
1118	N7140C	Reeve Aleutian	188A	21/1/60	D to Western AL. S to Reeve
1119	PP–VJU	Varig	188A	27/1/60	D to American AL as N6128A *San Diego*. S NOV–1–67
1120	N6129A	McCulloch International	188A	3/2/60	D to American AL. *Los Angeles*. S to McCulloch
1121	N6130A	McCulloch International	188A	17/2/60	D to American AL *San Francisco*. S JUN–4–69 to Lake Havasu City. S to McCulloch
1122	N6131A	McCulloch International	188A	17/2/60	D to American AL *Little Rock*. S MAY–30–69 to Lake Havasu City. S to McCulloch
1123	N6132A	McCulloch International	188A	19/2/60	D to American AL *Richmond*. S FEB–13–69 to Lake Havasu City. S to McCulloch
1124	PP–VJV	Varig	188A	24/2/60	D to American AL as N6133A *Baltimore*. S MAR–18–68
1125	CP–853	LA Boliviana	188A	25/2/60	D to American AL as N6134A *Memphis*. S APR–20–68
1126	PP–VJW	Varig	188A	22/3/60	D to American AL as N6135A *San Antonio*. S DEC–30–67
1127	CF–PAK	Pan Arctic	188A	24/3/61	D to Western AL as N7141C. S to Pan Arctic
1128	CF–ZST	Pacific Western	188A	17/5/61	D to Western AL as N7142C. S to Pacific W
1129	CF–IJV	Jet Air	188A	24/5/61	D to Western AL as N7143C. S to Jet Air
1130	N595KR	NCAR	188C	31/1/62	Built for Capital AL as N181H. D to Sports Aloft (L) as N185H. S to PSA as N175PS. S FEB–68 to King Investment Co. S to NCAR

C/n	Current Marks	Current Owner/operator	Model Series	Initial Delivery	Remarks
1131	N131US	Jet Set Travel Club	188C	9/3/61	D to Northwest. S to Jet Set Travel
1132	CF–NAZ	Nordair	188C	10/3/61	D to Northwest as N132US. S to Nordair
1133	N290F	Overseas National AL	188C	10/3/61	Built for Capital AL as N182H. L to US Navy 1961 as N181H. S PSA as N376PS in 1962. S MAY–12–68 to Universal AL as N863U. S to ONA.
1134	HR–TNL	TAN	188C	10/5/62	Built for Capital. D to Braniff as N9710C. S to Boeing APR–28–69. S 1970
1135	N182H	Ports of Call	188C	17/1/65	Built for Capital as N184H S to American Flyers. S to Ports of Call.
1136	N185H	American Flyers	188C	1/2/63	Built for Capital AL. WO at Ardmore APR–22–66
1137	PP–VLB	Varig	188C	14/3/61	D to Northwest as N133US. S JAN–26–70
1138	CF–IJR	Imperial Oil	188C	29/3/61	D to Northwest as N134US S to Imperial Oil.
1139	PP–VLA	Varig	188C	7/4/61	D to Northwest as N135US. S JAN–26–70
1140	N9744C	Reeve Aleutian	188A	3/2/61	D to Western AL. S to Reeve
1141	CF–PAB	Pan Arctic	188C	23/5/61	D to Northwest as N136US. S DEC–69 to Jet Air. S to Pan Arctic
1142	N137US	Northwest	188C	22/6/61	WO Chicago SEP–17–61
1143	LN–MOI	Fred Olsen AS	188A	15/2/61	D to Western AL as N9745C S to Fred Olsen
1144	N138US	Air Florida	188C	23/6/61	D to Northwest. S to Air Florida
1145	LN–FOH	Fred Olsen AS	188A	9/2/61	D to Western AL as N9746C. S to Fred Olsen
1146	N286F	Overseas National AL	188A	6/1/61	D to National AL as N5013K. S MAR–7–68 *Expediter*
1147	N118LG	Concare	188A	25/8/60	D to TAA as VH–TLC *Charles Sturt.* S to Concare
1148	N287F	Overseas National AL	188A	9/1/61	D to National AL as N5014K. S MAR–7–68 *Enterprise*
2001	N851U	Univeral AL	188C	29/9/59	N6934C before delivery to KLM as PH–LLA *Mercurius.* S JUL–68 WO MAR–19–72
2002	N359AC	Ayer Associates	188C	30/10/59	D to Qantas as VH–ECA *Electra.* S to Air California 1967. S to GATX/Boothe. S to Ayer
2003	N852U	Saturn Airways	188C	10/10/59	D to KLM as PH–LLB *Venus.* S AUG–7–68 to Universal AL. S Saturn
2004	N385AC	Intermountain	188C	30/10/59	D to Qantas as VH–ECB *Explorer.* S to Air California 1967. S to GATX/Boothe. S to Intermountain.
2005	–	Fred Olsen AS	188C	9/11/59	*Aotearoa*
2006	N853U	Saturn Airways	188C	19/11/59	D to KLM as PH–LLC *Mars.* S 1968 to Universal AL. S Saturn

Lockheed Electra

C/n	Current Marks	Current Owner/operator	Model Series	Initial Delivery	Remarks
2007	N1968R	Reeve Aleutian	188C	25/11/59	D to Qantas as VH–ECC *Endeavour.* S to Air New Zealand DEC–66 as ZK–CLX *Akaron.* S FEB–17–68
2008	N836E	Nomads	188C	3/12/59	D to Qantas as VH–ECD *Enterprise.* L to ANZ. S to Nomads.
2009	N854U	Saturn Airways	188C	16/12/59	D to KLM as PH–LLD *Jupiter.* S 1968 to Universal AL. S Saturn
2010	ZK–TEB	Air New Zealand	188C	18/12/59	
2011	ZK–TEC	TEAL	188C	14/12/57	WO MAR–27–65
2012	N855U	Universal AL	188C	30/1/60	D to KLM as PH–LLE *Saturnus.* WO AUG–24–70 Salt Lake City
2013	N856U	Saturn Airways	188C	16/2/60	D to KLM as PH–LLF *Uranus.* S APR–19–68 D to Universal AL. S to Saturn
2014	N857U	Saturn Airways	188C	25/2/60	D to KLM as PH–LLG *Neptunus.* L Martinair 1968, S 1968. D to Universal AL. S to Saturn.
2015	N858U	Saturn Airways	188C	16/4/60	D to KLM as PH–LLH *Pluto.* S JUN–14–68 D to Universal AL. S to Saturn
2016	N859U	Saturn Airways	188C	29/4/60	D to KLM as PH–LLI *Cercs.* S APR–3–68 D to Universal AL. S to Saturn.
2017	N860U	Saturn Airways	188C	14/5/60	D to KLM as PH–LLK *Pallas.* S MAR–13–68 D to Universal AL. S to Saturn.
2018	N861U	Saturn Airways	188C	1/12/60	D to KLM as PH–LLL *Orion.* S APR–2–68 D to Universal AL. S to Saturn.
2019	PH–LLM	KLM	188C	14/12/60	*Sirius.* WO Cairo JUN–12–61
2020		American Jet Industries	188C	14/1/61	D to Garuda Air as PK–GLA *Palem Bali.* S to AJI.
2021	PK–GLB	Garuda	188C	1/1/61	WO Menado FEB–16–67
2022		American Jet Industries	188C	15/1/61	D to Garuda AW as AK–GLC *Danau Tober.* S to AJI

Lockheed Hercules

C/n	Current Marks	Current Owner/operator	Model Series	Initial Delivery	Remarks
3587	60-5452	USAF	C–130B		Single example with FAA certification on APR–27–67 for use in support of C–5 programme
3946	PI–97	Philippine Government	382E		Prototype Model 382 civil demonstrator. FF as N1130E. Converted to prototype L–100–20, FF APR–19–68 and S to Flying 'W' as N50FW. S to Philippine Government
4039	SE–XBT	Forsvarets Materielverk	C–130		Single Swedish Air Force Hercules registered for use in Biafran air-lift
4101	N920NA	National Aircraft Leasing	382B		D to Continental AS as N9260R, OCT–65, S to Zambia Aír Cargoes AUG–66 as 9J–RCV. S APR–3–69 to Alaska AL as N920NA. S to National Aircraft Leasing. L to Saturn AW.
4109	9J–RCY	Zambia Air Cargoes	382B		D to Continental AS N9261R, NOV–65, To Zambia AUG–66. WO N'dola APR–11–68
4129	CF–PWN	Pacific Western	382F		D to Zambia Air Cargoes as 9J–RBW. S 1969 to National Aircraft Leasing. L to Pacific W
4134	N16ST	Saturn Airways	382B		L by Delta AL MAR–66, D to Alaska SEP–66 as N9263R. S to Saturn AW.
4137	9J–RBX	Zambia Air Cargoes	382B		WO N'dola APR–11–68
4144	AP–AUT	Pakistan International AL	382B		*City of Anchorage.* L to AREA 1968. WO MAY–16–68 Macuma
4146	N9267R	Alaska AL	382B	20/6/66	
4147	N9268R	Delta AL	382B	17/8/66	
4170	N9258R	Delta AL	382B	17/9/66	
4176	N9259R	Delta AL	382B	14/10/66	
4197	CF–PWO	Pacific Western	382B		N9269R before D to PWA FEB–67. L to TMA JUL–67, WO JUL–16–69 Caycaya, Peru
4200	N18ST	Saturn Airways	382B	23/3/67	D to Alaska AL as N9227R *City of Juneau.* S to Saturn AW
4209	N921NA	Alaska International AL	382B		D to Zambia Air Cargoes as 9JREZ. S 1969 to Interior Airways, now Alaska International
4221	N9248R	Airlift International	382B	30/6/67	WO OCT–11–70 McGuire AFB
4222	N13ST	Saturn Airways	382B	19/7/67	D to Airlift Int. as N9254R. S to Saturn AW. L to Alaska Int.
4225	N14ST	Saturn Airways	382B	6/9/67	D to Airlift Int. as N759AL. S to Saturn AW

Lockheed Hercules

C/n	Current Marks	Current Owner/operator	Model Series	Initial Delivery	Remarks
4229	N760AL	Airlift International	382B	3/10/67	L by Interior AW 1968. WO DEC–24–68, Anchorage
4234	N7999S	National Aircraft Leasing	382B		L by Delta 1969. S to National Aircraft Leasing. L to Saturn AW. Sub–L to Alaska Int.
4248	N9262R	National Aircraft Leasing	382B		L to Saturn AW. Sub–L to Alaska Int.
4250	N9266R	National Aircraft Leasing	382F		L to Saturn AW. Sub–L to Southern Air Transport
4299	N9232R	Southern Air Transport	382B		
4300	N9265R	Alaska International Air	382B		
4301	N7951R	Southern Air Transport	382B		
4302	PI–98	Philippine Government	382E		D to Flying W as N7592S. Re-reg N30FW. S to Philippine Govt.
4303	PI–99	Philippine Government	382E		D to Flying W as N92374. Re-reg N40FW S to Philippine Govt. L to James Bay Energy Corp.
4333	N17ST	Saturn Airways	382E		D as N7957S
4350	KAF317	Kuwait AF	382E		Formerly N7954S
4355	CF–PWR	National Aircraft Leasing	382E		L to Pacific Western
4358	N7985S	Peruvian AF	382E		
4361	CF–PWX	Pacific Western	382E		
4362	N7984S	Southern Air Transport	382E		
4364	N7986S	Peruvian AF	382E		
4383	N10ST	Saturn Airways	382E		
4384	N11ST	Saturn Airways			
4385	ZS–GSK	Safair Freighters			
4388	N12ST	Saturn Airways			
4391	N15ST	Saturn Airways			
4412	KAF318	Kuwait AF			
4450	956	SATCO–Peru			
4472	ZS–RSB	Safair Freighters			
4475	ZS–RSC	Safair Freighters			
4477	ZS–RSD	Safair Freighters			
4512	PI–100	Philippine Government			

Lockheed L-1011 TriStar

C/n	Current Marks	Current Owner/operator	Model Series	Initial Delivery	Remarks
1002	N301EA	Eastern Airlines		24/3/73	
1003	N302EA	Eastern Airlines		22/5/73	
1004	N303EA	Eastern Airlines		15/12/72	
1005	N304EA	Eastern Airlines		11/7/72	
1006	N305EA	Eastern Airlines		23/11/72	
1007	N306EA	Eastern Airlines		5/4/72	
1008	N307EA	Eastern Airlines		26/5/72	
1009	N308EA	Eastern Airlines		30/6/72	
1010	N309EA	Eastern Airlines		25/7/72	
1011	N310EA	Eastern Airlines		18/8/72	WO Everglades. DEC–29–72
1012	N311EA	Eastern Airlines		2/11/72	
1013	N31001	TWA		9/5/72	
1014	N11002	TWA		4/7/72	
1015	N11003	TWA		12/8/72	
1016	N11004	TWA		30/8/72	
1017	N11005	TWA		27/9/72	
1018	N11006	TWA		26/9/72	
1019	CF–TNA	Air Canada		13/12/72	D to Haas/Turner as N312EA. L to Air Canada.
1020	N313EA	Eastern Airlines		15/12/72	
1021	CF–TNB	Air Canada		14/1/73	
1022	N314EA	Eastern Airlines		2/1/73	
1023	CF–TNC	Air Canada		10/1/73	D to Haas/Turner as N315EA. L to Air Canada.
1024	G–BAAA	Court Line		28/2/73	
1025	CF–TND	Air Canada		9/3/73	
1026	N31007	TWA		7/4/73	
1027	CF–TNE	Air Canada		21/4/73	
1028	N31008	TWA		21/4/73	
1029	N31009	TWA		16/5/73	
1030	N31010	TWA		29/5/73	
1031	N31011	TWA		1/6/73	
1032	G–BAAB	Court Line		30/4/73	
1033	D–AERA	LTU		29/5/73	
1034	N31012	TWA		20/6/73	
1035	N31013	TWA		4/7/73	
1036	N31014	TWA		4/7/73	
1037	N316EA	Eastern Airlines		30/6/73	
1038	N317EA	Eastern Airlines		13/7/73	
1039	N318EA	Eastern Airlines		13/8/73	
1040	N319EA	Eastern Airlines		13/8/73	
1041	N701DA	Delta Airlines			
1042	N320EA	Eastern Airlines		1/9/73	
1043	N321EA	Eastern Airlines		20/9/73	
1044	N322EA	Eastern Airlines			
1045	N323EA	Eastern Airlines			
1046	N702DA	Delta Airlines			
1047	CF–TNF	Air Canada			
1048	CF–TNG	Air Canada			
1049	CF–TNH	Air Canada			
1050	N324EA	Eastern Airlines			
1051	N325EA	Eastern Airlines			
1052	N703DA	Delta Airlines			
1053	JA8501	All-Nippon AW			
1054	N326EA	Eastern Airlines			
1055	N327EA	Eastern Airlines			
1056	N328EA	Eastern Airlines			
1057	N704DA	Delta Airlines			
1058	CF–TNI	Air Canada			
1059	N31015	TWA			
1060	N41016	TWA			
1061	JA8502	All-Nippon AW			
1062	JA8503	All-Nippon AW			

Lockheed L-1011 TriStar

C/n	Current Marks	Current Owner/operator	Model Series	Initial Delivery	Remarks
1063	N15017	TWA			
1064	N10112	Pacific Southwest			
1065	N31018	TWA			
1066	N31019	TWA			
1067	CF–TNJ	Air Canada			
1068	JA8505	All-Nippon AW			
1069	CF–TNK	Air Canada			
1070	JA8506	All-Nippon AW			
1071	N705DA	Delta Airlines			
1072	N41020	TWA			
1073	CF–TNL	Air Canada			
1074	N706DA	Delta Airlines			
1075	N31021	TWA			
1076	N31022	TWA			
1077	N707DA	Delta Airlines			
1078	N708DA	Delta Airlines			
1079	N10114	Pacific Southwest			
1080	N31023	TWA			

NAMC YS-11

C/n	Current Marks	Current Owner/operator	Model Series	Initial Delivery	Remarks
2001	JA8611	NAMC	YS–11		FF AUG–30–62
2002	JA8612	NAMC	YS–11		Second prototype, FF DEC–28–1962
2003	JA8610	JCAB	104	30/3/65	*Chiyoda II*
2004	JA8639	Toa AW	101	10/4/65	
2005	JA8641	Toa AW	101	19/4/65	
2006	JA8640	JDA	106	15/5/65	*Shinju (Pearl)*
2007	JA8643	JDA	106	15/5/65	*Obsidian*
2008	52–1151	JASDF	103	30/3/65	
2009	52–1152	JASDF	103	30/3/65	
2010	PK–MYP	Merpati	102	29/7/65	D to All-Nippon AW as JA8644. S 1973
2011	PK–MYN	Merpati	102	16/9/65	D to All-Nippon AW as JA8645. S 1973
2012	PI–C–962	Filipinas Orient	107	19/10/65	
2013	PK–MYT	Merpati	102	4/10/65	D to All-Nippon AW as JA8650. S 1973
2014	JA8648	JDA	108	7/10/65	*Sango (Coral)*
2015	PI–C–963	Filipinas Orient	107	16/11/65	*Blue Lady*
2016	JA8651	JDA	108	8/12/65	*Seika*
2017	JA8653	JDA	108	8/1/66	*Diamond*
2018	62–1153	JASDF	105	4/3/66	
2019	62–1154	JASDF	105	28/3/66	
2020	JA8656	JDA	109	2/4/66	*Sapphire*
2021	JA8700	JCAB	110	24/1/67	*Chiyoda III*
2022	JA8662	JDA	109	12/5/66	*Ruby*
2023	JA8658	All Nippon AW	111	28/5/66	WO Matsuyama NOV–13–66
2024	JA8660	All Nippon AW	111	27/6/66	
2025	JA8661	All Nippon AW	111	29/7/66	
2026	JA8676	NAMC	120	28/4/67	FF as JA8676. L to LANSA as OB–R–893 *Manco Copac.* Rtd to NAMC MAY–13–69
2027	PI–C–964	Filipinas Orient	116	27/10/66	
2028	JA8666	Toa AW	114	28/9/66	
2029	JA8706	All Nippon AW	117	25/11/66	L to Hawaiian AL as N1145H DEC–1–66 to SEP–30–67. D to ANAW OCT–15–68
2030	JA8707	All Nippon AW	117	9/12/66	L to Hawaiian AL as N1146H DEC–12–66 to SEP–30–67. D to ANAW OCT–15–68
2031	JA8686	Toa AW	117	5/12/66	L to Hawaiian AL as N1147H DEC–12–66 to SEP–30–67 L to Aerolineas DEC–5–67 to AUG–15–68. D to Toa AUG–15–68
2032	JA8667	JDA	109	4/2/67	*Opal*
2033	205–9041	JMSDF	112	31/3/67	
2034	JA8668	All Nippon AW	111	30/9/67	
2035	JA8665	NAMC	120	15/4/67	L to LANSA as OB–R–857 *Sinchi Roca.* Rtd to NAMC SEP–69
2036	JA8672	Toa AW	129	5/4/68	Development aircraft for YS–11A before delivery
2037	JA8675	JDA	124	22/4/67	
2038	JA8678	Toa AW	114	5/7/67	
2039	PI–C–965	Filipinas Orient	121	1/7/67	JA8679 before D
2040	OB–R–895	LANSA	120	17/6/67	*Lioque Bopanqui*
2041	JA8680	NAMC	125	15/8/67	L to Cruzeiro as PP–CTA until NOV–3–68
2042	JA8681	NAMC	125	15/8/67	L to Cruzeiro as PP–CTB until DEC–2–68

NAMC YS-11

C/n	Current Marks	Current Owner/operator	Model Series	Initial Delivery	Remarks
2043	JA8682	NAMC	125	31/8/67	L to Cruzeiro as PP–CTC until DEC–18–68. L to VASP as PP–SMX
2044	JA8683	NAMC	125	31/8/67	L to Cruzeiro as PP–CTD until DEC–31–68. L to VASP as PP–SMY
2045	JA8684	Toa AW	128	25/11/67	L to Aerolineas DEC–5–67 to AUG–12–68. D to Toa NOV–6–68.
2046	OB–R–907	LANSA	126	2/12/67	FF as JA8685. L from NAMC *Mayta Capac*
2047	JA8720	JCAB	118		
2048	JA8711	Aeronautics College	115	2/11/67	
2049	JA8712	Aeronautics College	115	16/11/67	
2050	N156P	Piedmont	205	28/1/68	D as JA8685 *Blue Ridge* and *Sakura* later *Cherry Blossom*
2051	N158P	Piedmont	205	28/1/68	D as JA8687 *Tidewater*
2052	N162P	Piedmont	205	30/1/68	D as JA8688 *New River*
2053	N164P	Piedmont	205	9/2/68	D as JA8689 *Potomac*
2054	PP–CTE	Cruzeiro	202	25/3/68	
2055	PP–CTF	Cruzeiro	202	25/3/68	
2056	N169P	Piedmont	205	31/7/68	D as JA8690 *Albemarie*
2057	N159P	Piedmont	205	19/8/68	D as JA8691 *York River*
2058	205–9042	JMSDF	112	15/3/68	
2059	PP–SMJ	VASP	211	14/11/68	D as JA8692 WO Rio de Janeiro APR–12–72
2060	JA8693	All Nippon AW	208	27/3/68	
2061	N187P	Piedmont	205	31/8/68	D as JA8694 *Long Island*
2062	N189P	Piedmont	205	19/9/68	D as JA8695 *Cherokee*
2063	PP–CTG	Cruzeiro	202	4/6/68	
2064	PP–CTH	Cruzeiro	202	12/6/68	
2065	JA8696	Southwest AL	209	31/5/68	
2066	JA8697	All Nippon AW	208	18/5/68	
2067	JA8698	All Nippon AW	208	10/6/68	Originally allocated as –211 PP–SMJ for VASP
2068	PP–SMJ	VASP	211	30/10/68	JA8699 before D *Cuidade de Cuiaba* WO Rio de Janeiro OCT–23–73
2069	JA8715	Southwest AL	209	20/6/68	
2070	JA8714	NAMC	310		L to Korean AL 1969
2071	JA8713	JDA	307	14/7/68	
2072	CF–TAK	Transair	306	16/8/68	
2073	CF–TAM	Transair	306	19/8/68	
2074	82–1155	JASDF	305	28/8/68	
2075	N214P	Piedmont	205	21/9/68	JA8718 before D *Neuse River*
2076	PP–SMK	VASP	212	19/11/68	
2077	N218P	Piedmont	205	4/4/69	JA8721 before D *Roanoke River*
2078	JA8722	All Nippon AW	213	19/9/68	
2079	PP–SML	VASP	212	5/11/68	
2080	PP–CTI	Cruzeiro	202	23/10/68	
2081	PP–CTJ	Cruzeiro	202	15/11/68	
2082	PP–CTK	Cruzeiro	202	27/11/68	
2083	PP–CTL	Cruzeiro	202	28/11/68	
2084	PP–SMO	VASP	212		JA8709 before D
2085	JA8708	All Nippon AW	213	12/12/68	
2086	LV–JII	Austral–ALA	309		
2087	LV–JIJ	Austral–ALA	309	21/6/69	
2088					
2089	TU–	Air Afrique			
2090	JA8710	Southwest AL	214		
2091	PP–SMO	VASP	214		JA8716 before D
2092	JA8717	JAL	217		On L from JDA
2093	JA8701	JMSDF	207	4/69	

C/n	Current Marks	Current Owner/operator	Model Series	Initial Delivery	Remarks
2094	JA8726	All Nippon AW	213		
2095	JA8727	All Nippon AW	213		
2096	JA8728	All Nippon AW	213		
2097	JA8729	All Nippon AW	213		
2098					
2099					
2100					
2101					
2102					
2103					
2104	LN–	Mayair	300	12/69	JA8757 before L to Olympic AW as SX–BBG
2105					
2106	LN–	Mayair	300	1/70	L to Olympic AW as SX–BBH
2107					
2108					
2109	N219P	Piedmont		1/10/69	JA8740 before D *Pamlico*
2111					
2112	N224P	Piedmont		22/10/69	JA 8741 before D *Grand Strand*
2113	N245P	Piedmont		30/10/69	JA8742 before D *Croatan*
2114	N247P	Piedmont		10/11/69	JA8745 before D *Hickory*
2115					
2116					
2117	N254P	Piedmont		14/11/69	JA8746 before D *Pee Dee*
2118	N257P	Piedmont		4/12/69	JA8747 before D *Santee*
2119	N259P	Piedmont		16/12/69	*Shenandoah Valley*
2120	N268P	Piedmont		12/12/69	*Great Smokies*
2121	N269P	Piedmont		23/12/69	*Ohio Valley Pass*
2122	N273P	Piedmont			
2123					
2124	92–1157	JASDF	402		
2125		JASDF	402		
2126	N274P	Piedmont			
2127					
2128	TU–	Air Afrique	300		
2129	TR–	Gabon Republic	300		
2130					
2131					
2132					
2133					
2134					
2135					
2136					
2137					
2138					
2139					
2140					
2141					
2142					
2143					
2144					
2170	PK–PYV	Pertamina	600		
	PK–PYW	Pertamina	600		

Short Skyvan

C/n	Current Marks	Current Owner/operator	Model Series	Initial Delivery	Remarks
1828	G–ASCN	Shorts	1A		FF JAN–17–63 as Srs 1. Cvtd to Srs 1A and FF OCT–2–63. Grounded AUG–66
1829	G–ASCO	Shorts	2		Demonstrator, in Ansett–MAL colours. Grounded 1969
1830	G–ASZI	Shorts	3		FF as Srs 2. Cvtd to Srs 3 and FF DEC–15–67. Sc 1970
1831	G–ASZJ	Shorts	3		Cvtd from Srs 2. Srs 3 development aircraft and Skyliner demonstrator
1832	I–TORE	Aeralpi	2	8/6/66	WO Venice MAR–6–67
1833	G–ATPF	Southwest Aviation	2	16/8/66	D to Emerald Airways. Returned to Shorts 1967. L to SWA 1968. Rtd to Shorts 1969 and Sc
1834	G–AXCS	Shorts	2	10/10/66	D to Aeralpi as I–CESA. Rtd to Shorts MAR–69 and SC
1835	N731R	Remmert-Werner	2	13/10/66	D to Emerald Airways as G–ATPG. Rtd to Shorts and D to R–W JUL–67
1836	–	Shorts	2		Construction abandoned
1837	N4909	Remmert-Werner	2	20/4/67	Temporarily G–AVGO before D. L by Northern Consolidated 1968–70
1838	N10TC	Virginia Air Cargo	3	9/9/68	Built as Srs 2 VH–EIR for Ansett-MAL. G–AVJX before D. L to TAA 1968. Used by Forrestair 1969 S to Hicks, reg VH–FSG. S Virginia Air Cargo
1839	N33VC	Virginia Air Cargo	3		Built as Srs 2 VH–EJS for Ansett-MAL D to SWA as G–AWCS. S Virginia Air Cargo
1840	VH–PNI	Patair	3		
1841	N725R	Remmert-Werner	3	31/8/67	Built as Srs 2 VH–PNJ for Patair. Used by STOLines
1842	CR–LIF	CDA	3		Built as Srs 2 VH–EJT for Ansett-MAL. G–AWCT before D
1843	N20DA	Delaware Air Freight	3	28/9/67	L to Caribair 1969 by Remmert–Werner as N729R. S to Delaware Air Freight.
1844	N30DA	Delaware Air Freight	3	10/10/67	Temporarily G–14–1 before D to Remmert–Werner as N732R. S to Delaware Air Freight
1845	CF–GSC	Canadian Govt	3	5/12/67	D to Remmert–Werner as N734R. L to Dept of Energy, Mines and Resources.
1846	N4916	Wein Consolidated AL	3		D to Northern Consolidated
1847	N3419	Mackey International	2		G–AWKV before D to Remmert-Werner as N735R L to Cherokee 1969 L to Olympic

C/n	Current Marks	Current Owner/operator	Model Series	Initial Delivery	Remarks
1848	N70DA	Delaware Air Freight	3		Initially allocated 6Y–JFL for Air Caribbean. D to CAS as N3201, re-reg XW–PGA. S to Delaware Air Freight
1849	VH–PNJ	Patair	3		
1850	N4917	Wien Consoli-dated AL	3		D to Northern Consolidated
1851	PK–PSE	Pertamina	3		G–14–1 for first flight. D to Pertamina
1852	N50DA	Delaware Air Freight	3		FF as G–AWVM. L to Sadia as PP–SDO 1969. L to Caribair as N33BB 1970 S to Delaware Air Freight
1853	N60DA	Delaware Air Freight	3	3/69	FF as G–AWJM. L to Connellan AW 1969. S to Patair, reg VH–FSH. S to Delaware Air Freight
1854	N7978	International Air Cargo	3		FF as G–AWWS. D as CF–VAN. S to Pan Alaska, reg N7978. S to International Air Cargo.
1855	5S–TA	Austrian AF	3M	6/9/69	
1856	G–AWYG	Loganair	3	4/3/69	
1857	N40DA	Delaware Air Freight	3	6/69	FF as G–AXAD. D to Cherokee S to Caribair as N2OCK. S to Delaware Air Freight
1858	N21CK	Caribair	3	3/69	FF as G–AXAE. D to Cherokee as N3748
1859	N101WA	Interstate World AL	3	6/69	FF as G–AXAF. D to Cherokee S to Caribair as N22CK. S to Interstate World AL
1860	5S–TB	Austrian AF	3	6/9/69	
1861	N123PA	Pan Alaska	3	9/69	FF as G–AXAG
1862	–	Ecuastol-Ecuador	3	6/69	FF as G–ACXT D to Selkirk Air as CF–YQY. S to Ecuastol.
1863	N100LV	International Air Cargo	3	9/69	FF as G–AXCU. D to Barton Air Services as N100LY. S to International Air Cargo
1864	9M–AGG	Malaysian Air	3	30/6/69	D to Transair as CF–TAI. S to Malaysia Air Charter
1865	G–AXFI	Gulf Aviation	3	9/69	D to Alaska Leasing as N200LV. Rtd MAR–70. D to Gulf Aviation
1866	G–AXWU	Un Nigeria	3		L from Shorts
1867	G–AXPT	Shorts	3M		Military Demonstrator
1868	SAE–T–100	Ecuador Army AF	3		FF as G–AXNV. D to Pan Alaska as N23CK. S to Ecuador Army AF.
1869	SX–BBN	Olympia AW	3		FF as G–AXLB
1870	SX–BBO	Olympia AW	3		FF as G–AXLC
1871	T–701	Melanesian AF	3		FF as G–AXMO
1872	CF–NAS	Nordair	3		FF as G–AXLD
1873	N10DA	Delaware Air Freight	3		FF as G–AXLE
1874	PK–PSD	Pertamina	3		FF as G–AYDO
1875	902	Sultan of Oman's AF	3M		
1876	903	Sultan of Oman's AF	3M		FF as G–AYCS
1877	904	Sultan of Oman's AF	3M		
1878	905	Sultan of Oman's AF	3M		
1879	901	Sultan of Oman's AF	3M		FF as G–AYDP

Short Skyvan

C/n	Current Marks	Current Owner/operator	Model Series	Initial Delivery	Remarks
1880	906	Sultan of Oman's AF	3M		
1881	T–702	Melanesian AF	3M		
1882	T–703	Melanesian AF	3M		
1883	CF–QSC	Quester Air Surveys	3		
1884	9N–RAA	King of Nepal's Royal Flight	3		FF as G–AYIX
1885	G–AYJN	Gulf Aviation	3		
1886	G–AYJO	Gulf Aviation	3		
1887	PA–50	Argentine Naval Prefectura	3M		
1888	PA–51	Argentine Naval Prefectura	3M	2/6/71	
1889	PA–52	Argentine Naval Prefectura	3M	16/7/71	
1890	PA–53	Argentine Naval Prefectura	3M	16/7/71	
1891	PA–54	Argentine Naval Prefectura	3M	16/7/71	
1892	PK–PSC	Pertamina	3	24/5/71	FF as G–AYZA
1893	PK–PSA	Pertamina	3	7/7/71	FF as G–AYZB
1894	RAN–14	Nepal Army	3M	30/8/71	FF as G–AYZD
1895	907	Sultan of Oman's AF	3M	27/9/71	
1896	908	Sultan of Oman's AF	3M	25/10/71	
1897	21897	Thai Air Police	3M	9/6/72	FF as G–AZKL
1898	RAN–15	Nepal Army	3M	19/1/72	FF as G–AZHP
1899	909	Sultan of Oman's AF	3M	14/7/72	
1900	910	Sultan of Oman's AF	3M	14/7/72	
1901	LN–LPA	Airexecutive Norway	3		Was Short's Executive aircraft, reg G–AZRY before D
1902	21902	Thai Air Police	3M	26/6/72	FF as G–AZSR
1903	G–AZYW	British Airways – Scottish	3	8/3/73	
1904	PK–PSF	Pertamina	3	28/2/73	
1905	PK–PSG	Pertamina	3	5/1/73	
1906	1906	Thai Highways Board	3	30/9/72	FF as G–AZWX
1907	G–BAHK	Gulf Aviation	3	1/2/73	
1908	G–BAIT	British Airways – Scottish	3	20/3/73	
1909	XC–GAY	Pemex-Mexico	3	19/2/73	FF as G–BRID
1910	PK–PSH	Pertamina	3	25/3/73	
1911	XC–GAZ	Pemex-Mexico	3	9/4/73	FF as G–BRIE
1912	703	Singapore MoD	3M		
1913	700	Singapore MoD	3M	11/7/73	

Vickers Vanguard

C/n	Current Marks	Current Owner/operator	Model Series	Initial Delivery	Remarks
703	G–AOYW	Vickers-Armstrongs	950		Prototype FF JAN–20–59. Scrapped 1964.
704	G–APEA	British Airways	951	27/3/61	Formerly BEA. Was *Vanguard*
705	G–APEB	British Airways	951	17/3/61	Formerly BEA. Was *Bellerophon*
706	G–APEC	BEA	951	13/1/61	Was *Sirius* WO Aarsele, nr. Ghent OCT–2–71
707	G–APED	British Airways	951	30/1/61	Formerly BEA. Was *Defiance*
708	G–APEE	BEA	951	2/12/60	Was *Euryalus.* WO Heathrow OCT–27–65
709	PK–MVJ	Merpati Nusantara AL	951	12/12/60	D BEA as *Victory* S Templewood Aviation. L Merpati Nusantara AL
710	G–APEG	British Airways	953	19/5/61	Formerly BEA. Was *Arenthusa* Cvtd to Type 953C Merchantman
711	G–APEH	British Airways	953	21/6/61	Formerly BEA. Was *Audacious*
712	G–APEI	British Airways	953	20/7/61	Formerly BEA. Was *Indefatigable*
713	G–APEJ	British Airways	953	16/8/61	Formerly BEA. Was *Ajax* Cvtd to Type 953C Merchantnan
714	G–APEK	British Airways	953	16/9/61	Formerly BEA. Was *Dreadnought.* Cvtd. to Type 953C Merchantman
715	G–APEL	British Airways	953	7/10/61	Formerly BEA. Was *Leander* Cvtd to Type 953C Merchantman
716	G–APEM	British Airways	953	3/11/61	Formerly BEA. Was *Agamemnon.* Cvtd to Type 953C Merchantman
717	G–APEN	British Airways	953	14/11/61	Formerly BEA. Was *Valiant*
718	G–APEO	British Airways	953	27/11/61	Formerly BEA. Was *Orion* Cvtd to Type 953C Merchantman
719	G–APEP	British Airways	953	13/12/61	Formerly BEA Was *Superb* Cvtd to Type 953C Merchantman
720	G–APER	British Airways	953	16/1/62	Formerly BEA. Was *Amethyst*
721	G–APES	British Airways	953	24/1/62	Formerly BEA. Was *Swiftsure.* Cvtd. to Type 953C Merchantman
722	G–APET	British Airways	953	21/2/62	Formerly BEA. Was *Temeraire* Cvtd to Type 953C Merchantman
723	G–APEU	British Airways	953	30/3/62	Formerly BEA. Was *Undaunted*
724	CF–TKA	Air Canada	952	6/11/61	
725	SE–FTK	Air Trader	952	14/4/61	D to Air Canada as CF–TKB S to Air Holdings, reg G–AYFN. L Thor Flying Services, reg TF–JES. S Air Trader
726	CF–TKC	Air Canada	952	14/12/60	
727	G–AXOY	Invicta International	952	7/12/60	D to Air Canada as CF–TKD S to Air Holdings. reg G–AXOY. L to Thor Flying Services, reg TF–JEJ S to Invicta
728	PK–MVW	Merpati Nusantara AL	952	2/2/61	D to Air Canada as CF–TKE. S Air Holdings. S Templewood Avaition. L Merpati Nusantara AL

Vickers Vanguard

C/n	Current Marks	Current Owner/operator	Model Series	Initial Delivery	Remarks
729	G–AZRE	Invicta International	952	7/1/61	D to Air Canada as CF–TKF S Air Holdings. S Invicta
730	F–BUFT	Europe Aero Services	952	19/1/61	D to Air Canada as CF–TKG. S Air Holdings, reg G–AYLD. L Air Trader reg. SE–FTH. S Europe Aero Services
731		Europe Aero Services	952	18/2/61	D to Air Canada as CF–TKH S Europe Aero Services
732	CF–TKI	Air Holdings	952	10/3/61	D to Air Canada. S to Air Holdings Scrapped for Spares
733	G–AXOO	Invicta International	952	5/5/61	D to Air Canada. as CF–TKJ. S to Air Holdings, reg G–AXOO. S to Invicta
734	CF–TKK	Air Canada	952	24/5/61	
735	F–OCUA	Europe Aero Services	952	24/3/61	D to Air Canada as CF–TKL S to Air Holdings. S to Europe Aero Services
736	CF–TKM	Air Canada	952	27/4/61	
737	G–AXNT	Invicta International	952	5/5/61	D to Air Canada as CF–TKN S to Air Holdings S to Invicta
738	CF–TKO	Air Holdings	952	26/6/61	D to Air Canada as CF–TKO S to Air Holdings. Scrapped for spares
739	PK–MVR	Merpati Nusantara AL	952	16/6/61	D to Air Canada as CF–TKP S Air Holdings, reg G–BAFK. S Templewood Aviation. L Merpati Nusantara AL
740	G–AZUI	Air Holdings	952	12/8/61	D to Air Canada as CF–TKQ. S to Air Holdings, reg G–AZUI. Scrapped for spares
741	F–OCUB	Europe Aero Services	952	19/8/61	D to Air Canada as CF–TKR S to Air Holdings. S to Europe Aero Services
742	CF–TKS	Air Canada	952	28/10/61	
743	CF–TKT	Air Canada	952	7/10/61	
744	PK–MVC	Merpati Nusantara AL	952	11/7/62	D to Air Canada as CF–TKU. S to Air Holdings. L Air Trader, reg SE–FTI. S Templewood Aviation L to Merpati Nusantara AL
745	G–AXOP	Invicta International	952	7/7/62	D to Air Canada as CF–TKV S to Air Holdings. S to Invicta. WO Basle Mulhouse APR–10–73
746	CF–TKW	Air Canada	952	3/4/64	

Vickers Viscount

C/n	Current Marks	Current Owner/operator	Model Series	Initial Delivery	Remarks
1	G–AHRF	MoS	630		Prototype FF JUL–16–48 as VX211. WO at Khartoum AUG–27–52
2	VX217	MoS	663		Started as V609, G–AHRG. Completed with Tay Engines FF MAR–15–50 Scrapped
3	G–AMAV	MoS	700		Prototype long fuselage version FF AUG–28–50 Scrapped ARL 1958
4	G–ALWE	BEA	701	3/1/53	*Discovery* WO Ringway, Manchester Mar–14–57
5	G–ALWF	Cambrian Airways	701	13/2/53	D to BEA *Sir John Franklin* S to Channel. L to British Eagle. S to Cambrian Scrapped JAN 1972
6	G–AMNY	BEA	701	10/2/53	*Sir Ernest Shackleton.* WO Malta JAN–5–60
7	G–AMOG	Cambrian Airways	701	27/3/53	D to BEA *Robert Falcon Scott.* S Cambrian
8	F–BGNK	Air France	708	18/5/53	WO France DEC–12–56
9	G–AMOA	Cambrian Airways	701	17/4/53	D to BEA *Sir George Vancouver* S to Channel. L to British Eagle. S to Cambrian. WO Bristol JAN–19–70
10	F–BOEC	Air Inter	708	25/8/53	D to Air France as F–BGNL S to Maitland Drewery, reg. G–ARBY. L Silver City/ BUA. S to Air Inter
11	PP–SRI	VASP	701	24/4/53	D to BEA as G–AMOB *William Baffin* S to VASP WFS APR–8–70
12	F–BOEA	Air Inter	708	23/9/53	D to Air France as F–BGNM. S to Maitland Drewery, reg. G–ARER. L BKS Air Transport. L Silver City/ BUA. S to Inter Air. WO Southern France DEC–28–71
13	G–AMOC	Cambrian Airways	701	4/7/53	D to BEA *Richard Chancellor* S to Channel. L to British Eagle. S to Cambrian. WFS OCT–9–70 Scrapped DEC 1970
14	F–BOEB	Air Inter	708	29/10/53	D to Air France as F–BGNN S to Maitland Drewery, reg G–ARGR. L BKS Air Transport. L Silver City/ BUA. S to Inter Air
15	PP–SRJ	VASP	701	26/6/53	D to BEA as G–AMOD *John Davis.* S to VASP. WFS FEB–28–69
16	F–BGNO	Air Inter	708	12/12/53	D to Air France S to Air Inter.
17	G–AMOE	Cambrian Airways	701	13/7/53	D to BEA *Sir Edward Parry.* S to Channel. L to British Eagle. S to Cambrian. Scrapped JAN 1972
18	F–BGNP	Air Inter	708	21/12/53	D to Air France. S to Air Inter

Vickers Viscount

C/n	Current Marks	Current Owner/operator	Model Series	Initial Delivery	Remarks
19	PP–SRM	VASP	701	8/8/53	D to BEA as G–AMOF *Sir Martin Frobisher.* S to VASP. WO Santos Dumont OCT–31–66
20	G–AMNZ	Cambrian Airways	701	3/10/53	D to BEA *James Cook.* S Cambrian AW. Scrapped SEP 1971
21	G–AMOH	Cambrian Airways	701	14/10/53	D to BEA *Henry Hudson.* S to Channel. L British Eagle. S to Cambrian Scrapped NOV 1971
22	PP–SRL	VASP	701	5/11/53	D to BEA as G–AMOI *Sir Hugh Willoughby* S to VASP. WFS JUL–31–69
23	G–AMOJ	Cambrian Airways	701	30/11/53	D to BEA *Sir James Ross.* S to Channel S to Cambrian Scrapped DEC 1970
24	YV–C–AMB	LAV	701	22/12/53	D to BEA as G–AMOK *Sir Humphrey Gilbert.* S to LAV
25	G–AMOL	Cambrian Airways	701	1/1/54	D to BEA *David Livingstone.* S to Cambrian. WO Liverpool JUL–20–65
26	G–AMOM	BEA	701	27/1/54	*James Bruce.* WO Blackbushe JAN–21–56
27	G–AMON	Cambrian Airways	701	11/3/54	D to BEA *Thomas Cavendish* S to Cambrian WFS
28	G–AMOO	Cambrian Airways	701	19/12/53	D to BEA *John Oxenham.* S to Channel. L British Eagle S to Cambrian WFS DEC 1970. Scrapped FEB 1971
29	G–AMOP	Cambrian Airways	701	16/2/54	D to BEA *Mungo Park.* S to Cambrian Scrapped DEC 1971
30	G–APZB	Channel Airways	707	7/3/54	D to Aer Lingus as EI–AFV *St. Patrick* S to Tradair. S to Starways. L to British Eagle. S to Channel. Scrapped DEC 1969
31	VP–BCF	Bahamas Government	707	7/3/54	D to Aer Lingus as EI–AFW *St. Brigid* S to Eagle. (Bermuda) as VR–BBJ. S to Cunard Eagle as G–ARKH. S to Bahamas AW as VP–BCF. WFS DEC 1968
32	N7973	Bahamas Government	707	26/3/54	D to Aer Lingus as EI–AFY *St. Brendan* S to Eagle (Bermuda) as VR–BBH S to Cunard Eagle as G–ARKI. S to Bahamas AW as VP–BCE. WFS DEC 1968
33	F–BGNQ	Air Inter	708	27/5/54	D to Air France S to Air Inter
34	G–APZC	Channel Airways	707	3/4/54	D to Aer Lingus as EI–AGI *St. Laurence O'Toole,* S to Tradair, reg G–APZC L Kuwait AW. S to Channel Scrapped DEC 1969
35	F–BGNR	Air Inter	708	29/6/54	D to Air France. S to Air Inter
36	F–BLHI	Air Inter	708	30/6/54	D to Air France. S to Starways reg G–ARIR. S to Air Inter
37	F–BGNT	Air Inter	708	7/7/54	D to Air France. L Air Vietnam S to Air Inter

C/n	Current Marks	Current Owner/operator	Model Series	Initial Delivery	Remarks
38	F–BGNU	Air Inter	708	28/7/54	D to Air France. L Air Vietnam S to Air Inter
39	F–BGNV	Air Inter	708	19/8/54	D to Air France. S to Air Inter WO Lyons, AUG–12–63
40	CF–TGI	TransAir	724	8/12/54	D to TCA. S to TransAir. WFS JAN 1971
41	N–117H	Mercer Trucking Co	724	30/1/55	D to TCA as CF–TGJ. S to Mavarick Equipment and Cvtd to Type 744. S to Mercer
42	CF–TGK	Air Canada	724	25/2/55	Scrapped DEC 1969
43	CF–TGL	Trans Canada AL	724	9/3/55	WO Idlewild Airport NOV–10–58
44	VH–TVA	TAA	720	5/10/54	*John Batman.* WO OCT–31–54 in Australia
45	VH–RMQ	MacRobertson Miller AL	720	25/11/54	D to TAA as VH–TVB. *Gregory Blackland.* S to Ansett-ANA, reg VH–RMQ. S to MacRobertson. WO Port Headland DEC–31–68
46	VH–TVC	Ansett–ANA	720	8/12/54	D to TAA as *John Oxley.* S to Ansett-ANA. WO near Sydney NOV–30–61
47	VH–TVD	TAA	720	18/12/54	*Hamilton Hume.* WFS APR–28–67 Scrapped JUN 1970
48	VH–TVE	TAA	720	12/1/55	*Charles Sturt* later *John Ross.* WFS APR–2–67. Scrapped JUN 1970
49	VH–TVF	TAA	720	2/4/55	*Ernest Giles* later *Peter Warburton.* WFS JUN–30–67. Scrapped JUN 1970
50	F–BMCH	Air Inter	724	30/3/55	D to TCA as CF–TGM, S Air Inter. WO OCT–27–72
51	N18988	Eldee Inc	724	8/4/55	D to TCA as CF–TGN. S to Schenby Distilleries. S Kearney & Trecker, ctd. to type 744. S to Eldee Inc.
52	F–BMCG	Air Inter	724	1/5/55	D to TCA as CF–TGO. S to Air Inter
53	CF–TGP	Space Research Corp	724	19/5/55	D to TCA. S to Canadian DoT Scrapped by DoT OCT 1970 then S to Space Research Corp.
54	F–BMCF	Air Inter	724	5/6/55	D to TCA as CF–TGQ. S Air Inter
55	F–BNAX	Air Inter	724	21/6/55	D to TCA as CF–TGR. S Air Inter
56	CF–TGS	Air Canada	724	10/7/55	WFS
57	CF–TGT	Air Canada	724	4/8/55	Scrapped MAR 1969
58	CF–TGU	Air Canada	724	18/8/55	WFS MAY 1970
59	CF–TGV	Air Canada	724	15/9/55	WFS
60	CF–TGW	Air Canada	724	15/2/56	WFS JUNE 1970
61	PP–SRP	VASP	701C	19/10/54	D to BEA as G–ANHA *Anthony Jenkinson.* S to VASP. WFS FEB–28–69
62	PP–SRN	VASP	701C	21/11/54	D to BEA as G–ANHB *Sir Henry Stanley* S to VASP WFS FEB–28–69
63	G–ANHC	BEA	701C	19/12/54	*Sir Leo McClintock.* WO Anzio OCT–22–58
64	PP–SRO	VASP	701C	4/5/55	D to BEA as G–ANHD. *Sir William Dampier.* S to VASP. WFS FEB–28–69

Vickers Viscount

C/n	Current Marks	Current Owner/operator	Model Series	Initial Delivery	Remarks
65	PP–SRQ	VASP	701C	29/6/55	D to BEA as G–ANHE *Gino Watkins*. S to VASP. WO MAR–3–65
66	PP–SRR	VASP	701C	11/7/55	D to BEA as G–ANHF *Matthew Flinders* S to VASP. WO Friburgo SEP–4–64
67	YI–ACK	Iraqi Airways	735	13/10/55	*Ibn Fernas*
68	YI–ACL	Iraqi Airways	735	3/11/55	*Sinbad*
69	YI–ACM	Iraqi Airways	735	2/12/55	*Ibn Bottootah*
70	CF–GXK	Canadian DoT	737	28/3/55	
71	G–APTA	Channel Airways	702	28/7/55	D to BWIA as VP–TBK. L to Kuwait AW as G–APTA. L to Bahamas AW as VP–BBW S to Channel. Scrapped DEC 1969
72	G–APOW	Field AS	702	25/8/55	D to BWIA as VP–TBL. L to Kuwait AW as G–APOW. L to Bahamas AW as VP–BCD S to Field AS. Scrapped FEB–1970
73	G–APPX	Air International Charter	702	23/9/55	D to BWIA as VP–TBM. L to Kuwait AW as G–APPX. L to Bahamas AW as VP–BBV S to Field AS. L to British Midland. S to Air International Charter
74	G–ANRR	Hunting	732	11/5/55	L to MEA as OD–ACF. WO Frimley DEC–2–58
75	G–ANRS	British Eagle	732	15/6/55	D to Hunting as G–ANRS. L to MEA as OD–ACH. S Misrair, reg SU–AKY. S to British Eagle. Scrapped JUL 1969
76	SU–AKX	UAA	732	22/7/55	D to Hunting as G–ANRT. L to MEA as OD–ACG. L to Iraqi AW as YI–ADM. S to Misrair (UAA). WO Beirut FEB–28–64
77	G–AODG	British Midland	736	18/11/55	D to Fred Ohlsen as LN–FOF L to BEA as G–AODG. *Fridtj of Nansen*. L to MEA as OD–ACR. S to Airwork (BUA). S to British Midland. WO Castle Donnington. FEB–20–69
78	G–AODH	BUA	736	14/12/55	D to Fred Olson as LN–FOL L to BEA as G–AODH. *Roald Amundsen*. L to BWIA as VP–TBY. S to Airwork (BUA). WO Frankfurt OCT–30–61
79	VT–DWI	IAC	723	29/12/55	D to IAF as IU–683. S to IAC. *Gujrat* WFS JAN 1971
80	VT–DWJ	IAC	730	13/1/56	D to IAF as IU-684 *Raj Humsa*. S to IAC *Kerala*
81	YVC–AMT	LAV	702	4/11/55	D to BWIA as VP–TBN. L to Bahamas AW as VP–BCI. Sold to LAV
82	YS–O9C	TACA	763	6/11/58	WO Managua MAR–3–59
83	Not known	Chinese Government	734	20/3/56	D to Pakistan AF as J751. Sold to Chinese Govt.

C/n	Current Marks	Current Owner/operator	Model Series	Initial Delivery	Remarks
84	VH–TVG	TAA	720B	22/1/56	*William Hovell.* WFS OCT–13–67. Scrapped JUN 1970
85	SU–AIC	Misrair	739	23/12/55	WO DEC 1956 at Suez
86	SU–AID	Misrair (UAA)	739	4/2/56	WO at Wadi Halfa MAR–15–62
87	G–ATDU	British Eagle	739	27/1/56	D to Misrair (UAA) as SU–AIE. S British Eagle. *City of Liverpool.* Scrapped APL 1969
88	G–APJK	All Nippon Airways	744	15/6/55	D to Capital as N7402. S to Vickers. L to All Nippon. WO Itama Airport JUN–12–61
89	XR801	Shackleton AV	744	8/7/55	D to Capital as N7403. S to Vickers. L to All Nippon. as G–APKK. S to ETPS, reg XR801. S to Shackleton WFS DEC 1971
90	N7404	Capital Airlines	744	23/7/55	WO Chicago FEB–20–56. Rebuilt under c/n 301 as Type 757
91	CU–T–603	Cubana	755	16/5/56	Built as G–AOCA for Airwork. D to Cubana. WO NOV–2–58
92	G–AOCB	British Midland	755	5/6/56	Built as G–AOCB for Airwork. D to Cubana as CU–T–604. S Cunard (Bermuda), reg VR–BBL S British Eagle. S Invicta. S British Midland. Scrapped MAY 1970
93	G–AOCC	British Midland	755	30/6/56	Built as G–AOCC for Airwork D to Cubana as CU–T–605. S Cunard (Bermuda), reg VR–BBM S British Eagle. S Invicta. S British Midland. Scrapped JAN–12–69
94	YV–C–AMV	LAV	749	28/2/56	WO Merida JAN–25–71
95	YV–C–AMX	LAV	749	13/3/56	
96	YV–C–AMZ	LAV	749	27/3/56	WO Maracaibo NOV–1–71
97	VH–RMO	Ansett–ANA	747	27/9/55	FF as G–ANXV. D to Butler as VH–BAT *Warrel.* S Ansett–ANA, reg VH–RMO. L MacRobertson as *Oakover* WFS DEC 1968 Scrapped FEB 1971
98	7Q–YDK	Air Malawi	748	1/5/56	D to CAA as VP–YNA. *Malvern* S Air Rhodesia. S Air Malawi
99	VP–YNB	Air Rhodesia	748	17/5/56	D to CAA. *Matapos.* S Air Rhodesia
100	VP–YNC	Air Rhodesia	748	8/6/56	D to CAA *Mlanje* S Air Rhodesia
101	VP–YND	Air Rhodesia	748	2/7/56	D to CAA *Miveru* S Air Rhodesia
102	VP–YNE	CAA	748	18/7/56	WO Benghazi AUG–9–58.
103	N7405	United Air Lines	745	14/11/55	D to Capital, later VAL. WO Knoxville JULY–9–64
104	N7406	Cavalier	745	26/11/55	D to Capital, later VAL. S Cavalier WFS
105	N7407	Viscount International	745	7/12/55	D to Capital, later UAS. S to Viscount, WFS
106	N7408	Viscount International	745	23/12/55	D to Capital, later UAL. S to Viscount WFS

Vickers Viscount

C/n	Current Marks	Current Owner/operator	Model Series	Initial Delivery	Remarks
107	N7409	Viscount International	745	31/12/55	D to Capital, later UAL. S to Viscount WFS
108	N7410	Capital AL	745	15/1/56	WO Baltimore MAY–20–58
109	N7411	Viscount International	745	8/3/56	D to Capital, later UAL. S to Viscount WFS
110	N7412	Viscount International	745	23/2/56	D to Capital, later UAL. S to Viscount WFS
111	N7413	United Air Lines	745	23/2/56	D to Capital, later UAL. Scrapped FEB–29–68
112	HK.1320	Aeropesca	745	3/3/56	D to Capital as N7414. S Austrian AW, reg OE–LAN. *Johannes Brahms.* S to Aloha, reg N7414. S to Aeropesca. *Ciudad de Popayan*
113	N7415	Aloha Airlines	745	13/3/56	D to Capital as N7415 S Austrian AW reg OE–LAO. *Franz Lehar.* S to Aloha WO AUG–18–71
114	60S–AAN	Somali Airlines	745	20/3/56	D to Capital as N7416. S to Alitalia, reg I–LIRC. S Somali
115	N7417	Kearney Trecker	745	29/3/56	D to Capital, later UAL, S Kearney Trecker. Scrapped APL–23–68
116	G–AWGV	British Midland	745	30/3/56	D to Capital as N7418. S to Alitalia, reg I–LIRE. S to British Midland. Scrapped MAY 1970
117	N7419	Cathedral of Tomorrow	745	20/4/56	D to Capital, later UAL. S to Cathedral of Tomorrow
118	HK–1057	Aerolineas TAO	745	29/4/56	D to Capital as N7420. S to PAL as PI–C–773. L to Hawaiian AL, reg N745HA. S to Alitalia, reg I–LIRT. S to Aerolineas WO OCT–27–71
119	Not known	Aerolineas TAO	745	2/5/56	D to Capital as N7421. S to Alitalia, reg I–LITS S to Aerolineas. Scrapped JUL 1971
120	N7422	United Air Lines	745	7/5/56	D to Capital, later UAL. Scrapped JUN–5–68
121	N7423	United Air Lines	745	14/5/56	D to Capital, later UAL. Scrapped, donated to University JAN 1969
122	N7424	United Air Lines	745	19/5/56	D to Capital, later UAL. Scrapped, donated to University JAN 1969
123	N7425	United Air Lines	745	29/5/56	D to Capital, later UAL. Scrapped, MAY–7–68
124	G–ATTA	Northeast Airlines	745	31/5/56	D to Capital as N7426. S BKS Air Transport, reg G–ATTA. S Northeast AL. Scrapped NOV 1971
125	N7427	United Air Lines	745	12/6/56	D to Capital, later UAL. Scrapped APR–1–68
126	N7428	Cimarron Industries	745	20/6/56	D to Capital, later UAL. S Oral Roberts Evangelistic S Westenair. S Cimarron
127	N7429	United Air Lines	745	30/6/56	D to Capital, later UAL. WO Akron-Canton DEC–11–67
128	N7430	United Air Lines	745	2/7/56	D to Capital, later UAL. WO Washington NOV–23–62
129	N7431	United Air Lines	745	17/7/56	D to Capital, later UAL. WO Norfolk JAN–19–67

C/n	Current Marks	Current Owner/operator	Model Series	Initial Delivery	Remarks
130	CX–BHA	PLUNA–Uruguay	745	20/7/56	D to Capital, as N7432. S Alitalia, reg I–LIFS. S PLUNA
131	CX–BHB	PLUNA–Uruguay	745	26/7/56	D to Capital, as N7433. S Alitalia, reg I–LINS. S PLUNA
132	N7434	United Air Lines	745	3/8/56	D to Capital, later UAL. Scrapped JUN–10–68
133	N7435	Viscount International	745	17/8/56	D to Capital, later UAL. S Viscount. WFS
134	N7436	Viscount International	745	17/8/56	D to Capital, later UAL. S Viscount, WFS
135	N7437	Capital AL	745	31/8/56	WO Saginaw APL–6–58
136	N7438	Oral Roberts Evangelistic	745	6/9/56	D to Capital, later UAL. S Oral Roberts. Scrapped DEC–10–68
137	N7439	Viscount International	745	13/9/56	D to Capital, later UAL. S Viscount, WFS
138	N7440	Viscount International	745	24/9/56	D to Capital, later UAL. S Viscount WFS
139	N7441	Viscount International	745	23/9/56	D to Capital, later UAL. S Viscount WFS
140	TF–ISN	Icelandair	759	16/11/56	D to Hunting Clan as G–AOGG. S to Icelandair. *Gullfaxi* Scrapped MAY 1970
141	C–90–2100	Brazilian Air Force	742	7/11/56	D to Braathens as LN–SUN S to Brazilian AF. WO Santos Dumont DEC–8–67
142	CF–TGX	Air Canada	757	28/3/56	
143	CF–TGY	TCA	757	29/3/56	WO Toronto OCT–3–59
144	CF–TGZ	Air Canada	757	12/5/56	WFS
145	VH–RMP	Ansett–ANA	747	14/9/56	FF as G–ANYH for Butler AT. D as VH–BUT. *Warrawee II* Re-registered VH–RMP for Ansett. Scrapped FEB 1971
146	VH–TVH	TAA	756	3/6/57	*George Bass,* later *John Fawkner.* Scrapped JUN 1970
147	VH–TVI	TAA	756	9/6/56	*Matthew Flinders.* Scrapped JUN 1970
148	VH–TVJ	TAA	756	26/6/56	*John Forrest,* later *Ernest Giles.* Scrapped JUN 1970
149	TF–ISU	Icelandair	759	28/12/56	D to Hunting Clan as G–AOGH. S to Icelandair. *Hrinfaxi.* WO Fornebu APL–14–63
150	G–AOJA	BEA	802	14/2/57	WO Nutts Corner OCT–23–57
151	G–AOJB	British Airways	802	6/2/57	*Stephen Borough*
152	G–AOJC	British Airways	802	19/1/57	*Robert O'Hara Burke*
153	G–AOJD	British Airways	802	11/1/57	*Sebastian Cabot*
154	G–AOJE	British Airways	802	26/1/57	*Sir Alexander Mackenzie*
155	G–AOJF	British Airways	802	8/2/57	*Sir George Somers*
156	G–AOHG	British Airways	802	20/2/57	*Richard Hakluyt*
157	G–AOHH	British Airways	802	5/3/57	*Sir Robert McClure*
158	G–AOHI	BEA	802	11/3/57	WO near Glasgow JAN–19–73
159	G–AOHJ	British Airways	802	24/3/57	*Sir John Manderville*
160	G–AOHK	British Airways	802	5/4/57	*John Hanning Speke*
161	G–AOHL	British Airways	802	7/4/57	*Charles Sturt*
162	G–AOHM	British Airways	802	27/6/57	*Robert Machin*
163	G–AOHN	British Airways	802	1/5/57	*Alexander Gordon Laing*
164	G–AOHO	British Airways	802	4/5/57	*Samuel Wallis*

Vickers Viscount

C/n	Current Marks	Current Owner/operator	Model Series	Initial Delivery	Remarks
165	G–AOHP	BEA	802	17/5/57	WO Copenhagen NOV–17–57
166	G–AOHR	British Airways	802	4/6/57	*Sir Richard Burton*
167	G–AOHS	British Airways	802	22/6/57	*Robert Thorne*
168	G–AOHT	British Airways	802	3/7/57	*Ralph Fitch*
169	G–AOHU	BEA	802	11/7/57	WO Heathrow JAN–7–60
170	G–AOHV	British Airways	802	25/8/57	*Sir John Barrow*
171	G–AORD	British Airways	802	7/9/57	*Arthur Philipp*
172	EI–AOG	Aer Lingus	803	6/6/57	D to KLM as PH–VIA *Sir Sefton Brancker* S to Aer Lingus. *Finghin* WFS OCT–18–69
173	EI–AOJ	Aer Lingus	803	26/7/57	D to KLM as PH–VIB *Louis Bleriot* S to Aer Lingus. *Flannan.* WFS. NOV–1–70
174	EI–APD	Aer Lingus	803	28/8/57	D to KLM as PH–VIC *J. C. Ellehammer.* S to Aer Lingus *Fionnbharr* WFS NOV–1–70
175	EI–AOL	Aer Lingus	803	19/10/57	D to KLM as PH–VID *Otto Lilienthal.* S to Aer Lingus *Fionntan*
176	EI–AOF	Aer Lingus	803	19/10/57	D to KLM as PH–VIE *Ian Olieslagers.* S to Aer Lingus *Cathal.* WO Dublin JUN–22–67
177	EI–AOE	Aer Lingus	803	22/10/57	D to KLM as PH–VIF *Leonardo da Vinci.* S to Aer Lingus *Damhnait.* WFS NOV–5–70
178	EI–AOM	Aer Lingus	803	8/11/57	D to KLM as PH–VIG *Sir Charles Kingsford Smith.* S Aer Lingus *Feidhlim.* WO Wexford MAR–24–68
179	EI–AOI	Aer Lingus	803	23/11/57	D to KLM as PH–VIH *Wright Brothers.* S to Aer Lingus *Fearghal.* L. British Air Ferries
180	EI–AOH	Aer Lingus	803	23/12/57	D to KLM as PH–VII *Daidalos.* S to Aer Lingus *Fiachra.* WFS NOV–1–69
181	VH–TVK	TAA	756	18/1/57	Scrapped JUN 1970
182	PP–SRS	VASP	701C	27/7/56	D to BEA as G–AOFX *Sir Joseph Banks.* S to VASP WFS FEB–28–69
183	N905G	Holiday Air of America	764	4/12/56	D to US Steel as N905. S to Percell Jones. S to Gates Aviation. S to Union Assurance, reg N905G. S to Holiday Air
184	N906RB	Rogers Brothers	764	29/11/56	D to US Steel as N906. S to Rogers Bros. reg N906RB
185	XB–WOW	Grupa Cydsa	764	28/12/56	D to US Steel as N907. S to Percell Jones. S to Gates Aviation. S to Westernair. S to Grupa Cydsa
186	G–AWCV	British Midland	760	1/1/57	D to Hong Kong AW as VR–HFI. S to Malayan AW as 9M–ALY. S to Aden AW as VR–AAW. S to British Midland. Scrapped MAY 1970

C/n	Current Marks	Current Owner/operator	Model Series	Initial Delivery	Remarks
187	VR–AAV	Aden Airways	760	28/2/57	D to Hong Kong AW as VR–HFJ. S to Malayan AW as VR–SEE. S to Aden AW as VR–AAV. WO JUNE–30–67
188	XY–ADF	Union of Burma AW	761	27/7/57	
189	XY–ADG	Union of Burma AW	761	26/11/57	
190	XY–ADH	Union of Burma AW	761		D to UBA. L to Kuwait AW as G–APXN. L to MEA as G–APXN
191	N306	Standard Oil	765	11/2/57	
192	VT–DIO	Indian Airlines	768	19/8/57	WO Agra SEP–11–63
193	VT–DIF	Indian Airlines	768	26/9/57	WFS AUG 1970
194	VT–DIG	Indian Airlines	768	23/10/57	WFS FEB–9–71
195	VT–DIH	Indian Airlines	768	9/11/57	WO Colombo NOV–17–61
196	VT–DII	Indian Airlines	768	21/11/57	
197	VH–TVL	TAA	756	1/3/57	WFS AUG–19–69. Scrapped FEB 1971
198	XR.802	Shackleton Aviation	745	29/9/56	D to Capital as N7442. S Northeast AL. To Vickers as G–ARUU. S to MoA. WFS. DEC 1971
199	N7443	United Air Lines	745	5/10/56	D to Capital, later UAL. Scrapped FEB–13–68
200	N7444	United Air Lines	745	13/10/56	D to Capital, later UAL. Scrapped MAR–5–68
201	N923RC	Ray Charles	745	17/10/56	D to Capital, later UAL, as N7445. S East Coast Leasing. S Ray Charles
202	N7446	United Air Lines	745	23/10/56	D to Capital, later UAL. Scrapped JAN–16–68
203	N7447	United Air Lines	745	29/10/56	D to Capital, later UAL. Scrapped JAN–30–68
204	N7448	Viscount International	745	3/11/56	D to Capital, later UAL. S to Viscount. WFS
205	N7449	Viscount International	745	7/11/56	D to Capital, later UAL. S to Viscount, WFS
206	N7450	Viscount International	745	16/11/56	D to Capital, later UAL. S to Viscount, WFS
207	N7451	Aero-Flite	745	23/11/56	D to Capital, later UAL. S to Aero-Flite Scrapped MAY 1970
208	N7452	Westernair	745	30/11/56	D to Capital, laterUAL. S to Aero Flite S to Westernair. Scrapped MAY 1970
209	N7454	United Air Lines	745	11/12/56	D to Capital, later UAL. Scrapped JAN–9–68
210	N7455	United Air Lines	745	18/12/56	D to Capital, later UAL. Scrapped APR–9–68
211	N1898K	Kearney Trecker	745	13/12/56	D to Capital as N7456. S to Blaw Knox. S to Kearney Trecker
212	YS–28C	TACA	745	31/12/56	D to Capital as N7457. S to TACA
213	N7458	East Coast Leasing	745	6/1/57	D to Capital. S Grekenheimer Productions. S East Coast Leasing
214	N7459	Essex International	745	17/1/57	D to Capital. S Essex Int. Scrapped APR–17–68
215	N7460	United Air Lines	745	9/1/57	D to Capital, later UAL. Scrapped MAR–14–68
216	N7461	United Air Lines	745	1/2/57	D to Capital, later UAL. Scrapped FEB–27–68

Vickers Viscount

C/n	Current Marks	Current Owner/operator	Model Series	Initial Delivery	Remarks
217	N7462	Capital Air Lines	745	2/3/57	WO Richmond JAN–18–60
218	CF–THA	Wabush Mines	757	5/2/57	D to TCA. S to Canadian Inspection. S to Wabush Mines
219	CF–THB	Air Canada	757	29/1/57	
220	CF–THC	Air Canada	757	20/2/57	
221	CF–THD	Air Canada	757	22/2/57	WFS JUL 1969. Scrapped JAN 1971
222	CF–THE	Air Canada	757	5/3/57	WFS MAR 1969. Scrapped JAN 1971
223	CF–THF	Air Canada	757	14/3/57	
224	CF–THG	Air Canada	757	28/3/57	
225	G–APNF	North East	776	3/4/58	FF as G–16–4, Type 745. L to Aer Lingus as EI–AJW. L to BEA as G–APNF *Philipp Carteret*. S to Kuwait Oil Co. S to Kuwait AW as 9K–ACD. S to BKS AT as G–APNF. S to North East. WFS MAR–20–70 Scrapped NOV 1971
226	XC–FOV	Electrical Commission	798	27/2/59	FF as Type 745 Vickers demonstrator G–APBH. D Northeast AL as N6599C. S Essex. International, reg N1298. S North American Rockwell. S Travis Ward. S Westernair S Electrical Commission
227	SE–CNK	Skyline	784	14/3/58	FF as VH–TVO, L to TAA *David Lindsay* Returned to Vickers. S to PAL, reg PI–C–772. S to Falconair. reg. SE–CNK. S to Malmo Aero to Skyline
228	N24V	Ingersol Milling	793	27/3/58	FF as G–16–3, Type 745. L to Aer Lingus as EI–AJV. L to BEA as G–APNG *James Lancaster*. L to Kuwait AW. S to Royal Bank of Canada, reg CF–RBC. S to S. J. Groves, reg. N505W, S to Ingersol Milling
229	CF–DTA	Canadian DoT	797	28/10/58	FF as G–APFR Type 745 demonstrator. S to Canadian DoT
230	N776M	J. W. Mecom	798	2/10/58	FF as G–16–6, G–APLX Type 745 demonstrator. S to Northeast AL, reg N6595C. S to J.W. Mecom
231	N7465	United Air Lines	745	19/6/58	D to Capital, later UAL. WO Durham Airport NOV–28–67
232	HK.1319	Aeropesca	798	8/8/58	D to Northeast AL as N6590C S to Aloha AL, reg N7416. S Aeropesca. L to La Urraca
233	N1898T	Kearney Trecker	798	8/8/58	D to Northeast AL as N6591C. S to Blaw Knox. reg N820BK. S to Kearney Trecker
234	N6592C	Northeast Airlines	798	21/8/58	WO Boston NOV–15–61
235		Commerce International	772	26/10/57	D to BWIA as VP–TBS. S to Commerce International

C/n	Current Marks	Current Owner/operator	Model Series	Initial Delivery	Remarks
236		Commerce International	772	13/11/57	D to BWIA as VP–TBT. S to Commerce International
237		Commerce International	772	11/12/57	D to BWIA as VP–TBU. S to Commerce International
238		Commerce International	772	3/1/58	D to BWIA as VP–TBX. L to LAV as 9Y–TBX. S to Commerce International
239	OD–ACT	MEA	754	27/7/57	D to MEA. L Kuwait AW. WO Beirut DEC–28–68
240	VP–WAR	Air Rhodesia	754	7/9/57	D to MEA as OD–ACU. L to Jordainian as JY–ACI. S to Air Rhodesia
241	7Q–YDL	Air Malawi	754	27/9/57	D to MEA as OD–ACV. S to CAA, reg VP–YTE *Zambesi* later Air Rhodesia. S to Air Malawi
242	N7410	Aloha Airlines	754	9/10/57	D to MEA as OD–ACW. L to Kuwait AW. S to Aloha WO JUN–27–69
243	VP–YTE	Air Rhodesia	754	9/11/57	Intended as G–APCD. *St. Hilarion,* Cyprus AW. D to MEA as OD–ADD. L to Jordanian as JY–ACK. L to Overseas Holidays. S Air Rhodesia
244	OD–ADE	MEA	754	15/12/57	WO Ankara FEB–1–63
245	OD–ACX	MEA	754	1/1/58	WO Elarish Airport APR–21–64
246	TC–SEC	Turkish AF	794	21/1/58	FF as OD–ACY for MEA, not delivered D to THY. S to Turkish AF.
247	VT–DOD	IAC	779	30/4/57	D to Fred Olsen as LN–FOM. L Austrian AL, reg. OE–LAE. L BEA, reg G–ARSW. S to IAC. *Madras,* later *Mysore* WFS JUL–12–71
248	ZK–NAI	NZNAC	804	17/9/57	D to Transair (BUA) as G–AOXU. S to LOT, reg SP–LVC. S to NZNAC, cvtd to Type 807. *City of Palmerstone North.*
249	SP–LVA	LOT	804	24/9/57	D to Transair (BUA) as G–AOXV. S to LOT. WO Leige AUG–20–65
250	VT–DOE	IAC	779	25/4/57	D to Fred Olsen as LN–FOH L Austrian AL, reg OE–LAB. L to BEA, reg G–APZP. S to IAC. *Uttar Pradesh,* later *Maharashtra.*
251	VT–DOH	IAC	779	28/5/57	D to Fred Olsen as LN–FOI. L to Austrian AL. reg OE–LAC. L to SAS, reg LN–FOI. S to IAC. *Mysore,* later *Andhra Pradesh*
252	VT–DOI	IAC	779	9/8/57	D to Fred Olsen as LN–FOK. L to Austrian AL, reg OE–LAD. L to SAS, reg LN–FOK. S IAC *Punjab,* later *Madras.* WFS MAR–9–71
253	G–AOHW	British Airways	802	1/8/57	
254	G–AORC	BEA	802	27/8/57	WO Prestwick APL–20–58
255	G–AOYF	Vickers	806A		Prototype FF AUG–9–57. WO Johannesburg OCT–20–57

Vickers Viscount

C/n	Current Marks	Current Owner/operator	Model Series	Initial Delivery	Remarks
256	G–AOYG	Cambrian Airways	806	29/1/58	D to BEA. *Charles Darwin.* S to Cambrian
257	G–AOYI	Cambrian Airways	806	1/1/58	D to BEA. *Sir Humphry Davy* S to Cambrian
258	EI–AMA	Aer Lingus	808	9/12/57	D to Eagle as G–APDW, Type 805. To Eagle (Bermuda) as VR–BAX. S to Maritime reg CF–MJC. S Aer Lingus, cvtd Type 808. WFS JAN–6–70. Scrapped MAY 1972
259	G–AOYJ	Cambrian Airways	806	8/1/58	D to BEA *Edward Jenner.* L to Cyprus AW. S to Cambrian
260	PK–RVK	Mandala AW	806	12/2/58	D to BEA as G–AOYK *Edmund Cartwright.* L to Cyprus AW. S to Mandala. *Garunda Mataram*
261	G–AOYL	North East	806	14/2/58	D to BEA. *Lord Joseph Lister* S to BKS AT, to North East
262	G–AOYM	Cambrian Airways	806	19/3/58	D to BEA. *John London McAdam.* S to Cambrian
263	G–AOYN	Cambrian Airways	806	26/3/58	D to BEA. *Sir Isaac Newton* S to Cambrian
264	G–AOYO	North East	806	3/4/58	D to BEA. *Adam Smith.* S to BKS AT, to North East
265	G–AOYP	Cambrian Airways	806	16/5/58	D to BEA. *John Napier.* S to Cambrian
266	G–AOYR	North East	806	11/4/58	D to BEA. *Sir Richard Arkwright.* S to BKS AT, to North East
267	G–AOYS	Cambrian Airways	806	13/6/58	D to BEA. *George Stephenson.* S to Cambrian
268	B3001	Winner Airways	806	2/5/58	D to BEA as G–AOYT. *James Watt.* S to Winner
269	CF–THH	Air Canada	757	18/5/57	Scrapped MAY 1970
270	CF–THI	Air Canada	757	26/5/57	Scrapped Donated to Museum. DEC 1969
271	CF–THK	Air Canada	757	3/6/57	WO Seven Islands APR–7–69
272	CF–THL	Air Canada	757	16/12/57	
273	CF–THM	Air Canada	757	18/12/57	WFS
274	CF–THN	Air Canada	757	1/1/58	
275	CF–THO	Air Canada	757	24/1/58	
276	CF–THP	Air Canada	757	29/1/58	
277	CF–THQ	Air Canada	757	14/2/58	
278	CF–THR	Air Canada	757	27/2/58	WFS
279	CF–THS	Air Canada	757	1/2/58	
280	150	SAAF	781	16/6/58	
281	ZK–BRD	NZNAC	807	31/12/57	*City of Wellington*
282	ZK–BRE	NZNAC	807	31/1/59	*City of Auckland*
283	ZK–BRF	NZNAC	807	12/3/59	*City of Christchurch*
284	–	Italian Instituto Technico Aeronautico	798	22/9/58	D to Northeast AL as N6594C S to Alitalia, reg I–LIRG. Scrapped JUL 1971 for use as ground trainer
285	N7464	United Air Lines	745	20/2/58	D to Capital, later UAL. Scrapped SEP–5–68
286	G–AVED	North East	798	2/9/58	D to Northeast AL as N6593C S to Hawaiian AL, reg N746HA. S to TACA, reg. YS–07C. S to BKS AT, reg G–AVED, to North East
287	N7463	Capital	745	25/1/58	WO Baltimore MAY–12–59

C/n	Current Marks	Current Owner/operator	Model Series	Initial Delivery	Remarks
288	HS–ART	SAETA	798	31/10/58	D to Northeast AL as N6596C S to Alitalia, reg I–LIRM, S to SAETA. WO Cuena Airport JUN–3–70
289	EI–AJI	Aer Lingus	808	22/5/57	WFS OCT–20–69. Scrapped MAY 1972
290	EI–AJJ	Aer Lingus	808	10/1/58	WFS DEC–31–69. Scrapped MAY 1972
291	HB–ILR	Air Tourisme Alpine	808	21/2/58	D to Aer Lingus as EI–AJK. S SATA, reg HB–ILR. S Air Tourisme
292	VT–DIX	IAC	768	3/3/58	WO Jaipur AUG–9–71
293	VT–DIZ	IAC	768	18/3/58	WFS JAN–31–72
294	VT–DJA	IAC	768	21/4/58	
295	VT–DJB	IAC	768	22/5/58	WFS FEB–21–71
296	VT–DJC	IAC	768	6/6/58	
297	VP–WAS	Air Rhodesia	782	25/3/58	D to Iranian AL as EP–AHA. S to Air Rhodesia
298	VP–WAT	Air Rhodesia	782	16/4/58	D to Iranian AL as EP–AHB. S to Air Rhodesia
299	EP–AHC	Iranian AL	782	9/5/58	WO Isfahan FEB–14–65
300	SE–CNL	Skyline	784	10/5/57	D to PAL as PI–C770. S Falconair, reg SE–CNL. S Malmo Aero, to Skyline.
301	CF–THJ	Air Canada	757	30/5/57	Rebuild of C/n 90. WFS MAR 1969. Scrapped JAN 1971
302	CF–THT	Air Canada	757	1/3/58	WO Toronto JUN–13–64
303	CF–THU	Air Canada	757	8/3/58	WFS
304	CF–THV	Air Canada	757	21/3/58	
305	CF–THW	Air Canada	757	3/4/58	WFS
306	CF–THX	Air Canada	757	18/4/58	
307	CF–THY	Air Canada	757	3/5/58	
308	CF–THZ	Air Canada	757	15/5/58	
309	CF–TIA	Air Canada	757	13/6/58	
310	CF–TIB	Air Canada	757	11/6/58	
311	G–AOYH	North East	806	23/12/57	D to BEA. *William Harvey*. S to BKS AT, to North East
312	EI–ALG	Aer Lingus	808	5/3/58	D to Eagle as G–APDX, Type 805. To Eagle (Bermuda) as VR–BAY. S to Aer Lingus, cvtd Type 808. *Cirran*. WFS NOV–1–69. Scrapped MAY 1972
316	PP–SRH	VASP	827	11/8/60	FF as prototype Type 810, reg. G–AOYV. S to VASP after cvtd to Type 827
317	ZS–CVA	SAA	818	20/11/58	D to Cubana as CU–T–621. S to SAA, reg ZS–CVA. *Reitbok*. WO East London MAR–13–67
318	VH–TVR	Moorabbin Air Museum	818	11/4/59	D to Cubana as CU–T–622. S to TAA, reg VH–TVR. *John Murray*. WFS APL–11–70. Scrapped FEB 1971, presented to Museum
319	B2019	FEAT	818	18/8/59	D to Cubana as CU–T–623. S to Ansett-ANA, reg VH–RML. S to FEAT
320	N500T	Tenneco	835	24/9/59	FF as CU–T–624 for Cubana. D Tenneco
321	CX–AQN	PLUNA	768	13/5/58	
322	CX–AQO	PLUNA	768	13/5/58	
323	CX–AQP	PLUNA	769	13/5/58	WFS JAN–11–67. Scrapped JUL 1969

Vickers Viscount

C/n	Current Marks	Current Owner/operator	Model Series	Initial Delivery	Remarks
324	SE–CNM	Skyline	784	18/9/57	D to PAL as PI–C–771. L to TACA, reg YS–06C. S to Falconair. S to Malmo Aero, to Skyline, reg SE–CNM. Scrapped OCT 1971
325	60S–AAK	Somali AL	785	23/3/57	D to Alitalia as I–LIFE. S Somali AL
326	HK1061	TAO Colombia	785	17/4/57	D to Alitalia as I–LIFT. S to TAO. WFS SEP–6–69. Scrapped JUL 1971
327	HK1061X	TAO Colombia	785	26/5/57	D to Alitalia as I–LILI. S to TAO. WFS OCT–7–71
328	I–LAKE	Alitalia	785	30/8/57	WO Vesuvius MAR–28–64
329	HC–AVP	SAETA	785	30/6/57	D to Alitalia as I–LARK. S SAETA
330	–	TAO Colombia	785	28/7/57	D to Alitalia as I–LOTT. S TAO. WFS DEC–18–69. Scrapped JUL 1971
331	YI–ACU	Iraqi Airways	773	18/11/57	WO MAR–19–65
332	YS–08C	TACA	786	28/8/57	D to Kaysam as HK–943X. S to TACA. *El Centroamericano*
333	G–AVIY	North East	786	23/1/58	D to Kaysam as HK–946X. S to LANICA, reg AN–AKP. S TACA, reg YS–11C. S BKS AT, to North East. Scrapped OCT–1–69
334	N200Q	Merriweather	786	27/2/58	D to Kaysam as HK–947X. S to LANICA, reg AN–AKQ. S to Merriweather
335	AP–AJC	PIA	815	8/1/59	WO MAY–18–59
336	G–AVJA	British Midland	815	13/2/59	D to PIA as AP–AJD. S British Midland WO MAR–20–69
337	AP–AJE	PIA	815	17/3/59	WO Karachi AUG–14–59
338	D–ANUN	Nora Air Services	814	5/10/58	D to Lufthansa. L to Condor S Nora AS.
339	G–AWXI	British Midland	814	19/12/58	D to Lufthansa as D–ANOL. L to Condor S British Midland. WO JAN–22–70
340	D–ANAD	Nora Air Services	814	10/1/59	D to Lufthansa. S to Nora AS
341	D–ANIP	Nora Air Services	814	15/2/59	D to Lufthansa. L to Condor. S to Nora AS
342	503	Sultan of Oman	814	8/3/59	D to Lufhansa. L to Condor. S to Sultan of Oman
343	504	Sultan of Oman	814	26/3/59	D to Lufthansa as D–ANEF. S to Sultan of Oman. WFS APL–4–71. WO JAN–18–72
344	D–ANIZ	Nora Air Services	814	6/4/59	D to Lufthansa. S to Nora AS
345	C92–2101	Brazilian AF	789	23/12/57	
346	G–AZLP	British Midland	813	26/10/58	D to SAA as ZS–CDT.*Blesbok.* S to British Midland
347	G–AZLR	British Midland	813	26/10/58	D to SAA as ZS–CDU *Bosbrok.* S to British Midland
348	G–AZLS	British Midland	813	18/11/58	D to SAA as ZS–CDV. *Waterbok.* S British Midland
349	G–AZLT	British Midland	813	8/12/58	D to SAA as ZS–CDW *Roosbok* S British Midland
350	G–AZNA	British Midland	813	20/12/58	D to SAA as ZS–CDX *Wildebees.* S British Midland
351	G–AZNB	British Midland	813	10/1/59	D to SAA as ZS–CDY *Gemsbok.* S British Midland

C/n	Current Marks	Current Owner/operator	Model Series	Initial Delivery	Remarks
352	G–AZNC	British Midland	813	29/1/59	D to SAA as ZS-CDZ *Hartbees* S British Midland
353	N501T	Tenneco	812	10/5/58	D to Continental AL as N240V. S to Tenneco
354	N243V	Continental Airlines	812	13/6/58	D to Continental. L to Capital. WO Amarillo JUL–9–62
355	B2021	FEAT	812	10/5/58	D to Continental as N241V. S to Ansett-ANA as VH–RMK. S to FEAT
356	N242V	Continental Airlines	812	23/5/58	D to Continental AL. L to Capital. WO Kansas JAN–29–63
357	G–ATUE	Alidair Cargo	812	26/6/58	D to Continental as N244V. S to Channel AW. S to Alidair
358	G–AVIW	Alidair Cargo	812	8/7/58	D to Continental as N245V. S to Channel AW S to Alidair
359	G–AVHK	Channel Airways	812	1/8/58	D to Continental as N246V. S to Channel AW WFS MAY-19–70 Scrapped JUN–19–72
360	G–AVJZ	Channel Airways	812	16/9/58	D to Continental as N248V. S to Channel AW. WO Southend MAY–3–67
361	G–AVNJ	Channel Airways	812	2/10/58	D to Continental as N249V. S to Channel AW. L to Air Ferry. WFS Oct–23–69. Scrapped JUN–19–72
362	G–APPC	Channel Airways	812	24/10/58	D to Continental as N250V. S to Channel AW. WFS SEP–29–68. Scrapped JUN–19–72
363	G–AVHE	Channel Airways	812	5/11/58	D to Continental as N251V. S to Channel AW. L to Air Ferry. WFS MAY–30–70 Scrapped JUN–19–62
364	G–APPU	Channel Airways	812	23/3/59	D to Continental as N252V. S to Channel AW. WO Southend MAY–4–68
365	G–ATVR	Channel Airways	812	23/3/59	D to Continental as N253V. S to Channel AW WFS
366	G–ATVE	Channel Airways	812	10/4/59	D to Continental as N254V. S to Channel AW. WFS OCT–26–69 Scrapped JUN–19–72
368	D–ANAM	Lufthansa	814	17/4/59	WFS FEB–19–70. Scrapped JUL–1–71
369	D–ANAB	Lufthansa	814	29/4/59	WFS DEC–4–69. Scrapped JUL–1–71
370	4X–AVA	Arkia Airlines	814	3/5/59	D to Lufthansa as D–ANAC. S to Arkia AL.
371	XT–661	MinTech (RRE)	838	19/9/61	D to Ghana AW as 9G–AAV. S to MinTech
372	9G–AAW	Ghana Airways	838	21/10/61	
373	VH–TVM	TAA	756	4/7/58	Scrapped JUN 1970. *John Fawkner*
374	VP–YNI	Overseas Holidays	756	8/7/58	D to TAA as VH–TVN *William Dampier.* S to Botswana National, reg A2–ZEL. S to Overseas Holidays
375	G–AVJB	Kestrel International	815	31/8/59	D to PIA as AP–AJF. S to British Midland. S to Kestrel International

Vickers Viscount

C/n	Current Marks	Current Owner/operator	Model Series	Initial Delivery	Remarks
376	LX–LGC	Luxair	815	28/9/59	D to PIA as AP–AJG. S to Luxair. *Prince Guilleume* Scrapped DEC 1969
377	HC–ARS	SAETA	785	24/3/58	D to Alitalia as I–LIRS. S to SAETA
378	I–LIZT	Alitalia	785	4/4/58	WO Rome DEC–21–59
379	60S–AAJ	Somali Airlines	785	29/4/58	D to Alitalia as I–LIRP. S to Somali AL. WO Mogadishu MAY–6–70
380	HK–1058	Aerolineas TAO	785	15/5/58	D to Alitalia as I–LIZO. S to Aerolineas
381	G–APEX	North East	806	24/6/58	D to BEA. S to BKS AT, to North East
382	G–APEY	North East	806	18/7/58	D to BEA. S to BKS AT, to North East
383	CF–TIC	Air Canada	757	30/6/58	
384	CF–TID	Air Canada	757	8/3/59	
385	CF–TIE	Air Canada	757	20/3/59	
386	CF–TIF	Air Canada	757	28/3/59	
387	CF–TIG	Air Canada	757	2/5/59	
389	G–AVJL	Alidair Cargo	812	20/8/58	D to Continental as N247V. S to Channel AW. S to Alidair
391	N8989V	Super Valu Stores Inc	798	11/12/58	D to Northeast AL as N6597C S to Victor Comptometer, reg N3939V. S to Super Valu
392	N6598	Bendix Corp	798	8/1/59	D to Northeast AL as N6598C S to Ideal Basic Industries, S to Bendix
393	G–ATDR	British Eagle	739A	12/7/58	D to Misrair (UAA) as SU–AKN. S to British Eagle. *City of Glasgow.* Scrapped DEC 1969.
394	G–ATFN	British Eagle	739A	27/7/58	D to Misrair (UAA) as SU–AKO. S to British Eagle. *City of Truro.* WO Munich AUG–9–68
395	SP–LVB	LOT	804	24/4/58	D to Transair (BUA) as G–APKG. S to LOT. WO Warsaw. DEC–19–62
396	XW–TBN	LAO Air Line	806	12/7/58	D to BEA as G–APKF. *Michael Faraday.* S to LAO
397	PP–SRC	VASP	827	28/10/58	
398	PP–SRD	VASP	827	10/11/58	
399	PP–SRE	VASP	827	3/12/58	WO Congonhas SEP–15–68
400	PP–SRF	VASP	827	22/12/58	
401	PP–SRG	VASP	827	29/1/59	WO Rio de Janeiro. DEC–22–59
402	G–APND	British Midland	831	23/2/59	D to Airwork (BUA). S to British Midland
403	G–APNE	British Midland	831	17/3/59	D to Airwork (BUA). S to British Midland
412	G–APIM	Cambrian Airways	806	23/6/58	D to BEA *Robert Boyle.* S to Cambrian
413	PK–RVM	Mandala Airways	806	2/8/58	D to BEA as G–APJU *Sir Gilbert Blane.* S to Mandala
414	B2015	FEAT	832	12/3/59	D to Ansett-ANA as VH–RMG. S to FEAT
415	9M–AOE	Pelandok Airways	832	1/4/59	D to Ansett– ANA as VH–RMH. S to FEAT, reg B 2023. S to Pelandok
416	VH–RMI	Ansett–ANA	832	24/4/59	WO near Winton, SEP–22–66
417	B2017	FEAT	832	15/5/59	D to Ansett-ANA as VH–RMJ S to FEAT

C/n	Current Marks	Current Owner/operator	Model Series	Initial Delivery	Remarks
418	PK–RVL	Mandala Airways	806	4/4/59	Was prototype Type 806A. WO at Johannesburg (see c/n 255). Rebuilt as Type 806. D to BEA as G–APOX *Isambard Brunel* S to Mandala. *Prabu Prawidjaja*
419	G–ASED	Alidair Cargo	831	5/6/59	D to Airwork (BUA). L to Sudanair reg ST–ANN. S to BUA, reg G–ASED. S British Midland. S Alidair
421	D–ADAN	Air Commerz	808	7/1/59	D to Aer Lingus as EI–AKO *Colman.* S to Air Commerz
422	EI–AKK	Aer Lingus	808	31/1/59	WO Bristol SEP–21–67
423	D–ADAM	Air Commerz	808	20/3/59	D to Aer Lingus as EI–AKL. *Colmcille.* S to Air Commerz
424	4X–AVB	Arkia	833	18/6/59	D to Hunting Clan as G–APTB Later Transair (BUA). S to Arkia
425	4X–AVC	Arkia	833	29/6/59	D to Hunting Clan as G–APTC. later Transair (BUA) S to Arkia. Scrapped OCT–26–69
426	4X–AVD	Arkia	833	20/7/59	D to Hunting Clan as G–APTD. Later Transair (BUA) S to Arkia
427	SU–AKW	UAA	739B	7/3/60	WO near Elba SEP–29–60
428	ZK–BWO	NZNAC	807	20/5/61	*City of Dunedin*
429	TC–SEV	THY	794	1/8/58	WO Gatwick FEB–17–59
430	TC–SEL	Turkish AF	794	19/9/58	D to THY. S Turkish AF
431	TC–SES	Turkish AF	794	24/10/58	D to THY. S Turkish AF
432	TC–SET	THY	794	2/12/58	WO FEB–2–69
433	B2025	FEAT	816	23/5/59	D to TAA as VH–TVP. *John Gould*. S to Conley Aircraft Sales. S to FEAT
434	B2027	FEAT	816	17/6/59	D to TAA as VH–TVQ. *McDonall Stuart* S to Conley Aircraft Sales. S to FEAT.
435	501	Sultan of Oman	836	25/5/60	D to Union Carbide as N40N. S to RAAF, reg A6–435. S to Jetair, reg VH–EQP. S to Gates Aviation. S to Sultan of Oman
436	502	Sultan of Oman	839	15/5/61	D for use of Shah of Persia as EP–MRS. to Iranair. S to RAAF, reg A6–436. S to Jetair, reg VH–EQQ. S to Gates Aviation. S to Sultan of Oman
437	OE–LAF	Austrian Airlines	837	25/2/60	WO Moscow SEP–26–60. *Josef Haydn.*
438	XT–575	MinTech RRE	837	29/2/60	D to Austrian AL as OE–LAG *Franz Schubert.* S to MinTech
439	–	Shackleton Aviation	837	14/3/60	D to Austrian AL as OE–LAH *Anton Bruckner.* later *Franz Schubert.* S Shackleton
440	HK–1412	Uracca Lineas Aereas	837	21/3/60	D to Austrian AL as OE–LAK *Johann Strauss* S Shackleton S. Uracca AL
441	HK–1267	Uracca Lineas Aereas	837	14/5/60	D to Austrian AL as OE–LAL *W. A. Mozart* S to Shackleton. S to Uracca AL

C/n	Current Marks	Current Owner/operator	Model Series	Initial Delivery	Remarks
442	HK–1347	Uracca Lineas Aereas	837	3/8/60	D to Austrian AL as OE–LAM later OE-IAM. ***Ludwig V Beethoven.*** S to Shackleton. S to Uracca AL. WO JAN–21–72
443	PK–MVT	Merpati Nusantara AL	828	21/7/61	FF as G–ARKX. D to All-Nippon AW as JA8201. S to Merpati Nusantara
444	JA–8202	All-Nippon Airways	828	22/6/61	FF as G–ARKY. WO near Nagoya NOV–19–62
445	PK–MVG	Merpati Nusantara AL	828	2/9/61	FF as G–ARKZ. D to All-Nippon AW as JA–8203. S Merpati Nusantara
446	9G–AUU	Ghana Airways	838	26/11/61	
447	D–ANAF	Nora Air Services	814	1/1/62	D to Lufthansa. S Nora AS. Scrapped JAN 1972
448	PK–MVS	Merpati Nusantara AL	828	25/3/62	FF as G–ARWT. D to All-Nippon AW as JA–8205. S Merpati Nusantara. WO nr. Padang NOV–10–71
449	JA–8206	All-Nippon Airways	828	30/4/62	FF as G–ARWU. WFS APL–30–69. Scrapped DEC 1970
450	JA–8207	All-Nippon Airways	828	4/6/62	FF as G–ARWV. WFS AUG–31–69. Scrapped DEC 1970
451	402	CAAC	843	2/7/63	FF as G–ASDP. D as 84301.
452	404	CAAC	843	26/7/63	FF as G–ASDR. D as 84302.
453	406	CAAC	843	1/9/63	FF as G–ASDS. D as 84303.
454	408	CAAC	843	26/10/63	FF as G–ASDT. D as 84304.
455	410	CAAC	843	19/1/64	FF as G–ASDU. D as 84305.
456	412	CAAC	843	9/3/64	FF as G–ASDV. D as 84306.
457	HC–ASP	SAN–Ecuador	828	5/10/62	FF as G–ASBM. D to All-Nippon AW as JA–8208. S to SAN
458	HC–ATV	SAN–Ecuador	828	2/11/62	FF as G–ASBO. D to All-Nippon AW as JA–8209. S to SAN
459	PK–MVM	Merpati Nusantara AL	828	3/2/63	FF as G–ASBR. D to All-Nippon AW as JA–8210. S to Merpati Nusantara

Soviet Airliners

Insufficient detail of Soviet airliner production is available to make possible a listing of construction numbers, registrations and operators in the form adopted throughout the remainder of this book. Of the brief details given below, construction numbers related to particular registrations are shown in parentheses and individual aircraft names in italics.

Antonov An-10 Prototype SSSR-1957. Production models for Aeroflot in the range SSSR-11120 to 11229, and SSSR-34366 to 34825.

Antonov An-12 Production models for Aeroflot in the range SSSR-75613 to 75625, SSSR-11001 to 11130, 11340 to 11415 and 12952 to 12999, and SSSR-04343 to 04373.

Antonov An-24 Prototypes SSSR-L1959, -L1960. Production models for Aeroflot in the range SSSR-46202 to 46848.

Ilyushin Il-18 Prototype SSSR-L5811. Pre-production batch for Aeroflot, SSSR-L5812 to -L5830. Production models for Aeroflot in the range SSSR-74526 to 74268, SSSR-75400 to 75470, and SSSR-75499 to 75899.

Ilyushin Il-62 Prototypes SSSR-06156, -06176 and -06300. Production models for Aeroflot in the range SSSR-86650 to 86698.

Tupolev Tu-104 Prototype SSSR-L5400. Initial production batch SSSR-L5401 to -L5420. Production models for Aeroflot in the range SSSR-42307 to 42509.

Tupolev Tu-114 Prototypes SSSR-L5611 and -L5700. Production models for Aeroflot in the range SSSR-76459 to 76490.

Tupolev Tu-124 Production models for Aeroflot in the range SSSR-45000 to 45112.

Tupolev Tu-134 Prototypes SSSR-45075 and -45076. Production models for Aeroflot in the following ranges: Tu-134 : SSSR-65601 to 65649. Tu-134A : SSSR-65950 to 65970.

Tupolev Tu-154 Prototype SSSR-85000. Production models for Aeroflot in the range SSSR-85001 to 85042.

Yakovlev Yak-40 Prototype SSSR-1967. Production models for Aeroflot in the range SSSR-19661 to 19672 and SSSR-87591 to 87799.

Typical fleets of Soviet airliners, accurate details of which are known, are given below:

Ceskoslovenske Aerolinie

Il-18	OK-NAA	*Piestany*
	OK-NAB	*Kosice*
Il-188	OK-OAC	*Sliackupee*
	OK-PAE	*Karlovy Vary*
	OK-PAG	*Visoste Tatre*
	OK-PAH	*Marianske Lazne*
Il-62	OK-YBA	*Praha*
	OK-YBB	*Bratislava*
	OK-ZBC	*Ostrava*
	OK-ABD	
	OK-DBE	
Tu-104A	OK-LDA	
	OK-LDC	*Brno*
	OK-NDF	*Ceske Budejovice*
Tu-134A	OK-AFA	
	OK-AFB	
	OK-CFC	
	OK-CFD	
	OK-CFE	
	OK-CFF	
	OK-CFG	
	OK-CFH	

Egyptair

An-24B	SU-ANV
	SU-ANX
	SU-ANY
Il-18D	SU-AOX
	SU-AOY
Tu-154	SU-AXB
	SU-AXC
	SU-AXD
	SU-AXE
	SU-AXF
	SU-AXG
	SU-AXH
	SU-AXI

Interflug

An-24B	DM-SBA	(02206)
	DM-SBC	(02302)
	DM-SBD	(02210)
	DM-SBE	(02301)
	DM-SBF	(02304)
	DM-SBG	(02303)
	DM-SBH	

Soviet Airliners

Il-18	DM-STA	
	DM-STB	
	DM-STC	
	DM-STD	
	DM-STE	
	DM-STF	
	DM-STG	
	DM-STH	
	DM-STI	
	DM-STK	
	DM-STL	
	DM-STM	(10805)
	DM-STN	(10903)
	DM-STO	(10904)
	DM-STP	
Tu-124	DM-SDA	
	DM-SDB	
Tu-134	DM-SCA	(0502)
	DM-SCB	(0503)
	DM-SCD	(0702)
	DM-SCE	(0703)
	DM-SCF	(0904)
	DM-SCG	(0905)
	DM-SCH	(0906)
Tu-143A	DM-SCK	
	DM-SCM	(1904)

Malev

Il-18	HA-MOA
	HA-MOE
	HA-MOF
	HA-MOG
	HA-MOH
	HA-MOI
Tu-134	HA-LBC
	HA-LBE
	HA-LBF
Tu-134A	HA-LBI
	HA-LBK
Tu-154	HA-LCA
	HA-LCB
	HA-LCE

Polskie Linie Lotnicze

An-24	SP-LTA	
	SP-LTB	
	SP-LTC	
	SP-LTD	
	SP-LTG	
	SP-LTH	
	SP-LTI	
	SP-LTK	
	SP-LTL	
	SP-LTM	
	SP-LTN	
	SP-LTO	
	SP-LTP	
	SP-LTR	
	SP-LTS	
Il-18	SP-LSA	
	SP-LSB	
	SP-LSC	
	SP-LSD	
	SP-LSE	
	SP-LSF	
	SP-LSG	
	SP-LSH	
Il-62	SP-LAA	*Micolaj Kopernic*
	SP-LAB	*Tadevsz Koscuiszko*
	SP-LAC	*Frederyk Chopin*
Tu-134	SP-LGA	
	SP-LGB	
	SP-LGC	
	SP-LGD	
	SP-LGE	
Tu-134A	SP-LHA	
	SP-LHB	
	SP-LHC	